Animal death

Edited by Jay Johnston and Fiona Probyn-Rapsey

SYDNEY UNIVERSITY PRESS

First published in 2013 by Sydney University Press

Reproduction and Communication for other purposes

National Library of Australia Cataloguing-in-Publication Data

Title:	Animal death / edited by Jay Johnston and Fiona Probyn-Rapsey.
ISBN:	9781743320235 (pbk.)
	9781743320242 (ebook : epub)
	9781743323700 (ebook : kindle)
Notes:	Includes bibliographical references and index.
	Animal rights.
Subjects:	Animal welfare--Moral and ethical aspects.
	Animals.
	Human-animal relationships.
Other Authors/Contributors:	
	Johnston, Jay, editor.
	Probyn-Rapsey, Fiona, editor.
Dewey Number:	179.3

Cover image by Sidney Nolan, *Carcass*, 1953, enamel on composition board, 90.8 x 121.3 cm. Nolan Collection, managed by Canberra Museum and Gallery on behalf of the Australian Government.

Cover design by Miguel Yamin

Contents

List of figures	v
Acknowledgments	ix
*Foreword*The Hon. Michael Kirby AC CMG	xi
Introduction *Jay Johnston and Fiona Probyn-Rapsey*	xv
1 In the shadow of all this death *Deborah Bird Rose*	1
2 Human and animal space in historic 'pet' cemeteries in London, New York and Paris *Hilda Kean*	21
3 Necessary expendability: an exploration of nonhuman death in public *Tarsh Bates and Megan Schlipalius*	43
4 Confronting corpses and theatre animals *Peta Tait*	67
5 Respect for the (animal) dead *Chloë Taylor*	85
6 Re-membering Sirius: animal death, rites of mourning, and the (material) cinema of spectrality *George Ioannides*	103

7   Mining animal death for all it's worth
    Melissa Boyde   119

8   Reflecting on donkeys: images of death and redemption
    Jill Bough   137

9   Picturing cruelty: chicken advocacy and visual culture
    Annie Potts and Philip Armstrong   151

10 Learning from dead animals: horse sacrifice in ancient
    Salamis and the Hellenisation of Cyprus
    Agata Mrva-Montoya   169

11 The last image: Julia Leigh's *The hunter* as film
    Carol Freeman   189

12 Euthanasia and morally justifiable killing in a veterinary
    clinical context
    Anne Fawcett   205

13 Preventing and giving death at the zoo: Heini Hediger's
    'death due to behaviour'
    Matthew Chrulew   221

14 Nothing to see – something to see: white animals and
    exceptional life/death
    Fiona Probyn-Rapsey   239

15 'Death-in-life': curare, restrictionism and abolitionism in
    Victorian and Edwardian anti-vivisectionist thought
    Greg Murrie   253

16 Huskies and hunters: living and dying in Arctic Greenland
    Rick De Vos   277

17 On having a furry soul: transpecies identity and ontological
    indeterminacy in Otherkin subcultures
    Jay Johnston   293

About the contributors   307

Index   313

List of figures

Figure 2.1 Hyde Park Pet Cemetery, London (1997).   23

Figure 2.2 Overview of Hartsdale Pet Cemetery, New
York (2007).   24

Figure 2.3 Cat on grave at Cimetière des Chiens,
Asniere-sur-Seine, Paris (2011).   25

Figure 2.4 Gate to Heaven memorial, Cimetière des
Chiens, Asniere-sur-Seine (2011).   27

Figure 2.5 Barry at the gates of Cimetière des Chiens (2011).   29

Figure 2.6 Balu memorial stone, Hyde Park Pet
Cemetery (1997).   34

Figure 2.7 Tennis balls for Arry, Cimetière des Chiens (2011).   36

Figure 2.8 Dog memorial wall, Federal Park,
Annandale, Sydney (2010).   38

Figure 2.9 Grave at Hillside Animal Sanctuary,
Frettenham, Norwich.   39

Figure 3.1 *in vitero* installation, PICA. Image by Megan
Schlipalius.   45

Figure 3.2 *in vitero* logo. Image by Tarsh Bates and
Megan Schlipalius.   46

Figure 3.3 Inoculating *Candida* vessel, *in vitero*
performance still, 11 October 2011. Image by Megan
Schlipalius.   53

Figure 3.4 Tarsh with *Candida*. Image by Bo Wong.   54

Figure 3.5 Feeding *Drosophila melanogaster*. Image by
Megan Schlipalius.   58

Figure 3.6 *Drosophila melanogaster*: day 15. Image by
Megan Schlipalius and Tarsh Bates.   59

Figure 3.7 *Drosophila melanogaster*: day 56. Image by
Megan Schlipalius and Tarsh Bates.   59

Figure 3.8 *Hydra vulgaris* vessel with brine shrimp
hatchery. Image by Tarsh Bates.   61

Figure 3.9 Conducting audience research during *in
vitero*. Image by Tarsh Bates.   64

Figure 10.1 Salamis, Tomb 2: plan with finds in the
dromos in situ. After Karageorghis 1967, fig. VI.   173

Figure 10.2 Salamis, Tomb 47: skeletons of horses G
and H (first burial) in situ. After Karageorghis 1967,
fig. XXIX.   174

Figure 10.3 Terracotta horse-and-rider figurine dated
to Cypro-Archaic II (600–475 BC), provenance
unknown, Nicholson Museum.   184

Figure 13.1 Hediger's catalogue of 'death due to
behaviour' (1969, 179).   227

Figure 16.1 Dogs tethered in the designated dog yard,
Illulissat, June 2011. Photo: Monika Szunejko.   281

Figure 16.2 Dogs tethered on the ice, Inglefield Fjord,
Qaanaaq, June 2011. Photo: Monika Szunejko.   284

Figure 16.3 Cemetery, Qaanaaq, June 2011. Photo: Rick
De Vos.   285

Figure 16.4 Hunters and huskies, Inglefield Fjord,
Qaanaaq, June 2011. Photo: Monika Szunejko.   289

Figure 16.5 Dogs look out over Inglefield Fjord,
Qaanaaq, June 2011. Photo: Rick De Vos.   290

Acknowledgments

We would like to thank all the participants at the Animal Death Symposium at the University of Sydney, 12–13 June 2012. We gratefully acknowledge financial support provided by the School of Philosophical and Historical Inquiry at the University of Sydney. The School of Philosophical and Historical Inquiry supported both the symposium itself and also the publication of this book. Julie-Ann Robson and Jane Yan were especially helpful. We also thank the School of Letters, Art and Media for their help with the symposium venue, and particularly Professor Annamarie Jagose for launching the symposium. The Honourable Chief Justice Michael Kirby remains a fantastic supporter and patron of the Human Animal Research Network (HARN) at the University of Sydney and we are grateful for his willingness to contribute a foreword for this collection of essays. We would also like to thank our peer reviewers who provided reports on each submission received and the team at Sydney University Press for their dedication. And finally, thank you to the Canberra Museum and Gallery (CMAG) for granting permission to use an image of Sidney Nolan's incredible painting, *Carcass* (1953), on the front cover of this book.

Jay Johnston
Fiona Probyn-Rapsey

Foreword

The Hon. Michael Kirby AC CMG[1]

A chapter in this book by Carol Freeman extends the story told in Julia Leigh's novel *The hunter* (1999). That work was recently adapted as a film (Nettheim 2011). It tells a story of a man, sent to Tasmania to obtain genetic material from the last Tasmanian 'Tiger', for use in bio-warfare. It explores the impact of technology on animal life and does so under the shadow of the danger of species extinction. Julia Leigh's book is described by Freeman as unrelentingly 'bleak'. Some may feel the same about this book. It is about two subjects that most people spend their lives trying to avoid, preferring not to think of them: animal welfare and protection, and death. Put the two together and one has a combination likely to upset, repel and distress many readers in Australia and abroad.

Animals, for many, tend to be lovely playful things (even members of 'the family') found around the home; exotic things at zoos or in TV documentaries. Or useful things that live far away and die in circumstances unknown, because their purpose in life is their death: to provide their bodies for nourishment and other uses by the ascendant creature

M Kirby (2013). Foreword. In J Johnston & F Probyn-Rapsey (Eds). *Animal death*. Sydney: Sydney University Press.

---

1   Patron of Voiceless, one time Justice of the High Court of Australia and President of the International Commission of Jurists.

that sits at the top of the living species on earth. This is the creature described in several chapters of this book as the 'human animal'; to distinguish it from the 'nonhuman animal', destined to die before its natural time.

Fortunately, in the current age, famous writers and ethicists in Australia are reminding our people that it does not have to be so – that the huge industry of the killing of nonhuman animals could be abolished; should certainly be radically altered; and must, at the very least, be significantly reduced, if only for the benefit of humankind itself, its physical wellbeing and its moral sensibilities. These advocates of change include John Coetzee, a famous writer and scholar of fiction, laureate of the Nobel Prize for Literature in 2003, originally from South Africa but now living in Australia. And Peter Singer, the world famous philosopher, who was born amongst us and now enjoys global recognition in the fields of ethics and animal rights, recently awarded Australia's highest civil honour. He teaches from chairs to which he has been appointed at famous universities in the United States of America and Australia. These two leading thinkers, and many others, are showing that there is another pathway to a new and preferable relationship with animals, and that it is the very intelligence and capacity for ethical reflection of human beings that demands of them a new sensitivity in their interactions with other living species.

I stumbled into this context, partly by accident. A certain curiosity about it persuaded me to participate in launching a book on animal welfare laws in Australia and New Zealand. I launch and write forewords for so many books, on so many topics, that there was no certainty that the book on animal law would have a major impact. But impact it had: too much information; too many images to haunt my brain.

From the day that I launched the book on animal welfare, in May 2009, I have not eaten the flesh of any animal or fowl. This is possible. So books have power. Words convey moral dilemmas. Human beings are capable of being moral creatures. So it may prove with the present book. Dear reader, be warned. Reading about animal death may prove a life-changing experience. If you do not wish to be exposed to that possibility, read no further. Indulge yourself in the novels of Barbara Cartland. Select a book on statistics or pure mathematics. Do not torment your mind, as mine was tormented with cruel images inflicted on millions of sentient creatures every year, in the anthropomorphic conceit that humans are completely special – that they are created in the image of God Himself, and that every other living creature is a thing without a soul, that it is put on earth only to be useful or amusing to human beings. Books and voices can challenge us to rethink these barren illusions.

This new book is a kaleidoscope with an amazing and, at first, seemingly unconnected, collection of essays. They are bound together by nothing else than a link with the death of animals. To note a selection: George Ioannides describes the decomposition of a beloved dog Sirius and the beauty that could be found in the most unlikely places through film and cinema of these events. Anne Fawcett explores ideas of euthanasia and what, in real terms, this friendly word means for animals 'put to sleep'. Agata Mrva-Montoya recounts the discovery of the bones of animals in prehistoric funeral sites, silent witnesses to their unequal relationship with human beings over the millennia. Melissa Boyde draws parallels between the violent death of animals in the outback and the attitudes of the same protagonists to fellow humans. Fiona Probyn-Rapsey recounts the lives of white and albino animals, their whiteness influencing their relationship to death. Annie Potts describes the familiar chicken and how billions of these most social of animals are disparaged and abused, and denied their nature, in the mass production of food for humans. Matthew Chrulew takes us to the zoo. But is it a recreated Garden of Eden where the animals are gently tended and fed? Or is it a horror place, a kind of imprisonment, alien to natural animal existence? In a book of sombre messages, this one at least recounts stories of the improving sensitivity of zoos towards animals and to the dedication of modern zoos and their keepers to diminishing the pains and fears involved in premature animal deaths. Deborah Bird Rose examines the boundaries of multispecies death zones and does so in the context of species extinctions.

My description of several chapters in this book does scant justice to the new ideas and pressing thoughts that the authors offer to the readers. Some of the chapters are essentially literary and artistic in their objective. Others are scientific, empirical and factual. Not a few are allegorical and didactic. Some speak directly and sharply of the need for human change. Others do so with great subtlety and by allegorical images.

In the end, by concentrating our attention on death in animals, in so many guises and circumstances, we, the human readers, are brought face to face with the reality of our world. It is a world of pain, fear and enormous stress and cruelty. It is a world that will not change anytime soon into a human community of vegetarians or vegans. But at least books like this are being written for public reflection. Books like the one of animal welfare that changed my life are now being used to teach animal welfare law in a growing number of institutions of legal education throughout Australasia and the Western world. Laws are being enacted to prohibit the worst instances of corporatised greed and indifference to animal fear and needless pain. Organisations of citizens and passionate media are lifting their voices and causing protests, in an increasingly successful effort to focus attention on the duty that we humans owe to other sentient animals.

During my service as a judge in the High Court of Australia, two significant cases raised, indirectly, the issues of animal welfare and its advocacy: *Levy v Victoria* (1997) 189 CLR 579 and *Australian Broadcasting Corporation v Lenah Game Meats Pty Ltd* (2001) 208 CLR 199. More cases will come. Lawyers and other citizens will insist upon change. And books like this one will plant ideas in the human consciousness of our world. Such ideas will prove powerful. Experience, law and literature combine. They can change the world for all of the animals in it.

Sydney
18 February 2013

Introduction

Jay Johnston and Fiona Probyn-Rapsey

Animal death is a complex, uncomfortable, depressing, motivating and sensitive topic. For those scholars participating in human–animal studies, it is – accompanied by the concept of 'life' – the ground upon which their studies commence, whether those studies are historical, archaeological, social, philosophical or cultural. It is a tough subject to face, but, as we hope this volume demonstrates, one at the heart of human–animal relations and auman–animal studies scholarship.

The sheer scale of animal death is mind-boggling. The statistics are easily accessible and the rhetoric all too familiar: 'Animals become extinct. They are also killed, gassed, electrocuted, exterminated, hunted, butchered, vivisected, shot, trapped, snared, run over, lethally injected, culled, sacrificed, slaughtered, executed, euthanized, destroyed, put down, put to sleep, and even, perhaps, murdered' (Animal Studies Group 2006, 3). It is not that we do not know what is going on (the information is available if we care to look), but that many do not 'care to know' in the sense that Stanley Cohen uses that phrase. For Cohen, caring to know is knowledge plus acknowledgment of the moral and ethical consequences of that knowledge (2001). While killing animals is a 'defining aspect of human behavior' (Animal Studies Group 2006, 8), understanding the *ways* in which animal deaths are faced up to, ob-

J Johnston & F Probyn-Rapsey (2013). Introduction. In J Johnston & F Probyn-Rapsey (Eds). *Animal death*. Sydney: Sydney University Press.

scured, minimised, and rendered morally distant by cultural design (by which we mean ideas, arguments, representations and beliefs) is vital to bringing about change. This volume examines the cultural contexts in which animal death becomes the background noise of everyday life: routinised, normalised, mechanised and sped up. It also offers different strategies for intervention that highlight the need to sit with, contemplate and act with the discomfort brought on by confronting animal death. And so the volume considers not only the cultivation of indifference[1] and silence by various cultural mechanisms, but also responses that are possible and necessary, responses to the call of those who are, as Deborah Bird Rose describes, in the 'deathzone: the place where the living and the dying encounter each other in the presence of that which cannot be averted'. In this sense, this volume contributes to the scholarship on the subject by bringing the modes of recognition, acknowledgment (as well as forms of disavowal) to the foreground.

This volume emerges out of a symposium held at the University of Sydney on 12–13 June 2012 by Human Animal Research Network (HARN). The symposium brought together cross-disciplinary voices on animal death. These papers variously explored how animal and human death diverge and also connect in profound ways. The selection of papers reflects a genuine commitment by the editors to the transdisciplinary nature of human–animal studies, while also acknowledging that differences in discipline methodology and conceptual foundation always remain in the dynamics of such dialogue. This volume aims to open up discussion with scholarship that is challenging, insightful and diverse.

Deborah Bird Rose's chapter, 'In the shadow of all this death', contemplates questions of response-ability towards the dead and dying in a time of mass extinctions. Her elaboration of the 'deathzone', as a space of encounter between species, and a place where ideally none should be abandoned, underscores the necessity of confronting death as an ethical and political problem for individuals and species. She points out that a 'multispecies shadow' hangs over us all, connecting our lives and

---

1 'Cultivation of indifference' is a phrase used by Fiona Probyn-Rapsey in *Made to matter* (Sydney University Press 2013) to highlight the point that indifference does not arise simply through neglect or ignorance but is actively cultivated through various cultural mechanisms.

deaths not only to past and future generations of our own species, but also every other species too. Her chapter illustrates models for hope in what she calls 'crazy love', a form of radical multispecies relationality seen in passionate responses to the call of those imperilled. In the work of Levinas, Seamus Heaney, the story of the Moon and the Dingo from the Ngarinman people of the Northern Territory, Australia, and in the 'crazy love' expressed by Louise and Rick in their attention to a grieving Albatross pair, Rose finds examples of remarkable multispecies entanglement in the deathzone, where none is 'abandoned' to die alone. Such fidelity to the dead and to the imperilled marks a space of hope where our relationality, our being-with-others, does not leave us paralysed and alone, 'behind the corpse house, longing for those "we" have killed, and unable to save those "we" are now killing', but gives us resources with which to respond.

The question of whose deaths we mourn and how we pay our respects to the animal dead correlates with human–animal intimacy and proximity. As Hilda Kean observes in her chapter on pet cemeteries in London, Paris and New York, the memorialisation of beloved 'pets' by tombstone, plaque and monument are signs of a broader pattern of attachment between human and animal in life and also, by implication, in some kind of afterlife. But Kean also observes that these public commemorations of the animal dead go beyond the individual relationships formed between specific animals and humans. They also include public monuments erected to commemorate animals in war, memorial walls (such as that for the dogs in Glebe, Sydney), or monuments and plaques celebrating the bravery of particular animals. Kean discusses the commemoration of Sirius, a rescue dog who died in the aftermath of the World Trade Center bombing in 2001, as one example where the human–animal divide is challenged by such commemorative practices. What we can mourn and grieve for is indicative of what is possible between the species in life.

The issue of which animals we choose to mourn and those whose deaths are ignored or devalued is played out in Tarsh Bates and Megan Schlipalius' chapter. It records the artist's and curator's reactions to relationships with non-human organisms during an artistic installation. Responsibility towards maintaining life, confrontation with death and the aesthetics of engagement between human and organism (insects, fungi, plants and yeasts) in a gallery environment is evocatively recorded. The installation, dependent on the life and deaths of so many others, becomes an ethical conundrum. Bates and Schlipalius provide the reader (as they did the exhibition viewers) with an opportunity to sit with these dilemmas.

The staging of such dilemmas is the remit of Peta Tait's chapter 'Confronting corpses and theatre animals'. Here the vocabulary of the contemporary visual exhibition is counterpointed with the pseudo-presence of dead animals in selected theatre productions. The dead here are at turns entertainment, prop, education, spectacle: their presence bounded by diverse frames. Tait draws our attention to the way in which such framing speaks to the dead animal and confines the way an audience responds and proposes increased awareness of the sensory body's reactions.

Chloë Taylor's chapter highlights the ways in which animals that are not companions – such as the hunted or those who die on our roads, or are killed by other animals – are relegated to a very different ethical space. Taylor discusses a number of case studies that demonstrate a cultural habit of equating 'respect for the dead' with eating the corpse, not wanting to 'waste' the animal dead. She points out that while human death 'should entail notions of dignity, rituals of mourning, and abiding by the wishes of the deceased', respect for the animal dead can, for some, mean 'instrumentalising their corpses as much as we can'. This word 'respect' is subject to very different interpretations depending on the species one is, and the proximity of human and animal relationships involved.

The issue of proximity and the ability to mourn individual animal lives also informs George Ioannides' chapter and his analysis of Stan Brakhage's silent short film *Sirius remembered* (1959). Brakhage's film documents the decomposition of his dead dog, Sirius, over several seasons. Ioannides argues that this film attends to the material, embodied and affective life of Sirius and offers a ritual of mourning for a beloved subject. Ionnades departs from John Berger and Akira Lippit's diagnosis of the visual/cinematic animal as intrinsically linked to their disappearance in the world: 'where cinema, even more consummately than linguistic metaphor, "mourns" vanishing animal life, preserving or encrypting animality in an affective and transferential structure of communication'. But a film like *Sirius remembered*, Ioannides argues, complicates and supplements this spectral de-animation of animal life, because Brakhage's film moves animal life and death back towards materiality and affect, where the animal's life and death insists on its difference to the cinema's appropriation of animality as an ideal image of modernity's loss.

Melissa Boyde's chapter considers animal death in two novels and their film adaptations – *Wake in fright* (Kenneth Cook 1961/Kotcheff 1971) and Red Dog (De Bernières 2001/Stenders 2011). This chapter interrogates how cultural texts that use animal deaths as poetic devices can *simultaneously* marginalise and yet also make central the death of animals. Boyde points out that animal deaths in these texts function as a comment on human life, human feeling and companionship, while the animals whose bodies inhabit the textual space function as backdrop, their stories constituting a 'presumptive knowledge' that leaves the animals silent. Animal deaths in these films are routinised with little interrogation of human complicity in the poisonings and shootings that imperil animals from start to end. Highlighting the textual strategies of the *roman à clef*, with its generic potential to both conceal and reveal cultural secrets, Boyde turns her attention to how these texts minimise and obscure the lives and deaths of animals by 'bring[ing] to the surface animal matters embedded in these texts: deviation and disappearance, shame and shamelessness, and vested and invested interests'.

Jill Bough engages with the particularly Australian cultural myth of Simpson and his donkey to expose the gulf between the celebrated animal and its treatment in everyday society: a shameful gulf. While exploring the rich tradition of symbolism associated with the donkey, Bough articulates the tension between symbolic reverence and physical neglect.

Similarly, Annie Potts and Philip Armstrong deftly weave together the symbolic and the real life – real death – of chickens in 'Picturing cruelty: chicken advocacy and visual culture'. 'Picturing' here is the key: this chapter excavates the visual literacy of advocacy projects unpacking the cultural complexity and socio-political 'afterlife' of images.

Turning from what the symbolic and everyday treatment of animals can reveal about culture, a time, a place, Agata Mrva-Montoya looks to the material remains of horse sacrifice to propose a re-reading of cultural change in Cyprus. In this chapter the material evidence of animal death is employed to construct an alternate cultural history. Intersecting with current debates in archaeology and history, Mrva-Montoya interprets the material culture of animal death to temper histories built upon predominantly textual foundation.

Disparity in the rendering and reading of different textual formations underpins Carol Freeman's investigation of Julia Leigh's *The hunter* as novel (1999) and as film (Nettheim 2011). In a careful exegesis she mines the film's images for slippage in attitude towards the animal. Changes in emphasis and orientation are read against audience expectation and broader socio-cultural opinion. Animal–human relations, extinction and responsibility jostle one another in the packaging and repackaging of this thylacine tale.

The reluctance to discuss animal death, even though its place is undeniably central to our relationship to animals, marks institutions, theories and practices that produce the idea of 'surplus animals'; factory farms, the pet industry and zoos. All of these institutions grapple with animal death and all involve animal science practitioners. Anne Fawcett's chapter highlights the moral stresses faced by veterinary surgeons who, on a daily basis, are faced with the task of euthanising animals. Euthanasia is supposed to describe an assisted death in the context of poor quality of life and prevention of suffering. But, as Fawcett points out, the term is also misused to describe the deaths of animals who are deemed 'surplus', and who can no longer be looked after by their owners. Fawcett argues that such slippery (mis)use of this term has become normalised in veterinary practice and that it poses significant risks for animals facing death, and also for the vets and pet owners who allow it.

Matthew Chrulew's chapter highlights the place of death in the zoo. He points out that while zoos are reluctant to discuss death, it is intrinsic to their function as 'archetypally life-fostering' institutions. Chrulew discusses the zoo's relationship to death, not as something that can be hidden successfully (though the public hears very little of zoo deaths), but as an 'immediate product of scientifico-medical intervention, where one group survives (or indeed lives well) at the expense of another'. Chrulew uses the example provided by Heini Hediger, a mid-century zoo director, whose interest in managing death at the zoo marks a significant shift in the understanding of the role of zoos, and death within them. Chrulew agues that Hediger's 'analysis of "death due to behaviour" opened up captive and other animals' lives to a new domain of knowledge, power and biopolitical intervention'. Chrulew finds in Hediger an exemplary biopolitician whose work is best understood within the context of a shift from sovereignty to biopower, as elaborated by Michel Foucault.

Fiona Probyn-Rapsey's chapter 'Nothing to see, something to see: white animals and exceptional life/death' also attends to a biopolitical intervention into animal life in the form of standardisation, in particular the ways that an animal's appearance, specifically colour, affects its treatment in human hands. Struck by the standardisation of white broiler chickens, her chapter engages with the question of how their whiteness contributes to the de-individuation of animal life in intensive factory farming. Contrasting this with the fascination for albino animals, the essay examines the variability in how the white animal is marked for death in some contexts and exceptional life in others such as zoos, which foster rare and exceptional albino animals for purposes of trade and spectacle. Her chapter analyses how white animals 'are marked by the (non)colour of whiteness, caught not just *within* but *as* the space between death and life: whiteness as vulnerable hypervisibility and as exceptional life; to be made *more of* in order to be continually unmade'.

The 'state of death-in-life', found in the complexities of anti-vivisectionist thought in the Victorian and Edwardian periods is the focus of Greg Murrie's chapter. Not only articulating the often paradoxical positions taken by individuals and organisations to the issue, Murrie demonstrates the way in which such debates led to an expansion of perceived animal–human difference.

Drawing boundaries of difference between species and the (irr)rationales employed, forms the ground layer upon which Rick De Vos builds his analysis of the relationship between huskies and hunters in Greenland. Richly detailed fieldwork is recounted which presents both the dogs' contradictory socio-cultural positioning and De Vos' own embodied response to this predicament and its specific environmental context. As an 'arctic other', Greenland's status as a frontier place – part wild and part 'civilised' – is mirrored in De Vos' reading of the husky–hunter interaction: a relation that covets dependence and dissolution simultaneously.

Drawing together an unlikely coupling of contemporary spiritual subculture (Otherkin) and poststructuralist theory, Jay Johnston questions the usefulness of distinguishing between 'animal' and 'human' for individuals who understand themselves as simultaneously both. This chapters explores how, by claiming the animal as an aspect of their lived subjectivity, Therians (animal–human Otherkin) enact the simultaneous death of the animal and the human, while paradoxically reinforcing a generic and romanticised concept of the animal. The ethics involved are both promising and troubling.

In summary, the essays in this collection problematise animal death. Collectively they demonstrate that whether that death is an 'anonymous' fly or a beloved pet, whether it is deemed symbolic or real, or a conflux of the two, animal death is never simple. An increasingly mechanical and routinised event for so many nonhuman creatures, animal death is a departure point for a broader consideration of our lives with, and as, other animals.

Works cited

Animal Studies Group (Ed.) (2006). *Killing animals.* Urbana and Chicago: University of Illinois Press.

Cohen S (2001). *States of denial: knowing about atrocities and suffering.* Cambridge: Polity Press.

1
In the shadow of all this death

Deborah Bird Rose

We live in a time of almost unfathomable loss, and we are called to respond. We are called to respond to that which we cannot fully understand, and we are called to understand why and how we are called. We will be shaping our understandings as we shape our responses, and we will increasingly understand that our responses are offerings into the unknowable. We howl in the dark for the loss that surrounds us now, and for all that is coming. Our howling starts from within, from empathy, grief, and much more, and it reverberates beyond us. At the same time, other howls reach us and penetrate us, amplifying not only our voices but our meaning. As we are now within the sixth mass extinction event on earth, and as we are its cause, we are howling into, and from, an extremely complicated place: the shadow of the Anthropocene.

Seamus Heaney offers a poetic cry of grief and solidarity written in response to the death of his friend the Nigerian literary scholar and poet Donatus Nwoga. The poem 'A dog was crying tonight in Wicklow also' works with an African story of the great spirit Chukwu and the origins of death, connecting grief across continents through the fact that Wicklow is Heaney's home town. According to the story Heaney reports, human beings wanted to return from death; they didn't want to die forever. They told the dog to take this message to Chukwu, and the

DB Rose (2013). In the shadow of all this death. In J Johnston & F Probyn-Rapsey (Eds). *Animal death*. Sydney: Sydney University Press.

dog trotted off only to become distracted by another dog. Thus it was that the toad, who heard it all, went to Chukwu with a lie, saying that humans actually wanted to die forever. And Chukwu became enraged, so that nothing the dog or anyone could say would reverse his decision that death would be final. In Heaney's great words:

> And nothing that the dog would tell him later
> Could change that vision. Great chiefs and great loves
> In obliterated light, the toad in mud,
> The dog crying out all night behind the corpse house.
> (Heaney 2006)

Within the house of life, to use Heaney's elegant term, are all the creatures who are born to die, including the dogs. This is our condition as earth creatures: stated in the poetics of the ethical, *we* are *all* dogs crying behind the corpse house. We did not choose death, we bear the burden of the deaths of others, and we cry. We are creatures who cannot stop death or evade it, and cannot rescue others forever; we howl for the greatness of our responsibilities and we howl for our inadequacies.

Part One: The shadow that hovers over us all

In life and death we are never alone, either as individuals or as species. Others precede us, we come after, and thus we are in their shadow. James Hatley offers an important analysis of the inter-generational gifts that constitute the relationship between death and life through time. He holds that one's 'kind', that is, group or race, or species, is the result of 'an on-going series of ethical relationships' (2000, 60). One's kind only comes in the aftermath of generation, of one's being-birthed (219). In accepting the great fact that life always comes after the deaths of others, we understand ourselves to be in the shadow, and also in the debt, of those who came before. Without them we would not be alive. This shadow of the lives and deaths of all those who preceded us must also be understood as a multispecies shadow, immensely great and never fully knowable (Rose 2012).

Another story that addresses death and its place in life belongs to Ngarinman people whose homeland is along the Wickham River in the north-west part of the Northern Territory of Australia. I lived and learned from people in the communities of Yarralin and Lingara for many years, and the story of death was first shared with me by people who are now deceased. I am very much in their debt, and in their shadow.

This story of death involves the Moon and the Dingo, and it articulates the ethics of *our* place, that is the place of animals, within the shadow of death. As Daly Pulkara, and other Dingo lawmen, told the stories, the Moon's claim to fame is that he dies and returns as himself. Every month he disappears and every month he comes back. There is no death for the Moon. There is, however, a terrible loneliness. He has no mates, no fellow creatures; there is only the one Moon. So he offers Dingo eternal life, but there is a catch. The Dingo will have to become a sycophant of the Moon. The Dingo refuses, and so the Moon starts taunting him and daring him, urging him to die and return, to try to do as the Moon does.

'Die,' the Moon said. 'Die as I do and come back again in four days time.' The Dingo reckoned he couldn't do it. But the Moon kept daring him, and so he decided to take the gamble. As Daly told the story, the Dingo knew it wouldn't work, and his final words were: 'You can't see me come out in four days. I'll go forever.' And that is what happened.

Unlike the Moon, however, the Dingo was not alone. His mates were there too, and they called out to him: ' "What's the good, poor bugger? Come back, come back . . . " ' Again and again they called, but he was truly gone.

That was the first death, and its long shadow is with us today. Nobody wants to die, but there he was, this Dreaming Dingo, pressured into a contest he thought he would lose, and then abandoned by the Moon who had persuaded him. Daly and others heaped blame on the Moon: 'Why that Moon never go back and help him?' Daly asked. 'That Moon should have said: "Ah, that's bad. No good you stay dead like that. Why don't you come back again?" '

Along with the obvious task of giving an origin to the fact of death, this story tells us about that place where a living being is slipping inevitably into death: not yet dead, but not able to come back. This threshold is the death zone: the place where the living and the dying encounter each other in the presence of that which cannot be averted. Death is imminent but has not yet arrived. The Dingo has started to follow the Moon, and perhaps he hears the Moon laughing in triumph. I imagine he poured forth a great howling lamentation as he disappeared forever. But at the same time he would have heard his mates. Their voices, raised in the haunting harmonies of dingoes, were calling 'Come back, come back . . .'

The beautiful wailing voices of those who live on offer solidarity in the face of death. They tell us of two aspects of the condition of coming 'after'. We live after death in the sense that the deaths of others precede us. We come after that Dingo, and so we die. But there is more. We *live on* after the deaths of others. And so we live with the dying of others. As long as we live we are surrounded by death, and until it is time for our own death we are the ones who call out to the dying, who stay with the dying, but who do not accompany them into death. We go on living even as they are dying, and we go on living after they are gone.

The Moon and Dingo story offers a momentous ethical call which is stated as plain fact: we live in the world that exists after that first death. It articulates two courses of action: the Moon's course is to push others toward death and then abandon them. He finds triumph in hard-heartedness. The Dingo's course of action is to counter loss with mateship, to refuse to abandon others, to howl in solidarity. We are not the Moon, we don't live forever. We are social animals enmeshed in bonds of solidarity, and we are members of the wider family of those who cry behind the corpse house. Exactly here, where to be alive is to be implicated in the lives and deaths of others; exactly here we are called into an ethics of proximity and responsibility. Because we live after, we bear the burden of witness. In one sense, simply to be alive is to bear witness, by virtue of one's own embodied life, to the others who came before, but the actual ethical burden entails embracing those relationships. Here in the midst of life we are entangled within a particular kinship; we are beneficiaries of, and contributors to, the family of those who are born to die. The expression of our ethical lives will be visible in how we inhabit the death zone: how we call out, how we refuse to abandon others, how we refuse hard-heartedness, and thus how we embrace the precious beauty that permeates the house of life.

The stories of death that I have dealt with tell us that neither life nor death nor the threshold between is exclusively for humans. Thom van Dooren expresses this point eloquently: 'Death . . . positions all organisms (including humans; a point that shouldn't have to be made, but unfortunately often does), as parts of a broader multispecies community. Possibilities for life and death, for everyone, get worked out inside these entangled processes . . .' (2011, 48). In short, and again quoting van Dooren, we are 'interwoven into a system in which we live and die with others, live and die *for* others' (2002, 10). It is with the most precious complexity that the shadow of death is entangled within the house of life, and we are always implicated in encounters at the threshold.

Part Two: In the house of life

The philosopher Lev Shestov made the point that it takes a certain kind of craziness to love all that is doomed to perish. His context was a rave against 'reason', by which he meant scientific positivism, certain forms of rationality, and other aspects of modernity. He equated modernity's philosophical reason with a majestic and dispassionate unity that universalised truth and morality by suppressing the particular, the contingent and the ephemeral, including most especially the life that ends in death. He asserted that if we were to reject this universalising erasure of the particular, then there 'will break forth innumerable selfhoods that philosophy has kept in fetters during the course of thousands of years with their unsatisfied desires, with their inconsolable sorrows . . .' (Shestov 1982, 85).

In the face of these calls of desire and grief, Shestov urges us 'to learn anew to be horrified, to weep, to curse, to lose and find again the last hope'. That hope, for Shestov, is an 'enigmatic craziness' that he finds in relation to God (87). In following his logic, I argue for a kind of crazy love that is directed toward earth life (Rose 2011b, 108–11). This is exactly what is called for in the death zone, but not only there, and not only amongst humans. Throughout the whole of the house of life, crazy love springs forth in the face of death.

I will explore the practice of crazy love through a story of an albatross couple and their chick. The small part of the story I share here is the tip of a beautiful iceberg. It concerns Laysan albatross on the Hawaiian island of Kaua'i. These fantastic birds fly 80,000 or more kilometres annually to gather food from the North Pacific and raise their chicks on islands in the temperate waters around Hawaii. It is possible to walk amongst them, even when they are nesting. This in itself is a very odd experience for a human, accustomed as we are to the fact that so many other animals fear us and seek to get away from us.[1]

They mate for life, and show significant site fidelity as well, often returning to make nests where they were hatched. One couple raises one chick per year; they take it in turns to sit on the egg, each one going out to feed for several weeks while the other one takes their turn on the nest. The parent on the nest neither eats nor drinks while they wait for their mate to return – sometimes, as in this story, one parent may wait more than five weeks for his mate to relieve him (Safina 2002, 4–6).

Albatross go through an adolescence that lasts several years, and during this time one of their great activities is dance. They are courting, in ethological terminology, working out who they will partner with, but, as we will see, dance is communicative in contexts other than courting, and along with dance there is also a lot of vocalisation and grooming. The story of the particular couple I relate here is connected to the story of a human couple named Louise and Rick. Their home is situated on a bluff overlooking the ocean on the small island of Kaua'i, north-west of Oahu. Here the albatross couple courted and danced, and last year they built a nest and had their first egg together.[2] This was a new nesting location for albatross – there was no record of any albatross nesting here before. Louise and Rick said that they felt deeply honoured to have the birds select their yard for their nest. The nest was just inches from the house, and Louise and Rick observed the birds, the nest, and the egg over the next eight weeks. They cherished the fact that they were living so close to the albatross, and they asked some native Hawaiian friends to help name the birds. Accordingly, the female was

---

1   The albatross' lack of fear has contributed to their vulnerability to rapacious human desires for consumption – a desire for feathers for women's hats, for example, that drove one albatross species to the absolute edge of extinction, and a desire for albumen – used in photography – that fuelled an egg poaching industry on Midway Island that also had devastating effects on the North Pacific albatross. The population probably dropped from about 10 million to about one million birds (Safina 2002, 80–81, 183–84; Ruttle n.d.).

2   Rick, Louise and Hob Osterlund (from the Albatross Network) deduce that this was the first egg the couple had.

named Makana, meaning 'the freely given gift', and the male became Kūpa'a meaning 'steadfast, loyal, protector, good provider'.

Louise took notes on everything. She saw the egg being laid, she knew when the dad returned to give the mum a break. She knew when the dad started getting so weak, after five weeks of patient brooding, that he actually had to leave the egg. And she and Rick knew from albatross biologists that there was a grace period of about four days during which the chick would survive unattended, if a parent returned to continue incubating it. They waited tensely to see what would happen, and they were incredibly relieved when the mother returned after three days.

Not long after the mother returned, the father also came in. And by now it was clear to all that something was wrong with the egg. Here I take up the story in Louise's and Rick's own words.

Louise: When we came back to our house on the afternoon of the third day, we saw she was there, and then he came back on the 31st, 12 days later, and that's when the egg was broken. We think it had broken that morning, because I'd been watching it and it seemed okay.

That was when it was really sad. We did nothing but cry that whole day, pretty much. Because they, Makana and Kūpa'a, were out there mourning and crying. They were crying this most mournful . . .

Rick: *They* were crying!

Louise: We were *all* crying. You could tell it was a different sound. They were doing the 'sky moo', but instead of their 'oooh, oooh', it was 'aah, aah' [wailing]. It was sad. Awful. Just awful.

Rick: But she did sit on it for those 12 days, and she was talking to it and moving it, and then on the morning that he came back again, she got off the nest and the egg was flat.

Louise: The egg had been getting darker, too. The colour of it had changed. There was a chick inside, but it was dead. It was already kind of crushed a little, and mixed in with the dirt. You could see feathers, down.

Rick: So Kūpa'a came up, and Makana stood up to greet him, and it appeared that he understood what the situation was sooner than she did. Or, that he was able to accept it.

Louise: I don't think she knew before that, that the egg was broken.

Rick: She may have been in that trance state. So, she kept on trying to sit on it, and he would talk to her. He was starting to groom her. And she started to appear to realise that there was a problem with the egg, and they started to grieve. She really struggled to accept it – the loss of their chick. We can't do anything but anthropomorphise, because from their behaviour it appeared that she didn't want to accept that the egg was gone. And so she'd try to rearrange it in the nest, and she'd talk to it, and he would talk to it and then he would try to comfort her. Aah, it was difficult. And it was difficult for them. You could tell that they really struggled with their emotions.

Louise: It was just like he was saying, 'This is what's happened and you've got to accept it'. He would nuzzle her, and talk to her, and a couple of times she almost appeared to be saying 'Leave me alone' to him. She almost was just drawing back from his grooming, and you could just see that he was trying to get her to understand, and she knew but she didn't want to accept it. It really seemed very clear.

Rick: He wasn't making any effort to get her off so he could sit on the egg. So he really knew there was no reason to continue sitting on the nest. But he stayed with her for a good three, four hours.

Louise: He'd walk away a few times, and then he'd come back and try to comfort her. But it was a long time. Then about 12:30, she went out and walked over there, waited for the wind, took off, and then changed her mind. She just totally changed her mind, like saying 'I'm not going'. She crash landed and she ran back over here. She just couldn't leave . . . couldn't leave. And she sat on the nest. She sat on the nest a lot. And he kept trying to groom her and trying to get her to accept it, and it's like she knew it, but it was like she said 'I don't care'. He finally left at 1:10. She tried to leave three other times, and went back to the nest, and finally she left at 4:30. She'd get up, she'd walk out there, she'd look around. I couldn't tell if she was waiting for the wind to be right and she was ready, or if she was trying to decide if she should go yet. So she finally left about 4:30 in the afternoon.

Rick: They had left separately. Which makes the next part even more remarkable.

Louise: On February 9, that's about the time the egg would have hatched if it had lived, they came back.

Rick: Together.

Louise: Together. Yes. So how can you not think, I mean, it's just impossible not to think that they knew that that was the time it would have hatched. It's just too coincidental.

Rick: So they came back to the nest, they talked to the egg remains, and they grieved. They comforted each other.

Louise: Yes, they both went right over to the nest and started doing the same things they were doing when they realised that the egg was not going to hatch.

Rick: But they didn't try to sit on it. They talked to it.

Louise: Right, they talked to it.

Rick: And they grieved and they sat near the nest but they didn't sit on the nest.

Louise: Yes, they sat near it, around it. They'd get up and walk around, and then come back and sit near the nest. Talk some more. And that was really sad, too. They were there a few hours if I remember right.

Rick: There's no doubt they knew exactly what had been their egg. They weren't picking up a stone or talking to a stone, they were talking to the egg remains. But the story doesn't end . . . because they came back. They came back a week later, together. They went to the nest, they grieved for a while. And then they . . . they went out in the yard and they danced.

Louise: We've read, or someone's told us, that Laysan albatross only dance until they commit, until they decide that they are each other's mate. But they were dancing, and they clearly had decided before this that they were each other's mate. They were dancing just like teenagers, like young courting albatrosses do. And then they were around for probably another month.

Rick: They came back almost daily, and the appearance was that they were deciding where their nest was going to be next year. They walked all along the driveway here, and they'd pick a spot and they'd settle down, spend a couple of days there, and then try another spot.

The albatross left for the months they spend in the air, and, as of the time of writing, Louise and Rick are waiting for their return. In reflecting on these events, Louise again pointed to the difficulty and necessity of telling stories like this:

And even if our interpretation of it is wrong, it is clear that they were experiencing something, their behaviour was different, they have a relationship; there was clearly a process going on, even if it is not exactly as we interpret it; there was a process they were going through to relate what had happened, and get through what had happened.

The story of how Louise and Rick came to have these albatross dancing, mating and nesting in their yard is part of a wider story of multispecies conviviality. It is driven in part by a remarkable woman named Hob Osterlund who has organised the Kaua'i Albatross Network and who is indefatigable in her love and advocacy of albatross. The story is too long to tell fully here, but the main point is that many people in this area have so loved sharing their lives and properties with albatross that they are now involved in programs to assist the birds to relocate from places of potential harm to these places of relative safety. The most massive potential harm, of course, is sea level rise. Ninety percent of the Laysan albatross nest on Midway Island. If sea levels rise as anticipated due to anthropogenic climate change, their nesting ground will no longer exist (Safina 2002, 166–67).

People in Kaua'i and other islands are developing transitional ecologies that will help albatross form new fidelities to places where they will continue to be safe even in the event of sea level rise. They are enticed by decoys that give the impression of dancing albatross, and the decoys are accompanied by solar-panelled speakers, disguised as stones, that broadcast albatross sounds of happy dancers.

The crazy love that albatross demonstrate for their mate and chick encounters the crazy love of people who are doing all they can to help them thrive. Exactly here, within the shadow of the Anthropocene, exactly here we encounter the crazy love that keeps calling others back from the edge of disaster, and staying with those who grieve in the wake of death.

Part Three: Ethical poetics in the shadow of the Anthropocene

The philosopher Emmanuel Lévinas' life work has been summarised in the single phrase 'ethics as first philosophy'. He argued, again and again, the two sides of ethics: the entanglements that bring forth subjectivity, and the refusal to justify or ignore the sufferings of others (Bernasconi 1986; Lévinas 1989). This philosophy is, I believe, uniquely relevant to the Anthropocene, for Lévinas came to the view that if philosophy is to be capable of responding to violence, and to refuse the idea that might makes right, it must start with ethics. The heart of ethics is the call from the other. One only comes into becoming within the entangled worlds of life and death through others and though one's response and responsibility to others. One of the terms Lévinas uses to talk about the call is the face. Whether aural or visual, the other's claim on me arrives to interrupt my self-absorption and awaken me to my responsibility as a living subject, which is to say, as an ethical subject.

Lévinas' definition of the face that is particularly pertinent to my analysis is:

> the face is the most basic mode of responsibility. As such . . . the face is the other before death, looking through and exposing death . . . [T]he face is the other who asks me not to let him die alone, as if to do so were to become an accomplice in his death. Thus the face says to me: 'you shall not kill'. (Lévinas & Kearney 1986, 23–24)

There are actually two messages in this statement, and each deserves attention. There is the command against killing, and there is the plea not to be abandoned. Philosophers have devoted themselves primarily to the command not to kill, but the plea may be even more complex, requiring, as it does, that we save the lives we can save, and that we remain faithful to those whose lives we cannot save. As Judith Butler reads Lévinas, this plea awakens us to the precariousness of the lives of others, and thereby to the precariousness of all life (2004, 134).

A Dingo reading of Lévinas urges us to focus on the appeal not to be left to die alone. In pressing the significance of this plea, I am moved by how Lévinas subtly reminds us that actually and ultimately we cannot prevent the deaths of others. In practical and beautiful ways, however, we can refuse to abandon them. Sometimes, in fact, we may even be able to help them return from the death zone. The call of those in peril expresses their longing always for connection within the world of life. We are doubly responsible – first we have the responsibility to hear that call, and secondly we have the responsibility to respond to it.

The refusal to abandon others therefore depends in the first instance on appreciating that there is a call. There are many reasons why we do not hear the calls of others. Geographical distance may be a factor, but all too often there are cultural reasons such as, for example, the philosophical move to refuse the idea that animal deaths concern us. And there are certainly political reasons too – we may not know what is happening, or our ignorance may be strategic. Deliberate ignorance is explained and expressed vividly by David Clark when he writes of 'the alibis that always put the human somewhere else, doing something else when it comes to killing animals and dehumanized or animalized humans' (1999, 185). Perhaps these numerous factors lead to the atrophy of our ethical senses. Perhaps, as Richard Flanagan suggests, 'We have grown autistic to the natural world' (2012).

But in addition to these specific reasons, there is a larger issue that claims us: what is happening to other creatures in this era of mass anthropogenic death may be too large to think, too unprecedented to know how to imagine. And still we are called. For many reasons, then, we need an ethical poetics that brings us into proximities that awaken us both to others and to ourselves, and thus to our responsibilities. Such an ethical poetics will return us to the death zone, and to the crazy love that makes possible the refusal to abandon others.

One such expression of ethical poetics is Janet Laurence's exhibition 'After Eden'. It was shown first at the Sherman Gallery in Sydney and funded by the Sherman Contemporary Art Foundation. Let us enter the gallery, stepping from a hot and bright street into the calm, cool foyer. The gallery is lit as if night were suddenly upon us. When you walk in, your eyes have to adjust, and for a brief moment you are not sure where to put your feet. You wonder where the next step should be, and this uncertainty will be with you the whole time. It will become integral to the experience – not that you are lost, but that your certainty is off balance.

After that first disorienting moment when your body is out of kilter with its surrounds, you realise that something is near. As your eyes fumble to adjust, other eyes gaze at you. The installation of owls and nightjars is not so much a greeting as an enticement. These glowing eyes seem already to be at home, to know more than you, and to beckon. You have to remind yourself that they are not alive. In fact, every nonhuman body in this room is dead, but the depths of all this death will only enter your consciousness gradually.

A few steps bring you into a more open space and to your left you encounter a place of possible healing. Preserved bodies of koalas and Tasmanian devils are surrounded with vials, tubes, healing plants, and spills of blood. Already, before you have fully left the glowing eyes of owls, you are facing a death zone. Amongst the wounded are others who call out with tender care. Not just humans, but plants and water become part of the attempt to heal. The call to come back is visible in these healing gestures. But nothing you know about the future for koalas or devils leads you to sunny optimism. An exquisite tenderness arises here: whatever the outcome, care is offered.

Around you there is a distant call of an owl. Images move and reflect. Veils of gauze surround much of what you see, and there are also screens on which images are projected in ghostly beauty. And always there is this light, invoking the haunting sense that, in Richard Flanagan's evocative words, 'We live in the twilight of some terrible moment, the meaning of which we can only grasp at' (2012).

The burden of living in a world dominated by humans is becoming tangible. One starts to sense the incommensurate gap between our capacity to harm and our capacity to avert all that harm. In the section called 'Sanctuaried', Laurence uses film to allow us to see into a place where protection is both a blessing and a life sentence. Here are films of elephants and pandas. Exactly because the film is not representational, you realise that no representation can capture all this (Butler 2004, 144). Vision can behold, but cannot contain. The languid motion is close, slow, intimate, strange. Nothing can or should contain these images, for they bear witness and so offer an opening into ethics. We see them over and over, as if the lives continue, and continue, and I want to express something in the manner of a prayer: 'let them live', I think, 'let them live'. And 'if only', I think. 'If only' there were a world in which they did not have to carry all this weight. A world in which there were no chains across the elephant's shoulders and around their ankles, a world in which they could escape this liminal zone between the humans who seek to kill them and the humans who seek to save them.

Everywhere you look is a knife in the heart. I pulled up a stool and sat with the dingo in an area titled 'Love and extinction'. Taxidermy is clearly a fine and artful skill. This is *and* is not a dingo, and the dissonance between all that it is *and* all that it is not is troubling. The proximity of a photo of a Tasmanian tiger adds to the disturbance that is fracturing my sense of 'we'. 'I' am here – in all my inadequacy. I encounter myself as one who cries behind the corpse house, longing for those 'we' have killed, and unable to save those 'we' are now killing.

In the centre of the gallery we encounter a circular display bearing the title 'Anthropocene'. The shelves are layered, and the whole construction is surrounded by gauze. There are barn owls that look like mummies, and there are the delicate bones of flying foxes. There are the bodies of myriad brightly coloured little birds, in all the glorious delicacy of smooth feathers, tiny brittle beaks and feet, and the startling stillness of wings that beat no more. You can walk around, and around. You can look at every individual on every shelf, and in every group. You can think about every slender bone that once held up a leathery wing to beat through the night sky in search of blossoms and nectar. You can think of hoots and squabbles, songs and chirps. And you cannot find a depth that feels deep enough to be with them properly. Of course, you tell yourself, this is how it is in the house of life: everything that lives will die. We know this. But here, every creature bears a label. The section as a whole has a label too: 'Anthropocene'. The dead bodies are not allowed to decay: they are tagged, counted, described, and held in climate-controlled environments for safe-keeping. This 'Anthropocene' is a mirror. It seems that we are creatures who not only abandon life, pushing it over the brink and letting it go, but who also carefully curate the specimens.

Laurence's 'After Eden' offers another dimension to being 'after'. Recall that, in Hatley's analysis, to be after others is to be situated in cross-generational relationships such that one is always after others, and for the future. But in the face of the dead bodies, curated for posterity while the living creatures and species are lost to the world forever, we see a more terrible possibility of being after. This is the after of those whose living others are no more. It is the after of those who inhabit a crowded loneliness surrounded by superbly studied and curated dead bodies.

And yet, the bright little bodies grasp us and insist that we acknowledge that there is luminosity even here in this shadow of the Anthropocene. Laurence's 'After Eden' seems to want to capture the ambiguity of 'after', an ambiguity that includes after in the sense of forever gone, as well as the sense of always happening. We live after that first Eden in the sense that we are always outside the gates of paradise. And yet in so far as we still live in a world of (diminishing) life, Eden still surrounds us. Every creature is a fragment of creation, a chip off the great block of earth life. We live now at a threshold of generational transition in which the future will either collapse into death or will flourish in new life. Paradise is not wholly lost, Laurence seems to be saying. There was and is a world in which every song had a singer, and every singer had a home. Outside the gallery birds still sing, but in the chamber called 'Anthropocene' they are enshrouded by ghostly silence.

Part Four: In the shadow of Eden

I turn now to an Eden story that is taking place in close proximity. The expulsion part of the Eden narrative is one of the great stories of the Western world, and it is repeated again and again as we experience the trauma of loss, and seek to remake the world into some vision of paradise (Merchant 2004). We seem to want to hold to the conviction that if we could expel or exterminate all those who annoy us, our particular version of paradise would be secure. I am referring to huge issues of colonisation, extermination, dislocation, genocide, ecocide, speciocide and more. We know this story as ethnic cleansing, with visions of racial or religious purity, and we know it again and again in relation to animals. Let us consider the awful life prospects of animals who are condemned by the slippery label 'pest'. When an animal is declared a pest, death becomes its destiny. Suddenly, whatever it does is wrong in the eyes of those who are determined to get rid of it. And suddenly wherever it is, that is where it must not be. A purist vision arises at the Gates of Eden in which perfection is imagined to be always on a near horizon, and violent death lurks in powerful policy and practice cloaked in the aura of management.

The particular garden in which this violence in now being enacted is Sydney's Royal Botanic Gardens, and the species now being persecuted are flying foxes. The most common species in Sydney is the grey-headed flying fox (*Pteropus poliocephalus*). Like the other Australian *Pteropus* species, they navigate principally by sight, feed exclusively on plant foods, and are among the largest flying mammals on earth. With their long-distance capacity to pollinate and disperse seeds, they are a keystone species for native Australian forests and woodlands with which they are co-evolved. If flying foxes become extinct, either wholly or 'in the wild', that which remains of Australian native forests will also be imperilled. The great eucalypts that make south eastern Australia the unique place that it is depend in large measure on the work that flying foxes do for trees (Hall & Richards 2000; Booth et al. 2008).

For well over a century, whitefella settlers did their utmost to exterminate flying foxes. With government approval, they shot, poisoned, gassed, burnt, and electrocuted these creatures. They cut down their maternity camps, created a great variety of forms of harassment to drive them away, paid a bounty for the corpses, and even bombed them (Martin & McIlwee 2002; see also Rose 2011a). Flying fox numbers are plummeting at this time, they are listed as threatened, and they are federally protected. And yet, in Queensland the government issued a decree on 7 September 2012, Threatened Species Day, allowing all four species of flying foxes to be shot. There was legislation against cruelty to animals, and shooting had been deemed to be cruel, so the government had to exempt flying foxes from the cruelty legislation. Suddenly, it seems, pain doesn't matter if the creature experiencing it is unwanted, and suddenly, it seems, extinction doesn't matter either, if the creature tumbling into the abyss of loss is unwanted. In NSW, where Sydney is located, flying foxes are legally shot by orchardists who are issued licenses to do so, and they can now be legally harassed.

Flying foxes are notable for their site fidelity. Maternity camps are central to the future of flying foxes generations, for these are where mothers gather to give birth and congregate for protection of the young. The most spectacular Sydney camp is in the Royal Botanic Gardens. The trees the flying foxes have chosen to camp in are heritage trees, deemed to be valuable because of their rarity; they are non-native trees and they have suffered under the continuous presence of flying foxes (Leishman 2007). The Royal Botanic Gardens has a statutory duty to protect these specimens, and the only option they are prepared to adopt is to expel the flying foxes.

In 2010 the Botanic Gardens was granted permission by the federal Minister for the Environment to embark upon a 30-year process of expelling the flying foxes through the use of noise harassment. The procedure is designed to cause pain and distress. That is what it takes to break site fidelity: success depends on the trauma that can be inflicted upon flying foxes. There has been a lot of debate and protest, and every major point has been made: trees can be netted, it doesn't have to be either-or; a botanic gardens should be especially attentive toward a keystone species that is so crucial to trees; causing stress to a threatened species is not appropriate; expelling members of a threatened species from a maternity camp is not appropriate; stressing pregnant females is not appropriate; co-existence is possible, it would cost less than expulsion, and would set a benchmark for good practice. Nonetheless, the procedure started on 4 June 2012.

In Laurence's 'After Eden' we saw an image of ourselves as a species that pushes others into the death zone, abandons them, and then claims the bodies for specimens. Similarly, in the Botanic Gardens, 'asset protection' trumps living creatures, and specimens trump future generations. In a move that bears alarming similarity to the famous decree that 'death solves all problems' (attributed to Stalin), the problem of protecting trees is presented as amenable only to one solution: the elimination of flying foxes.

All this violence, vilification and trauma, and all this intransigent refusal to embrace co-existence stems from a will to power enacted on the bodies of flying foxes as they seek to sustain their lives in the garden that is their home. Those of us who raise our voices to try to stop the violence, and who are committed to not abandoning flying foxes in their time of persecution, find ourselves living with our own inadequacy, and living with the sense of shame that arises in the face of unstoppable cruelty.

It takes crazy love to keep defending the lives of the persecuted, and over time it puts us in a place of witness to the apparently unstoppable and the increasingly unimaginable. This is a place of emotional turmoil and exhaustion. In the eloquently understated words of one flying fox carer: 'we are not holding up very well here'.

I started by discussing unfathomable loss and the need to respond. It is clear that part of the response must be to our fellow humans who are at the front lines in the expanding death zones of the Anthropocene. In this terrible time we need blessings as well as exhortations, and yet every blessing must, I believe, be complicated by the knowledge of all this death. Peter Boyle's poem 'Dawn Ritual of Purification for families and descendants of those who participate in slaughter' is a guide to making peace; it homes in on our condition, and expresses the desire to be other than those who kill and those who abandon (2009, 91–92). The final portion of the poem pulls these themes into this time of death:

To the west
eyeing the west as an equal
eyeing the west as a mother
eyeing the west as your child
scatter the grain
scatter the bright joy of water
kneel
kneel do not speak
wait for the light that rises and sets
to touch you
wait for the winds that come
from the lands of all the dead
to filter around your ears
wait for their voices to enter you
wait till their voices speak
wait till the words
are fierce and tender
wait till the words
tear at the sinews of pain
till the words slice
through forehead and skull
till the heart is open to all words
the earth is struggling to say
Kneel longer
wait till their voices
cease
wait till the silence steadies you
speak
"Brothers"
speak
"Sisters"
speak
"I give back
I give back"

Acknowledgements

The research on which this paper is based was carried out under a grant from the Australian Research Council (DP110102886). Special thanks to Louise and Rick in Hawaii, and to albatross carer par excellence Hob Osterlund (www.albatrosskauai.org/wp/). Further thanks to Louise Saunders and other dedicated flying fox carers (www.bats.org.au/; www.dontshootbats.com/). Many of the ideas in this paper first took shape in conversation with members of the Extinction Studies Working Group during a week-long conversation in February 2012. Thanks to Michelle Bastian, Jeff Bussolini, Matt Chrulew, Rick De Vos, James Hatley, Jake Metcalf and Thom van Dooren. An anonymous referee gave me excellent advice as well as enthusiastic encouragement; I am grateful for both.

Works cited

Bernasconi R (1986). Lévinas and Derrida: the question of the closure of metaphysics. In R Cohen (Ed.). *Face to face with Lévinas* (pp181–202). Albany: State University of New York Press.

Booth C, Parry-Jones K, Beynon N, Pallin N & James B (2008). Why NSW should ban the shooting of flying foxes. Sydney: Humane Society International [Online]. Available: hsi.org.au/editor/assets/Actions/FFreport4Jan09.pdf [Accessed on 27 February 2013].

Boyle P (2009). *Apocrypha: texts collected and translated by William O'Shaunessy*. Sydney: Vagabond Press.

Butler J (2004). *Precarious life: the powers of mourning and violence*. London: Verso.

Clark D (1999). On being 'The last Kantian in Nazi Germany': dwelling with animals after Lévinas. In J Ham & M Senior (Eds). *Animal acts: configuring the human in Western history* (pp165–98). New York: Routledge.

Flanagan R (2012). Opening address for 'Janet Laurence: after Eden'. Unpublished manuscript.

Hall L & Richards G (2000). *Flying foxes: fruit and blossom bats of Australia*. Sydney: UNSW Press.

Hatley J (2000). *Suffering witness: the quandary of responsibility after the irreparable*. Albany: State University of New York Press.

Heaney S (2006). A dog was crying tonight in Wicklow also. *Poeziba* [Online]. Available: poezibao.typepad.com/poezibao/2006/02/seamus_heaney.html.

extrait 1, poezibao.typepad.com/poezibao/2006/02/anthologie_perm_8.html
[Accessed 27 February 2013].

Leishman A (2007). The history of grey-headed flying-foxes in the Royal Botanic
Gardens, Sydney [Online]. Available: www.sydneybats.org.au/index.php/
download_file/view/126/134/ [Accessed 3 May 2013].

Lévinas E (1989). Ethics as first philosophy. In S Hand (Ed.). *The Lévinas reader*
(pp75–87). Malden: Blackwell Publishing.

Lévinas E & Kearney R. (1986). Dialogue with Emmanuel Lévinas. In R Cohen
(Ed.). *Face to face with Lévinas* (pp13–33). Albany: State University of New
York Press.

Martin L & McIlwee AP (2002). The reproductive biology and intrinsic capacity
for increase of the grey-headed Flying-fox poliocephalus (Megachiroptera),
and the implications of culling. In P Eby & D Lunney (Eds). *Managing the
Grey-headed Flying-fox as a threatened species in NSW* (pp91–108). Sydney:
Royal Zoological Society of New South Wales.

Merchant C (2004). *Reinventing Eden: the fate of nature in Western culture*. New
York: Routledge.

Rose D (2011a). Flying foxes: kin, keystone, kontaminant. *Australian Humanities
Review*, Special issue. Unloved others: death of the disregarded in the time of
extinctions, R Deborah & T Van Dooren (Eds), 50: 119–36.

Rose D (2011b). *Wild dog dreaming: love and extinction*. Charlottesville: University
of Virginia Press.

Rose D (2012). Multispecies knots of ethical time, *Environmental Philosophy* IX
(1):127–40.

Ruttle G (n.d.) 'Wisdom' returns to Midway Atoll [Online]. Available:
www.redbubble.com/people/whalegeek/writing/
5400046-wisdom-returns-to-midway-atoll [Accessed 12 March 2013].

Safina C (2002). *Eye of the albatross: visions of hope and survival*. New York: Henry
Holt and Company.

Shestov L (1982). Speculation and apocalypse: The religious philosophy of
Vladimir Solovyov. In *Speculation and revelation*, (pp18–88). Athens: Ohio
University Press.

Van Dooren T (2002). Being-with-death: Heidegger, Lévinas, Derrida & Bataille
on death. Unpublished manuscript.

Van Dooren T (2011). Vultures and their people in India: equity and entanglement
in a time of extinctions. *Australian Humanities Review* 50: 45–61.

2
Human and animal space in historic 'pet' cemeteries in London, New York and Paris

Hilda Kean

This chapter will analyse the nature of three important historic animal cemeteries. These are the Hyde Park pet cemetery in London, Hartsdale pet cemetery outside New York, and the Cimetière des Chiens in Asnières-sur-Seine in Paris. Dating back to the late 19th century, these are the oldest animal cemeteries in their respective countries. Those in New York state and Paris still function as 'open' cemeteries. Animal cemeteries emphasise the importance of particular individual animals to individual humans. Although there are occasional references such as a plaque 'In memory of the millions of animals whose lives are taken for research and testing' (in Hartsdale) or to 'the strays and ill-treated creatures' (in the PDSA animal cemetery in Ilford, London), these are primarily sites of expression of emotion of humans towards personally known animals with whom at least one human shared their personal living space.

During the 19th century the status of domestic animals grew; and, in turn, so did the commemoration of animals after death. Despite their relatively short lives, 'pets were seen as being worthy of celebration with the visual language of permanence'. Thus Matthew Craske has described the work of artist Landseer, famous for animal paintings, who

H Kean (2013). Human and animal space in historic 'pet' cemeteries in London, New York and Paris. In J Johnston & F Probyn-Rapsey (Eds). *Animal death.* Sydney: Sydney University Press.

'in much the manner as a taxidermist, [was] commissioned to paint, as if in life, the corpse of a dog brought to his studio by a grieving owner' (Craske 2000, 42). As Diana Donald has astutely analysed, in Landseer's paintings each animal has a 'distinctive psychology' (Donald 2007, 144). His portraits of dogs were not 'banal portraiture' but 'emotive moral dramas, in which the mentality of animals, and its relationship to that of humans, were the real subject' (Donald 2007, 127). His popularity helped influence the way that domestic animals were seen as sentient beings (Kean 2000, 80–2). This depiction of animals was one influence on the initiation of public animal cemeteries but so too was the growing public – as well as private – memorialisation in civic and national sculpture at least in Europe and the United States of America (Kean 2011a; Michalski 1998, 7–8). In addition, such public animal cemeteries were also situated, as Philip Howell has discussed, 'within the same moral and spiritual framework as the reformed practice of interment, and the parallel growth of sanitary suburban cemeteries' (Howell 2002, 11). Here was an attempt to alleviate the status of animals not merely in the present but in some future afterlife. The *Strand Magazine* gave status to dogs by suggesting 'So intelligent and so amiable a dog assuredly deserves a Christian burial' ('A cemetery for dogs', *Strand Magazine* 1893, 625–33 as quoted in Howell 2002, 10). Certainly the sentiments famously expressed by Jane Carlyle on the death of her dog Nero were not hers alone: 'I grieve for him as if he had been my little human child' (Howell 2002, 13).

The three cemeteries have changed in different ways over the past century. The London Hyde Park Dog Cemetery as it was originally called (it also admitted the corpses of three small monkeys, and two cats) was established in 1880 in the part of the park that lies adjacent to Kensington Gardens (Gordon-Stables 1912, 257–59; Simpson 1902, 260). Although accounts vary as to the origins of the cemetery, either initiated by the Duke of Connaught (Gordon-Stables 1912) or through a favour of the gatekeeper to friends who lived nearby (Pet Cemetery 1997), it is evident that the cemetery was not run for profit but as a philanthropic gesture towards grieving animal owners. The acreage was small, being situated within the garden of Mr Winbridge the gatekeeper at the Victoria Lodge (Pet Cemetery 1997). Within a few years there was no further space and by 1902, when it contained some three hundred graves, it was permanently closed (Pet Cemetery 1997; Simpson

Figure 2.1 Hyde Park Pet Cemetery, London (1997).

1902, 257). Subsequently many animal cemeteries have been established in the London area (and elsewhere), including those run by
animal charities such as the renovated PDSA cemetery in Ilford which
both hosts memorials for individual animals deemed to have been heroes during the Second World War and the remains of thousands killed
by their human 'companions' at the start of the war (Kean 2013; Parker
2008). Since the early years of the 20th century, the Hyde Park cemetery
has no longer fulfilled its original function. It has nevertheless been
preserved as a heritage site although opportunities to visit have been restricted. (It became a heritage site and could be seen on 'Open House'
weekends one day a year but this opportunity to view is no longer available.)

By way of contrast the geographical location of the Hartsdale
cemetery, the oldest animal cemetery in the United States, founded in
1896, north of New York in Westchester County, is far from the centre
of the sprawling city. The original owner Dr Johnson was a veterinary surgeon. Apparently he was inspired by seeing similar cemeteries

23

Animal death

Figure 2.2 Overview of Hartsdale Pet Cemetery, New York (2007).

in London, Paris and Edinburgh.[1] He offered his apple orchard as a burial site for a friend's dog and then developed the ground as a business.[2] Initially five acres, the cemetery continues to function and grow. By 1920 some 3000 animals had been buried including dogs and cats, one lion, two monkeys, three ducks, one horse and a number of chickens ('Where good dogs go' 1920, 68). Today there are remains of nearly 80,000 nonhuman animals although in recent years it has also taken in cremated humans too, reaching by 2007 some 700 such ashes. The cremated remains, for example, of Sandra Rindner from New York City who founded 'Miss Rumple's Orphanage for Small Dogs' and who died in 2006 have been buried there along with the remains of four canine companions and one feline called Buzby.[3]

---

1 The small Edinburgh dog cemetery within the castle grounds was started during the 19th century as a burial place for regimental mascots and for the dogs of officers and is still tended as a memorial ground. 'Where good dogs go', 1920, 68.
2 Hartsdale Pet Cemetery and Crematory. Retrieved 13 March 2013 from www.hartsdalepetcrematory.com/aboutus.
3 'Founder of canine orphanage interred at Hartsdale', 2007, 2. Retrieved 3 June 2013 from site.mawebcenters.com/hartsdalepetcemetery/Newsletters/2007.pdf.

Figure 2.3 Cat on grave at Cimetière des Chiens, Asniere-sur-Seine, Paris (2011).

The Parisian cemetery that presumably inspired Dr Johnson was the Cimetière des Chiens in Asnières-sur-Seine, just outside the city of Paris on the left bank side of the Seine beyond the Clichy bridge. When it was founded in 1899 by Georges Harmois and Marguerite Durand the cemetery was on land occupied by rag and bone men ('chiffonniers'). Soon this site of discarded remains was transformed into an altogether more prestigious place commemorating animal death with the employment of the Parisian architect Eugene Petit as designer of the grand entrance to the cemetery (Cimetière des Chiens 2011). Outside the city this too was a place set apart from the everyday where humans could mourn animals. In recent decades the cemetery has expanded onto adjacent land. It also is a place for living animals. Feral cats are regularly fed within the cemetery by people listed by name within the cemetery who are regulated by the ADCC (Association de Défense du Cimetière de Chiens et Autres Animaux).

Rather than dispose of former family companions as waste, the establishment of specific burial grounds for animals also became 'infused with ... spiritual(ist) associations' (Howell 2002, 12). Initially – and later – public cemeteries for animals reflected the form of the commemoration found in contemporary human cemeteries. Thus, in London, funerals were conducted that included attendance by former canine friends (Gordon-Stables 1912, 257–58). Headstones were laid out in little rows and carried epitaphs; for example, as quoted on the headstone of 'Betty':

And when at length my own life's work is o'er,
I hope to find her waiting as of yore,
Eager, expectant, glad to meet me at the door.
(Gordon-Stables 1912, 258)

All three cemeteries include similar sentiments of hope of a future meeting. 'A bientôt au paradis', is but one Parisian example. As an early epitaph from Hartsdale records:

My Adored Zowi I do not cringe from death as much
Since you are gone, my truest friend.
Thy dear dumb soul will wait for mine
However long before the end
('Where the good dogs go' 1920, 68).

There are frequent visual representations of the gate to paradise. More recent burials reflect other religious sentiments, most notably those of Judaism, with small stones placed on the gravestone, as evident on the memorial to the rabbit Bunga in Asnières, or the Star of David on the memorial to Bethel 'good girl' in Hartsdale. As Norine Dresser has noted, if no specific animal rituals are available then pet owners tend to incorporate animals into rituals originally intended just for humans (Dresser 2000, 102). Thus markers will not be put on gravestones

Figure 2.4 Gate to Heaven memorial, Cimetière des Chiens,
Asniere-sur-Seine (2011).

of animals within a Jewish household until a year has passed (Dresser 2000, 100). However, the still functioning cemeteries at Hartsdale and Asnières have, in different ways, attempted to go beyond the creation of a site of personal mourning to a site that remembers the role of individual animals with the nation's and city's story.

National heritages

Dating to the early years of the cemetery, Barry, a 19th-century St Bernard dog, and national hero, was represented by a grand sculpture at the entrance to Asnières (Terhune 1937, 284). On the dog's back is a child he has rescued during the course of his work at the Hospice of Great St Bernard in the Alps. According to the story, he saved 40 people. He was killed by the 41st who, in an exhausted state, thinking him a wolf, stabbed Barry. Nevertheless the dog made his way back to the hospice to raise the alarm, directing a rescue party to the injured man before dying himself. Although the story has recently been debunked, the presence of a represented Barry is nevertheless an attempt to construct the cemetery as more than a site of personal mourning (Bondeson 2011, 190–95). This development of the cemetery as a broader heritage site is reinforced by the stone of 2006 to Moustache, remembering his death nearly two centuries before. Moustache, a black poodle dog prominent in Napoleon's campaigns in Austria and Spain, died from a cannonball in 1812. His plaque was erected by those who identified themselves as 'Amis du patrimoine Napoléonien' rather than as animal lovers as such.[4]

The first memorial in Hartsdale to go beyond a personal relationship with an individual animal was the 1923 statue of a nameless German shepherd dog, designed by Walter Buttendorf and sculpted by Robert Caterson, in 1923. This nameless dog wearing a red cross is sculpted alongside a soldier's battered helmet and canteen. It is dedicated to 'man's most faithful friend', the dogs who played their part 'in bringing peace and comfort to the men who were wounded on the battlefield.' This would be the first of several such memorials in Hartsdale. Recent plaques have included those to dogs who served during the Oklahoma bombing in 1995 and to Sirius. This rescue dog – who worked with David Lim, a police officer – was the only such dog to die in the aftermath of the attack on the World Trade Center in 2001. Lim had been trapped in the collapsed building and was one of the last survivors to be

---

4   By way of contrast, the statue of the Alaskan malamute dog, Balto, who brought lifesaving diptheria serum to the stranded people of Nome in Alaska, was not erected in New York's Central Park by people with connections to Alaska but rather by dog lovers living near the park (Kean 2009).

Figure 2.5 Barry at the gates of Cimetière des Chiens (2011).

rescued. Ironically Lim had left the dog behind in the basement while he rushed up as far as the 44th floor as he had not wanted to endanger Sirius. Lim was forbidden from going back to the basement to search for Sirius. The dog was found months later and brought up in a basket covered with the American flag, in a similar ritual to that enacted for human victims. Subsequently there was a memorial service attended by 400 people and 100 dogs.[5]

The location of such animal memorialisation is significant. Some countries, most notably Australia, have created national icons of certain animals in war, often in important memorial sites. In particular the

1936 Wallace Anderson 'Simpson and his donkey' outside the Melbourne Shrine of Remembrance and the 1988 version by Peter Corlett outside the Australian War Memorial in Canberra have ensured that this earlier iconography of the emerging ANZAC nation remains a central part of national commemoration that the founders of the Australian War Memorial in Canberra had established (Scates 2009, 159; Kean 2012b, 251–56). This Australian trend of commemorating animals' role in war in national sites of memory has been most recently perpetuated through the 2009 'Animals in War' memorial of Steve Mark Holland in the same location. Drawing on a bronze horse's head that was previously part of a memorial to the Desert Mounted Corps in Port Said in Egypt, destroyed during the Suez crisis, it pays attention particularly through an accompanying plaque to the various roles of animals who 'served alongside Australians' (Kean 2011b, 63).

However, such examples are in national sites of war memory where people go to remember and think primarily about the human war dead. Such landscapes are very different locations to those of memorials in animal cemeteries. The memorials to Moustache or Sirius, for example, will only be seen by those already sufficiently interested in nonhuman animals to be visiting an animal cemetery. Such memorials, while erected with respectful intentions, are unlikely to alert people generally to the importance of animals' role within a nation's heritage.

Blurring animal and human space

This raises the question of the extent to which such cemeteries are 'animal' places. In discussing 'nature's spaces', for example, Steve Hinchliffe has suggested that they are not 'straightforwardly independent of the societies with which they co-exist. A better spatial imagery than an island of natural facts untouched by people will be needed' (Hinchliffe et al. 2005, 33). In thinking more expansively about a continuum between animals included and excluded within 'everyday space', Philo has argued that companion animals are readily accepted into such places

---

5   '15 seconds of hell: K-9 officer lives through North Tower collapse'. CNN.com. Retrieved 13 March 2013 from edition.cnn.com/SPECIALS/2002/ america.remembers/stories/heroes/lim.html.

(Philo 1995, 677). Animal cemeteries are, I suggest, places of over-lapping, if not competing, geographies in which human and animal are blurred in various ways. In discussing animal memorialisation in Australia, Rose Searby, for example, has talked of the way in which me-morial landscape is 'co-constructed by humans and animals, something that can enable a repositioning of animals in relation to humans and result in the creation of a new framework of reference for memori-alising animals' (Searby 2008, 120). Certainly in some sense one can define these animal cemeteries as animal places, since they contain the corpses or cremated remains of animals. But these corporeal remains are never seen. All that is visible are human words and iconography and sometimes a photo of the animal when alive or an engraved represent-ation in stone.

To an interested visitor – rather than a former companion – the physicality of the animal is, in some ways, less important that the way in which the animal is described, usually by an individual or couple of humans. Human emotions towards a dead animal are dominant but, as many of the inscriptions suggest, such sentiment is reflective of a re-lationship crossing species boundaries. As James Serpell has observed, 'human–pet relationships are unique because they are based primarily on the transfer or exchange of social rather than economic or utilitarian provisions' (Serpell 2005, 131). There are narratives that describe an in-dividual's behaviour or characteristics, or even, in a few instances, the prizes won by pedigree cats or dogs such as 'Ici Reposent les Premiers Komondors de France de Bergers Hongrois Celebres Champions Na-tionaux Internationaux et Mondiale'.

Across time the dominant sentiments are of the value the human has derived from the relationship. Typical examples range from the epitaph to Barrie in London: 'In life the firmest friend, The first to wel-come, Foremost to defend' or 'Minouche, my best pal' in Hartsdale in 1937, or Bébé 'Toi, notre chien, plus humain qu'un humain . . .' in As-nières this century. In many instances – again across time – the animal death provides the human with an opportunity to talk about their own condition that has been ameliorated by the now dead animal. Thus the early gravestone to Douchka 'compagne fidele dans mes jours de tristesse et de solitude 1894–1907' and 'A notre petit Marquis si fidele mort le 24 Juillet 1923 a l'age de 9 ans notre seul ami'. This continues in the recent past, for example, in the epitaph to a small black dog: 'Sophie mon bébé nous avons eu 17 ans d'amour toi et tes petites soeurs vous avez remplacé l'enfant que je n'ai pas eu. Je t'aime a jamais. Ta petite Mère'. Such outpourings are not exclusively French. Thus in Hartsdale Trixie is described in 1987 as 'very best friend' and in Hyde Park Puck Lee was described, 'In a false world thy heart was brave and true'.[6] In discussing animal–human relationships and their representations generally, it is important to look at the broader cultural and chronological contexts. The relationship is not constant (Brantz 2010, 10–11; Kean 2012a, 58–60). Nevertheless, strikingly, but perhaps not surprisingly, there is the overwhelmingly constant feature of a positive and emotional engagement. While fashions in memorial stones or the language of loss may shift, an underpinning sentiment does cross time. It is the human expressing emotion, often addressed to the dead but deemed receptive animal. Morris, Knight and Lesley have noted, 'That pet owners believe more in animal emotion is likely due to the extent to which they have engaged socially with their own animals' (2012, 221). This understanding continues after the animal's death.

Changing contexts: emotion and language

Clearly such epitaphs illustrate human emotion towards the dead animal; but they do more than that. The cemetery itself has certain conventions: not least that those visiting will be sympathetic to the idea of remembering animal companions. It is a space that provides a safe location for humans to convey positive emotion towards this particular animal–human relationship. Such emotion may more generally be subject to ridicule or derision. Although interactive websites or obituary pages of newspapers may provide opportunities for the expression of loss, they are so 'public' and detached from physical space that it is impossible to easily 'monitor' visitors. This has been analysed by Jane Desmond in relation to pet obituaries covered in some American newspapers where their proximity to human obituaries has been seen as

---

6 Gordon-Stables 1912, 259. Another example drawn from the Berkshire Park animal cemetery to the west of Sydney is 'Our beloved son Ewark Suen now that you're away from us we will never feel the same. An essential part of our life is missing and nothing else can take your place, mummy and pappa'.

demeaning towards people (Desmond 2011). Companion animals – other than pedigrees who have genealogical breed charts that record the names of their parents and grandparents etc. – routinely have only one given name. The assumption is that they are looked after within a particular family and that if a surname is needed at all it will be that of the humans. Thus although the names of pet animals are always stated, the names of the humans are not. Indeed it is quite unusual to have a full name. Exceptions include 'Mrs Jennie M Owen's Black Pomeranian Rags' in Hartsdale from 1921 or the grand black marble stone of Alfred Anthony D'Elia in which (as at 2007) 21 cats were remembered by name. Thus human sentiments can be expressed anonymously in a quasi-public place. A particularly striking example is on the stone in Hyde Park to 'Fritz Omnia Veritas' with underneath 'Balu son of Fritz poisoned by a cruel Swiss'. The sentiments expressed can be quite revealing about the condition of the human. As in the examples suggested above, it can include declaring oneself to be friendless apart from animal companionship. The 'animal space' in fact permits the most personal of human statements of their *own* condition and past emotional state.

In a cemetery in Western culture, whether human or animal, language is key. As I have discussed elsewhere concerning human gravestones in the 19th century, texts from the Psalms were often employed for those suffering from a long illness. For example, 'I waited patiently for the Lord and he inclined unto me and heard my cry' (Kean 2004, 65). Thus the dead person would be seen to speak. In this example I considered the way in which a woman who was illiterate in life became transformed in death as articulate and literate, thus maintaining a material presence in the village where she had lived and died for some centuries after her death. As Ranciere has discussed, 'The availability of writing – of the "mute" letter – endows any life, or the life of anybody, with the capacity of taking on meaning, of entering into the universe of meaning' (as quoted in Kean 2004, 66).

Recently, in an insightful work, Tom Tyler has critically explored anthropomorphism as a form of anthropocentrism, and different philosophical debates on the nature of language as a symbol of a divide between animals and humans (Tyler 2012, 63ff). Traditionally the possession (or not) of language – defined as an exclusively human attribute – was what was deemed to distinguish humans from animals. This was

Figure 2.6 Balu memorial stone, Hyde Park Pet Cemetery (1997).

challenged most famously by Bentham who attempted to define not language as a dividing line but to employ other senses, notably pain, as a shared experience (Kean 2000, 21–2). In animal cemeteries there is no attempt to make the dead animal speak: rather s/he is a focus for the words of a grieving human. This follows on from the nature of the relationship between a known individual human and a known individual animal. Those forming strong bonds with companion animals understand that there is a form of communication in various ways between humans and animals within a household – even if for scientists this is a relatively new phenomenon (Bradshaw 2011, 210–23).

In the 19th century, Bentham was seeking, amongst other things, to move away from what apparently distinguished humans and animals to what drew them together. Yet at that time, 'speaking animals' were routinely employed by animal welfare campaigners to convince people of the need for humane attitudes. Keri Cronin has carefully explored visual images used by 19th-century campaigners against animal cruelty. In order to invoke sympathy in humans yet to be convinced of the value of animal welfare, animals were depicted as speaking. Such images included the popular image of a Newfoundland dog (famous for rescuing people from drowning), taken from a Landseer painting, used in anti-vivisection propaganda with the slogan 'Save me! I would save you' (Cronin 2011, 214). As Cronin analyses, an imagined voice and agency underscored the fact that nonhuman animals were sentient beings (220). Similarly Teresa Mangum has argued that, in contemporary poetry exploring emotion towards animal loss, 'the human speaker finds himself or herself fighting to articulate the unique dignity and importance of an animal in part to explain to *themselves* and to others how a human could feel such deep grief at the loss of a "mere animal" ' (Mangum 2007, 162; my emphasis).

Writing of the more recent period, Davis et al. have argued that in the 21st century losing a pet is seen as qualitatively similar to losing a beloved human (Davis et al. 2003, 58). The difference is the way in which that loss might be expressed and where. Emotion has been expressed in pet cemeteries from the from the turn of the 19th and 20th centuries onwards: no attempt to explain grief is needed because of the location. The place, the physical landscape of the cemetery, is itself a celebration of a particular personal cross-species relationship. Justification is not needed; nor are measures to convince the unsympathetic of the existence of the sentience of animals. Animals do not need to 'speak' from beyond the grave to convince particular humans that they have consciousness – in this context it is a given. Although an animal 'voice' is absent, many traces of the animal's activities and sense of agency are present. Former actions of animals within a domestic space are recorded as well as the human response. Thus in Asnieres Arry is remembered by a glass bowl containing tennis balls and Iris described

Figure 2.7 Tennis balls for Arry, Cimetière des Chiens (2011).

as 'Aux pieds ailes'. (In the Berkshire Park pet cemetery to the west of Sydney, in language reminiscent of Thomas Hardy's poem about his own epitaph, Cleo Cotton is remembered for her observations within the landscape: 'sunshine, plants, soil, grass and insects. She used to notice such things'.)[7]

Adrian Franklin has argued that in recognising the needs of others and possibilities of mutuality the 'animal–human relation is not one characterised simply by strong sentiments, but also unconsciously challenging and dissolving the human–animal boundary itself' (Franklin 1999, 86). While such dissolving may be found in the emotional engagement expressed in animal cemeteries in some way, there are also sharp divisions: the human is still living and thus able to express emotion or hopes for the future, while the dead animal, obviously, is not. However, the sight of feral cats wandering through Asnières and being

---

7 'He was a man who used to notice such things'. 'Afterwards' in Hardy 1970, 521.

fed amongst the graves also reinforces the cemetery as a place of safety for animals.

Despite the growth in number of animal cemeteries, domestic animals remembered publicly in these ways are still in a minority. There are new forms such as internet remembrance; for example, the websites Gone Too Soon (www.gonetoosoon.org/) or Rainbow Bridge (www.rainbowbridge.com/) that are often explicitly religious or spiritual in tone. Physical 'unofficial' sites such as the memorial wall in the Federal Park in Annandale in Sydney are secular in character. Brief details of the dog's name and dates are written on one of the brick arches near where dogs and humans play. Thus this acts as a signifier of death but within a place not removed from the everyday, in an animal–human place of leisure.

Recently those working with abused or abandoned animals have started to explore the ways in which domestic animals may mourn other animals. Julie Ann Smith of the House Rabbit Society, a rescue society founded in 1988, suggests that rabbits eventually come to understand that their partners are dead by grooming or lying by them (Smith 2005, 190). However, she does not know, she says, whether the rabbit acting in this way will know that this will happen to her/him in the future, albeit concluding that 'animals may understand their own experiences in their own ways' (Smith 2005, 200).

Perhaps one of the most interesting developments in commemorating animal death is the burial ground that exists at the Hillside Animal Sanctuary, in England, just outside Norwich. The sanctuary takes in and look after thousands of abandoned 'farm' animals and horses and donkeys and also undertakes investigations into animal cruelty, particularly in farming. As they state on their website, 'Although at Hillside we have given sanctuary to over 600 horses, ponies and donkeys, most of our residents have been rescued from the farming industry'.[8] (It routinely exposes atrocious conditions even in farms given RSPCA approval.) Animals are not killed but live out their days safely. They are then buried in a small graveyard in the centre of the sanctuary adjacent to the fields where cows graze. The graves are simple, but large, and adorned with modest wooden crosses.

---

8   Hillside Animal Sanctuary. Retrieved on 13 March 2013, www.hillside.org.uk.

Figure 2.8 Dog memorial wall, Federal Park, Annandale, Sydney (2010).

In a discussion at the end of the collection *Killing animals*, Diana Donald noted that 'perhaps the absolute basic distinction is between those kinds of killing that are wilfully invisible, removed from the consciousness of the perpetrators and excluded from the sight of anyone else, and those that are in some way commemorated or represented?' (Animal Studies Group 2006, 198). What is striking about the Hillside example is that the type of animal usually killed in a slaughterhouse and whose corpse is eaten is taking on the status of a companion animal or human being very visibly in a cemetery form. Such an 'afterlife' of dead animals within a cemetery is a very different place to that discussed in a recent collection of 'afterlives' of animals, particularly in natural history museums. In this context, Geoffrey Swinney argues, 'animals were appropriated and reconstructed in humans' image'. They were 'anthropomorphized and fashioned to embody human emotions and values ... Death allows such roles to be consolidated, and the postmortem reconstruction of an animal is both material and epistemological' (Swinney 2011, 221).

In a cemetery animals are not taxidermised; nor are they being represented for some sort of human edification or enlightenment. Although the physical space is public, it is simultaneously personal: the appropriate response to the dead animal is an emotional one rather

Figure 2.9 Grave at Hillside Animal Sanctuary, Frettenham, Norwich.

than intellectual. It is also a place of visible animal death – and the animal has not been killed for food or sport or scientific experimentation. We tend to see animal cemeteries in some ways as a given since they partly mirror human cemeteries, which is perhaps why so little scholarly attention has been paid to them. However, if we consider them in relation to the way in which most nonhuman animals on the planet meet their end and are used after death, perhaps we might see them as places not only worth visiting but thinking about more carefully.

Acknowledgments

Thanks to: Edward C Martin Jr and staff at Hartsdale pet cemetery; Paul Ashton, Pauline O'Loughlin and Katrina Fox for introducing me to the Berkshire pet cemetery and the memorial wall in Federal Park, Glebe.

Works cited

Animal Studies Group (Ed.) (2006). *Killing animals*. Urbana and Chicago: University of Chicago Press.

Anon (2007). Founder of canine orphanage interred at Hartsdale (2007). *Friends of the Peaceable Kingdom in Hartsdale* 11: 2. [Online]. Available: www.petcem.com/Newsletters/2007.pdf [Accessed on 13 March 2013].

Bondeson J (2011). *Amazing dogs: a cabinet of canine curiosities*. Ithaca, New York: Cornell University Press.

Bradshaw J (2011). *In defence of dogs*. London: Allen Lane.

Brantz D (2010). *Beastly natures: animals, humans and the study of history*. Charlottesville, VA: University of Virginia Press.

Craske M (2000). Representations of domestic animals in Britain 1730–1840. In J Wood and S Feeke (Eds). *Hounds in leash: the dog in eighteenth and nineteenth century sculpture* (pp40–53). Leeds: Henry Moore Institute.

Cronin JK (2011). 'Can't you talk?' Voice and visual culture in early animal welfare campaigns. *Early Popular Visual Culture*, 9(3): 203–23.

Cimetière des Chiens, Asnières sur Seine (2011). *Map and guide*, Asnières-sur-Seine: Cimetière des Chiens.

Davis H, Irwin P, Richardson M & O'Brien-Malone A (2003).When a pet dies: religious issues, euthanasia and strategies for coping with bereavement. *Anthrozoos*, 16(1): 57–74.

Desmond J (2011). Deaths and the written record of history: the politics of pet obituaries. In L Kalof & GM Montgomery (Eds). *Making animal meaning* (pp99–111). East Lansing: Michigan State University Press.

Donald D (2007). *Picturing animals in Britain 1750–1850*. New Haven: Yale University Press.

Dresser N (2000). The horse bar mitzvah: a celebratory exploration of the human–animal bond. In A Podberscek, E Paul & J Serpell (Eds). *Companion animals and us* (pp90–107). Cambridge: Cambridge University Press.

Franklin A (1999). *Animals and modern cultures: a sociology of human–animal relations in modernity*. London: Sage.

Gordon-Stables L (1912). The dogs' cemetery in Hyde Park. *The Animals' Guardian*, November: 257–59.

Hardy T (1970 [1930]). *The collected poems of Thomas Hardy*. London: Macmillan.

Hinchliffe S, Kearnes M, Degen M & Whatmore S (2005). Urban Wild Things: a cosmopolitical experiment. *Environment and Planning D: Society and Space*, 23: 643–58.

Howell P (2002). A place for the animal dead: pets, pet cemeteries & animal ethics in late Victorian Britain. *Ethics, Place & Environment*, 5(1): 5–22.

Kean H (2000). *Animal rights: political and social change in Britain since 1800*. London: Reaktion Books.

Kean H (2004). *London stories: personal lives, public histories*. London: Rivers Oram Press.

Kean H (2009). Balto, the Alaskan dog and his statue in New York's Central Park: animal representation and national heritage. *International Journal of Heritage Studies*, 15(5): 413–30.

Kean H (2011a). Traces and representations: animal pasts in London's present. *The London Journal* 36(1): 54–71.

Kean H (2011b). Commemorating animals: glorifying humans? Remembering and forgetting animals in war memorials. In M Andrews, C Bagoti Jewitt & N Hunt (Eds). *Lest we forget: remembrance and commemoration* (pp60–70). Stroud: History Press.

Kean H (2012a). Challenges for historians writing animal–human history. What is really enough? *Anthrozoos*, 25th Anniversary Supplement: S57–S72.

Kean H (2012b). Animals and war memorials: different approaches to commemorating the human–animal relationship. In R Hediger (Ed.). *Animals and war* (pp237–62). Boston: Brill.

Kean H (forthcoming 2013). The people's war on the British home front: the challenge of the human–animal relationship. In E Dardenne & S Mesplède (Eds). *Representing animals in Britain*. Manchester: Manchester University Press.

Mangum T (2007). Narrative dominion or the animals write back? Animal genres in literature and the arts. In K Kete (Ed.). *A cultural history of animals in the age of empire* (pp153–74). Oxford: Berg.

Michalski S (1998). *Public monuments: art in political bondage 1870–1997*. London: Reaktion Books.

Morris P, Knight S & Lesley S (2012). Belief in animal mind: does familiarity with animals influence beliefs about animal emotions? *Society and Animals* 20(3): 211–24.

Parker G (2008). The Dickin medal and the PDSA animal cemetery. *After the Battle* 140: 46–55.

Pet Cemetery (1997). *Pet Cemetery, Hyde Park*. Open House leaflet. London: The Royal Parks.

Philo C (1995). Animals, geography, and the city: notes on inclusions and exclusions. *Environment and Planning D: Society and Space*, 13: 655–81.

Scates B (2009). *A place to remember: a history of the shrine of remembrance*. Melbourne: Cambridge University Press.

Searby R (2008). Red Dog, horses and Bogong moths: the memorialisation of animals in Australia. *Public History Review* 15: 117–34.

Serpell JA (2005). People in disguise: anthropomorphism and the human–pet relationship. In L Daston and G Mitman (Eds). *Thinking with animals: new perspectives on anthropomorphism* (pp121–36). New York: Columbia University Press.

Smith JA (2005). 'Viewing' the body: towards a discourse of rabbit death. *Worldviews: Environment, Culture, Religion* 9(2): 184–202.

Simpson F (1990 [1902]). Cat and dog London. In *Edwardian London*, vol. 1 (pp254–60). London: Village Press. First published in G Sims (Ed.). *Living London*, Cassell & Co.

Swinney GN (2011). An afterword on afterlife. In SJMM Alberti (Ed.). *The afterlives of animals* (pp219–34). Charlottesville: University of Virginia Press.

Terhune AP (1937). *A book of famous dogs*. Garden City, New York: Doubleday, Doran & Co.

Tyler T (2012). *Ciferae: a bestiary in five fingers*. Minneapolis: University of Minnesota Press.

Where good dogs go (1920). *New York Times*, 4 July: 68.

3
Necessary expendability: an exploration of nonhuman death in public

Tarsh Bates and Megan Schlipalius

How do we deal with the death of so-called lower order nonhumans: insects, fungi, plants, yeasts? How do we deal with this death if we have cared for them? *in vitero* was an artistic research project investigating the embodied nature of relationships between human and nonhuman organisms. These relationships were explored through an aesthetic of care, that is, the embodied experiences that sustained proximity and care offer to reveal the complex and contradictory relationships between human and nonhuman organisms. In *in vitero* the aesthetic experiences of care were explored through engagement with eight scientific model organisms. This project necessitated prolonged physical attention and care of living creatures, negotiating the ethics of the scientific and artistic usage of other species by humans and their life and death in our care. It was an attempt to engage in what aesthetics philosopher and cultural theorist, Wendy Wheeler (1999, 127) describes as 'ways of "rethinking human beings" and readdressing the world . . . a wholly serious and creative attempt "to imagine differently reconstituted communities and selves" '.

The central focus of *in vitero* was the relationships that humans can develop when spending time with and caring for nonhuman bodies

T Bates & M Schlipalius (2013). Necessary expendability: an exploration of nonhuman death in public. In J Johnston & F Probyn-Rapsey (Eds). *Animal death*. Sydney: Sydney University Press.

that are very different to each other and us. Inevitably death occurred during the performance, while on display or when the organisms were killed soon after project completion. This paper explores differing relationships with the critters cared for, in particular with *Candida albicans* (candida), *Hydra vulgaris* (hydra) and *Drosophila melanogaster* (drosophila), and the utility and 'necessary expendability' of the organisms in this biological art project. The diverse experiences and responses to the deaths of these organisms necessitated by the distinct roles of artist and curator/audience researcher are described.

Death as a design feature: the artist . . .

in vitero was a durational performance occurring in two locations: a scientific laboratory at the University of Western Australia (UWA) and a public art gallery at the Perth Institute of Contemporary Art (PICA). After four and a half months in the laboratory, where I was intimately engaged with the organisms, learning how to live with them and take care of them, the project moved into the art gallery and was open to the public for the remainder of the performance. The critters[1] were installed in the gallery in customised vessels and I lived in the gallery with them for 70 days (Figure 3.1). Audience research was conducted during this phase by curator Megan Schlipalius.

Model organisms are liminal creatures, ideally situated for an exploration of the ambiguous nature of care: simultaneously same and different, their bodies stand in for the human body while remaining nonhuman. I chose eight model organisms that are radically Other in appearance and apparent mindfulness from humans for this project, hoping that their otherness would provide a significant contrast and make the ambiguities and ambivalences of our engagement clear. These organisms were *Arabidopsis thaliana* (thale cress), *Caenorhabditis elegans* (soil nematodes), *Candida albicans* (thrush), *Daphnia pulex* (wa-

---

1 'Critters' is a term used during this project as synonymous with 'organisms'. 'Critters' is adopted from Donna Haraway to complicate taxonomic categories: 'Critters are always relationally entangled rather than taxonomically neat. I pray that all residual tones of creation have been silenced in the demotic *critter*.' (Haraway 2008, 330). For Haraway, 'critters' include non-biological agents.

Figure 3.1 in vitero installation, PICA. Image by Megan Schlipalius.

ter fleas), *Drosophila melanogaster* (fruit flies), *Hydra vulgaris* (hydra), *Neurospora crassa* (red bread mould), and *Physarum polycephalum* (slime mould) (Figure 3.2). Each critter was radically different from the human animal in:

- anatomy, including size, number of legs (or absence of), cell type (plant, insect, amoeba), eye structure (including lack of eyes)
- environment (soil, water, human body)
- reproductive strategy and sexuality (asexuality, parthenogenesis, cloning, budding, immortality).

Unlike encounters with cats, dogs and other familiar mammals which are visibly similar to us and hence evoke a strong sense of empathy, engagements with radical difference tend to elicit disinterest at best and violent disgust at worst. This project endeavoured to encourage interest and familiarity with these scientifically important but often ignored organisms, in order to examine the possibilities for modes of interaction other than disgust or disinterest.

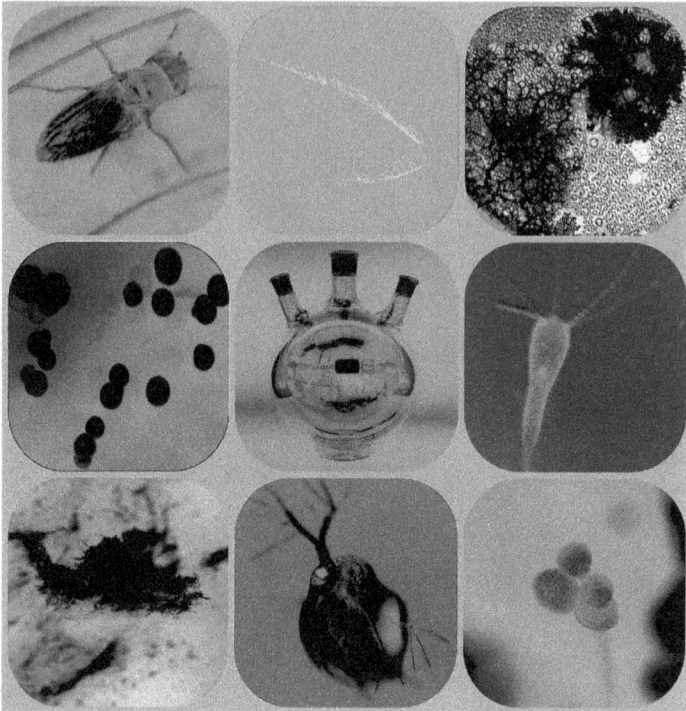

Figure 3.2 in vitero logo. Image by Tarsh Bates and Megan Schlipalius.

Human scientists conduct experiments with these organisms partly because of their size: they are easy to contain, manipulate and cultivate in confined spaces. They are also chosen for their short lifespans: the effects of manipulations can be seen relatively quickly as they reproduce and die between three days and eight weeks (depending on the species, with the notable exceptions of hydra and slime mould).[2] These critters are cared for by scientists to be available for knowledge production (experiments) and are then manipulated and sacrificed for those experiments: they are bred to be killed. For Gilles Deleuze and

---

2　These species are considered immortal, although not invincible, that is, they do not die unless they are injured and killed by an external factor (Cooper 2003).

Felix Guattari, these organisms are 'animals with characteristics or attributes', that is, they 'serve the purposes of science' (cited in Baker 2000, 125). As such, they are not considered worthy for becoming-with; they are too banal to offer the transcendence of the wild. However, as liminal beings, simultaneously Self *and* Other, subject *and* object, I believe that these critters offer a unique opportunity to explore the complexities of inter-species relationships.

This project imported living nonhuman organisms into a public art gallery, shifting them from the normalising spaces of 'natural' habitat, science laboratory and domestic home, where our assumptions about and behaviours toward these critters are invisible. Relocating the organisms into a gallery space revealed complex power relationships and ethical dilemmas which challenged human complacency and complicity by putting their lifecycles on display: the births, deaths and in-betweens. Seven months incorporated several generations of each nonhuman species as the average lifespan was two to six weeks. Consequently, I became familiar with the different stages of each life and navigated the simplicities and complexities of inevitable deaths. The short life spans of these organisms and my incompetence made death an inevitable experience during *in vitero*. I did not ritualistically mourn these deaths, but did experience regret for those killed through my clumsy attempts at care.

The critters cared for during *in vitero* did not look back at the human carer/viewer, or their looking was imperceptible. Most did not have faces, let alone eyes. Individuals of two of the species could not even be seen by unassisted human eyes. The inability of these organisms to 'look back' extends explorations of human/nonhuman relationships. For the most part previous considerations are of 'higher' animals, mostly mammals. Jacques Derrida famously saw his own radical otherness in the eyes of his pet cat (Derrida & Wills 2000). His shame at perceiving his nakedness violently confronted him, enabling a 'felt transformation' into his animality. Heidegger cannot understand the lion; Nagel imagines feeling like a bat; Haraway coevolves with her dogs. In art, coyotes, rats, pigs, rabbits, mice, elephants, sharks, apes and horses have variously been used to reinforce or challenge the human/animal dualism.[3] In all these encounters, the gaze and faciality of these animals were crucial: they look back; their resemblance to us felt as a challenge to complacency and neglect.

Much has been written about the gaze of the animal nonhuman Other: Sherryl Vint states that 'to be a citizen, a majority in Deleuze and Guattari's terms, is precisely to exclude the voice and gaze of the ... animal' (Vint 2005, 296). For Lévinas, 'the face-to-face relation, my exposure to the face of the other' is the site of responsibility for the Other (cited in Bruns 2007, 712). The returned gaze of Derrida's cat disturbed his subjecthood. Haraway (2006, 111) argues that 'the truth or honesty of non-linguistic embodied communication depends on *looking back* and greeting significant others, again and again.' Bioanthropologist Barbara Smuts describes her becoming-baboon through the visual: ' "At the beginning of my study, the baboons and I definitely did not see eye to eye" ... They [the baboons] frequently looked at her, and the more she ignored their looks, the less satisfied they seemed ... "I neither knew how to look back nor that I lacked the habit" ' (cited in Haraway 2006, 108). *in vitero*, however, explored the vital question: how do we recognise ourselves in the myriad nonhumans which do not 'look back'?

in vitero drew from a long history of the containment of human and nonhuman organisms for both entertainment and science, exploring the power relationships and species understandings inherent in these activities. The Victorian/Edwardian period was an important reference for this project as much private collecting and categorising of nonhuman specimens from the colonies occurred during this time, concurrent with the rise of the amateur naturalist and Darwinian evolutionary theory. Natural history museums were established in order to collect and categorise new world specimens and opened for public viewing, spawning a new industry of vitrines, cabinets for containment and public display (Barber 1985). The new museums rejected the non-hierarchical, chaotic cabinets of curiosity (Wunderkammer), adopting an aesthetic reflecting the Enlightenment drive for categorisation and order: drawers and boxes separating species from one another, glass display cases that combined particular species and facilitated viewing, and collections of specimens en masse.[4] Botanical illustration flour-

---

3   This is by no means an exclusive list.
4   A specimen included in a Wunderkammer was by definition unique and 'aberrant'. The new sciences required mass collection of similar specimens to identify the majority as the norm and hence as a species.

ished during this period and radical cultural changes occurred as a result of scientific discoveries: religious doctrine and the assumption of human separation from and dominion over nature were undermined; humans became animal. Anxieties fuelled by this collapse required methods to distinguish contemporary, civilised humans from their animal lineage; museums contributed to and validated this separation. Victorian middle-class drawing rooms were common locations for ferneries and fish tanks enabled by the inventions of the Wardian case and the glass fish tank (Whittingham 2012).[5] Freak shows and menageries displayed the aberrant human alongside the exotic nonhuman.[6]

Like the organisms in museums and menageries, the organisms contained within the glass vessels in this project had been captured by scientists, bred to promote human knowledge, and then displayed for entertainment in a public art gallery. They were sourced from scientific research laboratories, having been bred for experimentation. These organisms were not my collaborators. I was highly aware of the power imbalance between myself and the creatures, in laboratory and gallery: they did not choose to participate; they were my 'victims/slaves'. However the project also committed me as a 'slave' to these organisms: I was responsible for sustaining their lives which necessitated dealing with their deaths.

---

5   The Wardian case was a small, portable glasshouse invented by English botanist Nathaniel Ward and subsequently used to transport live botanical species around the world, opening up a new trade in living specimens not previously possible. The first live specimen was transported in a Wardian case from Australia to England in 1833 (Hershey 1996). They rapidly became popular for botanists and gardeners and enabled exotic humid ferneries in the cold drawing rooms of Western Europe and the United States. The vessels of *in vitero* are contemporary Wardian cases, transporting live model organisms from the exotic scientific laboratory to the public gallery.

6   Coco Fusco argues that these displays acted as an important form of public education, as 'living expressions of colonial fantasies and helped to forge a special place in the European and Euro-American imagination for nonwhite peoples and their cultures'. Fusco provides a fascinating summary of the displays of humans at this time (Fusco 1994).

Care and death

Repeated domestic rituals of care occurred during the performance
of *in vitero*: I regularly fed and cleaned the organisms and removed
creatures which had died through my neglect or ineptitude, or because
of their short lifespans. I consciously decided not to publicise these
activities: it was never 'feeding time at the zoo' or a funeral. Their deaths
were not memorialised, unlike the wartime deaths of beloved pets
and other animals described by Hilda Kean in this volume. I rejected
the 'killing rituals' of Tissue Culture and Art Project (tc&a) sculptural
works. tc&a collaborators Ionat Zurr and Oron Catts publicly kill their
tissue cultured sculptures at the end of an exhibition. For them 'the
Killing Ritual enhances the idea of the temporality of life and living art,
and our responsibility as manipulators to the new forms of life' (Zurr
& Catts 2003, 12). Although I may have given up opportunities to raise
questions about 'the temporality of life and living art' and challenge assumptions about 'our responsibility as manipulators . . . of life', I wanted
to reflect the banal nature of domesticity. The feeding and/or killing
of these organisms is not celebrated or mourned during scientific research; we do not lament the death of a fly in our fruit bowl, mould in
our bathroom, or the treatment of a candida infection; we do not debate the implications of habitat destruction for *Daphnia pulex* or hydra.
The rituals of care and death happened during *in vitero*, I was conscious
of them, but did not draw particular attention to them.

Candida albicans (candida) is an organism symbiotic with humans,
a single-celled yeast which is one of many species of microorganisms
that make up the intestinal and urogenital flora of humans; without
it we would have difficulty digesting as it breaks down sugars in the
bloodstream (Sears 2005). As an organism which is an opportunistic
pathogen of vaginal tracts in particular, candida is culturally gendered
without itself having a gender or even a sex. Many women have intimate, embodied and emotional relationships with this microscopic
creature which usually involves trying to kill it. Candida signifies the
leaky bodies of women: the excess, the abject, the undisciplined.[7] I became fascinated by this organism as a site of the gendered quality of

---

7   Refer to Margrit Shildrick and Julia Kristeva for discussions of leaky and abject
female bodies.

our relationships with nonhumans and what might become apparent through caring for it instead of trying to kill it – to domesticate it.[8]

Special consideration was required to care for and exhibit *Candida albicans* due to its status as a Class 2 human pathogen (Standards Australia 2010). Consequently I was required to complete a Health, Safety and Environment Assessment and Control of Work form to ensure that no humans were contaminated during laboratory handling and exhibition. This form included a detailed risk assessment and design of a double containment transport and exhibition system in compliance with the Office of Gene Technology Regulations and the Australian Standard for laboratory safety. As part of this assessment I had myself tested for candidiasis (thrush) before and after the project (the results of which were negative).

I also compiled a Risk Minimisation Plan which included emergency contact information, a description of project locations and associated risk activities, risk minimisation measures, a list of Personal Protective Equipment (PPE), a Spill Hazard Kit (SHK), an Incident Report Form, and a description of the *in vitero* Risk Minimisation Induction. The following is an excerpt from the *in vitero* Risk Minimisation Plan:

This risk minimisation plan has been written to address the possible risks associated with handling one of the project species *Candida albicans*, as it is classified as a Risk Group 2 human infectious organism under the Australian/New Zealand Standard S2243.3:10. It must be noted that *Candida albicans* is present as one of many harmless organisms that live in the mouth and gut of humans. Under normal circumstances, *Candida* lives in 80% of the human population with no harmful effects. It is not airborne and can only be contracted by touch. Humans with a healthy immune system are unlikely to be infected, but those with compromised immune systems may be susceptible to infection. Consequently special handling is required if exposure occurs.

---

8   The gendered aspect of our relationships with nonhumans is a recent area of scholarship and is discussed particularly by Donna Haraway, Nina Lykke and Tora Holmberg. The specific relationship with *Candida albicans* is the subject of my current PhD research.

This plan was provided to all emergency contacts associated with the project and gallery management, and was included in the SHK located in the gallery. An induction was conducted with emergency contacts and with gallery staff to ensure that they were aware of actions to take to minimise human contamination.

Care of the candida in the laboratory was an intimate undertaking (Figure 3.3). Following care instructions, I subcultured it every three to four days in a biosafety cabinet in a PC2 laboratory to ensure a ready supply of nutrients. In the ritualised environment of the PC2 laboratory, with my lab coat, gloves and sterilising ethano, I became highly aware of my actions when caring for these critters: flaming the inoculation loop to sterilise it; stroking the agar plate to remove a colony; streaking the colony onto a new plate in the accepted four quadrant streak method;[9] brushing my hair out of my eyes with the back of my gloved hand; pushing my glasses back up my nose; wrapping the streaked plate with parafilm to prevent contamination; jumping off my chair; opening the incubator; turning the plate upside down to prevent condensation; placing the plates on the incubator shelf; coming in every day to check growth and contamination. I experimented with different media, and one fascinating care activity involved the preparation of blood agar plates, which required sheep's blood sampled from the sheep of a local farmer, provided in a 100mL bottle with anti-coagulant. The blood was added to the liquid agar at 70°C for 'chocolate' agar plates and 55°C for blood agar plates; the blood of the living sheep is 39°C.

My relationship with the candida transformed following installation in the gallery (Figure 3.4). Although I could not subculture it in the gallery, I watched it grow within the custom-made, double-contained, temperature-controlled display unit (35°C). I had become habituated to its cultural valency, and audience reactions renewed my awareness of our ambivalent relationship with it. My care actions also differed in the gallery. I had to remove it from the display incubator, place it in a

9   In microbiology a sample is rubbed across the surface of an agar plate in order to produce an uncontaminated colony of the desired microbe. This colony can then be used to further propagate new colonies for experimentation. The four quadrant streak method is the most common protocol used to produce uncontaminated colonies (Katz 2008).

Figure 3.3 Inoculating Candida vessel, in vitero performance still, 11 Octo-
ber 2011. Image by Megan Schlipalius.

double contained transport unit, carry it through the gallery, strap it
into my car and drive it to the lab for subculturing. Subculturing into
the vessel was challenging as I had to customise an inoculation loop to
extend through the necks down onto the agar surface. I did not bother
with the streak pattern as I was not trying to isolate colonies, but was
attempting to cover the agar. I sterilised the transport unit, packed the
newly subcultured vessel into the unit, strapped it into my car, drove it
back to the gallery, walked it through to my studio, sterilised the display
incubator, and installed the vessel back in the exhibition unit. Following each subculturing, the residue candida had to be destroyed. This
was achieved by rinsing the vessel with bleach for ten minutes and then
autoclaving.[10] I did not regret its destruction, partly because it continued in the new vessel.

The fate of the critters following completion of the project was a
significant aspect of negotiating death during the project. I encouraged
interest in adoption (which was usually treated as a joke) and was can-
did about the requirement to kill the candida and the likely culling of

Figure 3.4 Tarsh with Candida. Image by Bo Wong.

the other critters. I found that my regret about the organisms' deaths became less extreme towards the end of the project. The reasons for this were complex, but most obviously because I was so exhausted by the end of the 70 days of relentless exposure in the gallery that I was relieved I no longer had to take care of them; in fact, I unremorsefully killed most of them.[11] I had also become habituated to their deaths, complicit in perceiving them as dispensable, as 'bare life'.[12] This project enacted a human/nonhuman necropolitics as described by Achille Mbembe. In *Necropolitics* (2003, 12), Mbembe asks:

---

10   An autoclave is used to sterilise equipment and supplies by subjecting them to high pressure saturated steam at 121°C for around 15–20 minutes. The process is also used in medical and research facilities to sterilise medical waste prior to disposal. All bacteria, viruses, fungi, and spores are inactivated during the process (Block 2001).

11   Except the *Daphnia pulex* which were adopted by Megan.

12   Refer to Giorgio Agamben for a discussion of bare life as a mode of biopolitics. Agamben (following Aristotle) describes 'bare life' as physiological, life 'that may be killed and yet not sacrificed' (1998).

Under what practical conditions is the right to kill, to allow to live, or to expose to death exercised? Who is the subject of this right? What does the implementation of such a right tell us about the person [organism] who is thus put to death and about the relation of enmity that sets that person [organism] against his or her murderer? . . . What place is given to life, death, and the human [organism] body? How are they inscribed in the order of power?

These critters are the invisible and the undesirable: pests and weeds; so small we don't notice their presence, let alone death (unless they get out of control, in which case we try to kill them). The irony of caring for an organism we usually try to kill was a significant attribute of my relationship with the candida in particular. Through this project I became increasingly interested in the experience of cohabiting with nonhuman organisms that are potentially threatening to human health. Our first response is usually to kill them. The intimacy of caring for the candida certainly shifted my awareness of my actions towards threatening organisms: not necessarily so that I wouldn't kill mosquitos, cockroaches or even candida itself, but I am much more aware of the ambiguities of those decisions.

Death as responsible action: the curator . . .

For an emerging curator, *in vitero* was both demanding and exciting. This was my first opportunity to work with an artist who was operating with life as a medium. Most of my experience with art exhibitions had been from four years working at the Holmes à Court Gallery. The vast majority of artwork at this gallery was of the more 'traditional' media and materials – paintings, sculptures, photography, textiles and the occasional assemblage of found objects and mixed media. I was used to the usual dilemmas of selection, juxtaposition, and interpretation, and practical conservation issues such as light levels and length of time on display. Now I was faced with new dilemmas: organism needs (light, food and water); audience access versus health and safety; the potential – and in many cases inevitable – death of organisms on display.

My experience with this project revealed that curating biological art is vastly different to being a viewer. I was placed in a position of responsibility to the artist, the public and the host institution. I became acutely more aware of the practical and ethical issues at play when you move life into an art gallery. Yet alongside this responsibility, the project revealed a pleasure in working intimately with living art that is constantly dynamic, evolving and continually in a state of flux. At times curating *in vitero* was more like curating a miniature zoo with 'keeper' Tarsh giving me updates and progress reports on the wellbeing, or not so wellbeing, of each type of organism.

As this was an artistic project, I had additional responsibilities that came with being in an art gallery. Primarily, I had to ensure the safety of other artwork housed in the gallery at the same time. One of the first issues that I was concerned about when working with living media was practical: what to do about potential escapee organisms? As a keeper of cultural collections in museums and art galleries, I was well aware of damage that can be caused by insects, moulds and excess moisture. I was also teaching museum conservation at the time of the project, so I was acutely aware of potential problems. Deliberately introducing and caring for living things in a gallery is quite contradictory to what is taught in curatorial studies. I often felt like a hypocrite – preaching one thing in the morning and then breaking the 'rules' in the afternoon.

One of the critters that Tarsh was working with was *Drosophila melanogaster* or fruit fly. Therefore one of my initial concerns was to reduce the risk of fruit fly escapees. I did not want to see fly speck on the sculptural works installed in the gallery next door to our room. Or have faecal matter turn up on the large, expensively produced and gilt framed photographs on display downstairs. I knew from experience the damage insect faecal matter can cause to art. The only thing for it was to limit and kill escapees. This had impacts on the caring behaviours and the way that the drosophila were fed. Tarsh became quite fast in her technique of squeezing the foam stoppers to drop fresh yeast into the vessel (Figure 3.5). Although audiences were invited to spend time and take care of the organisms, I was not comfortable with other people feeding the fruit fly, so this task was solely undertaken by Tarsh and feeding was kept to a minimum. A vinegar trap was set up in the space to attract and kill escapees, hopefully before they left the room. Death in this instance for me was a necessity and the most responsible way to deal with escapees.[13] I did not delight in their death – it was essentially a means to an end. Nor was I upset or concerned about their deaths as I knew there were still plenty of living flies for audiences to interact with and experience. Short life cycles, prolific breeding and sheer numbers enabled me to be unconcerned about the deaths of individual flies.

Audiences generally were not concerned about fruit fly deaths. During the course of the project, fruit fly carcasses built up in the bottom of the vessel, slowly changing the colour of the base of the flask (Figure 3.6 and 3.7). Newly hatched maggots ate and underwent metamorphosis amongst the carcasses of previous generations. Their containment was not seen as problematic or unethical due to their status as pests. In fact their containment was often seen as a positive thing; it seems that fruit flies have generally a low status in the Australian psyche. Very little sympathy was shown towards the fruit fly despite being the most biologically complex organism on display (apart from Tarsh of course, representing *Homo sapiens*). Most of the time the fruit fly vessel was described as 'gross' or 'disgusting'. It was even a little threatening for some visitors. As one young writer said to me:

> This one is probably the most disgusting. I feel like I could live in all of them but not this one . . . it looks like it would attack you.

Curator's guilt, or the case of the *Hydra vulgaris*

Like the other organisms, the hydra was set up in the space within the customised scientific vessel on top of the table and the food source and 'instruments of care' on the shelf underneath (Figure 3.8). For the hy-

---

13 These dilemmas of escaping organisms or deaths on display are rarely discussed by artists and curators of bioart. For example, the fate of the 200 live crickets in Nigel Helyer's artwork *Host* during the 2011 *Visceral* exhibition is not mentioned in the exhibition promotional material. It is difficult to ascertain whether any died while on display. Little is said about the use or death of organisms until there is public or media pressure such as with the 'butterfly fiasco' in the 2012 Damien Hirst retrospective which placed the host organisation, in this case the Tate Modern, into the role of defending the choice to exhibit the artwork in question, rather than evoking considered discussion. See Nikkhah (2012) and Brooks (2012) for media response to the Hirst exhibition.

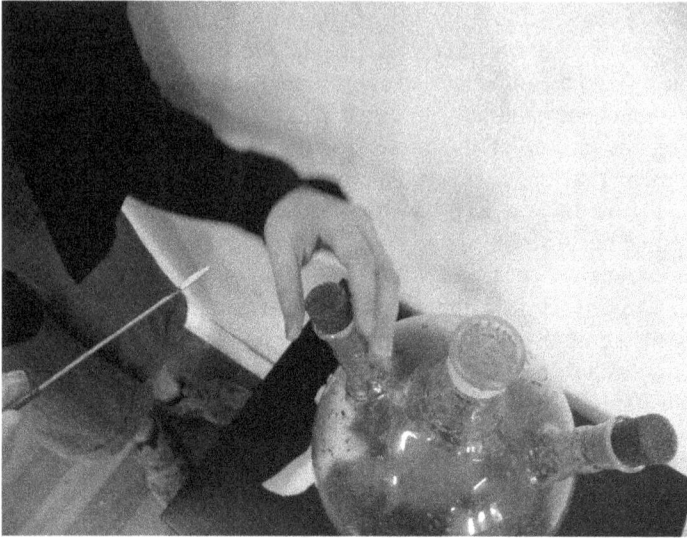

Figure 3.5 Feeding Drosophila melanogaster. Image by Megan Schlipalius.

dra this involved a hatchery for brine shrimp, which were provided as live food. During the course of the project the hydra became more and more, for want of a better word, 'unhappy'. By day 20 of the 70 day project their bodies shrank down to tiny white sticks and their tentacles became shorter. Their foot which they used to attach themselves to surfaces had become smaller. It appeared after a while that they were not eating. Tarsh began to speculate why they were not thriving. Vibrations of the table and vessel and lack of attachment to the vessel were theorised as possible reasons. On day 21 Tarsh attempted to improve their condition by trying to reduce table vibrations and kept feeding them 'just in case'. After a few days of uncertainty Tarsh finally declared that they were dead. As the project was not even halfway through, I asked Tarsh to order some more hydra from the scientific supplier as I was keen to have all the organisms for audiences to encounter. Although not large or highly dramatic, hydra are fascinating little critters. They are not usually encountered in day-to-day life, nor kept in fish tanks or aquaria, and I was disappointed that people would not get the opportunity to engage with them.

Figure 3.6 Drosophila melanogaster: day 15. Image by Megan Schlipalius and Tarsh Bates.

Figure 3.7 Drosophila melanogaster: day 56. Image by Megan Schlipalius and Tarsh Bates.

Dead organisms seem to be an obvious failure in an experiment in the aesthetics of care. I appreciated that death was an inevitable part of the project but I wasn't ready to give up having live hydra. 'Live-ness' is what makes biological art projects such as this interesting and powerful. I also enjoyed and appreciated the discussions with audiences the hydra evoked. The live food eaten by the hydra, encountered by most people as 'sea monkeys', was a great springboard for debates and conversations about breeding animals for food and the ethics of live food. They also provided opportunities for viewers to participate and become implicated in the project and the decisions to feed one creature to another. As Catts and Zurr (2011) explain, '[t]he participatory engagement with the processes of life is a visceral experience and implicates everyone involved – including the gallery visitor – into the larger picture of the technoscientific approach to life'. These opportunities would have been lost by accepting the death of the hydra. The tiny hydra were serving me well in my role as audience researcher.

Unfortunately, the replacement hydra did not survive for long. This time I accepted the loss of the critters and instead talked about the death of the hydra with audiences. Initially this was an uncomfortable experience, much to Tarsh's delight. I felt guilty that I no longer had living hydra for people to encounter. It felt wrong not to have thriving, healthy organisms and I felt like I was confessing when I explained that they were dead. As a curator I felt that we were not providing the experience that we had 'promised' to audiences. Hydra were mentioned in the exhibition text and images of hydra were used in our promotion. I felt that we were not giving people the 'full' experience or what was 'promised' by our publicity: audiences were not getting what was said on the label.

I became aware that there was increasing confusion about what a hydra was. The brine shrimp in the vessel were often mistaken for being the hydra (even when the hydra were alive) as they were brighter in colour and more mobile. I often corrected this if there was the opportunity, as this was not intended to be a hoax piece – none of the critters were 'fakes'. Tarsh, on the other hand, was less concerned about perceptions of 'reality and truth' and was more interested in subjective experiences and how audiences responded to her authority and trusted her as an 'expert'. She allowed confusion between shrimp and hydra, and dead hydra for live.

Figure 3.8 Hydra vulgaris vessel with brine shrimp hatchery. Image by Tarsh Bates.

For me, however, one of the exciting or interesting things about bioart is that it is 'real'. Cells really are cells, candida is actually candida, hydra is living hydra. This live-ness shifts the art from being representational into a new space of being literally alive, adding power to its symbolic qualities. As Jens Hauser suggests, 'biological art touches on the visceral at the same time that it produces meaning. It does not only picture or represent but gives a feeling of being linked to the presence of a holistic *bios'* (2007, 34). The experience is qualitatively and experientially different; like the difference between experiencing a taxidermied animal in a lifelike pose and one that is alive.[14] In my role as curator, I felt ethically that I should assist in clarification, rather than support or promote misunderstandings.

When talking to audiences, there was not always a serious tone to the project (Figure 3.9). At the risk of saying something taboo, a considerable amount of humour occurred when it came to discussing the deaths of the organisms. The organisms selected are not commonly cared for, so showing any reverence or sentimentality towards their death was seen as amusing. The deaths of the hydra were often a source of jokes. Tarsh would introduce the hydra vessel as: 'Hydra, well. It was. It's immortal but I managed to kill it ... twice.' Visitors would laugh along with her at this rather glib explanation. I too ended up joking about Tarsh's incompetence in caring for such a 'simple' organism. These jokes were only possible due to the low status of these organisms. It was also a poignant indication of our position of privilege and power over who gets to live and who gets to die, when, where and how.[15] I strongly doubt that we would have been able to make similar jokes if the model organism was a frog, rat or rabbit.

Is respect enough?

The majority of visitors had few qualms with the display of death in this context. The decomposing dead fruit flies were generally ignored and only occasionally commented on as 'disgusting'. Dead plants were overlooked and the carcasses of *Daphnia pulex* not commented upon. A number of visitors drew parallels with the use of animals by humans such as in farming or in science, accepting the inevitability of these deaths. Containment and presentation of life was more explicitly discussed than the death of organisms:

---

14   This ties in to a larger debate on viscerality, embodiment and the performativity of matter. See Ionat Zurr and Oron Catts, Elizabeth Grosz, Donna Haraway, and Karen Barad, among others.
15   Refer to broader discussions of biopower by Foucault and Agamben and its corollary, necropolitics, by Achilles Mbembe.

Although this is only my second visit, I still feel like an outsider. Outside the glass looking in, drawing on what I already know about life on display (humans omitted) from [a] scientific context and trying to distance myself from that understanding. They are perceived by me to be objects of curiosity and manipulation, and, strangely I feel ok about that relationship, even though it is unfair, maybe with more time I would care? Or would I? *(audience feedback in exhibition comment book 2011)*

Only a few of our viewers found the containment and utility of the live organisms in this art project an uncomfortable experience and voiced their concerns:

Interesting stuff. A whole new world. No material deserves to be locked up. Its [sic] human beings' attempt to control what is by nature uncontrollable. An illusion of control. In reality, freedom is/comes with birth (pre/post). *(audience feedback in exhibition comment book 2011)*

Death was generally implicit in audience questions and discussion rather than a direct topic of conversation or comment: people often asked 'What is going to happen to them at the end?' Death was generally treated as something that was going to happen later rather than already sitting in front of them in a vessel.

Figure 3.9 Conducting audience research during in vitero. Image by Tarsh Bates.

in vitero explored the possibilities for conceiving of a nonhuman Other as a socially active partner, not as foreign or threatening, or with a 'desire to ecstatically fuse with it' (Gardiner 1996, 131). *in vitero* was not a becoming-animal, humans are always-already animal; rather, this project attempted to negotiate alterity through acts of care which necessitated acknowledgement of a nonhuman Other and which also maintained the autonomy of those involved. Michael Gardiner suggests that in a relationship based in dialogic alterity 'the self garners a new awareness of, and respect for, otherness . . . the mixture of distance and communion in the relation of self and Other allows the uniqueness and independence of each interlocutor to be respected and maintained' (1996, 131). This enacting of alterity is what Donna Haraway and Luce Irigaray consider taking the Other seriously, in thinking and rethinking it seriously, 'questing for new vocabularies, new forms of openness . . . openness to the animal' (Baker 2000, 188–89). For *in vitero,* taking the Other seriously means taking responsibility for an 'asymmetrical and non-reciprocal' relationship, responsibility that is not contingent upon reciprocity or justice, or based on utilitarianism or Kantian-based absolutist ethics, but is situated and relational (Gardiner 1996, 122–23). A significant aspect of this responsibility is the contradictory and fraught politics of necessary and inevitable death of the invisible and expendable.

Acknowledgements

This project was made possible by support from SymbioticA, Centre for Excellence in Biological Art, the University of Western Australia and the Perth Institute of Contemporary Art.

Works cited

Agamben G (1998). *Homo sacer: sovereign power and bare life.* D Heller-Roazen (Trans.). Stanford, CA: Stanford University Press.
Barber L (1985). *The heyday of natural history, 1820–1870.* New York: Doubleday.
Baker S (2000). *The postmodern animal.* London: Reaktion.
Block SS (2001). *Disinfection, sterilization, and preservation.* Philadelphia: Lippincott Williams & Wilkins.
Brooks K (2012). Damien Hirst butterfly fiasco: artist kills 9,000 in the name of art, *The Huffington Post* [Online]. Available: www.huffingtonpost.com/2012/10/16/damien-hirst-kills-9000-b_n_1970627.html [Accessed 1 February 2013].
Bruns GL (2007). Becoming-animal (some simple ways). *New Literary History,* 38(4): 703–20.
Catts O & Zurr I (2011). *Visceral: the living art experiment.* Exhibition Catalogue. Dublin: Science Gallery
Cooper M (2003). Rediscovering the immortal hydra: stem cells and the question of epigenesis. *Configurations,* 11(1): 1–26.
Derrida J & Wills D (2002). The animal that therefore I am (more to follow). *Critical Inquiry,* 28(2): 369–418.
Fusco C (1994). The other history of intercultural performance. *TDR,* 38(1): 143–67.
Gardiner M (1996). Alterity and ethics. *Theory, Culture & Society* 13(2): 121–43.
Haraway D (2006). Encounters with companion species: entangling dogs, baboons, philosophers, and biologists. *Configurations,* 14(1/2): 97–114.

Haraway D (2008). *When species meet.* Minneapolis: University of Minnesota Press.

Hauser J (2007). *Still, living.* Exhibition Catalogue. Perth: Biennale of Electronic Arts.

Hershey D (1996). Doctor Ward's accidental terrarium. *The American Biology Teacher,* 58: 276–81.

Katz DS (2008). The streak plate protocol. *Microbe Library* [Online]. Available: www.microbelibrary.org/component/resource/laboratory-test/3160-the-streak-plate-protocol [Accessed 12 March 2013].

Mbembe A (2003). Necropolitics. *Public Culture,* 15(1): 11–40.

Nikkhah R (2012). Damien Hirst condemned for killing 9,000 butterflies in Tate show, *The Telegraph* [Online]. Available: www.telegraph.co.uk/culture/culturenews/9606498/Damien-Hirst-condemned-for-killing-9000-butterflies-in-Tate-show.html [Accessed 1 February 2013].

Sears C (2005). A dynamic partnership: celebrating our gut flora. *Anaerobe,* 11(5): 247–51.

Standards Australia (2010). AS/NZS 2243.3:2010 *Safety in laboratories.* Part 3: Microbiological safety and containment.

Vint S (2005). Becoming other: animals, kinship, and Butler's, 'Clay's Ark'. *Science Fiction Studies,* 32(2): 281–300.

Wheeler W (1999). *A new modernity? Change in science, literature and politics.* London: Lawrence and Wishart.

Whittingham S (2012). *Fern fever: the story of pteridomania.* London: Francis Lincoln.

Zurr I & Catts O (2003). The ethical claims of bio art: killing the other or self-cannibalism? *Australian and New Zealand Journal of Art: Art & Ethics* 4(2): 167–88.

4
Confronting corpses and theatre animals

Peta Tait

This chapter compares the presentation of dead animals in Gunther von Hagens' unique 'Animal inside out' exhibition with the staging of animal bodies in recent theatre productions. Von Hagens' exhibitions present actual body parts and Jane Desmond (2008, 348) aligns these with a 'theatre of the dead' created with taxidermy specimens. The theatre form, however, commonly presents replicas of animal bodies. Given ethical controversy over von Hagens' anatomy exhibitions of specially treated plastinated bodies, the use of fake animals in theatre would seem to be more indicative of 21st-century pro-animal sympathies.

This discussion considers the purposeful presentation of dead animals, using cognitive interpretations and ideas of the phenomenology of the body in viewing them. In a response to Desmond's conceptual framing, the discussion contrasts the 'Animal inside out' exhibition in London with two original Australian realist plays because a focus on dead animals sets a theatrical precedent within Australia's inherited realist theatre tradition, and possibly also in English-speaking theatre since it differs from the deployment of living animals in contemporary performance or live or dead animals in visual arts installations.[1] While not condoning von Hagens' exhibition, this chapter explains that it had

P Tait (2013). Confronting corpses and theatre animals. In J Johnston & F Probyn-Rapsey (Eds). *Animal death*. Sydney: Sydney University Press.

a stronger bodily impact than that achieved through theatre because looking at a dead body is not the same as viewing a lifelike replica. It argues that confronting, unpleasant encounters focus attention on animals. The underlying contention here is that looking at animals evokes body-based responses in viewers, and these are, in the extreme, palpable, viscerally felt sensations. Accordingly, graphic depictions of animal death have a physiological as well as cognitive impact. But theatre in particular additionally situates animals in narratives that evoke emotions – emotions are connected to the arousal of bodily feelings. Thus the larger point is that awareness of sensory engagement and unpleasant bodily reactions should be regarded as diverging from human-centred emotional narratives, and this distinction has implications for the targeted effort to turn around social attitudes to animals in human worlds.

Dead animals

I visited von Hagens' exhibition 'Animal inside out' at London's Museum of Natural History after having previously viewed 'Body worlds', which presented plastinated human corpses.[2] I probably expected a comparable experience: motivated by curiosity, I walked through a very crowded 'Body worlds' space, making an effort to see the exhibits and pondering concerns about how the human bodies were obtained while observing a diverse public in attendance. On reflection, the human exhibits seemed almost benign because the experience of viewing 'Animal inside out' unfolded in quite unexpected ways. The first major difference was the visual effect of the exhibits. On entering the exhibition, I stopped in surprise in front of a brilliantly coloured shark; a

---

1 See Phelan (1993) and Carlson (2003) for distinctions between the three art forms of theatre, performance and visual art. A pro-animal focus on dead animals is uncommon and, as far as can be established, arguably contributing to the English-speaking theatre precedent. The focus on living animals in theatre is apparent: for example, the Melbourne Theatre Company staged Edward Albee's *The goat, or who is Sylvia?* in 2003 after its successful New York season (Chaudhuri 2007).
2 The author viewed 'Animal inside out' on 13 July 2012; 'Body worlds', Melbourne, August 2010. Author's thanks to Marlowe Russell for her help.

mass of capillaries and veins were bright red. The second difference was the sparse attendance for London so that there was an unobstructed close encounter – entry had been ticketed with set viewing times to accommodate crowds. The third major difference happened through felt responses.

As I slowly walked through the exhibition of about 90 bodies and body parts, I began to feel queasy and, by the end, this feeling had turned into mild nausea. This dissipated soon after leaving the exhibit. What produced such a strong physical reaction? The chemical process of plastination replaces body fluids with silicon, acetone and resin, so there could have been something toxic lingering in the environment. Alternatively, did the idea of what was being viewed make me particularly sensitive so there was a physical reaction? One metaphor presented itself in the widely used phrase for how a social or psychological realisation is said to make someone 'sick to the stomach'. The sensory impact of this exhibition of dead animals was experienced through bodily feelings and perhaps arose from a combination of chemical, cultural and physiological reactions. Regardless, the unpleasant visceral responses to this exhibition could not be ignored.

Although it was human made, the exhibition was like entering an unknown world. An encounter with a plastinated corpse involved standing and confronting an anonymous animal body or body part. The philosophical phenomenology of Maurice Merleau-Ponty (1995) has influenced my approach to the ways that spectators receive body-based performance over two decades and, most recently, in an application to the reception of trained animal acts (Tait 2012). Merleau-Ponty insightfully theorises the underlying, if under-recognised, physicality of social responsiveness to others. His starting point involves subjective reactions – that is, an impression of individual interiority – followed by the process of perceptually moving outward into the phenomenal world of other bodies and objects. The notion of bodily reaching out is encapsulated by Merleau-Ponty's ideas of responses to the movement and action of other bodies, and how a 'body schemata' absorbs and replicates their 'motility'. Thus sensory processes denote the reversibility of the visible world. Merleau-Ponty explains about the lack of separation between lived experience and the world around: 'it would be better to say that the body sensed and the body sentient are as the obverse and the reverse, or again, as two segments of one sole circular course

... since the world is flesh' (1995, 138). These concepts recognise how the separate senses are active conditions and converge so that sight can seem to cross over into touch. This idea of a sensory intertwining with the surrounding world is proposed in an idea of a perceiving body within a visible field (1995, 142). Although Merleau-Ponty (2004) does apply his thinking to human encounters with nonhuman animals, the discussion does not extend to dead animals. Drawing on Merleau-Ponty's concepts to consider von Hagens' exhibition, it might be argued that the viewing of dead animals stimulated sensory responses in a viewer that were then internalised in a 'circular course'. A live body to dead body encounter involved a perceiving sensory body responding to preserved dead flesh.

While not necessarily updating ubiquitous taxidermy, von Hagens' exhibition can certainly be located within the museum tradition of displaying animal specimens (Alberti 2011). This may account for the comparatively smaller attendance at the animal anatomy exhibition, since the public are accustomed to seeing animal bodies in natural history museums. Perhaps the entry fee was a barrier – the rest of the museum was free and was crowded and it was only mid-morning. Or it is possible that the exhibition was under-advertised or seemed too educational or lacked the novelty of the human body in 'Body worlds'. Regardless, von Hagens' exhibition of animal bodies utilised stands and glass cases as if it were a scientific display which confirmed the blurred distinctions between museum, education and leisure time activity (Macdonald 2011), even though only one exhibit at the end had traces of the quasi-environmental settings frequently used in older-style taxidermy displays. The exhibition was structured one-way so that viewers encountered the exhibits and spaces in a similar order. The species order was approximately as follows: a squid, an octopus, two shark bodies, a sheep, a goat, a rabbit, a chicken, a duck, three reindeer, a horse head sliced in three and opened out, a second horse body, a goat with a baby, a sequence of organs, two ostriches, an elephant, a giraffe and a gorilla. The organs included animal hearts, a nervous system, a digestive system, brains, testes and a fetus. The two sharks were the first of several dual encounters with the same species body presented in different positions and colours: there was a pale cream shark shape and the aforementioned bright red one.

What made this exhibition suitable for such a pre-eminent national history museum? Sharon Macdonald points out that museum practices must cater for plural publics and while concerned with economic viability and competitive prestige, she contends they remain 'inherently political' within practices that implicate identity politics (2011, 48). The latter as yet may not fully extend to awareness of the politics of identities in the human–animal hierarchy. Von Hagen's displays were dead animal bodies without decay, described as anatomy display and presented in a quasi-clinical style, although it was the venue that conveyed an educational purpose. But they might also be contrasted with taxidermy skin and fur displays. In her analysis of von Hagens' 'Body worlds', Jane Desmond (2008) finds that the effect of plastination is the opposite to that sought by taxidermy which preserves the outer skins of dead animals in poses within environmental settings to create an illusion of realism. The outer surface is preserved to appear lifelike in fake natural settings. In contrast, plastination reverses the elements on display by showing the preserved innards. The inner substance of an animal body was being presented in 'Animal inside out' as either muscles and veins and/or skeletons or capillary and veins with some of an outer layer of skin peeled back. The shark exhibit brought to mind Damien Hirst's shark in a perspex box, which was, by coincidence, concurrently remounted in his retrospective at London's Tate Modern, although this was a shark's outer body surface.[3] Called *The physical impossibility of death in the mind of someone living* (1991), it was supposed to evoke fear, and it certainly had sensationalist impact even though the title suggests a philosophical dead end whereby the perception of the viewer cannot reach beyond the embodied physicality of living. The purpose of this type of dead animal exhibition still remains ambiguous. Irrespective of the ethical validity of continuing to put dead bodies on show in museums (Alberti 2011) or art galleries (Baker 2006), the deadness in 'Animal inside out' even in a natural history museum seemed excessive.

The exhibition was outside common social anthropomorphic relations and their compartmentalised encounters. Plastination removed the familiar surface of the animal body, the habitual sight and site of encounters between species. Stark moments with an animal body that

---

3 The author viewed it in the exhibition 'Damien Hirst' at Tate Modern on 12 July 2012.

looked so completely different obliterated familiar habituated responses derived from repeated exposure to animal images in representation designed to arouse selective emotional feelings. This presented an inverse too: the shark swimming freely in television programs about sea life; filmed sheep, horse or goat grazing calmly on a farmed spacious landscape; and the highly photographed African elephant roaming open plains (Chris 2006). Only the iconic misunderstood and endangered species, the gorilla, was given touches of a setting, posed marooned on a small collection of twigs, a token concession that seemed especially misplaced. The elephant exhibit was like encountering a new species. Cultural images of these animal species were turned inside out.

While dead bodies exhibited over decades in museums seemed to have provided minimal challenge to human control over animal lives, 'Animal inside out' brought questions about the origins of the animals and the quality of their life to the fore. A whole body needed to be processed prior to decomposition, and therefore soon after death, and this must have been organised because the exhibition presented a mixture of domesticated and wild animal species. Was someone merely waiting for the animals to die naturally? The domestication of animal species might produce a false impression that the human utility of animals was justifiable – and perhaps life on a farm did eventually suit some bred species. But as Harriet Ritvo points out in her essays on domestication, 'anthropomorphism is problematic, since it implicitly disparages the possibility that humans and nonhumans share perceptions, behaviours, and responses' (2010, 8, original emphasis). Yet paradoxically, anthropomorphic projection about animals can also lead to the notion of sameness so that the assumed right of humans to control the life and death of other animal species comes unravelled. Thus humans would no longer have the unquestioned right to put animal bodies on display for leisure activities.

The reddened muscle and discoloured white fat was contained inside a body shape which made each animal species easily recognisable. Some were posed as if ready for action, which in itself drew the eye. The sensory impact of viewing exposed fat and muscle substances was compounded by the great diversity of the body shapes that contained them. Could this exhibition also disrupt habitual patterns of perceiving other species bodily? Drawing on Merleau-Ponty's argument that the embodied subject is engaged in a continual process of sensing the external world, it is clear that an observing body was confronted with an animal body shape that was additionally revealing inside substances of muscle, bone and veins. The process of perceiving, bodily, was potentially turned inside out.

In his exploration of the phenomenology of human and animal living body encounters, Ralph Acampora explains that humans are aware that they are most vulnerable at a somatic level through accidents, injuries and illness within life, but that this awareness should facilitate the development of more positive ongoing human–animal relations (2006, 130). What happens when somatic awareness is confronted with the converse situation of animal death? Perhaps such an encounter is better able to remind humans of somatic vulnerability. In both 'Body worlds' and 'Animal inside out', viewers were being confronted by somatic stasis; the living body had been turned into an inert object. The encounter with a range of three-dimensional shapes seemed to increase an impression of catering to ghoulish human voyeurism as viewers moved in, amongst and around variously large and small flayed exhibits. These were like an extension of the creations of repulsive nightmares in horror films. But the plastination preservation process manipulated an encounter with deadness so that this was cognitively recognisable but viscerally chilling because it was outside everyday sensibility. It compelled attention but seemed to obviate empathetic responses. Exhibits were repulsive and did not spark emotional sympathy.

The red blood effect intermittently looms large in memory. The effort to display the multitude of criss-crossed veins of an individual animal with a red dye resin had a powerful sensory impact. A viewer was being shown how blood was contained in the veins, in a hyper-realist impression. Vivid brightness, contradictorily, signifies vitality in blood. Viewed within the severed dead body shape, it was as if this was the fresh red blood of the newly killed animal, cut open. It had the effect of suggesting that the viewer was encountering the animal soon after death and might be complicit in the animal's death.

Did a viewer's pulse rate change in this process of looking at dead animals? The multiple ways in which the internal movement of blood is subjectively experienced was potentially confronted within a sensory enfolding of a bloodied corpse. Such a pulsating blood to static blood encounter might make for uncomfortable and stomach-churning sensations.

The exhibition space was a repulsive world filled with dead animals. The intention of 'Animal inside out' was unclear beyond the premise that humanity has the right to display the dead remains of other species for its own leisure activity – such exhibitions need to be challenged at a broad societal level. Although it was probably not the intended outcome, by exposing what is not seen, the exhibition had the potential to bodily upset at an individual level and potentially confirms a similar potency arising from the viewing of photographic and media images of animal death. The unseen way that animals live and die in the human social world was inverted through focused attention on dead animals. Sensory aversion and repulsion may usefully jolt viewers into a different type of awareness.

Theatre fakes

Can the use of replica animal bodies, which would seem to be the more ethical practice, deliver comparable impact? The ways in which two original productions in Australian theatre with pro-animal politics specifically depicted dead animals is discussed below and contextualised in relation to comparative examples that used animal replicas. Animals can be represented directly or indirectly in theatre since the idea of an animal species can be present when the animal body is absent. Similarly ideas of animal death can be conveyed through the dialogue or with an object prop which is made to appear realistic. The two theatrical depictions focused on dead animals were coincidentally produced around the same time. The plays bring questions about dead animals in human lives to the fore, even though the purpose of each diverged; *The call* by Patricia Cornelius (2009) was orientated to disadvantaged humans working in an abattoir and *Letters from animals* by Kit Lazaroo was primarily centred on animal extinction. The works are discussed here because their content, and their respective intriguing, if somewhat flawed, small innovative productions highlight divergent approaches to staging dead animals in theatre.

The longstanding aesthetic problem of whether to theatrically represent the animal body onstage, alive or dead, was compounded by the invention of turn-of-the-20th-century naturalism in theatre that demands a lifelike visual realism. Australian theatre adopted these

European and English theatre traditions. While productions of Henrik Ibsen's (1999) *The wild duck* from the late 19th century could conveniently use spoken dialogue to refer to shot ducks and a living captive duck off stage, Anton Chekhov's (1991) ironic response with *The seagull* requires a shot bird onstage, and has been commonly staged with a realistic prop. But throughout the 19th century, a variety of domesticated animal species had been integral to the traditional circus dominated by equestrian acts, and circus animal acts regularly appeared on theatre stages along with the acts by human impersonators of animals. Although 20th-century realist theatre dispensed with live animal acts, the range of animal species in circus increased greatly with the addition of trained wild animals from the 1890s and, despite ongoing pro-animal opposition, circus continues to present animals performing human-derived action (Tait 2012). Animal performance was theatrically constructed to provoke a range of emotions from fear and excitement to delight and amusement. Meanwhile, the presence and social function of animals became oblique in 20th-century modernist theatre that depicted symbols and metaphors through dialogue. It should be noted that drama about environmental issues might also be tracked back to Chekhov's (1991) *Uncle Vanya*, first staged in 1898, although it implies that the farming of animals was part of the growing problem of deforestation. With several notable exceptions, modernist drama was generally preoccupied with the human condition and avoided troublesome issues of how to stage animals, live or fake.

An encounter with a replica of a life-size rhinoceros that was created for a 2007 London production of Eugene Ionesco's modernist absurdist play of the same name, and retained within a museum, further illustrates the comparison here between 'Animal inside out' and the impact of animals in Australian realist theatre.[4] In this instance, the rhinoceros would probably have been a surprising and strange arrival on stage since the play has the metaphoric rhinoceros represented only with heads, and the incongruity of full bodily presence would have focused audience attention. Fake animal bodies in theatre can have a striking impact. Since the outer body of this replica seemed almost

---

4 The author viewed this exhibit in the Theatre section of London's Victoria and Albert Museum, 13 July 2012. *Rhinoceros*, translated by M Crimp, was in the repertory of the Royal Court Theatre in the second half of 2007.

real with the simulation of the colour and texture of the animal's hide, the theatrical imperative to fabricate a rhinoceros body to seem lifelike might be compared to that of taxidermy's preservation of outer skins. But an extended encounter with the rhinoceros was neither sickening nor mired in complex ethical conflicts. Instead a close encounter with a three-dimensional large grey replica of the species body was enjoyable. The use of a replica in human entertainment might draw attention to the species, but, paradoxically, such substitution could also be counter-productive for the living animal. Conversely the utility of actual animals for viewing can breach ethical limits although theatre still does not generally challenge these limits.

In a realist production of Patricia Cornelius' *The call* in Melbourne in 2007, dead animal bodies were realistically replicated.[5] The production's minimalist staging with plastic crates and no set only deviated in two scenes in an abattoir, when it showed a row of dead animal carcasses on a factory line. Regardless of the visual effectiveness of these replica dead bodies, the assembly line was a memorable feature of the production. *The call* is about young people in small town Australia who leave school early with limited social options – the women are often pregnant, and the men work in factories. In a narrative about the character Gary's conversion to Islam, the male characters take drugs and treat work in an abattoir or on a caged chicken farm as interchangeable with other factory work, although the killing of animals has the lowest status. The increasing scale of the industrial production of animals for meat consumption relies on less skilled or migrant labour (Burt 2006). In the pro-animal politics of this play, the slaughtering of animals provided a commentary on human disadvantage, the trap of poverty, and different religious attitudes so that the dead animal replica was symbolic of a social convergence of human and animal misery.

The production's meat assembly line was visually prominent but not somatically potent. Prop replicas of birds, fish and animals in theatre represent realness that can be cognitively appreciated but deliver only limited bodily impact. It is possible to speculate that the replica might actually negate reactions to deadness, since the idea of realness can be received without visceral confrontation.

---

5 The author viewed *The call* at the Fairfax Studio, 23 November 2007. This was produced by the Melbourne Workers' Theatre and directed by Andrea James.

Live animals are once again appearing on stage in theatre and in contemporary performance, and with some ethically questionable practices in the latter (Orozco 2013), although without feats and tricks as once happened. The comparable absence of animals in modernist visual art that was discerned by John Berger had been reversed in postmodern visual art some years earlier and often with live animals (Baker 2000). Theatrical attention has slowly turned to the question of the animal, and species identities across performance forms including circus (Chaudhuri 2007 [Derrida]; Peterson 2007; Tait 2012). An animal might be a subsidiary element within a human story in theatre, but some precedents with a horse or dogs generate complex commentaries (Kelleher, Ridout, Castellucci, Guidi & Castellucci 2007). Consequently it is probably not surprising to find an Australian Belvoir St Theatre production of *The wild duck* in 2011–12, directed by Chris Ryan, presenting a living duck on stage. The production had a set with a glass wall between the audience and performers, and the Melbourne season coincided with the opening of the duck-hunting season in Victoria.[6] Live animals standing on stage might seem like objectification for human voyeurism or at least a sensationalist gesture, but an animal body on stage is a truer depiction of a species and invariably takes the complete focus away from human performers. This stage presence may serve to heighten the visibility of the species outside the theatre.

Jane Goodall (2008) explores ideas of how intangible human presence is recognised within theatre texts historically but suggests that this concept can only be grasped through ideas of embodiment. Her exploration of human presence indirectly provides one justification, if not necessarily a strong one, for the bodied presence of animals in theatre. But animal presence raises a conundrum in relation to the ethics of presenting live animals in an environment such as theatre with several hundred people that might sensorily and bodily upset an animal in order to fulfill a larger purpose of drawing attention to the plight of the species.

While contemporary performance and visual art has returned to presenting live animals in an era when new circus has rejected animal

---

6 The author viewed the production at the Malthouse Theatre, 6 March 2012, and reviewed it for the Australian Animal Studies Group AASG Bulletin March 2012.

performers, most theatre continues to eschew the dead animal of ritual and rite associated with its founding early Greek theatre. The dead animal remains a ghostly offstage presence.

Animal absence

It is difficult to gauge the extent to which 21st-century theatre and performance practitioners accommodate contemporary attitudes to living animals and the politics of speciesism (Singer 1995; Cavalieri 2001), and grapple with developments in the fraught politics of ethical relations (Sunstein & Nussbaum 2004). To date, clear responses in Australia only seem apparent in theatre texts that consider the future. The fish (prop) falling out of the desert sky at the start of Andrew Bovell's (2008) *When the rain stops falling* signals the effect of climate change sometime in the future without elaboration. In Kit Lazaroo's futuristic play, *Letters from animals*, most animal species have become extinct.[7] This narrative countenancing the death of other species is imbued with loss and grief.

Lazaroo's play suggests that the issue of species survival is an extremely urgent one. *Letters from animals* comments directly on animal lives and practices in the present by forecasting a future in which human acquisitive aggression and animal disease eradication have had apocalyptic consequences in an environmental disaster that obliterates nearly all other animal species. It also indirectly suggests that the deadly implications of climate change for other species are often obscured by human preoccupation with the impact on its own kind. In a female-only future, lone scientist Queenie, living in a house flooded by a river, resists the inquisitive questions of the bureaucrat Shelley, from the Ministry of Satisfaction, but she is deceived into handing over her precious collection of bird bones by the youthful and completely devious Gretel. Human performers also personify the voices of the remembered scavenger cockroach, rat and vulture, species metaphor-

---

7 The author viewed *Letters from animals* at the Storeroom, 25 November 2007. This was produced by Here Theatre at the Storeroom, directed by Jane Woollard with cast, Queenie and rat (Glynis Angell), Gretel and cockroach (HaiHa Le), Shelley and vulture (Georgina Capper).

ically associated with death. But in the extreme circumstances whereby some humans live on, they join the species associated with death. Over the other side of the river is a secret renegade laboratory that attempts to preserve remnants of other species and even bring some to life. Queenie has managed to hide the smallest of life forms to release into the river, which does promise renewal if not necessarily hope for humans; human survival is limited by the sludge that must be pumped out of habited areas. The interdependency of species becomes a transparent point. In this apocalyptic world, humans have lost more than the words for animals and knowledge about them, they have lost their freedom along with their imaginative and creative capacity – the longstanding way in which animals embody human thinking and emotional feeling. The play crystallises fears for the future by taking to a logical conclusion the warning that, unless humans change, there will be devastating consequences. Absence is central to the narrative because it is about biodiversity and species loss and animal death. Hence the embodied presence of animals in human worlds was emphasised through bodily absence.

The purpose of *Letters from animals* was to draw attention to the obliteration of other species. As well as the vulture, rat and cockroach voices, the theatrical staging included quirky oversized, cardboard two-dimensional animal, insect and bird shapes to make a post-apocalyptic world explicit. In production, the play could have been much shorter without losing its significance and some staging choices needed revisiting, but strong performances brought the unimaginable implications of the futuristic world to the fore. The performers climbed over upturned buckets and angled surfaces in a precarious way to visually reinforce their condition. The design conveyed a return to everyday manual technologies and equipment that were not fuel-dependent, although pumps still kept the black chemical sludge away until they began breaking down at the play's end as the most deadly species was gradually killing itself.

Animal impersonation is a further (and longstanding) option alongside these other representational modes. The 21st-century return to a human playing an animal suggests an alternative strategy used in theatre, contemporary performance and visual arts to deliver species presence but obviate detrimental effects of using animals. An anthropomorphic rendition of an animal body by a human performer may seem like a reasonable response to ethical concern about presenting living animals to make a point. In 2007, performance artist Mark Wallinger won the Turner Award, Britain's top contemporary art award, for *Sleeper*, in which he wandered around an art gallery in a brown bear costume for two and a half hours (*The Australian*, 5 December 2007, 3). If incongruous visibility was central to this performance suggesting a bedroom world of dreams, it also evoked social fondness for cuddly (replica) toy bears, although any reference to the plight of living bears was probably more oblique. Further, the pervasive social expectation that animals in representation embody human emotional feelings may circumvent a strategy of attracting attention to living animals. In the 2010 production of Jenny Kemp's *Kitten*, sea species were presented through recorded sound and a polar bear played by a human appeared in a teasing ironic depiction that evoked human fondness for images of white bears. Kemp's oeuvre spans theatre and contemporary per-formance and is often inspired by visual art (Varney 2011). In this performance text, the central figure is the ex-singer, Kitten, a widow grieving for her partner, Jonah, who has gone missing at sea. Jonah researched whales and other species, and the spoken text of *Kitten* is about environmental destruction and species survival. As it follows the trajectory of the female character's grief for Jonah, it unfolds an idea of human grief over other species. Given that this production was titled *Kitten*, emblematic of an extremely anthropomorphised domesticated species, and there were frequent references to other species throughout as well as recorded whale calls and the appearance of a polar bear, it is surprising to encounter minimal or only passing comment on these theatricalised animals in some responses to the performance.[8] It was as if the animal species went unnoticed in a human-centric focus that missed the point. Why? It is possible this was due to the way that the human story highlighted emotions, and Kitten's grief and trauma over

---

8   See M Pereira, review of *Kitten* [Online]. Available: www.australianstage.com.au/reviews/miaf/kitten--jenny-kemp-1946.html [Accessed 25 May 2012]. Several reviews of *Kitten* were critical and did not mention its central theme of animal loss and extinction; see C Boyd [Online]. Available: chrisboyd.blogspot.com.au [Accessed 25 May 2012]; A Croggan, theatrenotes.blogspot.com.au/2008/10/miaf-big-game-three-kitten.html [Accessed 25 May 2012]. Varney acknowledges the bear as a manifestation of Kitten's bipolar mental health (2011, 226).

the death of her husband was unmistakable. A performance of grief over the death of a family member might be unquestioningly accepted as socially gendered, and this was the dominant emotional motif in the narrative. Perhaps these emotional dynamics completely overshadowed haunting animal audio presence for some spectators and the implicit inference of madness and grief over animal death. As well, the projection of human emotions onto animals may become literalised with animal impersonation.

The examples given here confirm that when animal species are made the central identities in a dramatic world, they are hard to miss. But even where there was a meaningful commentary about animals, associated with strong emotional responses between human characters, animals did not necessarily become the focus of attention. The evocation of emotional responses on behalf of animals may be unreliable. While emotion is connected to body-based feelings, and although emotions are embodied and objectified within larger social patterns, specific emotional feelings remain unpredictable in their evocation and interpretation. Human emotions may even obscure animal identity. While sensory effects can have a body-based impact, connections between reasoning and physiologies of feeling are not automatic. Unchallenged, habitual patterns of emotional responses to animal species who embody human emotions may continue to distort responses (Tait 2012). Emotional narratives cannot be assumed to maximise attention for animal species because of how animals have been habitually assimilated into human social worlds in representation and surrounded with human emotional feelings.

Conclusion

Where theatre continues to present animals integrated into human worlds through its stories and framed by the emotional expression arising from spoken word delivery, they remain abstract symbolic and metaphoric entities. They continue to be enveloped by human emotions as theatre's anthropomorphic processes camouflage the separate worlds inhabited by animals. Some contemporary performance has turned attention to embodied presence and it is hoped that this might be indicative of a larger pattern of orientation in society which lessens the need to repeatedly present living animals. The urgent issue of species survival requires all possible interventions.

The experience of 'Animal inside out' was quite different to that of seeing lifeless replicas in theatre productions or cognitively interpreting animal identities without embodied presence in dramatic narratives. It was impossible to avoid the issue of animal death, even though the exhibition's intention was unclear. The human was placed in a world filled with animals – albeit one fabricated by humans – which turned around how species remain unseen in a human world. The exhibition disrupted the familiar process of pleasant viewing and thus, paradoxically, increased awareness of animals. A species-to-species encounter happens with and through lived body experience and, as argued here, a body-to-body encounter can be surmised to also happen at a level of physiological responses. Bodily confronting an actual animal body, dead or alive, potentially resists the emotional processes of species conflation. The body-based habitual pattern of calm, pleasant responses if not stronger, affectionate responses to images of animals was completely obscured by three-dimensional grotesque bodies without skins. The sensations of a human body responding to a preserved corpse were turned inside out. The viewing of dead animal bodies became literally sickening.

Works cited

Acampora RR (2006). *Corporal compassion: animal ethics and philosophy of body*. Pittsburgh: University of Pittsburgh Press.

Alberti SJMM (Ed.) (2011). *The afterlives of animals*. Charlottesville and London: University of Virginia Press.

Animal Studies Group (Ed.) (2006). *Killing animals*. Urbana and Chicago: University of Illinois Press.

Baker S (2000). *The postmodern animal*. London: Reaktion Books.

Baker S (2006). You kill things to look at: animal death in contemporary art. In Animal Studies Group (Ed.). *Killing animals* (pp69–99). Urbana and Chicago: University of Illinois Press.

Bovell A (2008). *When the rain stops falling*. London: Nick Hern.

Burt J (2006). Conflicts around slaughter in modernity. In Animal Studies Group (Ed.). *Killing animals* (pp120–44). Urbana and Chicago: University of Illinois Press.

Carlson M (2003). *Performance: a critical introduction*. New York: Routledge.
Cavalieri P (2001). *The animal question: why nonhuman animals deserve human rights*. Oxford: Oxford University Press.
Chaudhuri U (2007). (De)Facing the animals. *The Drama Review*, 51(1) (T193): 8–20.
Chekhov A (1991). *Five plays*. R Hingley (Trans.). Oxford: Oxford University Press.
Chris C (2006). *Watching wildlife*. Minneapolis: University of Minnesota Press.
Cornelius P (2009). *The call*. Sydney: Currency Press.
Desmond J (2008). Postmortem exhibitions: taxidermied animals and plastinated corpses in the theaters of the dead. *Configurations*, 16(3): 347–78 [Online]. Available: muse.jhu.edu/journals/configurations/v016/16.3.desmond.html [Accessed 13 March 2013].
Goodall J (2008). *Stage presence*. London: Routledge.
Ibsen H (1999). *An enemy of the people; The wild duck; Rosmersholm*. J McFarlane (Trans.). Oxford and New York: Oxford University Press.
Kelleher J, Ridout N, Castellucci C, Guidi C & Castellucci R (2007). *The theatre of Societas Raffaello Sanzio*. London: Routledge.
Kemp J (n.d.). Kitten, unpublished script courtesy of the author.
Lazaroo K (n.d.). Letters from animals, unpublished script courtesy of the author.
Macdonald, S (2011). Expanding museum studies: an introduction. In Sharon Macdonald (Ed.). *A companion to museum studies* (pp44–66). Malden, MA; Oxford, UK: Blackwell.
Merleau-Ponty M (1996). *Phenomenology of perception*. C Smith (Trans.). London: Routledge.
Merleau-Ponty M (1995). *The visible and the invisible*. A Lingis (Trans.). Evanston: Northwestern University Press.
Merleau-Ponty M (2004). *The world of perception*. O Davis (Trans.). London: Routledge.
Orozco L (2013). *Theatre and animals*. Basingstoke: Palgrave Macmillan.
Peterson M (2007). The animal apparatus: from a theory of animal acting to an ethics of animal acts. *The Drama Review*, 51:1 (T193): 33–48.
Phelan P (1993). *Unmarked*. London: Routledge.
Ritvo H (2010). *Noble cows and hybrid zebras*. Charlottesville: University of Virginia Press.
Singer P (1995 [1975]). *Animal liberation*. London: Pimlico.
Sunstein CR & Nussbaum MC (Eds) (2004). *Animal rights: current debates and new directions*. New York: Oxford University Press.
Tait P (2012). *Wild and dangerous: animals, emotions, circus*. Basingstoke: Palgrave Macmillan.

Varney, Denise (2011). *Radical visions 1968–2008: the impact of the sixties on Australian drama*. Amsterdam: Rodopi, see Chapter 7.

5
Respect for the (animal) dead

Chloë Taylor

JM Coetzee's novel, *Disgrace*, includes the remarkable scene of the protagonist – previously indifferent to nonhuman animals and condescending towards animal welfarists – taking upon himself the task of incinerating the corpses of unwanted dogs who have been killed at the local animal shelter. Although he observes that there are more 'productive ways of giving oneself to the world', such as 'persuad[ing] the children at the dump not to fill their bodies with poisons', he perseveres in his task in order to spare the bodies of the dogs the indignity of being treated like garbage by the dump employees. He cremates the dogs individually, 'For his idea of the world, a world in which men do not use shovels to beat corpses into a more convenient shape for processing' (Coetzee 1990, 146). In the literature on Coetzee's novel, the ethical motivation behind this scene has been described as 'unfathomable' and 'ridiculous' (see Willett 2011). These judgments support the intuition of Coetzee's character himself, according to which it is of dubious importance to concern oneself with the dignity of dead animals when there are live animals, and especially live humans, who would benefit from our efforts.

In this chapter I explore whether we should be concerned about the dignity of dead animals, and about the dignity of the ways in which

C Taylor (2013). Respect for the (animal) dead. In J Johnston & F Probyn-Rapsey (Eds). *Animal death*. Sydney: Sydney University Press.

animals currently die. My initial assumption in approaching this topic was that the dominant Western worldview has no ethics of respect for the animal dead, and that an ethics of respect for the animal dead was incompatible with a society that systematically eats and otherwise instrumentalises nonhuman animal bodies and corpses. I thought that it was for this reason that attempting to give dignity to dead dogs might strike Coetzee's character and readers alike as an absurd and 'unfathomable' gesture. As I worked, however, things came to seem more complicated, as the word 'respect' continually crops up to describe our treatment of dead animals, and in particular to describe acts (such as hunting and eating hunted animals) which, if done to humans, would never be considered respectful. I am now inclined to think that the dominant Western worldview *does* contain an ethics of respect for the nonhuman animal dead but, with the complex exception of companion animals, this ethics prescribes using the bodies of dead animals so that their deaths are not for nothing. In this context, 'wasting' is the ultimate act of disrespect to the dead. Such an ethics is in opposition to our ethics of respect for the human dead which entails dignifying and mourning the dead, abiding by their wishes as these were expressed in life, and eschews instrumentalising corpses except when such instrumentalisation accords with the dead person's wishes, as in the case of organ donation.

In the first section of this paper I tell a series of stories about eating the dead, as these are some of the stories that complicated my thinking about this topic. In particular, I am interested in the idea that we can eat the dead respectfully. I then draw on these stories to suggest that there exists an ethical apartheid between the deontological thinking about humans, including the human dead, and the utilitarian thinking about other animals, including their corpses, which characterises Western thought. In the third section, I suggest that the utilitarian ethics of respect for the nonhuman animal dead is problematic because it forbids mourning, and I draw on Judith Butler's work to argue that we will only be able to improve the lives of other animals once we have recognised those lives as grievable.

Stories

In his novel, *Immortality*, Milan Kundera (1999) tells a story about the death of Salvador Dalí's beloved companion rabbit. Kundera writes:

When they were already quite old, the famous painter Salvador Dalí and his wife, Gala, had a pet rabbit, who lived with them and followed them around everywhere, and of whom they were very fond. Once, they were about to embark on a long trip, and they debated long into the night what to do with the rabbit. It would have been difficult to take him along and equally difficult to entrust him to somebody else, because the rabbit was uneasy with strangers. The next day Gala prepared lunch and Dalí enjoyed the excellent food until he realized he was eating rabbit meat. He got up from the table and ran to the bathroom where he vomited up his beloved pet, the faithful friend of his waning days. Gala, on the other hand, was happy that the one she loved had passed into her guts, caressing them and becoming the body of his mistress. For her there existed no more perfect fulfillment of love than eating the beloved. Compared to this merging of bodies, the sexual act seemed to her no more than ludicrous tickling. (Kundera 1990, 96)

A student of mine tells me that her Aboriginal grandmother used to make her and her siblings eat the animals they killed. According to my student, who is now a vegan and animal activist, this eating of the animals she killed instilled an ethics of respect for animal life in her.

Ben Ehrenreich's short story, 'What we eat' (2004), tells a tale of a boy and his father who live alone in the countryside.[1] The father, like my student's grandmother, makes his son eat any animals he kills, and he tells his son that this is 'only right and just besides' (Ehrenreich 2004, 96). In this case, however, being made to eat the dead is traumatising for the child. It starts with insects and continues with a bird and a squirrel. When the son, now a teenager, accidently backs his car over his pet dog, the father butchers the dog and cooks him, expecting his son to eat

---

1 This story has been made into a short film by Jennifer Liao, also called 'What we eat'. I am grateful to Jennifer Liao for sending me a copy of her film. For information on Jennifer Liao's films, visit: www.jenniferliao.com.

the flesh. Soon after, the son, distraught, flings himself in front of his father's car, fork and knife in hand, and pretends to be dead on impact. As the father peers at his son's prone and broken body on the road, the son opens his eyes and asks, 'What were you gonna do?'

A friend of mine, Lisa, was walking in the forest in the Yukon when her dog ran off and attacked a gopher. The gopher was still alive but mangled and panting with fright and pain when Lisa reached her. Lisa decided that the best thing to do was to put the gopher out of her misery. She hit the gopher with an axe, attempting to decapitate her. Unfortunately, the gopher did not die from the first blow and Lisa had to hit her repeatedly before she perished. Tormented by this scene of suffering, Lisa was determined that her dog should eat the gopher since he had initiated her death. The dog had no interest in eating the gopher, however. Lisa therefore cooked the gopher on a camp stove with potatoes and carrots, and tried to serve the stew to her dog. The dog treated this mixture suspiciously and remained reluctant to eat.

My friend's landlord is a pilot who works for a small airline, flying American hunters from Montréal to Northern Québec to hunt, and flying them back to the city with trophy items such as antlers from the animals they have killed. The hunters leave the animal carcasses behind, only interested in their trophies. After depositing the hunters in Montréal, the pilot returns to the north and flies the animal carcasses to First Nations reserves where they are used for food, clothing, and other purposes. The way in which this story was told to me, and in which I received it, was that there is one morally repugnant aspect of this pilot's job – flying the Americans up north and back to facilitate their trophy hunting – and one morally redeeming aspect of his job – bringing the animal corpses to the native reserves so that they can be used.

One of my colleagues is a hunter. His website features a photo of himself standing triumphantly over the body of a deer he has killed. I am told that his Facebook page includes additional photos of himself holding up dead animals and parts of dead animals. He writes about hunting from an environmental ethics perspective. When I was hired, he presented himself to me as an ally, similarly concerned with animal ethics. He believes that by hunting he is being morally exemplary because he avoids supporting factory farms, and he does not waste any part of the animals' bodies that he kills. He makes household items out of their fat, fur, skin and bones, as well as eating their flesh and blood.

Other hunters argue that what makes their killing of animals respectful is that, unlike people who purchase animal flesh in grocery stores, they are willing to take responsibility for the deaths they cause; they look the animals they kill in the face.[2]

In *Consuming grief: compassionate cannibalism in an Amazonian society*, Beth Conklin (2001) provides a detailed study of funereal cannibalism in the society of the Wari'. Also called endocannibalism, funereal cannibalism is the ritualised eating of one's dead and is distinct from both hunger cannibalism and exocannibalism, the eating of one's enemies. While some Amazonian societies ate their dead family members for similar reasons to those that Gala Dalí gave for eating her rabbit, the Wari' ate, not their blood kin or spouses, but their in-laws. The reason for eating one's in-laws was not to incorporate or retain them, and was not aimed at satisfying any nutritional needs or desire for flesh. The Wari' ate the rotting and roasted meat of their in-laws with reluctance, amidst wailings of grief, overcoming disgust out of respect for the dead and their families. The Wari' considered it undignified to be placed in the ground and are sad to think of someone they love being buried. They did not want to be buried, and they did not want to think of their loved ones buried, and so they ate their in-laws because that is what they would have wanted done to them, and because that is what they expected their in-laws to do when their own family members died. The Wari' had similar views about eating other foods as they have about eating their dead. In each case, whether the food was human flesh, nonhuman animal flesh, or plant, the Wari' believed that it wants to be eaten and will feel disrespected if it is not: the Wari' tell a story of a dropped kernel of corn that longed to be planted so it could grow and be consumed, and another story of a pig who bewailed the fact that her roasted flesh was not shared with more Wari'.

Philosopher Val Plumwood notes that the 'human supremacist culture of the West' contrasts with Aboriginal worldviews in setting humans outside of nature and denying that we are part of the food chain. Plumwood notes that 'Horror and outrage usually greet stories of other

---

2   This argument was made, for instance, by Michael Adams in his presentation, 'Hunters heart: social and cultural dimensions of hunting in Australia' which was presented at the Animal Death conference at the University of Sydney on 12 June 2012.

species eating humans. Even being nibbled by leeches, sandflies, and mosquitos can stir various levels of hysteria' (Plumwood 2000, 7). When she was attacked by a crocodile while canoeing alone in East Alligator Lagoon in the Australian wetlands, Plumwood writes:

> I glimpsed a shockingly indifferent world in which I had no more significance than any other edible being. The thought, 'This can't be happening to me, I'm a human being. I am more than just food!' was one component of my terminal incredulity. It was a shocking reduction, from a complex human being to a mere piece of meat. Reflection has persuaded me that not just humans but any creature can make the same claim to be more than just food. (2000, 7)

Both Aristotle and Aquinas illustrate Plumwood's argument that the Western 'concept of human identity positions humans outside and above the food chain, not as part of the feast in a chain of reciprocity but as external manipulators and masters of it: Animals can be our food, but we can never be their food' (ibid.). Aristotle writes:

> We may infer that, after the birth of animals, plants exist for their sake, and that the other animals exist for the sake of man, the tame for use and food, the wild, if not all at least the greater part of them, for food, and for the provision of clothing and various instruments. Now if nature makes nothing incomplete, and nothing in vain, the inference must be that she has made all animals for the sake of man. And so, in one point of view, the art of war is a natural art of acquisition, for the art of acquisition includes hunting, an art which we ought to practice against wild beasts (Aristotle 1941, 1137)

For Aristotle, more complex souls correspond with higher forms of life, and it is natural for higher forms of life to eat lower forms of life, but unnatural for lower forms of life to eat higher forms of life. Since, according to Aristotle, humans, having reason, have more complex souls than other animals, and all animals, with their capacities for sensitivity and locomotion, have more complex souls than plants, it is natural for animals to eat plants and for humans to eat animals, but not for animals to eat humans or for plants to eat animals. It would seem that the insectivorous plant, the mosquito who sucks human blood, and the bear who eats a human are thus all behaving unnaturally. Aquinas would take up Aristotle's argument and translate it into Natural Law theory. He writes that

> Now the order of things is such that the imperfect are for the perfect . . . Things, like plants which merely have life, are all alike for animals, and all animals are for man. Wherefore it is not unlawful if men use plants for the good of animals, and animals for the good of man . . . wherefore it is lawful both to take life from plants for the use of animals, and from animals for the use of men. (*Summa theologica* II, II Q64, art. 1, cited in Singer 2002, 193–94)

In contrast with the lawfulness with which humans eat animals, animals who eat humans act unjustly:

> Savagery and brutality take their names from a likeness to wild beasts. For animals of this kind attack man that they may feed on his body, and not for some motive of justice. (*Summa theologica* II, II, Q159, art. 2, cited in Singer 2002, 194)

The result of this longstanding belief that animals who eat humans are behaving unnaturally and unlawfully is a sense of 'outrage' when other animals treat humans as food, and this outrage frequently results in the execution of such predators. In a case that occurred recently in Canada, a murderer who had skipped parole and was on the run in a remote logging area in British Columbia died of natural causes in his car. His corpse was discovered by a black bear, who pulled it out the open window of the vehicle and partially consumed it. Hunters came across the cache of human remains being guarded by a bear and reported the incident to authorities. Although the bear did not kill the murder convict and although it was not known before the necropsy whether the bear guarding the corpse was the one who had eaten it, he was referred to as 'the prime suspect' and 'the offending bear' and was 'euthanized [sic]' because he had 'lost its [sic] fear of humans'.[3]

Ethics for the dead

What this series of stories suggests – but also problematises and offers alternatives to – is a tendency in the dominant Western worldview to believe that it is respectful to kill nonhuman animals if we instrument-alise their cadavers, but that animals (including other humans) should never instrumentalise human corpses, and certainly not for food. In the case of nonhuman animals it is often thought to be worse to 'waste' their bodies than to use them, and using their bodies after death re-deems their killings or makes them morally acceptable. Burying or cremating the animal dead is either a waste of food or, as in the case of Coetzee's dogs, a waste of our moral time and effort. Thus hunters who eat their kill are considered less morally repugnant than trophy hunters, and, although the practice is rare, adults who make children eat the nonhuman animals they kill believe that they are teaching them respect for animal life. Importantly, 'wasting' nonhuman animal bodies means that *humans* fail to use them since, if we were to leave the dead animals where they fell, they *would not* go to waste; they would be consumed, but it would be nonhuman animals who would consume the corpses.[4]

If we think about it, these are curious intuitions. Returning to the case of Lisa, her dog, and the gopher, why exactly was it respectful to the gopher to ensure that her body was eaten by her predator, when gophers do everything in their power to avoid being captured by pred-ators? Instrumentalising an animal's cadaver is certainly not respectful in the usual sense of abiding by a being's wishes or respecting her autonomy as it was expressed in life. While Lisa took the situation with the gopher to an extreme that most people would not, and although the case is peculiar in that it treats the dog as a moral agent who must take responsibility for his deed, I think we can nevertheless understand

---

3   Why failure to fear humans, even dead humans, should be a capital offence for a predator the size of a black bear is unclear. For newspaper articles concerning this case, see: www.heraldsun.com.au/ipad/bear-killed-for-eating-murderer/story-fn6s850w-1226384085656; news.nationalpost.com/2012/06/01/man-whose-dead-body-was-eaten-by-bear-turns-out-be-convicted-murder-reported-missing/; news.nationalpost.com/2012/06/04/bear-euthanized-on-suspicion-of-eating-murderers-remains/.
4   I thank Deborah Bird Rose for this point, which she raised in the discussion period for this paper at the Animal Death conference in Sydney.

Lisa's intuition that it would have been better if the gopher's death had served some purpose beyond fleeting canine recreation. It goes without saying that Lisa's reaction – and ours – would have been different if the dog had killed a human. If she had butchered a human's corpse and stewed it with carrots and potatoes, so that the human didn't die for nothing, this would have landed Lisa in an asylum or charged under Canadian law with committing an act of indignity against a corpse.

Returning to my hunter colleague, while from a utilitarian perspective we can easily see that he is doing less harm to animals than if he bought his meat at the grocery store, we can once again question whether he would apply his arguments to humans. Would he see a murderer of humans who took trophy photos over his victims' corpses, posted them online, and made useful products out of their cadavers, as morally exemplary? How would he compare his own behaviour to that of Luca Magnotta, the Montréal murderer who recently filmed the beheading and dismembering of his victim, posted the videos on the net, and cannibalised some of his victim's body parts? Magnotta was charged with committing acts of indignity against a human corpse, and yet, with my colleague, he could defend himself by arguing that he was not supporting factory farms to get his meat and that he did not 'waste' the corpse of the individual he killed, and thus was morally exemplary in comparison to people who buy their meat in the store and do not look their victims in the eye – reducing those animal victims, in Carol Adams' terms, to 'absent referents' (Adams 1990).

The absurdity of these comparisons indicates that the utilitarian ethics for the nonhuman animal dead that I have been describing is in stark contrast to our intuition that killing humans to use their bodies is never a sign of respect for our fellows, never morally redeems their killing, and indeed makes these killings particularly heinous. Killers of humans who eat or use their victims' bodies, who take remorseless responsibility for the deaths they have caused, who take and circulate photos of their victims, are seen as especially loathsome. Ben Ehrenreich's short story, 'What we eat', highlights the tensions involved in believing that those who eat the animals they kill are respectful of animal lives and inculcate an ethics of respect in their children. The story points out that we do not think it is respectful of the dead to eat them when the dead are our children, humans, or pets. In these cases, as is illustrated by the example of Salvador Dalí, the idea of eating the dead sickens and appalls.

Put simply, the dominant Western worldview is deontological with respect to dead humans and utilitarian with respect to dead animals of other species. Appropriately then, Coetzee's character questions the 'productivity' of spending time cremating the corpses of dogs. This is not a question that we ask ourselves when we participate in human funerals, although then too there are other ways that we could be spending our time that might be more useful to the world. Companion animals create a dilemma for this system, as we are not prepared to use their bodies, but nor does our society tolerate the mourning of their deaths.[5]

Two of the stories that I told offer a contrast to this system of opposed ethics. Val Plumwood's experience of being attacked by a crocodile led her to the insight that our abhorrence for being food for other animals explains

> why we now treat so inhumanely the animals we make our food, for we cannot imagine ourselves similarly positioned as food. We act as if we live in a separate realm of culture in which we are never food, while other animals inhabit a different world of nature in which they are no more than food, and their lives can be utterly distorted in the service of this end. (Plumwood 2000, 7)

In contrast to this state of affairs, Plumwood argues for a 'respectful, ecological eating', that would entail recognising both our own edibility and the fact that other animals are not reducible to their edibility. This would mean not destroying or otherwise managing nonhuman animals who kill humans for food, as Plumwood resisted having the crocodile who attacked her killed; she not only dissuaded rangers from hunt-

---

5 I recognise the existence of pet funerals and pet cemeteries; however, such practices are often seen as something one does for children, or (as shall be argued in more detail below) are seen as childish, comical or overly sentimental acts on the part of adults. Although degrees of sympathy for such practices may vary, they are not respected or required the way that mourning for the human dead is. There is also no practice of granting employees leave from work to care for their dying pets or to mourn their deaths.

ing down the crocodile who had attacked her, she also attempted to limit the publicisation of the attack for fear that it would result in the increased management of crocodile populations more generally. Plumwood recognised that the attack on her had been neither unnatural nor unlawful, however terrifying and disorienting it had been. When Plumwood died (years later), her friends gave her a 'green burial', placing her in the ground in such a way that she could easily be accessed by worms and other fauna. Although in Australia it is illegal to bury a human without a coffin, Plumwood's friends chose a cardboard coffin and rejected a worm-resistant lining for her shroud. This burial was in accordance with Plumwood's wishes, and expressed her recognition and acceptance of the fact that humans are food for other animals. At the same time as this burial recognised Plumwood's edibility, the respect that was granted to her wishes recognised that she was more than just edible. It is this simultaneous recognition of our edibility and more-than-edibility that Plumwood argued we owe to other animals.

Like Plumwood following her encounter with a crocodile, the Wari' understood that their bodies could be food for others, and that they were made of edible flesh just like other animals. Admittedly, it cannot be said that the Wari' treated the eating of humans just like the eating of corn and pigs; the Wari' grieved while they ate other Wari', but not when they ate corn, enemy flesh, or nonhuman animals. They did not kill their own community members to eat them, and the primary purpose of killing their enemies was also not to eat them, whereas they did kill corn, and nonhuman animals for food. When the Wari' killed humans prior to eating them, these were enemies, and then the eating was considered disrespectful (it involved bad 'table manners'), and it was an expression of disdain to eat a human in the same way that one ate an animal (without elaborate 'table manners') (Conklin 2001, 130–31). In contrast, eating corn, pigs and in-laws was considered respectful, and the eating of in-laws was set apart by the particularly meticulous 'table manners' that it required (for instance, the use of utensils to handle the meat). Consuming human flesh thus introduced a number of complications into the Wari' ethics of eating, and yet, whether dealing with humans, other animals or corn, and with the exceptions of their enemies, the Wari' ate the dead at least in part for the same reason: because they believed that this is what the dead would have wished. Eating the dead, moreover, was compatible with intense practices of mourning.

Mourning other animals

Little has been written about our obligations to the dead in the literature on animal ethics. This is in contrast with the literature on human ethics, where much has been written on this topic. Clare Palmer offers an explanation for why ethicists do not worry about dead animals, and about seeking reparation for dead agricultural animals specifically. She writes that this question

> raises such peculiarly complicated nonidentity and counterfactual problems that it is hard to make sense of any reparation-like claims here . . . inasmuch as there are concerns about wrongful harms to agricultural animals, these are generally about ongoing harms. In that case, an argument to stop harming, rather than an argument for reparation-like responsibilities, has priority: it would be strange, after all, to recommend reparation for a harm that is still being committed, if there is some way of stopping the harm. (Palmer 2010, 102)

As in the case of Coetzee's dogs, worrying about dead animals is described as 'peculiar', 'strange', and an unwise way of investing our moral energy. While Palmer is discussing justice for farm animals, we might think that her argument could be applied to the question of respect for dead animals more generally. It might be thought that it makes little sense to worry about respect for the human or nonhuman animal dead when suffering and indignities in life are ongoing.

In fact, however, our attempts to give dignity to the corpses of humans through rituals of mourning, even when harm is ongoing, are *not* considered inexplicable or absurd. Respectful ritualisation of the disposal of human bodies is the norm, even in times of war, and the desire for these ceremonies is understandable *at all times*. In contrast, those who have funerals for nonhuman animals are often not simply considered unwise, but abnormal and childish. To dignify a nonhuman animal's corpse rather than to use it is to confuse species. Such confusion is understandable only on the part of children. In *Abnor-*

mal, Michel Foucault argues that the infantile is the mark of pathology; the mentally ill not only have the legal status of minors, but all mental disorders are thought to involve some manner of being delayed in a childhood state (Foucault 2003). The infantile is thus pathologised, a sign of danger in a biopolitical society. In Foucault's publication of archival material concerning a 19th-century matricide, Pierre Rivière, we read psychiatrists observe that Rivière's elaborate funeral for a pet bird was an indicator of mental illness: Rivière was *too old* to have engaged in such behaviour and he did so with children (Foucault 1992). This bird funeral, the psychiatrists agree, indicated Rivière's arrested development and, among other symptoms, made his later slaughter of his mother and siblings predictable to a trained medical eye.

Philosopher Kelly Oliver (2009, 303) observes that when she dedicates her books to dead cats, her friends warn her that she won't be taken seriously as an intellectual. This advice, like the psychiatric analysis of Pierre Rivière, shows that our failure to grieve other animals and to dignify their deaths does not simply reflect a species-inclusive situation in which such matters cannot be prioritised when the plight of the living demands our attention. Rather, it reflects the fact that the ethical apartheid between humans and nonhuman animals reserves mourning for humans and infantilises and thereby pathologises those who violate the rule. Eulogies for, commemorations of, and ritualised mourning of nonhuman animals thus have an air of mimicry about them, as if the mourner were play-acting at ceremonies for humans, and such fantasy on the part of an adult is psychologically worrisome in a culture where the childish marks pathology.

The problem is that this renders nonhuman animals ungrievable, and this in turn makes their lives less 'real'. Dead pets and those who loved them are left in limbo since it is neither socially acceptable to mourn them nor to eat or otherwise use them. We are expected to do and feel nothing, to get a new pet and be back at work the next day. Alice Kuzniar (2006) suggests that humans who lose companion animals are melancholy because of the cultural prohibition on mourning. For the most part, we do not grieve the nonhuman animal dead, and even animal activists focus on the living rather than memorialising and seeking reparation for the dead. Drawing on Judith Butler's (2006) work on mourning, however, I would argue that being ungrievable in death means that one's life will not be recognised as a life. This means that so long as we do not grieve nonhuman animals, the instrumentalisation of their lives, and not only of their corpses, will continue.

In 'Violence, mourning, politics', Butler writes, 'if a life is not grievable, it is not quite a life; it does not qualify as a life and is not worth a note. It is already the unburied, if not the unburiable' (2006, 34). Butler is writing of a situation in which, as in the case of nonhuman animal deaths, mourning has been forbidden. She cites George W Bush's claim, ten days after 9/11, that the time for mourning was over, that it was the time for 'action to take the place of grief' (29). This is not unlike Palmer's argument that so long as the plight of nonhuman animals remains dire, we must worry about justice to the living rather than the dead. Butler, however, is suggesting that in these political contexts, far from being something to be suspended in favour of action, mourning is a crucial source of ethical and political insight, allowing us to experience our commonality with others who have been set outside the sphere of the human. Butler specifically considers the lives that were lost but not publicly grieved on and after 9/11 – queer American lives, Afghan lives, Palestinian lives. Although Butler is not thinking of those who have been set outside the human, the grievable, because they are in fact *not human*, I would suggest that we might also think about the political uses of grief for other animals.[6] The animal liberation movement, like the communities of which Butler writes, is a movement that suffers 'innumerable losses' and for which mourning could be 'dramatic' (28), if it did not suspend grief for the dead in favour of the living. Grieving for nonhuman animals acknowledges the fact that the lives of other animals are indeed lives. In contrast, if we perpetuate the suspiciously self-serving view that it is respectful of nonhuman animals to instrumentalise their corpses, when our own bodies and those of beings we love can never be so treated respectfully, we are also likely to perpetuate the view that it is respectful to raise and to kill nonhuman animals for the sole purpose of such instrumentalisation.

---

6   For an article in which I make a related argument, see Taylor (2008).

Conclusions: ethics for the living

I would suggest that the system of two ethics for the dead that I have described in this paper, as well as the ambivalent position of companion animals in this system, is an extension of ethical attitudes towards the living in Western thought. While instrumentalising humans is generally seen to be precisely what makes an act immoral, approaches to animal ethics are overwhelmingly utilitarian. We see this in the case of laboratory experimentation: while animal ethicists lament that much experimentation on nonhuman animals does not *even* result in any useful information, and millions of animals are thus tortured and killed for scientific experiments that are frivolous, inconclusive, redundant, and that do not result in any publications, it is debated whether it is moral to make use of knowledge that was derived from Nazi experiments on human beings. The implication is that experiments on nonhuman animals are *worse* if they do not result in any useful information, whereas highly useful information derived from experiments on human beings should perhaps not be used because of the moral violence through which it was obtained.

The tendency to be utilitarian in our ethical thought about nonhuman animals, while deontological with respect to human ethics, is explicit in the work of a number of moral philosophers. Martha Nussbaum (2007) argues that utilitarianism is a particularly useful theory for animal ethics, although she develops a neo-Kantian or Rawlsian approach to a number of human ethical issues. For his part, Robert Nozick baldly prescribes 'utilitarianism for animals, Kantianism for people' and Jeff McMahan endorses the view that nonhuman animals are 'freely violable in the service of the greater good' while human persons are 'fully inviolable' (cited in Donaldson & Kymlicka 2011, 20). For each of these authors, it seems, we may mix and match ethical theories depending on the species involved. In fact, it could be that certain human capacities, such as being able to imagine the children that we might have had, makes certain acts, like involuntary sterilisation, cruel to humans in a way that they are not for members of some other species (although how we could ever know if cats and dogs regret their infertility is unclear to me). While I want to acknowledge that such an argument *might* be made for some acts concerning some live human and nonhuman animals, I would reject any categorical ethical division such as I have described in this chapter, and such as is declared by Robert Nozick, whether we are considering the living or the dead. In particular, in this chapter I have wanted to problematise the view that while respect for the human dead should entail notions of dignity, rituals of mourning, and abiding by the wishes of the deceased, respect for the nonhuman animal dead should entail instrumentalising their corpses – and the more we instrumentalise them, the less we waste, the more respectful we are. Although this chapter has argued that there are some contexts in which eating the dead, whether human or other animal, may be respectful, arguments about 'not wasting' the animal dead seem to be a blatantly speciesist way in which we justify doing what we want to other animals while feeling good (or at least less bad) about it. Moreover, I have argued that how we treat the dead has direct implications for how we treat the living: the system of using non-human animals that forbids mourning means that nonhuman animal lives lack value as lives. As the instrumentalisable rather than the griev-able, nonhuman animals, like the humans we do not mourn, cease to be lives with which we can empathise, and then the terrifying situation emerges in which violence cannot even be recognised as violence.

Works cited

Adams C (1990). *The sexual politics of meat: a feminist-vegetarian critical theory*. New York: Continuum.

Aristotle (1941). *Politica in the basic works of Aristotle*. New York: Random House.

Butler J (2006). *Precarious life: the powers of mourning and violence*. New York: Verso.

Coetzee JM (1990). *Disgrace*. New York: Penguin.

Conklin B (2001). *Consuming grief: compassionate cannibalism in an Amazonian society*. Austin: University of Texas Press.

Donaldson S & Kymlicka W (2011). *Zoopolis: a political theory of animal rights*. Oxford: Oxford University Press.

Ehrenreich B (2004). What you eat. In D Eggers & V Mortensen (Eds). *The best American nonrequired reading* (pp96–106). Boston and New York: Houghton Mifflin Harcourt.

Foucault M (2003). *Abnormal: lectures at the Collège de France: 1974–1975*. New York: Picador.

Foucault M (1992). *I, Pierre Rivière, having slaughtered my mother, my sister, and my brother . . .: a case of parricide in the nineteenth century.* Lincoln, NE: University of Nebraska Press.

Kundera M (1999). *Immortality.* New York: Harper Perrenial.

Kuzniar A A (2006). *Melancholia's dog: reflections on our animal kinship.* Chicago: University of Chicago Press.

Nussbaum M (2007). *Frontiers of justice: disability, nationality, species.* Cambridge, MA: Harvard University Press.

Oliver K (2009). *Animal lessons: how they teach us to be human.* New York: Columbia University Press.

Palmer C (2010). *Animal ethics in context: a relational approach.* New York: Columbia University Press.

Plumwood V (2000). Surviving a crocodile attack [Online]. Available: www.utne.com/2000-07-01/being-prey.aspx [Accessed 27 January 2013]. Large sections of this article are reprinted from Plumwood V (1996). Being prey. *Terra Nova* 1(3): 32–44 and Plumwood V (2007). Tasteless: towards a food-based approach to death. *The Forum on Religion and Ecology Newsletter* 1.2.

Singer P (2002 [1975]). *Animal liberation.* New York: Harper Collins.

Taylor C (2008). The precarious lives of animals: Butler, Coetzee, and animal ethics. *Philosophy Today,* 52(1): 60–72.

Willett C (2012). Ground zero for a post-moral ethics in J M Coetzee's *Disgrace* and Julia Kristeva's *Melancholic. Continental Philosophy Review,* 45(1): 1–22.

6
Re-membering Sirius: animal death, rites of mourning, and the (material) cinema of spectrality

George Ioannides

This chapter aims to map out the theorisations of spectrality and materiality, and of presence and non-presence, which attend the representation of the dead animal body on film. Through an exploration of the work of John Berger, Akira Lippit and Jonathan Burt, I argue that the filmic image of animal death is a form of 'rupture' (Burt 2000, 11) in the field of visual representation. This chapter begins with the notion of the visual animal, explicated through the work of Berger, to reveal when, how, and why the transformation of animals into absent referents takes place. It then tracks the genealogies of spectrality, in accordance with the work of Lippit, and those of materiality, in accordance with the work of Burt, that adhere to the question of what it means to screen the death of an animal. Concepts of the spectral animal suggest that there is no proper death of the animal and no death as such in cinema, but instead, a phantasmic spectacle linked to cinema through its repetitive function of (re)animation. Notions of the material animal, however, speak of the affective agency of the cinematic animal vis-à-vis its human observer, including the material-semiotic, historical, embodied traces that leave open issues of grief and mourning for the nonhuman animal's now-absent presence. Is the dead animal on screen, therefore,

G Ioannides (2013). Re-membering Sirius: animal death, rites of mourning, and the (material) cinema of spectrality. In J Johnston & F Probyn-Rapsey (Eds). *Animal death*. Sydney: Sydney University Press.

to be understood as spectral, a phantasm, captured on film and en-shrined in loops of movement? Or is there something more corporeal at play, the materiality and contingency of an individual animal that left a trace that is embodied and that should, perhaps, be mourned? It is here, in the confluence of these suppositions, that this chapter seeks to find a space for a more nuanced theorisation of the simultaneous spectrality and materiality of the dead animal body on film. This will be demon-strated through a close reading of *Sirius remembered* (1959), a short silent film by the American avant-garde filmmaker Stan Brakhage, that shows the body of his dead pet dog decomposing in the forest, and which highlights the necessity to view the undeadness of the spectral subject, and the material corporeality of the pictured subject, when ex-amining animal death on screen. The visual animal attests to spectrality as well as materiality, signalled by its absent presence (and present ab-sence) in today's human–animal entangled condition.

The visual animal

I begin with the eminent art historian and novelist John Berger's essay 'Why look at animals?' (1980), published over three decades ago, which remains a landmark exploration of modernity's relationship to animals and the vicissitudes of their cultural and conceptual visibility (see Pick 2011, 103). The central thesis of Berger's piece concerns the gradual fading of the modern animal from everyday life; according to Berger, 'everywhere animals disappear' (1980, 26), and the most obvious mani-festation of this thesis can be seen in the gradual yet recently acceler-ated disappearance and destruction of many forms of animal life from our planet. A differing manifestation of this thesis of 'disappearance,' however, concerns the *representation* of animals, and it is this mediat-ised line of inquiry into animal death which shall be taken up in this chapter.

For Berger, industrial capitalism ruptured the once intimate re-lationship between humans and other animals; the intensification of agriculture distanced farmers from their livestock, and urbanisation separated city-dwellers from wild and rural nature (Armstrong 2011, 175–76). 'Real' animals disappeared and were 'effaced,' to be replaced by forms of virtual animality such as spectacle, anthropomorphic representations, and animal imagery, where animals were either overlaid with metaphors of human characteristics or became the bearers of purely human concerns. As the 'animals of the mind' could not 'be so easily dispersed' (Berger 1980, 15), therefore, the material marginalisation of animals in modernity was accompanied by the proliferation of *conceptual* animals where, as they vanished from physical reality, they multiplied in the human psyche (Armstrong 2011, 189). 'One could suppose', Berger argued, that such innovative visualisations of animals 'were compensatory' (1980, 26); animals have here disappeared in their 'essential original form' and have been replaced by 'symbols' (Aloi 2012, 12; see also Armstrong 2011, 175–76, 188–89). Yet even these virtual animals 'have been coopted into other categories so that the category *animal* has lost its central importance' (Berger 1980, 15). When industrial modernity is thought through with animals, then, 'animals are always the observed. The fact that they can observe us has lost all significance. They are the objects of our ever-extending knowledge' (16). As Anat Pick so eloquently states, the disappearance of animals from daily life has rendered them completely visible by *re*-presenting them as objects of mastery and knowledge, an action that, ironically, has only intensified under the conditions of their endangerment (2011, 104). It is here where the Bergerian thesis of the representative 'disappearance' of animals bleeds into, and creates a space for, an investigation of the presence of death, dying, and decomposition found at numerous levels of inquiry into animal representation.

The spectral animal

Akira Lippit's work professes its debt to Berger in the opening sentence of his book *Electric animal*: 'Everywhere animals disappear' (2000, 1). Lippit follows Berger in his account of the way modernity dissolves the empirical animal into pure spectrality, proposing a link between animals and technology, and showing that the fate of the animal in modernity is bound up with its representation as a filmic image: 'animals never *entirely* vanish' but 'exist in a state of *perpetual vanishing*' (2000, 1). For Lippit, 'animals enter a new economy of being during the modern period, one that is no longer sacrificial in the traditional sense of the term but, considering modern technological media generally and the cinema more specifically, *spectral* (2000, 1). Moreover, in his follow-up article published in *Film Quarterly*, Lippit states: 'Cinema is an animal, animality a form of technology, technology an aspect of life. A life forged in the radical reanimation of the conditions of vitality as such' (2002, 20). In the words of Nicole Shukin, therefore, Lippit 'theorises animals as undying spirits that survive their mass historical "vanishing" within modernity to be reincarnated in the technological media' (2009, 40–41). As animals vanish from historical modernity, a spirit or trace of animality is salvaged by the media of technology, where cinema, even more consummately than linguistic metaphor, 'mourns' vanishing animal life, preserving or encrypting animality in an affective and transferential structure of communication (Lippit 2000, 196; see also Shukin 2009, 40–41). Such a structure of human–animal communicative affect, that survives the historical disappearance of animals to transmigrate into the cinematic apparatus (Shukin 2009, 41), is evinced by the early cinematic concern with documenting animal death and is demonstrated by the early pioneer of film Thomas Edison's *Electrocuting an elephant* (1903).

In January 1903, Edison helped choreograph the public electrocution of Topsy, a six-tonne elephant on exhibit at Coney Island's Luna Park. Topsy was electrocuted with 6,600 volts of alternating current (AC) to propagandise the mortal dangers of George Westinghouse's competing system of electricity, at the same time as promoting Edison's own 'safer' system of direct current (DC). Indeed, Topsy's execution came to constitute several seconds of some of the earliest live footage captured by moving picture cameras. The 60-second film-clip shows the elephant moving into the foreground of the shot and shuffling its feet, which then begin to smoke as she is administered a surging bolt of electricity. In quick succession the animal collapses, briefly quivers, and is rendered motionless (Sheehan 2008, 120). To say here that the film merely documents the death of the elephant, according to Lippit, is not quite true. Instead, an uncanny transference has taken place through the recording of the event of death, illuminating a 'spectral metaphysic of technology' (2002, 13). The film recording, as it were, 'transfers the anima of the animal, its life, into a phantom archive ... The animal survives its death as a film, as another form of animal, captured by the technologies of animation' (Lippit 2002, 13, 19; see also Sheehan 2008, 120). No longer present in the flesh, animals such as Topsy are instead 'recorded, captured on film, enshrined in loops of movement', neither dead nor alive but spectral, phantasmic, undead (Reinert 2012). Modern technology, in this reading, appears as 'a massive mourning apparatus, summoned to incorporate a disappearing animal presence that could not be properly mourned' (Lippit 2000, 188). Animal death on film preserves the presence of an animal that cannot 'properly' die. Supposedly oblivious to its own death, impossible to mourn, and dislocated from its own materiality, it is transformed into flickering loops and circuits of light and motion (Reinert 2012).

What is meant here, however, by a 'proper death'? In the concluding discussion of *Killing animals* by the Animal Studies Group, Jonathan Burt writes that 'it's almost as though the closer and closer you get to animal killing, the more everything begins to fall apart, perspective and everything'. To this, Steve Baker adds: 'And language' (2006, 209). For Lippit, in the filmic image of death, the animal dies beyond the reach of language, so it cannot 'die' as such. It cannot die because, according to particular philosophical discourses of the animal, it does not possess language, and therefore cannot know or name its death. A 'canonical figure of the undead animal' thus takes shape across a variety of texts that 'in different ways consign animals to a spectral existence outside of the possibility of language', and outside of the horizon of death (Shukin 2009, 134; see also Lippit 2000, 27–73). Georges Bataille states, for instance, that 'What marks us [humans] so severely is the *knowledge* of death, which animals fear but do not *know*' (1991, 82). According to Martin Heidegger, furthermore, 'To die means to be capable of death as death. Only man [sic] dies. The animal perishes. It has death neither ahead of itself nor behind it' (1971, 178). Here, language 'brings consciousness and with it, the consciousness of consciousness and its absence, or death. In this light, to have language is to have death. Without language, according to this sophism, animals have neither consciousness nor death' (Lippit 2002, 11).[1] The animal never 'dies', moreover, because its purported inability to die is reflected in cinema's essential feature, its *reanimating* function, where cinema

---

1 Of note is Lippit's continuation of this quote: 'It should be stated definitively . . . that animals do have language. Philosophical conceptions of language, linked to untenable notions of subjectivity, consciousness, and self, have failed to accommodate the language of animals as language' (2002, 11–12).

repeats 'each unique death until its [the animal's] singularity has been erased, its beginning and end fused into a spectral loop' (Lippit 2002, 12). In that manner, against 'the impossibility of animal death, cinema provides artificial life, anima, animation, and the possibility of reanimation' (Lippit 2002, 12), keeping the animal 'alive'. Separated from the consciousness of language, therefore, the animal cannot undergo a 'proper death'.

The material animal

Lippit's analysis of animals as supposedly incapable of death shows the animal 'persisting as spectre and trace in the body of cinematic technology' (Pick 2011, 108). Jonathan Burt in his *Animals in film* (2002), however, posits a divergent theorisation of the visual animal, one that sees the cinematic animal as acutely suspended 'on the borderline between technological artifice and corporeal reality' (Pick 2011, 116; see also Burt 2001, 2005, 2006). Lippit's *Electric animal* (2000), according to Burt, tends to regard the animal as a 'pure sign', which, in turn, '*reinforces* at a conceptual level the effacement of the animal that is perceived to have taken place in reality even whilst criticising that process' (2002, 29; see also Burt 2005, 215). The theory that the animal is becoming increasingly 'virtual', that its fate is to disappear into technological reproduction to become nothing more than imagery, would make sense 'were it not for the fact that this imagery is not uniform but unavoidably fragmented, both in terms of the technical variety of its reproduction and in terms of the various conflicts around the image itself' (Burt 2002, 87). By emphasising the existence of a variety of (at times contrasting) constellations of looks between humans and animals, and of different regimes of visibility for the animal in the modern public sphere, the visual animal is reclaimed as a potentially positive presence (Pick 2011, 108). The *agency* of the cinematic animal is asserted, not in the sense of animal subjectivity, but in terms of the animal's affective power vis-à-vis the human observer in its material, corporeal form (Pick 2011, 109).

It is of note that the animal bodies that Lippit discusses are technologically enshrined and encrypted in much more material ways than he allows; until well into the last century, for instance, film photography depended on the properties of gelatine, a substance rendered from animal bodies (Shukin 2009). According to Shukin, 'it is here, in the material convolutions of film stock, that a transfer of life from animal body to technological media passes virtually without notice'; the 'material-symbolic rendering of animals . . . helped to leverage cinema into historical existence' (2009, 104). Moreover, the subjects that are photographed, or filmed, affectively touch on the general conditions of material being. Filmed photographs show not just the undeadness of the spectral subject, but also the materiality and contingency of the aforementioned subject-animal (Pick 2011, 114–15).

Nonhuman animals are also material-semiotic and historical presences with whom we live our lives; as animals are inextricably bound up with human activity, they are historical not only *like* humans, but *with* them (Csicsery-Ronay 2010, 152). Humans and animals here interact with interdependent embodied traces, where these animals and the traces that they create function as historical actors of their own. In attempting to write about (dead) animals, then, we must depend on 'tracks, trails, or traces – those material-semiotic remnants . . . and often unintentional indexes of a now-absent presence' (Benson 2011, 3). In the presence of death, we must instead forge a relationship with the embodied traces of past animal life, including a relationship open to notions of grief and mourning. Humans, to be sure, often grieve the dogs and other animals they live with; they grieve them not necessarily because they are humanised, but because they transcend boundaries of kin and kind by becoming integral to their lives as social partners (rather than as 'resources') (Weil 2012, 115).[2] There are those who have lived with animals and are 'undone' by the animals they have lost, and many have witnessed animals who similarly seem to lose a part of themselves when they lose their animal others (see Weil 2012, 144; Butler 2004, 23; and Stanescu 2012). Contra Lippit, who valorises cinema as a salvaging apparatus that shelters or encrypts vanishing 'animal traits as a gesture of mourning' (2000, 196), it is thus evident that animals can be mourned by and like humans themselves. Lippit problematically elides the persistent materiality of the dead animal body on film; at the same time, however, he marvellously manages to capture

---

2   See Chur-Hansen et al. (2011) for the rites and rituals particularly associated with companion animal death that might leave traces of certain animals 'behind'.

some crucial aspect of the condition of animals in our vicissitudinous modernity, where the animal image is understood as a symptom of a deeper, more permanent loss.

Indeed, in taking such embellishments of Berger, Lippit, and Burt's theories into the realm of the visual representation of animal death, we see it as a form of 'rupture' (Burt 2000, 11) in the field of representation. An attempt must be made to think through the co-constitutive spectrality and materiality of visual animal death and the dead visual animal, and it is an examination of *Sirius remembered*, a 12-minute silent short made in 1959 by the filmmaker Stan Brakhage that, this chapter argues, offers such a realisation.

Sirius and spectrality

For this film, *Sirius remembered*, Brakhage placed the body of his deceased dog, Sirius, in the woods near his house and filmed the corpse at various stages of decomposition over several seasons, where it froze in the winter and rotted in the spring. The title of the film puns on the memory and reconstruction of Sirius and his extremities (or 'members').[3] In Brakhage's own words:

> There are three parts to the film: first there is the animal seen in the fall as just having died, second there are the winter shots in which he's become a statue covered with snow, and third there's the thaw and decay. That third section is all REmembered where his members are put together again. All previous periods of his existence as a corpse, in the fall, the snow, and the thaw are gone back and forth over, recapitulated and interrelated. (1963; quoted in Elder 1998, 214)

Of note in this discussion of the film is Brakhage's attempt to *reanimate* Sirius, and it is here, through its filmic techniques, that the film's representation and reanimation of the dead animal finds the greatest correlation with Lippit's theories of the filmic revivification of the dead or

---

3 The film exists in two parts online; see 'Andyfshito' (2007a; 2007b).

dying animal through cinema's essentially reanimating, captive, and re-petitive function.

Particularly in this film but also throughout his *oeuvre*, Brakhage develops a powerful set of devices for emphasising motion and, as befits the subject of spectrality, for disembodying movement. The film is defined by a formal reflexivity that continuously calls attention to Brakhage's direct intervention in every frame, through gestural camera movement, painting and scratching on the film emulsion, and rapid-fire editing (see Kase 2012, 4). According to R Bruce Elder, only 'in a small portion of the shots' that appear in the film is the camera 'static (or nearly static)', and often Brakhage's 'camera movement is very rapid'; Brakhage employs various means 'to create a difference between successive frames we perceive as a "jitter" '; the footage of Sirius was shot on black-and-white but printed on colour stock, so that the images of the film take on a very faint and 'ghostly' appearance; he sometimes 'blurs objects, either by defocusing or by swish-panning, to the end of de-realising objects and presenting pure motion'; he sometimes 'com-poses his frames so that large areas are dark, with just a small portion illuminated'; and sometimes the exposed subject matter 'is such a small portion of the whole' that we cannot identify it, and 'so we see the frame as a modulator of coloured light rather than as an image' (Elder 1998, 276–77). These devices have the powerful effect of converting the film from a medium that we first experience visually, to virtual kin-aesthetic phenomena (Elder 1998, 277).[4] Moreover, because 'there is often little consistency either in the content or in the visual forms that Brakhage presses into' this work, we sometimes have the impression, while watching his film, that 'any sort of image could follow any other sort … Every successive shot appears as new and independent of those that preceded it' (Elder 1998, 272). *Sirius remembered* thus elicits the sense of a continuous 'presence', where 'perpetually regenerating forms that appear always on the brink of collapse but regenerate themselves at the beginning of each cut' are used to engender such a sensation (Elder 1998, 271). Each new shot marks a new beginning, the affective equi-valent of rebirth.

---

4   Additionally, and of interest, see Tyler (1972, 204–05) for his negative review of the film as 'a monotonously overexpanded rhythmic cycle of film shots on a strictly limited theme'.

Sirius' rebirth is formed in the film's constantly re-generating compositions. The images are rapidly edited together into a repetitive and,
in the words of Lippit, *looping* framework, so that the film 'conveys
the impression of death from many [different] angles rather than ever
lingering on a single view or a single perspective' (Howard 2011). An
affective immediacy is achieved by camera movements that desperately
attempt to reanimate Sirius; the editing of frames whose startling jux-
tapositions strike directly upon the viewer's senses (Shukin 2009, 102).
The film features horizontal panning shots of Sirius' decaying corpse
as it lays in a field, with the camera literally swung over and across
the body to propel it back into motion, and vertical pans of the trees
and the sky of different lengths and velocities of movement (Kashmere
2004, 81) suggest the passage of Sirius' spirit away from the terrestrial
towards the transcendental.[5] In addition to generating the silent film's
rhythmic pulse, these 'opposing back-and-forth camera movements
cause visual tension, obscuring our ability to "make sense" of the image.
This tactic dovetails with the aims of defamiliarisation, to refresh perception and recast the familiar in an original light' (Kashmere 2004,
81). Through repetition and counterpoint (achieved through inter-cut-
ting stilled close-ups of Sirius' disfigured face) we are able to complete
the picture in our mind's eye, to see it 'fresh', so to speak (Kashmere
2004, 81). Later, shots panning left and right, up and down, are su-
perimposed to create a polyphonous rhythm. P Adams Sitney notes
that the 'second half of the film elaborates an intricate harmonics as
the two layers of fugue-like rhythms play against one another' (2002,
171). *Sirius remembered* is thus rhythmically tortured in its constant
repetition, where the images of Sirius' corpse 'have the quality of genuine apparitions' because of the way they 'interrupt the camera's wildly
swooping arcs'; they are 'experienced as perceptual events that impinge
on the viewer's entire sensorium', where we find and re-find meaning
through a process of re-encounter (Camper 2001, 70). The film, indeed,
here evinces a high level of congruence with the spectral economy of
the representative animal as exemplified by Lippit, transforming its ref-
erent into an enduring undead state; 'in the world of cinema, the animal
lives on, survives' (Lippit 2002, 18–19). This theory of filmic animal

---

5   Of note is how Brakhage (1963) saw his films as preoccupied with 'birth, death,
sex and the search for God' (quoted in James 2005, 3).

death thus gains great momentum in an examination of the corpse of Sirius, reanimated as it is by repetitive loops of light and motion.

Sirius and materiality

It must be argued, however, that the emphasis on Sirius' spectrality is to be tempered with an awareness of his *lived* materiality. It is true that the film views the corpse of Sirius *as* a corpse, 'as nature or the real that resists history as it resists being drawn into narrative' (Weil 2012, 38). Flies and maggots disregard death to eat from Sirius' flesh, and the film proceeds to investigate the processes of life after death in the form of endless transformations of the body as it is eaten and weathered away; it is a study of time and especially of the incremental moments between life and death, if not of life *in* death (Weil 2012, 104). Death happens 'not in a moment, but over time, denying the moment of "perishing" that for Heidegger defines animal death' (Weil 2012, 106). Changes in weather, light, the earth, register on the body of Sirius, whose tactile materiality is brought into sharp focus. It is here, therefore, that a more nuanced theorisation of visual animal death can be put to work, one that accounts for the animal that once existed within the temporal logics of its owners and of the human and nonhuman others who came into contact with him; an animal that was loved, cared for, and mourned for.

It is interesting to note that Sirius, unlike some other nonhumans, left an embodied and historical trace of his life which, aside from the film itself, was captured in the words of certain humans who knew him. There are the words of Brakhage himself who, in his annotations to *Sirius remembered*, states:

I was coming to terms with decay of a dead thing and the decay of the memories of a loved being that had died and it was undermining all abstract concepts of death. The form [of the film] was being cast out of probably the same physical need that makes dogs dance and howl in rhythm around a corpse. I was taking song as my source of inspiration for the rhythm structure, just as dogs dancing, prancing around a corpse, and howling in rhythm structures or rhythm-intervals might be considered like thebirth [sic] of some kind of song. (2001, 226)

Furthermore, in a three-page tribute poem by the filmmaker Chick Strand for a collection of essays, photographs, personal statements, and reminiscences about Brakhage, we do not just see, but *sense*, the traces left by Sirius. Strand ruminates:

I remember Sirius/black dog/white dog/brown/speckled/dotted/ longtail, short tail/long hair or not, ears up, down, nose to the air, into a hole, alert/sniffing/dem bones, dem bones/drinking from the hose/the basso in the neighbourhood choir imitating ghost dogs/the smell of him/shaking himself dry, ears flapping/oh yes, he is loved and cared for . . . / . . . his dog tags tinkle and I am reassured/I love his . . . matted fur, his thunder and loving grunts . . . /Sirius-ur dog fell down somewhere in the forest having found his secret dying place, or what was pushed, dragged, knocked down shot down and the life went out of him/the man finds him like that, and sniffs him, brother dog/and time and the elements return the animal to the earth/the man watches and re-members. (2005, 150–51)

It is thus evident, through such a trace, that *Sirius remembered* creates a beautiful, loving rite and ritual of mourning and meaning-making out of death, and the relation to the mutable, fallible, yet material nonhuman subject-body (see Plate 2008, 72). The simultaneously dead and undead body of Sirius is transposed through the camera of Brakhage, which is then perceived by the cinematic body of the film viewer. Brakhage mourns, but the hope is that we mourn *with* him, to be moved to a corporeal response that may be no response at all, the effect of an immediate experience to the ritualised cinematic event (Plate 2008, 72, 77). Indeed, the 'energy' of Brakhage's film, the 'speed' that characterises it, the 'discontinuities' it incorporates, the 'out-of-focus' shooting and swish-pans which make the shot's subject-matter of Sirius difficult to identity, the sense of the 'form-in-evolution' it imparts (which elicits the feeling that it 'could take unlikely turns or depart in unforeseen directions'), work to 'rivet the viewer's attention into the visual flow' (Elder 1998, 452). Brakhage's film elicits a strong sense of scopic identification, encouraging the viewer to enter into his film, to merge with its energy, and to participate in the flow of his shooting (Elder 1998, 451-52).

It is hoped that we *feel* every abrupt change that the film undergoes, every cut or every shift in intensity or direction (Elder 1998, 452). Brakhage crowds our viewing experience with the everyday, the 'mundane' and the material in images that, shot through filters or projected out of focus, painted over or captured at an unnatural angle, make us look differently, affectively, at the materiality of such subjects as 'a dog' (Sheehan 2012, 120-21). The confrontation with the actualised body of Sirius, transposed through the camera, in the terms of Burt and in contrast to Lippit, *agentially* affects the aesthetically and synaesthetically perceiving human body. The capacity of the cinematic image is not simply to represent a sense of the material contingency of the body of Sirius, but to make it present on the screen, giving movement to stillness as a form of remembrance, simultaneously rendered spectral, yet material.

Conclusion

Overall, via the confluence of the theories of animality, mortality and visuality analysed above, the animal comes to be more than a spectral and passive object of the human look, embodying the 'extreme collapse between the figural and the real' as questions about the cinematic animal and animal death arise at the point at which 'fiction and reality collapse into one another' (Burt 2002, 44, 161). This is not because animals metaphorise a human ontological lack; the history of the visual animal in connection with death attests to plenitude *as well as* spectrality signalled by the animal image, arising in the correlation between cinema and the corporeal (Pick 2011, 109). In the visual representation of animal death or a dead animal, we witness the undeadness of the spectral subject, linked to cinema's looping process of animation, re-animation, and the repetitive multiplicity of the animal and its death. Yet we also see the materiality and contingency of the pictured subject, an individual animal that left an embodied trace, a subject to be considered and mourned on its own terms, within or without the networks of human–animal relations and the human(s) behind the camera. *Sirius remembered* demonstrates this all too well in its looping, repetitive reanimation and filmic, regenerating compositions of Sirius as spectral subject, as well as, simultaneously, its affective ritualisation of mourning and its attentiveness to Sirius as material, historical, and embodied.

Works cited

Aloi G (2012). *Art and animals*. London and New York: IB Tauris.

'Andyfshito' (2007a). Stan Brakhage – *Sirius remembered* (1959) [Part 1/2] [Online]. Available: www.youtube.com/watch?v=luO9uTzYi3s [Accessed 9 January 2012].

'Andyfshito' (2007b). Stan Brakhage – *Sirius remembered* (1959) [Part 2/2] [Online]. Available: www.youtube.com/watch?v=dWfk6KjqiNQ [Accessed 9 January 2012].

Animal Studies Group (Ed.) (2006). Conclusion: a conversation. In *Killing animals* (pp188–209). Urbana and Chicago: University of Illinois Press.

Armstrong P (2011). The gaze of animals. In N Taylor & T Signal (Eds). *Theorizing animals: re-thinking humanimal relations* (pp175–99). Leiden and Boston: Brill.

Bataille G (1991). *The accursed share: an essay on general economy*. Vols 2–3. R Hurley (Trans.). New York: Zone Books.

Benson E (2011). Animal writes: historiography, disciplinarity, and the animal trace. In L Kalof & GM Montgomery (Eds). *Making animal meaning* (pp3–16). East Lansing: Michigan State University Press.

Berger J (1980). Why look at animals? In *About looking* (pp3–28). London: Bloomsbury.

Brakhage S (1963). *Metaphors on vision*. PA Sitney (Ed.). New York: Film Culture.

Brakhage S (2001). *Essential Brakhage: selected writings on filmmaking by Stan Brakhage*. BR McPherson (Ed.). New York: Documentext.

Burt J (2001). The illumination of the animal kingdom: the role of light and electricity in animal representation. *Society & Animals: Journal of Human-Animal Studies*, 9(3): 203–28.

Burt J (2002). *Animals in film*. London: Reaktion Books.

Burt J (2005). John Berger's 'Why look at animals?': a close reading. *Worldviews: Global Religions, Culture, and Ecology*, 9(2): 203–18.

Burt J (2006). Morbidity and vitalism: Derrida, Bergson, Deleuze, and animal film imagery. *Configurations*, 14(1–2): 157–79.

Butler J (2004). *Precarious life: the powers of mourning and violence*. London: Verso.

Camper F (2001). Brakhage's contradictions. *Chicago Review*, 47–48(4): 69–96.

Chur-Hansen A, Black A, Gierasch A, Pletneva A & Winefield H (2011). Cremation services upon the death of a companion animal: views of service providers and service users. *Society & Animals: Journal of Human-Animal Studies*, 19(3): 248–60.

Csicsery-Ronay I (2010). After species meet. *Humanimalia*, 1(2): 143–54.

Elder RB (1998). *The films of Stan Brakhage in the American tradition of Ezra Pound, Gertrude Stein, and Charles Olson*. Ontario: Wilfrid Laurier University Press.

Heidegger M (1971). The thing. In *Poetry, language, thought* (pp163–86). A Hofstadter (Trans.). New York: HarperCollins.

Howard E (2011). *The wonder ring/Reflections on black/Sirius remembered. Only the cinema* [Online]. Available: seul-le-cinema.blogspot.com.au/2011/07/wonder-ringreflections-on-blacksirius.html [Accessed 12 March 2013].

James DE (2005). Introduction. Stan Brakhage: the activity of his nature. In DE James (Ed.). *Stan Brakhage: filmmaker* (pp1–19). Philadelphia: Temple University Press.

Kase JC (2012). Encounters with the real: historicizing Stan Brakhage's *The act of seeing with one's own eyes*. *The Moving Image*, 12(1): 1–17.

Kashmere B (2004). Freedom of expression: John Coltrane, Stan Brakhage, and the American avant-garde, 1957–67. Unpublished Masters Dissertation. Montreal: Concordia University.

Lippit AM (2000). *Electric animal: toward a rhetoric of wildlife*. Minneapolis and London: University of Minnesota Press.

Lippit AM (2002). The death of an animal. *Film Quarterly*, 56(1): 9–22.

Pick A (2011). *Creaturely poetics: animality and vulnerability in literature and film*. New York: Columbia University Press.

Plate SB (2008). *Religion and film: cinema and the re-creation of the world*. London and New York: Wallflower.

Reinert H (2012). Face of a dead bird – notes on grief, spectrality and wildlife photography. *Rhizomes: Cultural Studies in Emerging Knowledge*, 23 [Online]. Available: www.rhizomes.net/issue23/imre/index.html [Accessed 12 March 2013].

Sheehan P (2008). Against the image: Herzog and the troubling politics of the screen animal. *SubStance*, 37(3): 117–36.

Sheehan RA (2012). Stan Brakhage, Ludwig Wittgenstein and the renewed encounter with the everyday. *Screen*, 53(2): 118–35.

Shukin N (2009). *Animal capital: rendering life in biopolitical times*. Minneapolis and London: University of Minnesota Press.

Sitney PA (2002). *Visionary film: the American avant-garde, 1943–2000*. 3rd edn. New York: Oxford University Press.

Stanescu J (2012). Species trouble: Judith Butler, mourning, and the precarious lives of animals. *Hypatia: A Journal of Feminist Philosophy*, 27(3): 567–82.

Strand C (2005). Brakhage package. In DE James (Ed.). *Stan Brakhage: filmmaker* (pp150–52). Philadelphia: Temple University Press.

Tyler P (1972). *The shadow of an airplane climbs the Empire State Building: a world theory of film.* Garden City: Doubleday.

Weil K (2012). *Thinking animals: why animals studies now?* New York: Columbia University Press.

7
Mining animal death for all it's worth

Melissa Boyde

This chapter considers the death of animals in the novels and film adaptations of *Wake in fright* (1961/1971) and *Red Dog* (2001/2011). Both texts have several things in common: they are set in Australian mining towns – in *Wake in fright* it is Bundanyabba, a fictional town with echoes of Broken Hill, New South Wales, and in *Red Dog* it is Dampier in the Pilbara region of Western Australia – and in both the death of animals is central to the narrative: in *Wake in fright* it is the massacre of kangaroos and in *Red Dog* it is the death of a dog from strychnine poisoning. *Red Dog*, written by Louis de Bernières, is a collection of stories based on an Australian kelpie known as Red Dog who famously wandered throughout mining towns in the Kimberley district of Western Australia. Kenneth Cook's novel *Wake in fright* tells the story of what happens to John Grant, a young schoolteacher, en route from his outback post to a summer holiday in Sydney which he never reaches. Instead, he experiences what has been described as 'an orgiastic weekend of blind drunkenness, gambling, male rape and savage kangaroo hunting' (O'Loughlin 2009).

A recent scholarly article suggests that the kangaroo massacre in the film of *Wake in fright* is 'a surrogate for the actual historical massacres of Australia's Indigenous peoples' (Docker 2010, 61), while in

M Boyde (2013). Mining animal death for all it's worth. In J Johnston & F Probyn-Rapsey (Eds). *Animal death*. Sydney: Sydney University Press.

an interview the director of *Red Dog* suggests that his film, although ostensibly about a dog, is 'about the people and what the dog did to the people' (Pomeranz 2011). In both of these accounts the animals' lives, and their deaths, are obscured. As Mary Allen suggests, 'metaphorical far outnumber the literal animals in literature' (Allen 1983, 6). In light of Derrida's suggestion that 'metaphor always carries its death within itself', the common critical approach in textual studies to metaphorise nonhuman animals may well contribute to a cultural elision of living animals (Derrida 1982, 271). Susan McHugh, following Derrida's work in 'The animal that therefore I am', points out: 'nonhuman traces serve as deconstructive elements that betray human attempts at self-representation, and ultimately elaborate the logic of substitution through which the animal's sacrificiality (its real and representational consumption) supports the human' (McHugh 2011, 9). A consideration of elements of the textual strategies of the *roman à clef*, the novel with a key, which provides traces of culturally contentious or secret matters through its generic capacity to conceal and yet simultaneously to reveal, opens up further ways to read the representations of animal death in *Wake in fright* and *Red Dog*. The excavation undertaken in this paper of the textual deaths of Red Dog and of the hunted kangaroos brings to the surface animal matters embedded in these texts: deviation and disappearance, shame and shamelessness, and vested and invested interests.

Wake in fright

The novel *Wake in fright* became a bestseller when it was published in Australia and the United Kingdom in the 1960s but it failed to sustain long-term critical interest. The film version of *Wake in fright*, although gaining critical acclaim and being chosen for the Cannes Film Festival as the official Australian entry in 1971, was neither a box office success in Australia, nor in America or Europe where it was released under the title *Outback*.[1] On its initial release critics called it 'violent realism', and

---

1 There was one exception: 'The only place that *Wake in fright* worked at the box office was Paris, where it ran for months in one cinema in an English print, with French subtitles' (Galvin 2009).

suggested it 'will shock and disgust and trigger off tidal waves of indig-
nation from those who still believe our outback is the backbone of the
nation' (Galvin 2009). On its re-release 40 years later, in a digitally re-
stored format, film critic David Stratton called it 'a great milestone in
Australian cinema history' and both he and film critic Margaret Pomeranz agreed it shows 'something that Australia embraces as part of
its ethos, this hard drinking, wild mateship . . . treating women badly'
(Stratton & Pomeranz 2009). Clearly the film makes strong connections with contested concepts of Australian identity. But what about the
kangaroos? As John Simons notes, 'perhaps no other animal is quite so
closely identified with a country and a culture', but this identification is
fraught with the kinds of contradiction which are embedded in the film
(Simons 2013, 181).

Deviation and disappearance

The narrative of *Wake in fright* is driven by deviation. Grant's thwarted
journey to Sydney for the long summer holiday becomes instead a journey into the unknown, starting with a drunken binge in and around
a mining town called Bundanyabba, after he loses all his money in a
two-up game held in a back room packed with sweaty, intoxicated men,
mostly miners. Grant's night out progresses to a drunken gathering at
someone's home where he meets alcoholic misfit Doc Tydon, a group
of hard drinking mine workers, and the host's daughter Janette, who
Kate Jennings remarks 'keeps a house that the *Women's Weekly* would
praise but who is remarkably free with her favours' (Jennings 2009). At
one point during the evening Janette leads Grant outside, into the bush,
where she attempts to seduce him but instead, both a sexual ingénue
and overcome by alcohol, Grant 'rolled off her body and knelt in the
scrub and vomited and vomited, painfully and noisily in abject humi-
liation' (Cook 2001, 87). The other men's attitudes to women ('we've all
had little episodes with Janette' (Cook 2001, 92) is symbolised, in the
film version, by a pregnant golden labrador about to give birth who has
only just been acquired by Dick, one of the drunken miners. The men
make sexual jokes in relation to the paternity of the as yet unborn puppies:

The CAMERA PANS dizzily 360 degrees around the room . . . three or four men . . . are gathered around a pregnant bitch arguing about the time of delivery . . .
TYDON: You the father?
The group roars with laughter.
JOE: No chance. He only does it to sheep.[2]
More laughter.
TYDON: She'll have pups by morning.
JANETTE comes in . . .
JOE: Who's the father?
JANETTE: Don't know. She's a slut this little bitch. She'll take anything.
The men laugh . . .
CUT to black. (Jones 1969, 57–58)

The next scene explicitly relies on metaphor:

During this period of black, we begin to hear the insistent buzz of a house-fly . . .
[Cut to next morning and close up of Grant waking up in Tydon's bedroom]
CUT to what he sees: a corrugated tin ceiling from which hangs a twisted strip of sticky fly-paper. A recently embedded fly struggles to escape. (Jones 1969, 58)

This image of the fly clearly does not relate to any of the nonhuman animals in the film – it is a metaphor for Grant's predicament, an instance of what McHugh refers to as 'the metaphorical animal's ways of inhabiting [texts] without somehow being represented therein' (6). The final sentence of the preface in the screenplay states: 'the film is about a moth, imprisoned in a world of light' (Jones 1969). The metaphor of the moth demonstrates 'the power to exclude that lies implicit in the power to name' (Altman 1990, 504). The overt focus on the human, wrought in this way, provides insight into why the labrador disappears from the

---

2   A handwritten annotation next to this line in the script notes 'different line for TV version' (Jones 1969, 57)

story after this scene – for despite the proliferation of animals in the narrative they are 'made to disappear' (Baker 2000, 22).

Tydon, referring to his and Janette's status as outsiders, says to Grant:

> We break the rules, but we know more about ourselves than most people. We do research into the wilder shores of animality. No . . . not animality. Animals are not so lucky. (Jones 1969, 64)

What follows shows some of the unlucky animals. In the lead up to the drunken kangaroo massacre, the miners pick up Tydon and Grant and they all pile into the car with a greyhound shoved in the back to be used to chase and pull down kangaroos. Along the way a fox is shot at and killed from the vantage of a pub verandah while the publican, unperturbed, brings out the beers. There are diseased rabbits and rotting cow and/or horse carcasses scattered throughout the landscape (Jones 1969, 90).

In a scene which lasts eight minutes, actual footage of a kangaroo hunt is edited to appear as a hunt within the storyline of the film. The film's director, staying faithful to Cook's account of the kangaroo hunt, made an arrangement with professional shooters to film one of their hunts. But as he recounts:

> From 6pm until 2am they were killing with great efficiency. Suddenly, around two in the morning, they started to miss and wound the animals. It was horrendous. The kangaroos were rolling around on the ground, and they were chasing the wounded kangaroos and putting them out of their misery. I learned that they had drunk a half of bottle of whiskey. Some of the footage that I shot was so repulsive, heinous, and bloody that there was no way I could even use it. (Monroe 2012, 2)

In the film and the novel the miners, Tydon and Grant are all hungover from the night before, but still drinking beer and getting drunk again. Early in the hunt the men come upon a mob of kangaroos. When a lone kangaroo moves toward the car the driver 'yells like a madman' and crashes the car into the animal. The injured kangaroo is not visible in the frame but its breathing and movement can be heard offscreen –

until Dick pulls out a knife and bends down, then silence. Tydon takes his knife and cuts off the animal's testicles:

JOE (to Grant): Doc eats them, reckons they're the best part of the roo.
DICK (to Grant): Haven't you tried 'em Grant.
GRANT: No.
DICK: Better than oysters. Put lead in your pencil. (Jones 1969, 69)

As day turns into night they shout, drive like maniacs, shine spotlights on the animals, shoot, stab, eviscerate and skin the animals, and laugh and drink. The hunt culminates with Grant's frenzied stabbing of an injured young kangaroo, urged on by the other men.

The film starts and ends with disclaimers:

All characters and events depicted in this film are fictitious. Any similarity to actual events or persons, living or dead, is purely coincidental.

Cook, who worked in Broken Hill in the early 60s (as a radio journalist for the ABC), indicated that the story may well be more 'real' than the disclaimer suggests: 'Cook told an interviewer that all of the characters of the novel were libelous recreations of actual people' (Galvin 2009).

In contrast the 'Producer's note' at the end of the film states that at least one 'event' is not fictitious:

The hunting scenes depicted in this film were taken during an actual kangaroo hunt by professional licensed hunters. For this reason and because the survival of the Australian kangaroo is seriously threatened, these scenes were shown uncut after consultation with the leading animal welfare organizations in Australia and the United Kingdom.

This statement, which not only seems to contradict the disclaimer at the start of the film, and which stands in stark contrast to the usual disclaimer that no animal was harmed in this film – instead stating that they were – may conceal more than it purports to reveal. The combination of the main elements of this statement – calling the shooters professional, intimating an interest in animal conservation and stating that there was consultation with unnamed animal welfare organisations in two countries – creates a context of care that allows the brutality of the kangaroo deaths to be revealed and a potential for abnegation of responsibility, a potential for shamelessness.

In light of the real events that are shown – the brutal deaths of animals – it seems relevant that the context for the rest of the film is disguise. The humans, the town, the events are all presented under the thin veil of secrecy offered by the roman à clef which Cook's comment, that he based the novel on real people, indicates. The back cover blurb on the 2001 reprint calls *Wake in fright* 'a portrait of fear and loathing in Broken Hill', not the fictional name, Bundanyabba, given in the novel. Certainly the novel has *à clef* elements. A central function of the *roman à clef* is that it conceals what is culturally sensitive or unacceptable, while revealing the same things to an 'in the know' or coterie audience who can identify people, places and events (Boyde 2009). For example, the genre was taken up by lesbian and gay writers at times when homosexuality was otherwise rendered a cultural secret and its practices considered shameful (Boyde 2010). In *Wake in fright* the disclaimer and the producer's note indicate that there are layers of revelation and disclosure. For an 'in the know' reader they highlight the contradictory discourses surrounding, and affecting, these (iconic) native animals: '[A kangaroo] is simultaneously a wonderful thing and a nuisance. It is a national symbol and a piece of meat on a plate' (Simons 2013, 103).

What may appear to some as deviant behaviour (the pleasure taken in the hunt and slaughter of animals and the emotional indifference of the hunters to their suffering) is displaced in the novel and film onto what at the time was (and possibly still is) more widely accepted as cultural deviation – an incident which occurs between Grant and Tydon after the kangaroo hunting episode.

Shame and shamelessness

Silvan Tomkin writes that: 'Like disgust, [shame] operates only after interest or enjoyment has been activated, and inhibits one or the other or both' (Sedgwick 2003, 39). Does anyone feel any shame for any of what happens in *Wake in fright*? Grant is the only person who appears to feel shame but it is not for the death of the animals. Instead his shame is linked to homosexuality – a sexual encounter with Tydon which in the film is visually linked to the hunt:

INT. TYDON'S BEDROOM NIGHT.
TYDON has switched on the light . . . The light is held so that it is shining into GRANT'S face, and he stands, hypnotized by it . . .
TYDON circles behind GRANT, as GRANT circled behind the little kangaroo, the camera matching the movement in the same way . . .
TYDON takes GRANT by the chin, tilting his head back and seizing his throat with the other hand. GRANT struggles . . .
GRANT gives up, and they are completely still, except for their exhausted breathing.
The music stops.
The overhead light is swinging gently, to and fro.
[Cut to next scene] TYDON'S BEDROOM DAY. (Jones 1969, 83)

As in so many other films in the decades prior to the 1970s, homosexuality is a present absence, inferred but not shown. Yet, for the protagonist of this film the homosexual encounter is a trigger that causes him initially to consider killing Tydon and then to turn the rifle on himself. Hidden from view – did it happen, was it mutual, was it rape as several critics claim (or does the gentle to and fro movement of the overhead light indicate otherwise?) – the secrecy of the sexual encounter between the two men moves the focus off the explicit representation of the kangaroo shoot. The massacre, like the *roman à clef*, both fiction and reality (real footage edited together with fictional film footage), is the only incident where Grant shows pleasure or excitement. At one point the novel reveals Grant's thoughts on his companions who, despite (or perhaps more precisely because of) their drinking and their pleasure in killing animals, he seems to admire:

it was remarkable that two men like the miners would associate with [Tydon]. With all their faults they were men, and Tydon was a twisted, revolting creature'. (Cook 2001, 115)

Although for some critics the hunt is overwhelmingly 'hard to watch' (Docker 2010, 62), it is, I suggest, made easier by being displaced onto the secret of homosexuality where shame is contained in the protagonist. Shame about the death of animals is further deflected by the information in the 'Producer's note'. Shame, as queer theorist Sally Munt (2008) points out, has a dimension of cultural politics.

Tomkins suggests that 'the vicarious experience of shame, together with the vicarious experience of distress, is at once a measure of civilization and a condition of civilization' (Sedgwick & Frank 1995, 162). Near the end of the novel, schoolteacher Grant discards the books, a symbol of civilisation, which he has been carrying in his suitcase. Shortly after, stumbling through the red dust landscape, he shoots a rabbit, takes out his knife and 'slit[s] the skin around the neck and peel[s] it off the body like a glove' before cooking and eating it. Grant's only regret is that he wishes he 'had thought to provide himself with salt' (Cook 2001, 139).

Red Dog: vested and invested interests

Red Dog, written by Louis de Bernières, is a collection of stories based on the (deceased) real-life dog called Red Dog, an Australian kelpie known as the Pilbara Wanderer. The novel was made into a film of the same name which was released in 2011. Like *Wake in fright, Red Dog* is set in an outback landscape, the Pilbara region of Western Australia, home to extensive open cut mining operations run by the Rio Tinto mining group. It is also the area where mining magnate and wealthiest woman in the world Gina Rinehart, dubbed the Pilbara Princess, is establishing the Roy Hill mine.[3] Like the glimmering red cliffs laden with iron-ore spotted from the air long ago by Rinehart's father Lang Hancock, which for him held the promise of untold wealth, Red Dog shimmers on page and on screen – the question arises who profits from his life and his death?

Mining industries are currently running advertising campaigns which put a glossy spin on their industry depicting it as glamorous,

---

3   According to the *Business Review Weekly's* (*BRW*) 2012 Rich 200 list.

in the outback vernacular mode, with promotional style shots of hu-
man/wildlife interactions and of 'lifestyle' activities such as rounding
up cattle (the cattle industries also thrive in this region, providing stock
for the contentious live animal export industry). Mining industry com-
panies Rio Tinto, Woodside and Westrac partially funded the film,
which was shot around the port town of Dampier, built in the early
1960s for the mining industries. Current mine workers were used as
extras in the film. The CEO of Rio Tinto, commenting on their investment in *Red Dog*, calls it: 'an exciting opportunity to showcase our
industry, our people and the story of the Pilbara to the world' (*Screenwest* 2010). Throughout the film there are many shots of the mining
town and surrounds – mining equipment, open cut mine landscapes
and mine workers are repeatedly shown, often with upbeat music on
the soundtrack. Unlike the miners in *Wake in fright*, the miners in *Red
Dog* look clean, happily hardworking and relatively sober.

On the outskirts of Dampier is a statue of Red Dog with a plaque
which states it was 'erected by the many friends he made during his
travels'. As Stephen Miller points out, 'dog memorials can be found
scattered throughout Australia' (Miller 2012, 36). Australian kelpies
have several – Red Dog at Dampier, a bronze statue of a kelpie at Ardlethan in the Riverina (NSW) which claims to be the birthplace of the
Australian kelpie (a mixture of strains of working collies and dingoes)
and where the Kelpie Dog Festival is held each year. Another Australian kelpie statue is at Casterton in Victoria where a counter-claim
was made that it was 'the birthplace of the foundation bitch of the Kelpie breed' with a statue erected outside the town hall (Miller 2012, 36).
'The Australian Kelpie Muster' is now held there each year with com-
petitions such as Fattest Dog, Dog Most Like It's Owner, and Kelpie
Pinball – which suggest (to some) a fun family day (Pedigree Australian
working dog muster 2012). But it is also about business, with a working
dog auction held where dogs are bought and sold – since inception of
the event, the auction has achieved over one million dollars in sales.

The film of *Red Dog* made much more for its investors – it was the
highest-grossing Australian film of 2011, taking $21.3m, and the most
popular local film since *Australia* (2008) (Bodey 2012). *Red Dog* was
awarded Best Film at the Australian Academy of Cinema and Television Arts awards 2011, and there are plans to develop *Red Dog* as a stage
musical. Marketed as a 'family film', *Red Dog* offers a feel-good look at

the life of a dog who throughout the length of the film lies dying from a man-made poison widely used in the Pilbara region to kill wild dogs (Code of Practice 2009). It seems ironic that many of these so-called wild dogs are, like Red Dog, a mixture of the native dingo and imported breeds. Classified as pests, the state government of Western Australia allocates $14 million per annum to, in the words of the premier, 'fight the wild dog issue' which allegedly affects both the pastoral and mining industries (ABC Rural 2012; ABC Rural 2002).

Deviation and disappearance

The novel on which the screenplay is based has a linear structure, comprising a series of stories about Red Dog's adventures, leading to a final chapter, 'The last journey', in which Red Dog, found on the roadside writhing in agony, is driven to the local police station while a vet is called. When it is discovered that the local vet is away, the policeman, Bill, decides he should shoot Red Dog who is 'raddled with the poison' (107). But the policeman can't bring himself to pull the trigger – Red Dog is his 'old and well-loved friend' (105). Instead Red Dog's friends 'arrived one by one to take it in turns to hold onto him and quell the convulsions during the long hours until the vet's arrival' (108). Throughout the night they drink tea and reminisce about Red Dog's life in the Pilbara and his journeys in search of his so-called 'one true master', John, who died in an accident when his bike hit a kangaroo (unlike the human and the dog, there are no sentimental stories on the death of this native animal). After being kept in a coma for two and a half days by the vet and administered anti-convulsant drugs every time the shaking and writhing started up, Red Dog seems to pull through. But the strychnine has caused brain damage and he cannot stand up, so one by one his friends say their goodbyes before the vet administers a fatal dose of morphine (108).

The film shows his death differently. It opens with truck driver Tom arriving at the outback pub where he sees a silhouette through opaque glass of a man with a gun in his hand and hears a voice saying 'hold his bloody head still'. The structure of the film weaves the present tense of Red Dog's last night with flashbacks of episodes in his life told by his friends, who instead of sitting with him gather in the hotel bar. Essentially these stories comprise scenes of Red Dog hitching rides, meeting

John, John's romance with Nancy, John's accidental death and Red Dog's wandering in search of him. At the end of his lectures, published as 'The animal that therefore I am', Jacques Derrida says 'I can die, or simply leave the room' (Derrida qtd in Wills 2009, 34). At the end of the film version of *Red Dog*, the eponymous protagonist does both – he leaves the room and shortly after he dies. The events leading to this moment, and the representation of his death, constitute a major deviation from de Bernières' novel. Following Derrida, David Wills refers to:

> the space that opens once another being has turned its back, left the room, or died. A being is, indeed, by virtue of inhabiting that dorsal space, by being behind the being that has left it behind in order that it might be. It *is* in the space of the unknown, of what cannot be known, for presumptive knowledge about how a being is is precisely what prevents a being from being as it is. (Wills 2009, 41)

The film is made up from presumptive knowledge about Red Dog which I suggest prevents 'a being from being as it is', inserting instead human interpretation rendered as real. Like the book, in the film Red Dog's 'friends' tell stories that are ostensibly Red Dog's stories and which comprise the episodic narrative of the film. In a notable deviation from the novel, the friends literally turn their backs on the dying dog – they become so buoyed up by the stories they tell that they break into song and dance and fail to see Red Dog struggle to his feet and leave the pub by the back door.

Both the novel and film have disclaimers that, like those of *Wake in fright*, offer somewhat conflicting statements about what is real in the narrative. Like *Wake in fright*, the *Red Dog* disclaimers indicate *roman à clef* features, providing a veil over that which is culturally contentious:

> The real Red Dog was born in 1971, and died on November 20th 1979. The stories I have told here are all based upon what really happened to him, but I have invented all of the characters, partly because I know very little about the real people in Red Dog's life, and partly because I would not want to offend any of them by misrepresenting them. The only character who is 'real' is John. (de Bernières 2001)

De Bernières' disclaimer in the author's note is on the surface rather standard but the statement that the stories about the dog 'are all based upon what really happened to him' seems contradictory – how can an event happen to Red Dog that doesn't depend on the participants involved in those events and the characters who represent them?[4]

Fiction combined with fact (although unverifiable by Red Dog himself, not only because he is dead but because he is a dog) and characters who are 'real' with inverted commas (de Bernières', not mine) are features of the *roman à clef* and this novel has *à clef* features – the 'Author's note' is itself a key. Over the past 400 years writers have adopted the *roman à clef* for political or social commentary, disguising and simultaneously disclosing (to an 'in the know' reader) the identity of well-known people (Boyde 2010). Despite the cover the *roman à clef* affords, a number of the writers and/or publishers of *romans à clef* have been charged with libel. As readers 'in the know' (for example, from the field of animal studies) would understand, the majority of nonhuman animals are culturally positioned as outsiders, with all the associated implications of that status. Several of de Bernières' stories in the novel reveal negative human impact on animals: Red Dog is badly injured falling off the back of a ute – as de Bernières notes, 'these were common mishaps for Western Australian dogs' (83) and Red Dog is found 'dragging himself along the road' with blood coming from bullet wounds in his haunch, shot by someone unknown (43). On the long journey to the vet 'the men couldn't help noticing how many kangaroos and wallabies had been hit by cars, and lay dead in horrible attitudes at the side of the tarmac' (48). When one of the men says 'they should do something about it', his mate replies: 'they jump fences . . . and anyway the farmers want them run over, right enough' (48).

Like the film version of *Wake in fright*, the film *Red Dog* also has disclaimers:

No animals were harmed in the making of this motion picture. The animals featured in this production were handled with care and concern for their safety and wellbeing.

---

4 I am indebted to my colleague Dr Alison Moore for this insight.

Is it for animal welfare reasons alone that, in the scene in which the miners drive Red Dog to the vet after he has been shot, there is no trace of what is known as 'roadkill' even though this is detailed in the novel? The figures in just one of Australia's six states estimate that 2.55 million animals are killed by cars per year (Ramp 2004, 5). The vast numbers of animals injured and killed in this way and the lack of public interest causes ecologist Dan Lunney to raise the question of 'whether driving in rural areas is a de-facto ritual of wildlife slaughter' (Lunney 2012). The episode described in the novel in which one of the miners in the car counts 'ten [dead animals] in five k's' (48) on the roadside is changed in the film – the dead animals are erased and replaced with a pristine stretch of road alongside which an almost three kilometre iron ore train rolls purposefully by – a symbol of what the film's director calls 'the engine of Australia' (Maddox 2011).

There is a further disclaimer at the end of the film: 'The *Red Dog* film has been inspired by events, which may or may not have happened, but have become Pilbara Outback folklore. All the human characters in this film are invented, fictitious and imaginary.'

In the film version of *Red Dog*, his life and his death by strychnine poison, posited as potentially real according to 'folklore' and through the statement that only the human characters are fictitious, are simultaneously disclosed and hidden. This is effected not only through deviations from novel to film but also through the deflection of the disclaimer – no animals were harmed etc. which, like the disclaimer in *Wake in fright*, suggests a sense of cultural responsibility on the issue of animal welfare. In reality poisons such as strychnine and 1080 are routinely used to kill so-called feral animals. Any other animal who can't read the warning signs posted in baited areas and who takes the bait becomes collateral damage – an open cultural secret.

Shame and shamelessness

Is there any sense of shame depicted in the film about the death of Red Dog from strychnine poisoning? It is a poison with no antidotes and which 'results in muscular convulsions and eventually death through asphyxia or sheer exhaustion', that is, after prolonged pain and suffering (Code of Practice 2009, 6).

In this film, what Eve Kosofsky Sedgwick calls 'the double move-ment shame makes: toward painful individuation, toward uncontrol-lable relationality' is figured in terms that strike out the animal suffering and death (Sedgwick 2003, 37). The 'uncontrollable relationality' that might reasonably be caused by the shame of Red Dog's death by man-made poison (and could, for example, prompt a review of that wide-spread method of killing 'feral' animals) instead creates a consolidation of conventional family values. The foregrounded (albeit sanitised) rep-resentations of animal suffering and death remarkably become 'feel-good' family entertainment.

This is what happens: although close to death, somehow Red Dog manages to get up and leave not only the room but the building, unseen by his friends. The camera follows his final journey which includes mul-tiple shots of the enormous freight train carrying iron ore from the mines to the port (which Rio Tinto lent to the film crew for an entire day's shoot). When the vet discovers he is gone, a search ensues and again mining apparatus is noticeably present in most of this sequence of shots: the port, a mining truck, the miners, huts and the miners. Red Dog is finally found lying dead at John's gravesite, known in the film as 'his master', in a highly romaniticised reunion of man and dog. (If Red Dog knew all along that John was dead and where his grave was, why did he go a-wandering in search of him?) Unlike the depiction of the mining town in *Wake in fright*, 'with its sweltering heat, choking dust, swarming flies' (Jennings 2009), in *Red Dog* the mining town comes out looking like a place of opportunity and renewal, where heterosexuality reigns supreme – most of the central mine worker characters find love, marriage and even children, and the regeneration extends to a Red Dog look-alike kelpie puppy given to Nancy by her new beau Tom whom she first meets in the bar while Red Dog is dying in the back room.

The director Kriv Stender's view that 'a dog is just a dog and that's what I loved about the idea of the movie . . . it was really more about the people and what the dog did to the people' contributes to the domin-ation of the human relationships in the film's narrative, exemplified by the filmic separation of dog and humans in the scenes which constitute the present of the film – the events in the bar while the dog lays dying (Pomeranz 2011).

Certainly the song Red Dog's friends are singing and dancing to in the bar reveals that the film is all about the humans, and the mining:

Way out west where the rain don't fall
Got a job with a company drilling for oil
And I'm never gonna leave
Living and a-working on the land
What a change it's been
From working that nine to five
How strange it's been
At last I get the feeling that I'm really alive. (The Dingoes 1973)

Red Dog leaves the room precisely at the moment when the singing and dancing in the bar reaches a crescendo. He is unseen by his so-called friends who all have their backs to him. Although this moment is structured as celebratory – the rousing music, the joyful stories, the romance of the new love for Nancy, the human bonds and friendship forged – for those in the know about the repercussions of such cultural elisions of animals the scene becomes something quite different. It takes on the nature of a wake – with, I suggest, the shamelessness of a wake held while a body is still living and breathing – it is a 'wake in fright'.

Postscript: Koko, the dog who starred in Red Dog, *died in December 2012 of congestive heart disease, aged seven.*

Works cited

ABC Rural (2012). Wild dog numbers in WA force some farmers out of livestock and PGA calls for bounty. [Online]. Available: www.abc.net.au/rural/content/2012/s3478621.htm [Accessed 8 February 2013].

ABC Rural (2002). Wild dogs an increasing problem in the Pilbara. [Online]. Available: www.abc.net.au/rural/sa/stories/s687430.htm [Accessed 8 February 2013].

Allen M (1983). *Animals in American literature*. Urbana: University of Illinois Press.

Altman M (1990). How not to do things with metaphors we live by. *College English*, 52(5): 495–506.

Baker S (2000). *The postmodern animal*. London: Reaktion.

Bodey M (2012). Dog of a year for box office but wizard works his usual magic. *The Australian* 23 January [Online]. Available: www.theaustralian.com.au/

arts/film/dog-of-a-year-for-box-office-but-wizard-works-his-usual-magic/
story-e6frg8pf-1226250782234 [Accessed 11 February 2013].

Boyde M (2009). The modernist roman à clef and cultural secrets, or, I know that
you know that I know that you know. *Australian Literary Studies*, 24(3–4):
155–66.

Boyde M (2010). 'Cultural secrets and the *roman à clef*'. In L D'arcens & A Collett
(Eds). *The unsocial sociability of women's life writing*. UK: Palgrave Macmillan.

Code of practice for the safe use and management of strychnine in Western
Australia (April 2009). Western Australian Departments of Health and
Agriculture and Food [Online]. Available: www.agric.wa.gov.au/objtwr/
imported_assets/content/pw/chem/strychnine_code.pdf [Accessed 20 June
2012].

Cook K (2001) [1961]. *Wake in fright*. Melbourne: Text Publishing.

De Bernières L (2001). *Red Dog*. Milson's Point, NSW: Random House Australia.

Derrida J (1982). White mythology: metaphor in the text of philosophy. In
Margins in philosophy. Alan Bass (Trans.) (pp207–71). Chicago: University of
Chicago Press.

Dingoes, The (1973). *Way out west* song. Copyright Mushroom Records 1974.

Docker J (2010). Epistemological vertigo and allegory: thoughts on massacres
actual, surrogate and averted — *Beersheba*, *Wake in fright* and *Australia*. In F
Peters-Little, A Curthoys & J Docker (Eds). *Passionate histories: myth,
memory and Indigenous Australia* (pp51–72). Canberra: Australian National
University ePress.

Galvin P (2009). Dreaming of the devil. *Wake in fright* DVD booklet. Sydney.

Jennings K (2009). Home truths: revisiting *Wake in fright*. In *The Monthly*. July.
[Online] Available: www.themonthly.com.au/
monthly-essays-kate-jennings-home-truths-revisiting-039wake-fright039-1779
[Accessed May 22 2012].

Jones E (1969). *Wake in fright: a screenplay. Based on the novel by Kenneth Cook.*
Australia: Group W Films NLT.

Lunney D (2012). Roadkill: an ecologist's view of an unresolved issue in wildlife
management. Abstract. In *Animal death conference programme*. University of
Sydney.

Maddox G (2011). Iron men. *Sydney Morning Herald* [Online]. Available:
www.smh.com.au/entertainment/movies/iron-men-20110714-1hei0.html
[Accessed 29 March 2012].

McHugh S (2011). *Animal stories: narrating across species lines*. Minneapolis:
University of Minnesota Press.

Miller S (2012). *Dogs in Australian art: a new history of antipodean creativity*.
South Australia: Wakefield Press.

Monroe J (2012). *Wake in fright*: director Ted Kotcheff talks drunk actors, kangaroo hunts and how Sly Stallone saved Rambo. [Online]. Available: www.complex.com/pop-culture/2012/10/ ted-kotcheff-wake-in-fright-director-interview/ [Accessed 15 November 2012].

Munt S (2008). *Queer attachments: the cultural politics of shame*. Aldershot, England; Burlington, VT: Ashgate.

O'Loughlin T (2009). Oz wises up to its horror heritage. *The Guardian*, Friday 19 June [Online] Available: www.guardian.co.uk/film/2009/jun/19/ wake-in-fright-horror-film [Accessed 11 February 2013].

Pedigree Australian working dog muster (2012) [Online]. Availabile: www.kelpies-casterton.org [Accessed 20 August 2012].

Pomeranz M (2011). *Red Dog* interviews: Margaret Pomeranz speaks with director, Kriv Stenders. *At the movies* [Online]. Available: www.abc.net.au/ atthemovies/txt/s3272053.htm [Accessed 11 February 2013].

Ramp D (2004). Sharing the environment: counting the cost of wildlife mortality on roads [Online]. Available: www.awrc.org.au/uploads/5/8/6/6/5866843/ nwcc-ramp-s-040726.pdf [Accessed 10 July 2012].

Red Dog (2011). Film. Kriv Stenders (Dir.). Distributor: Roadshow.

Screenwest (2010). Resources sector backs *Red Dog*. 10 March [Online]. Available: www.screenwest.com.au/go/news/resources-sector-backs-red-dog [Accessed 10 April 2012].

Sedgwick EK (2003). *Touching feeling: affect, pedagogy, performativity*. Durham: Duke University Press.

Sedgwick EK & Frank A (1995). *Shame and its sisters: a Silvan Tomkins reader*. Durham: Duke University Press.

Simons J (2013). *Kangaroo*. London: Reaktion Books Ltd.

Stratton D & Pomeranz M (2009). *Wake in fright* review. *At the movies* [Online] Available: www.abc.net.au/atthemovies/txt/s2590361.htm [Accessed 11 April 2012].

Wake in fright (2009 [1971]). Film. Ted Kotcheff (Dir.). DVD. Distributor: Madman Entertainment.

Wills D (2009). The blushing machine: animal shame and technological life. *Parrhesia* 8: 34–42.

8
Reflecting on donkeys: images of death and redemption

Jill Bough

At the recent funeral at Palmdale on the Central Coast of NSW of Elizabeth Harris, a fellow donkey enthusiast, her cortege, led by her two
donkeys, served as a reminder of the special link between humans and
donkeys, not only in life but also in death. As an active member of
the local donkey sanctuary, her donkeys, like so many companion donkeys, including my two, were rescued. These much loved animals once
again reminded me that donkeys are so much more than hard working
beasts of burden or gentle companions. The human-like qualities accorded them have placed them in a special relationship with humans who
construct them as symbols, both in this life and the next. Donkeys had
particular symbolic and spiritual meaning in ancient cultures of the
Middle East, while their association with Jesus in the New Testament
has seen them regarded as an allegory of human suffering and of hopes
for salvation. The link between the donkey as victim and as saviour is
nowhere more pronounced than in Australia in the modern era, as is
the gulf between the representation of the symbolic animal and that
of the mass of donkeys. The celebrated iconic image of Simpson, 'the
man with the donkey', a symbolic appropriation of the spirit of Anzac
that places the donkey in a special place in the nation's heart, veils the

J Bough (2013). Reflecting on donkeys: images of death and redemption. In J
Johnston & F Probyn-Rapsey (Eds). *Animal death*. Sydney: Sydney University
Press.

reality of actual donkeys slaughtered in their thousands. However, as individual animals they are also seen as humble sufferers of hardship, victims of cruelty and neglect, deserving of rescue and care,[1] associations which further link them with human death. As archaeologist Howard Williams has observed, these qualities render donkeys:

> as intimately linked with human death and the dead, and, in particular, hopes for their resurrection. Asses are therefore good to think about and good to care for. Yet they are also good to mourn and commemorate, and good to remember with. (Williams 2011, 223)

His words remind me of a special place where donkeys are indeed 'good to mourn and commemorate, and good to remember with'. Not unlike the lush greenery of the cemetery gardens, through which the cortege is processing, I am reminded of the fields back home in the southwest of England and, of course, donkeys. I had been aware of the link between donkeys and death (although had not thought about it consciously) since childhood in England. Being a lover of all things donkey, I often visited the Donkey Sanctuary at Sidmouth in Devon (The Donkey Sanctuary, n.d.). This is indeed a donkey heaven – for donkeys and for people – both physically and symbolically, where both are commemorated. At the sanctuary, the human–animal bond is everywhere evident and the boundary between them is broken down in life and in death. Rescued donkeys are available to watch and handle, to stroke and groom. Individual donkeys are also remembered in death with a plaque, with their names and histories written down for visitors to read.

The sanctuary has a large number of memorials within its grounds commemorating those humans who choose to have their ashes buried at the sanctuary, 'down amongst the donkeys'. Human and animal commemoration is merged in the memorial trees, benches and plaques placed beside paths on which the public meander. Howard Williams claims that the principal memorials at the sanctuary 'are the living (rescued and nurtured) donkeys themselves, non-human agencies by which the dead are remembered' and that the sanctuary 'is clearly regarded by some as a "sacred" and "spiritual" place where people, pets

---

1 See, for example: www.donkeywelfare.com.au/ and www.donkeyshelter.org.au/ Rescue.html.

and donkeys live on through trees, benches and fields and are comforted by the presence of the living donkeys' (Williams 2011, 222).
The belief that life will continue after death is evident in many of the
inscriptions. One plaque for example, reads: 'Now you're free from
pain, You can walk with the donkeys, To watch the sea, Always in our
thoughts.' Several examples illustrate the powerful connection created
between the human dead and the redemptive qualities of the rescued
donkeys.

Ancient cultures

The practice of including donkeys in funerary rituals and sacred places
is as old as their domestication at least 6,000 years ago. Ancient draw-
ings and texts suggest that donkeys have had religious importance and
symbolic and spiritual meaning for humans from their earliest use, as
they feature significantly in the iconography of the mythologies and
religions of different cultures. Donkey burials are recorded over 2000
years in the Near East. The earliest burials occur in ancient Egypt in the
third millennium BC where they are always interred adjacent to elite
human tombs. In Iraq and Syria donkeys are also associated with elite
human graves dated to the mid to late third millennium BC. Donkeys
tend to be buried within the actual tomb with draught equipment and
goods buried alongside them. (Way 2011).

Archaeological evidence indeed points to the fact that donkeys
held a special status in the funeral practices of the ancient world. Queen
Shubad of Ur, for example, had her team of draught donkeys buried
with her (Adolf 1950). In his historical survey of Near Eastern texts,
Kenneth Way concludes that 'it is evident that donkeys held a very special status in the ceremonies of both life and death' (Way 2011, 150).
He found that donkeys functioned, amongst other things, as 'funerary
furnishings', included amongst the goods needed by the deceased in
afterlife: 'It makes sense that a donkey intended for post mortem use
would have to be interred as an intact animal' (Way 2011, 152). They
may also function as offerings to the deities to secure a welcome in the
afterlife, an explanation suggested by the findings of incomplete donkey
remains. Different archaeologists offer different possible explanations
for donkey burials, complete skeletons and part skeletons. Manfred

Bietak, for example, suggested that they represent the draught teams employed in the ceremony (Bietak 1981). However, donkeys were associated with death in a number of ancient texts, which suggests a more religious or ceremonial explanation. Although in these texts the donkey features most prominently as a beast of burden, they are also symbolically associated with divination and death.

Ancient cultures in the Middle East, especially those that developed around the Fertile Crescent during the Bronze Age, depended on the donkey for transport. Archaeologists claim that 'the domestication of the donkey from the African wild ass transformed ancient transport systems in Africa and Asia and the organisation of early city states and pastoral societies' (Rossel et al.2008). Because donkeys can carry heavy loads and operate in semi-desert conditions with little food or water, they enabled pastoralists, their goods and their herds to move further afield. The changing nature of human societies, from hunters and herders, to those based on agriculture resulted in changing attitudes towards donkeys, despite the fact that they remained central in all aspects of domestic life and in trade between the emerging states. Donkeys' close and complex relationships with humans set them apart from other domesticated animals; their multiple functions were significant factors in establishing their unique status in life and in death. As historian Richard Bulliet found: 'the sacred aura surrounding the donkey far exceeds that of any other domestic animal in the region' of Western Asia (Bulliet 2005, 159).

The recent discovery of ten complete 5000-year-old donkey skeletons at the burial site of Abydos points to the high regard in which donkeys were held in the days of the Old Kingdom. For the ancient Egyptians, Abydos was one of the holiest sites and gateway to the underworld, a popular place of pilgrimage and burial. Situated in the Nile Valley 480 km (298 miles) south of Cairo, it is famous as the burial place of the earliest Egyptian kings and as the cult place of the god Osiris, himself a mythic king of Egypt and ruler of the Land of the Dead. The donkeys' burials and their location in the high-status area of the North Cemetery indicate that they were highly valued, their contributions to the daily lives of the ancient Egyptians recognised as they took their place alongside the kings of Egypt in their burial chambers. This elite status reinforces the economic importance of the donkey to the first pharaohs, land-based transport, and integration of the early Egyptian state (Rossel et al. 2008). However, it was as a source of spirituality, sustenance and companionship and an essential element of the cosmic order that they continued as companions into the afterlife.

Donkeys' economic value, close relationship with humanity and association with religious practices has resulted in specific symbolic connections and perceived human attributes distinct from other species. In the pastoral/nomadic environment of early Israel, their use in ceremonial rites as well as their importance in agricultural work and use as both pack and riding animal were significant factors in establishing the unique status of the donkey in biblical literature.[2] Their further association with divination and death saw the donkey as a divine symbol and as an agent for Yahweh (Way 2011, 199). The story of Balaam's ass in the Old Testament (Numbers 22: 21–35) is arguably the most significant of these references. She is the only animal in the Bible to be granted the power of speech by God. Not pleased with Balaam's behaviour, God sends an angel. Only the donkey sees the angel at first and she is given the power of speech to complain to her master, whom she has carried faithfully, about her harsh treatment. The angel tells Balaam that the only reason he did not kill him was because of the donkey. A less well-known passage featuring a donkey as a divine agent is the story of a disobedient prophet from Judah (Kings 1:13). As he is riding home on his donkey, the man is mauled by a lion while the donkey is unharmed. Both animals then stand by the dead prophet to make clear his death is a judgement from God. As subjects of divination, part of the donkey's role was as a mediator with the unseen spirit world.

The complex and contradictory relationships between humans and donkeys that still exist today were evident from these early days of their domestication. While their valuable role in everyday life as beasts of burden continued, their symbolic representation was to change over time and context (Bough 2011a). In the days of the Old Kingdom in ancient Egypt, the donkey had once been considered a holy animal, associated with the mighty desert god, Seth. Their ears, represented as two feathers, became a symbol of supremacy; sprouting from the royal sceptre, they acted as a reminder that all power derives from Seth, who

---

2   One concordance to the Bible, for example, lists 153 references to the donkey, more than any other animal: Robert Young, *Analytical concordance to the Bible* (Grand Rapids, MI, 1982).

was often depicted with a donkey's head, his sexual potency symbolised by the donkey (Bulliet 2005, 151). The virility of the ass was a life-giving force. However, although once a powerful and revered god of the desert, Seth fell from grace, and with him the status of the donkey. Both were infamous for their licentious behaviour and both were associated with the desert. Seth was transformed into a dark power, the god of storms, chaos and evil. He was later linked to the evil Typhon by the Greeks and both came to be identified with demonic forces. During an Egyptian festival, as recorded by Plutarch, both donkeys and men with sandy, or Typhonic, colouring, resembling that of the wild ass, were pushed over cliffs. This was claimed to be in retribution for the murder of Osiris (Johnson 2011). The associations between donkeys and their representations in the rituals surrounding both life and death were conflicting and complicated and usually led to their neglect and harsh treatment in everyday life.

However, since the Middle Ages, donkeys have been considered by many to be noble and holy animals, largely because of their associations with Jesus. Specifically, the prominence of the ass in the New Testament of the Bible has made their character an allegory for human suffering and hopes for salvation. As Williams says of the rehabilitation work at the Donkey Sanctuary, it is 'extended after death and the biblical associations of donkeys may help to facilitate this afterlife imagining' (Williams 2011, 235). Donkeys are linked with the birth of Jesus and with his death and have been referred to as the bearer of the salvation of the world. Two are mentioned symbolically in the Gospel story, one coming from the north and bearing the pregnant Mary to Bethlehem, where, according to legend, an ass and ox stood over the crib; the other taking her to Egypt to escape the slaughter of the innocents and so saving Jesus' life. In particular, the image of Jesus' triumphal entry into Jerusalem on a donkey on Palm Sunday, on the first day of the last week of his life, is one of the most enduring Christian symbols in Western culture. For Christians, the death of Jesus was not the end but represented a new beginning. This is essential in appreciating the significance of the donkey to suffering, death, hope and redemption. The ties with Christianity are so strong that legend has it that the cross on the donkey's back came from the shadow of the Crucifixion, a living symbol that the donkey has carried through the centuries.

Warfare

In the secular, modern world, donkeys have come to be regarded as sufferers of hardship and victims of human cruelty, deserving of our care, associations which have again linked them with human death. Elizabeth Svendsen (the founder of the Devon Donkey Sanctuary) claims that the place of the donkey in British popular mortuary culture originates with warfare (Svendsen 2009). This becomes especially apparent in the statues that commemorate donkeys at war. A bronze statue of a donkey stands alone in the centre of the walled Russell Memorial Garden at the Donkey Sanctuary. The sculpture is the sanctuary's war memorial: 'Dedicated to all those donkeys and mules who have lost their lives in war.' Donkeys have been an important means of transport in most theatres of war since the time of their domestication. They were exploited by Greek and Roman armies in their thousands, mainly as pack animals but also for riding and pulling chariots. Indeed, in particularly challenging environments, such as Afghanistan, they are still used in human warfare to the present day (McLaughlan 2005). The 'Animals in War' memorial in Hyde Park in London (2004) features bronze statues of a donkey and mule as the centrepiece. Carrying First World War military equipment, they not only represent the vast numbers that died in the Great War but all animal suffering in human conflicts. We now commemorate not only the humans who died and suffered in war but also the animals that suffered and died alongside them.

Simpson and the donkey

There are histories which record the contribution of animals in human warfare and, at times, individual animals are remembered for their acts of bravery (e.g. Ambrus 1975; Baynes 1925; Clutton-Brock 1992). Focusing on the individual animal rather than the group can create a greater understanding and sense of empathy.[3] In Australia, of course, we have Murphy, Simpson's donkey. Memorials to 'the man and the donkey' feature in many towns around Australia while statues of them

---

3   A recent example is the film *War horse* (2012) directed by Stephen Spielberg.

stand outside the Shrine of Remembrance in Melbourne and the War Memorial in Canberra. Here we see the donkey both as a victim of war and as saviour. Out of the horrors experienced at Gallipoli in 1915 stepped the reassuring sight of the man and the donkey, carrying a wounded soldier to safety. The donkey's association both with life and hope and death and redemption is evident in a complicated mix of reality and religious symbolism. The mythology surrounding the image of man and donkey is deeply rooted in the Christian tradition (Cochrane 1992). Not only is the image evocative of Jesus riding a donkey on Palm Sunday, it is also reminiscent of the Good Samaritan helping a wounded stranger. Melded in the realistic image of the donkey carrying a soldier to safety and possible life is the powerful Christian message of service, sacrifice and redemption.

Perhaps the best known memorial to Simpson and the donkey stands at the entrance of the War Memorial in Canberra (1988). The striking, realistic, larger-than-life bronze statue of Simpson and the donkey carrying a wounded soldier was designed and built by the well-known sculptor Peter Corlett. It offers a scene of compassion rather than killing – Corlett likened it to Christ entering Jerusalem. It is the donkey that validates this connection. The realistic portrayal of the group emphasises the drama of the events as men and donkey make their way to get aid. We can see the soldier's pain and stress, Simpson, composed and supportive, but it is the donkey who bears most of the weight. He is small compared to the men, yet sturdy and calm although he seems to stagger under his heavy load as he leans forward. With the Red Cross insignia on his headband, he represents compassion in the face of danger on this perilous journey. The iconic image of man and donkey held a reassuring message for those suffering and dying – and for those grieving at home. The combination of the ordinary bloke and the humble donkey together in the face of the carnage of war calmly going about their business of rescuing fallen soldiers was an inspiring image of bravery and hope. There was hope that a soldier/son/husband/brother may be saved by his journey on the donkey's back. For the many that were not saved, comfort may be found in the belief that their deaths were not in vain, that they died so that others might live (Bough 2011b).

Wild donkeys in Australia

The link between the donkey as symbol and as a 'real' animal that has played an active part in a country's history is nowhere more pronounced than in Australia (Bough 2008). Although we commemorate one special donkey in Australia on 25 April every year, and many are kept as companion animals, the outlook for the species is not so positive. A recent article in a hunting magazine highlights the fate for donkeys in some regions of Australia today. Shot from helicopters, they wander around for weeks in agony, their jaws shot off, slowly starving to death (Penfold 2011). One hunter reported that on one station alone they shot 23,500 donkeys. Complete eradication of wild donkeys in Australia is the government's aim. How is it that donkeys, long instrumental in the life of human cultures, have come to be condemned to death in this way?

Donkeys were brought to Australia by the British in the latter half of the 19th century as they colonised the land in their search for land and minerals. Great teams of donkeys hauled goods across the outback and were instrumental in the success of the vast pastoral stations in some of the harshest areas of the continent. However, with the advent of motorised transport in the 1930s, they were no longer economically viable and were set free to fend for themselves (Bough 2008). Donkeys are well adapted to life in arid areas because they are derived from wild stock originally inhabiting northern Africa. They can survive a water loss equal to 30 per cent of their body weight, the same degree of tolerance as a camel, and can drink enough in two to five minutes to replace the loss (Hoy 2000). As they are more tolerant of dehydration and heat than Brahmin cattle, a favoured breed for the conditions of the Top End, donkeys can wander further from water and they can also feed on poorer scrub; indeed, they prosper under the adverse conditions of the outback (Letts 1979).

Donkeys thrived and multiplied as they ran wild and were deemed 'pests' by pastoralists as they competed with cattle and sheep for feed. Furthermore, as an 'introduced' and now 'useless' animal, no longer under the control of the colonists, they became 'feral pests' and eventually 'destructive vermin' to be destroyed. Since being declared 'vermin' in 1948 in the Northern Territory, eradication programs have seen them shot, trapped and poisoned in their hundreds of thousands, especially in the adjoining areas of north-eastern Kimberley of WA and the Victoria River District of the NT. As Keith Thomas has argued in a different context:

> Wild animals which were deemed as useless, or which made the mistake of competing with man on his own ground were universally classified as vermin that needed to be exterminated at every possible opportunity. (Thomas 1983, 25)

Estimates of feral population numbers vary enormously. In 1959 it was reported that shooting teams in the East Kimberley area had destroyed over 20,000 donkeys over the previous three years (McDonald 1959). In 1964 the Western Australia government estimated that at least 100,000 roamed the eastern half of the Kimberley. In 1988, large herds often outnumbered cattle on some stations in the Kimberley region, which carried 5000 cattle and 10,000 donkeys despite the fact that over the preceding decade 164,000 donkeys had been shot (Terry 1963). Although other methods such as poisoning and trapping were sometimes used, the remoteness and difficult terrain makes shooting from helicopters supposedly 'the most effective and practical method' in the campaign to eradicate the donkey (Senate Select Committee on Animal Welfare 1991). It is claimed that shooting from helicopters is 'a humane and efficient technique in the remote country of the Kimberley. It permits the shooter to follow donkeys into inaccessible areas and to make sure no wounded animals escape' (Agriculture Protection Board 1981). An observer who joined the helicopter shooting team at Halls Creek witnessed one marksman killing 50 donkeys in 30 minutes (*Western Australian*, 11 April 1981). Is killing wild donkeys from helicopters humane? Personal evidence would suggest that this is not the case. One shooter explained that firing from helicopters on a small moving target is not so easy and it will sometimes take five shots to bring down a donkey foal (Cohen 1989). Others tell of wounded donkeys wandering around for weeks before they die a slow and painful death.

The latest weapon used in the war against feral donkeys is the 'Judas Collar' Program begun in the southern Kimberley in 1994. Several donkeys, usually jennies (females), are fitted with a tracking device collar and are then released to join groups in the area. The 'Judas donkeys' are familiar with the area and are part of the social structure of the target mobs, so they lead the shooters to the herds.[4] The donkeys found with the Judas donkey are then shot, leaving her to locate other donkeys in the area. Over 270 radio collars were fitted in the Kimberley and five years later the Agricultural Protection Board reported that they were over half way to achieving their aim of complete eradication (Johnson 1999). Figures for 2007 showing the numbers of donkeys shot on West Kimberley pastoral leases using the Judas Program were 25,520. Mick Everett, the Biosecurity Officer for the region, reported that the program had been completed for many of the properties, that is, there were no donkeys remaining, while the situation was still being 'monitored' on some stations, and 'continuing' on several more (Everett 2007).

Jonathan Burt has noted that animals that are treated as symbols and icons are paradoxically placed 'outside history' (Burt 2001, 203). He argues that limiting the history of the animal to a human framework as textual, metaphorical animal, reducing it to a mere icon causes the 'effacement' of the animal. As has been shown here, representing the donkey as symbol and icon and as metaphors for human characteristics 'effaces' the 'real' animal and fails to portray the donkeys' actual place in history. Furthermore, we label those animals to suit human shifting values: they can be 'companion' or 'beast of burden', 'expendable' or 'vermin'. Inconsistent and changing representations influence how the animal is valued and treated. The donkey may be symbolically associated with divination and human rituals surrounding death; however, their actual existence has all too often been accorded little recognition or respect. Certainly, the place of the donkey in Australia's history has largely been ignored, their significance overlooked. Arguably, the only well-known donkey is Murphy of Anzac. However, this 'special' donkey is of little interest in his own right, only as a symbol of the service and mateship of the 'digger' melded with Christian belief in redemption. Meanwhile, the rest of his kind has been placed not only 'outside history' but, it would seem, outside our 'field of vision' or scope of empathy. The mass destruction on an enormous scale of 'feral' donkeys continues, largely unrecorded and unopposed. The fate of the Judas jenny seems particularly sad. Taking advantage of her social nature, the method turns the jenny into a harbinger of death: wherever she

---

4   This is once again reminiscent of Holy Week when Judas led the soldiers to arrest Jesus in the Garden of Gethsemane – and betrayed him with a kiss.

goes, death follows. Humans have turned her into a betrayer of her own kind. She soon learns to keep away from other donkeys. Psychologically damaged by what she has witnessed, she remains isolated. As Deborah Bird Rose so eloquently argues:

> She becomes the creature without fellow creatures, the creature for whom being-with-others has lost its purchase. The jenny's options are devastating, and like a prism in the sun her choice continues to show the moral putrefaction of Judas work. (Rose 2008, 66)

As I watched the two jennies standing sentinel outside the crematorium at Palmdale, seemingly aware of the solemnity of the occasion, I thought of those other jennies far away at the other end of Australia. Alone and traumatised, without human or donkey company, they await the final bullet.

Works cited

Adolf H (1950). The ass and the harp. *Speculum*, 25(1): 49–57.

Agriculture Protection Board (1981). Feral donkey: advisory leaflet no 71. Perth.

Ambrus VG (1975). *Horses in battle London*. London: Oxford University Press.

Baynes EH (1925). *Animal heroes of the Great War*. London: Macmillan.

Bietak M (1981). *Avaris and Piramesse: archaelogical exploration of the Nile Delta*. London: British Academy and Oxford University Press.

Bough J (2008). Value to vermin: the donkey in Australia. Unpublished PhD thesis, Newcastle University.

Bough J (2011a). *Donkey*. London: Reaktion Books.

Bough J (2011b). Murphy and Simpson: Lest We Forget. Between the representation and the reality lies the shadow. Paper presented at the 'Animals, people – a shared environment' conference, Brisbane.

Bulliet R (2005). *Hunters, herders and hamburgers: the past and future of human–animal relationships*. New York: Columbia University Press.

Burt J (2001). The illumination of the animal kingdom: the role of light and electricity in animal representation. *Society and Animals*, 9(3): 203–28.

Clutton-Brock J (1992). *Horse power: a history of the horse and the donkey in human societies*. Cambridge, MA: Harvard University Press.

Cochrane P (1992). *Simpson and the donkey: the making of a legend*. Australia: Melbourne University Press.

Cohen J (1989). Genocide of the Kimberley donkeys, *West Australian*.

Everett M (2007). *Summary of donkey control in the West Kimberley: Pastoral Memo - Northern Pastoral Region*. Derby: AGWEST.

Hoy A (2000). Remains of the bray. *The Bulletin with Newsweek*, 118(6249): 46.

Johnson A (1999). Kimberley collars on Judas donkeys. Savanna Links, 9, March–April [Online] Available: savanna.org.au/savanna_web/publications/savanna_links_issue9.html?tid=29413 [Accessed 7 May 2013] .

Johnson SF (2011). The question of the magician: an exploration in the role of the magician in ancient Greek and Roman literature and material culture. *Senior Capstone Projects*, Paper 6.

Letts G (1979). *Feral animals in the Northern Territory*. Darwin: Department of Primary Production, NT Government.

McDonald PJ (1959). The donkeys are doomed. *Journal of the Department of Agriculture*, 8(2): 180–82.

McLaughlan P (2005). Gas guzzlers replaced by hay burners: pack animals help fight war on terror. *Veterans Magazine*, 8–11.

Penfold B (2011). Australia: What happens to dead donkeys in Australia? *HuntNetwork* [Online]. Available: huntnetwork.net/modules/news/article.php?storyid=6061&keywords=hunting [Accessed 12 December 2011].

Rose B (2008). Judas work: four modes of sorrow. *Environmental Philosophy*, 5(2): 51–66.

Rossel S, Marshall F, Peters J, Pilgrim T, Adams M & O'Connor D (2008). Domestication of the donkey: timing, processes and indicators. *PNAS: Proceedings of the National Academy of Sciences of the USA*, 105(10): 3715–20.

Senate Select Committee on Animal Welfare (1991). *Culling of large feral animals in the Northern Territory*. Canberra: Parliament House.

Svendsen E (2009). *The complete book of the donkey*. Shrewsbury: Kenilworth Press.

Terry M (1963). Exotic pests? We've got the lot. *People*, 14: 12–15.

The Donkey Sanctuary (n.d.). Together we can help end the suffering [Online]. Available: www.thedonkeysanctuary.org.uk/ [Accessed 7 July 2012].

Thomas K (1983). *Man and the natural world: changing attitudes in England, 1500–1800*. London: Allen & Lane.

Way K (2011). *Donkeys in the biblical world: ceremony and symbol*. Winona Lake, Indiana: Eisenbrauns.

Williams H (2011). Ashes to asses: an archaeological perspective of death and donkeys. *Journal of Material Culture*, 16(3): 219–39.

9
Picturing cruelty: chicken advocacy and visual culture

Annie Potts and Philip Armstrong

In December 2004, scientists announced they had cracked the first complete genetic code of a bird: over 20,000 genes had been found to comprise the genome sequence of the Red Jungle Fowl, the wild progenitor of all chickens. Immediately there was speculation about how the mapping of the chicken genome could benefit humankind; it was claimed that manipulation of embryonic growth with the assistance of new knowledge about the chicken genome would lead to advances in dealing with human developmental diseases such as cleft palate and muscular dystrophy, as well as DNA changes associated with human ageing. 'The chicken is really in an evolutionary sweet spot', stated Richard Wilson, director of the international team that mapped the genome. 'It's at just the right evolutionary distance from all the other genomes we already have to provide us with a great deal of fresh insight into the human genome' (Wilson, cited in Purdy 2004). It was also announced that understanding the genetic code of chickens would greatly advantage those in agribusiness: one of the researchers enthusiastically declared that this new information about chickens would act as a ' "bible" for those who seek to breed [even] faster-growing birds, lower-fat breasts and more prolific egg-layers' (Mestel 2004). While the

A Potts & P Armstrong (2013). Picturing cruelty: chicken advocacy and visual culture. In J Johnston & F Probyn-Rapsey (Eds). *Animal death*. Sydney: Sydney University Press.

scientific community applauded the discovery of the chicken genome, chicken advocates lamented the exposure of these birds to further scientific experimentation and commercial exploitation. For, while the blueprint of the Jungle Fowls' genome may offer insights into gallinaceous origins, and open a new window on the ancient history of life on this planet, its discovery also undoubtedly seals chickenkind's continued manipulation and abuse as a 'utility object' in human hands.

To give some idea of the extent of chicken exploitation today: it is estimated that worldwide over 50 billion chickens are killed for meat each year. America kills around 23 million broiler or meat chicks per day, around 10 billion per year; while in the United Kingdom 860 million broiler chicks and 30 million 'end-of-lay' hens are killed annually. Australia kills at least 500 million broiler chicks each year for meat, having raised 96% in intensive systems, while 11 million battery hens produce 93% of the nation's eggs (Potts 2012). Australians refer to the modern poultry industry as 'technology's child', because the changes in the use of machinery and technology undertaken by commercial chicken farmers within the past century have been dramatic and immense (Dixon 2002, 83). Such changes included the invention of incubators and brooders (which separated mother hens from eggs and hatched chicks), and the creation of highly mechanised barn and cage systems that permitted intensive automated farming of chickens for both meat and eggs. Technical 'advances' in slaughterhouses, along with modifications to the ways in which meat from chickens was packaged and marketed, also allowed increasing numbers of birds to be 'processed' at a time.

Modern poultry farming rapidly transformed chickens, who over many centuries and cultures had been revered for their beauty, bravery and devotion to parenthood, into the least respected and most exploited creatures on the planet (Potts 2012).[1] The word 'chicken' has now come to symbolise cowardice, and the hen, whose love for her chicks was once so admired, has become a dispensable egg-making machine. Instead of a natural lifespan of up to 12 years, the typical farmed chick today will live about four to six weeks, never having experienced sunshine, rain or grass, and will arrive at the slaughterhouse still uttering the cheeping sounds and coated with the premature down of chicks. Most consumers of chicken meat do not realize they are eating juvenile birds (a fact not widely publicised by the poultry industry);

perhaps some would still not care much if they did know this fact, for in modern societies chickens have become de-natured, de-personalised and even de-animalised. This latter point is evident in the nonchalant ways Western consumers approach chicken meat. An important technique for disguising the origins of meat (and reducing the likelihood of consumers feeling disconcerted about eating once living creatures) is to remove skin, feathers and bones; this process, referred to by Kubberod (2005) as 'de-animalisation', also applies to offal and organs. In addition, the meat from an animal is often given another name from the creature it is derived from; for example, pig becomes pork or ham, and cow becomes beef. However, in poultry industry studies chicken meat is rarely classified by consumers as potentially or borderline repulsive because chickens, as a result of industrialisation, are no longer considered significant sentient beings to start with. They are 'chicken' before and when they are eaten; consumers comfortably consider them as food even while they are alive.

It is also commonplace in Western culture to ridicule the deaths of chickens for food production. Hence American Dick Clark's cartoon strip once featured the 'joke': 'Where did Paul Simon get the idea to write "Mother and Child Reunion"? From a chicken-and-egg dish at a

---

1   While chickens are exploited primarily for food, they are also utilised in myriad other ways. For example, the chicken provides the most popular 'farm animal model' in studies of arthritis, cardiovascular disease, cystic fibrosis, skin disorders, eye diseases, muscular dystrophy, viral infections such as HIV, and vaccine testing (Fox 1997, 88). Vivisection on chickens has also involved growing tooth buds in the jaws of newly hatched chicks (chickens do not have teeth in nature), developing facial abnormalities (such as two beaks), transplanting brain tissue from quails into chicks (to ascertain whether chicks will then prefer a mother quails' calls). Pain research on chicks has included confining 1-14-day-old Leghorns to hot plates to determine whether older or younger chicks jump faster when exposed to more heat (Hughes 1990; Hughes & Sufka 1990). Agricultural experiments focus on improving the economical benefits of poultry farming. Scientists have shaved hens (in studies on heat stress), cut off the wings and legs of newly hatched chicks to establish how much growers could save in food costs if they had to feed smaller broiler chicks, and created featherless birds for intensive farming in hot climates. The poultry industry also supplies fertilised eggs to schools in order that children may follow the hatching and development of chicks as part of their education (chicks are commonly discarded following this exercise). Chickens are also used by the US military to detect chemicals in Iraq; the birds, who travel on army vehicles, succumb if exposed to deadly toxins (Davis 2003).

Chinese restaurant' (Adams 2003, 150);[2] while *The Christchurch Press*, the daily newspaper of the city where we live, recently featured a piece on the fun of barbecuing by a regular columnist who joked that 'whole chickens (deceased) cook beautifully on the barbecue when you insert a full can of beer up their rear ends and stand them to attention in a row over the grill' (Bramwell 2006, 23). The conjoining in contemporary culture of chickens' principal role as merely 'food' with a total disregard for their sentience is also starkly evident in a recent advertising campaign named Subservient Chicken run by Burger King to promote the company's range of chicken meat sandwiches. Subservient Chicken centred on a website featuring a person dressed in a cartoon chicken costume; users commanded the chicken to perform over 300 pre-recorded activities, such as 'Riverdance', 'Lay Egg', 'Yoga', and 'Spank'. The chicken obeys when an instruction is typed over Burger King's campaign slogan 'Get chicken just the way you like it'. Subservient Chicken attracted 20 million hits within one week, and won gold at the 2005 Viral Awards granted to successful advertising campaigns (Anderson 2009). Jokes about the subservience of chickens extend to the arena of pranks: in 'chicken roping' contests in the United States, girls and boys compete to see who can lasso and rope a chicken's feet quickest once birds are lowered into a rodeo ring; the chickens at these events are also whipped by small ropes and submitted to various forms of suspension 'for fun'.

These activities testify to the levels to which chickens have sunk in the worlds of symbolism and the human imagination: dim-witted comic chickens are made to spank themselves, actual dead chickens have cans of beer stuffed up them to make them explode, and live chickens are pursued around a rodeo ring by children learning to have fun by exercising cruelty towards, and domination over, terrified birds. These examples demonstrate the need for public education as well as sanctuary for chickens in contemporary Western societies. Chicken activism

2   This story is actually provided as one of the possible meanings 'behind the lyrics' of Simon's song; and it may certainly be the case that an omelette presented to Simon at a restaurant in New York's Chinatown sparked his thinking about separation between mothers and offspring; however, most analysts of the lyrics to 'Mother and child reunion' speculate Simon approached this subject with more seriousness and sensitivity than traditional 'hen and egg' jokes afford.

works to challenge ignorant ideas about and disrespectful treatment of *Gallus gallus*, to promote compassion for these most abused of birds, and to resurrect accurate understanding of chickens as sentient and intelligent creatures. What follows is an historical overview of some of the ways in which chicken activism over the past 50 years or so has utilised visual culture, especially provocative imagery, to raise awareness, educate the public, politicise and lobby against the miserable lives and deaths of the majority of the planet's chickens. In particular we focus on the beginnings of modern 'imagery' activism in the work of the British group Chickens' Lib, the rise of the open rescue movement, the important place of internet activism, and the works of artists campaigning against the exploitation of chickens.

Chickens' Lib

The modern-day use of eye-catching visuals to challenge the treatment of chickens in Western societies emerged in a serious way in the early 1970s when a group of outraged women protested on the steps of Whitehall Place in London, before the premises of the Ministry of Agriculture, Fisheries and Food (MAFF).[3] A few days earlier, one of these women had talked her way into obtaining a couple of 'spent' battery hens destined for slaughter and consumption in the East End. These hens were also present at the protest. Contained in a makeshift 'sample' battery cage built by the woman's husband, they provided visual testament to the condition of hens farmed intensively for their eggs throughout the United Kingdom. This brazen action, occurring at a time when the second-wave women's movement was on the rise, helped to launch the public face of another newly formed activist group, Chickens' Lib. Led for many years by independent poultry welfare researcher Clare Druce, and her mother Violet Spalding, Chickens' Lib was the first organisation to dedicate its activities primarily towards raising awareness of intensive chicken farming practices. For decades, Chickens' Lib confronted consumers with the truth behind the eggs

---

3   Philip Armstrong (2007) points out how even earlier protests, such as the Old Brown Dog demonstration in London in 1905, appealed to visibility (in this case, of the human protestors rather than actual animals).

they ate each morning and the meat they bought for dinner, and lobbied government and agribusiness to change the living and slaughter conditions of farmed chickens in Britain.

The appearance over 30 years ago of the rescued battery hens on the steps of MAFF in London provided the urban public with perhaps their first glimpse of the 'real lives' of hens confined in cages. This tactic, instigated by Druce as a provocative, effective way to draw attention to 'the hens behind the eggs', remains crucial in contemporary animal activism, and especially in exposés of intensively farmed animals. From very small beginnings – in fact, just Druce and a handful of supporters with the determination to show the misery of factory farmed chickens to the world – this group grew to impact hugely on the British scene and also influence North American activism.[4] One British chronicle even wrote in 1979 that the names Violet Spalding and Clare Druce might

> mean nothing to most people, but in the corridors of Whitehall they are names that can cause shudders of fear ... known to halt a whole morning's work at the Ministry of Agriculture, they have demonstrated in Whitehall addressing ministry officials by loudspeaker, appeared on television in their own programme [and] been threatened with prosecution by the police ... Chickens' Lib may sound like a joke but it isn't. (Druce, personal communication, 2010)

The legacy of Chickens' Lib continues today in the various ways that advocacy for chickens relies on visual impact to raise awareness and gain public support. The employment of pictures in animal activism per se has been considered important not least because of the notion that animals are unable to speak for or represent themselves; thus compassionate people attempt to represent on their behalf (Burt 2002). Images work especially well for issues relating to companion animals and wild animals, particularly those considered charismatic, such as the great apes, big cats and cetaceans. According to James Jasper, this is because such 'categories' of animals provide powerful 'condensing symbols' that

---

4   Karen Davis, head of the world's foremost advocacy group for poultry (United Poultry Concerns) credits Druce with having led the way for today's campaigners against cruelty towards chickens (personal communication, 7 August 2008).

aid political or ethical protests because they appeal to a variety of viewers and address issues and concerns deemed acceptable for public debate (Jasper 1997). Managing visual impact is more complex when dealing with chicken exploitation as these birds are not readily viewed as charismatic or in any way 'special' by the general population (as previously mentioned, they are more likely to be seen as trivial, stupid, dispensable – 'meat' even before death). Nor are chickens likely to elicit in viewers a 'cute response' – that is, an emotional nurturing response triggered by 'infant' animals like fluffy kittens or playful puppies (Genosko 2005). In popular culture chickens tend to be anthropomorphised as dim-witted and silly characters, or they appear as cute yellow chicks with no clear relation to the grim realities of chicken adulthood. In meat or egg advertising chickens seem ridiculously jovial; readers will be familiar with signage showing happy caricatured chickens pointing to eateries selling chicken meat, as if these birds are personally delighted to be on the menu. Over 30 years ago cultural theorist John Berger argued convincingly that 'real' animals had largely vanished in Western culture, having been replaced with other animal images, such as those we see now in cartoons, movies, and marketing. This phenomenon, he contended, worked to divorce humans from more authentic and respectful relationships with actual animals, to replace the animal *as animal* with the animal as spectacle (Berger 1980). We suggest that while Berger's position is still valid in many ways, it has also been (helpfully) complicated by newer theory on the place of animals in visual culture (Baker 1993; Burt 2002; Armstrong 2007; Malamud 2010). Recent thinking on animal representation informs analysis of chicken advocacy presented below.

Show and tell in chicken activism

Effective political campaigns against poultry farming and other forms of chicken exploitation have, since Chickens' Lib, relied heavily on visual exposure, particularly spectacular footage. Activism disrupts the concealment of experimental or intensively farmed chickens which routinely occurs in the domains of technoscience and agriculture. As urban-centred commodity capitalism has developed over the last two centuries, it has increasingly demanded that images of animal suffering be removed from public view; thus meat producers attempt to conceal the origins of the billions of McNuggets™ and KFC Wicked Wings™ consumed each year, whereas those protesting the immense exploitation of chickenkind expose these unpalatable facts about the poultry industry and mass chicken meat consumption. Consequently, the struggle between these two sides of the animal-use debate have often been played out in the arena of visual culture, and have involved attempts to regulate or liberate the power of the seen and the unseen.

One highly successful strategy employed by activists has involved using raw footage of actual animals in order to reveal the avian suffering and pain 'behind the scenes'. For instance, Kentucky Fried Cruelty, a campaign run by the American-based organisation People for the Ethical Treatment of Animals (PETA), strives to expose the misery behind the chicken meat sold at thousands of KFC outlets worldwide. To this end, Kentucky Fried Cruelty's webpage shows 'undercover investigations' of abuse towards chickens filmed on named farms and slaughterhouses across America, as well as India, Germany, Australia, New Zealand and the United Kingdom. In 2004, Kentucky Fried Cruelty was responsible for bringing into the public arena material secretly filmed within a Maryland slaughterhouse owned by Perdue Farms Incorporated, one of KFC's main suppliers of chicken meat in the United States. In the film, live chicks at the plant are kicked and thrown by employees, and are still conscious when their bodies enter the scalding tanks. Such real-time footage draws the public eye to precisely those realities that are usually eclipsed from the consumer's view: namely, the stages of the industrial processing sequence that turn animals into meat.

Open rescue

While protest demonstrations involving live hens still occur, such as those conducted by the women from Chickens' Lib during the organisation's formative days, these can now reach far beyond local media or the eyes of those in the immediate vicinity. The internet is now the most significant resource for animal activism; rapidly reaching millions around the globe, its contribution to global educative activism is immense. Publicising scenes such as those at the Perdue plant may involve secretly filmed footage by undercover groups, streamed live or later released online. Clandestine operations were until the 1990s commonplace among those identifying as animal liberationists; however, more recently, the public exposure of conditions within battery farms is the result of footage obtained during 'open rescues', which, as the name implies, involve the very visible release and care of incarcerated and mistreated chickens. Open rescues are conducted by teams of individuals who are identifiable at all times; the human faces of rescuers are not hidden, nor are their names necessarily concealed. The moral premise underlying open rescues is that 'it is wrong to knowingly let any individual, regardless of their species, die an unnecessarily slow, agonizing and painful death', and rescue workers are required to act as professionally and carefully as 'colleagues in other rescue areas such as fire fighters, state emergency services or ambulance personnel' (see www.openrescue.org). Property is not vandalised or destroyed; only non-violent methods of emancipation are employed.

Openrescue.org states the immediate objective of documented rescues carried out in factory farms is to liberate individual chickens who are suffering, but the confrontational visual coverage accompanying such daring emancipations also helps capture public attention and highlight issues related to intensive farming and slaughter practices. If rescuers are caught and charged with trespass or theft, this can work to their advantage as trials are opportunities to broadcast stories about conditions on chicken farms to the unknowing public. Open rescue is now a worldwide phenomenon with teams operating in Germany, Austria, the Czech Republic, Scandinavia, North America, Australia and New Zealand (Jones 2006). The pioneer of the global open rescue movement, Australian Patty Mark, led the first open rescue fronted by Animal Liberation Victoria in 1992. Mark's approach is staunch: as well as challenging the cruelty inherent in intensive poultry farming (a subject that more readily attracts the sympathy of the public), she ensures open rescues reveal the fallacies behind free-range chicken meat and eggs, reasoning that 'it is poor use of our time to engage with animal industries, big business and governments trying to encourage them to treat the animals who are at their mercy "better". The real work isn't negotiating with the animal industries, but with educating the public' (Mark 2006).

In terms of effectiveness, visual campaigns against battery farming have an advantage over broiler chick campaigns. Activism on behalf of layer hens is more readily amenable to visual representation, because 'a snapshot of three or four featherless hens in a cramped cage' provides the kind of potent 'condensing symbol' identified by Jasper; such an image immediately embodies the key elements of the case against battery farming: that extreme confinement and sensory deprivation cannot but degrade the birds' physical and behavioural wellbeing. The plight of chicks raised for meat is not so easily explained through pictures of broiler sheds as these juvenile birds retain their feathers, are not kept in cages, and, because they appear plump, may even be labelled 'greedy' (Franklin 1999). However, savvy activism exploits these very features of broiler chicks in order to educate the public about those 'uncomfortable' issues cleverly disguised by the chicken meat industry, such as the fact that broiler chicks are still technically 'babies' when slaughtered and eaten; that they suffer from painful conditions brought on by selective breeding for rapid massive weight gain; and that they may be unable to stand for days, even weeks, before their lives are ended. Instead of using a snapshot image of broiler chicks in a shed, the fate of broilers can be visually demonstrated by juxtaposing a 'meat chick' at one and six weeks of age with another breed of chicken at the same stages of life, a strategy used by New Zealand animal advocacy group Save Animals From Exploitation.

Because the suffering of chickens in the commercial meat industry is less easily condensed into a potent image, another important strategy in advocacy for these birds involves asking people to *imagine* being broiler chicks. This approach was used by Pulitzer-Prize winning author Alice Walker in a letter she wrote on Mother's Day 2004 addressed to David Novak, then CEO of Yum! Brands, the parent company of KFC (see Walker's letter below).[5] While the once-hidden living (and dy-

---

5 'Suppose in a future life you come back as a chicken. You are small and fuzzy and scared. You feel heavy and hot, suffocating because you are constantly drugged; your body forced to grow so large and fast your bones cannot support it: they begin to break . . . Your body, broken though it is, and smeared with excrement that left it because you were so afraid as you died, is plucked of its sickly covering of feathers, cut up, and sent to the place where it will be covered with white flower and herbs, fried in hot fat, and presented to human families who have no way of knowing they are eating – bringing into their own bodies (and spirits) – the deep suffering, fear and misery of your largely unlived life'. (Walker 2004)

ing) conditions of intensively farmed chickens are now increasingly in evidence – thanks to the world wide web and open rescues – people still have to be motivated to investigate and educate themselves. To this end, the participation of celebrities such as Walker in public protests assists to attract a wider audience. Thus, organisations such as PETA enlist popular culture icons to front particular campaigns; for example, celebrities as diverse as Oprah Winfrey, Pamela Anderson, P!nk, Sir Paul McCartney, the Dalai Lama, Ryan Gosling and Emmylou Harris are all enlisted as speakers against KFC.

Activist art

Historically, the production of artworks has been integral to some of the most exploitative connections humans have had with animals (such as farming and hunting) (Burt 2008); it has also been important as a vehicle for protest against such practices. Most well-known artworks involving chickens tend to contain familiar renditions of these birds, portrayals which are more or less easily recognised within certain cultural contexts and commonly shared ideas about 'chicken-ness' and what chickens represent. For example, chickens may portray the rural (American folk art), pastoral (European art), or stand for characteristics of pride and strength (Japanese folk art). The chickens in such works are more or less conventional depictions of what a culture (and artist) assumes about chickens; in the Western context traditional art tends to objectify chickens in accordance with cultural assumptions about the *gallus gallus domesticus* species (Potts 2012). However, art also exists in which the image and/or idea of the chicken evokes a sense of the unfamiliar, aiming to challenge the viewer. Such works disrupt conventional use of chickens in art by associating chicken motifs with other, often less sanguine, versions of chickens' lives or appearances; or by using chickens as metaphorical or subliminal media for human concerns.

Jonathan Burt (2008, 5) argues that art since the 1960s – especially performance and environmental art – has 'transformed the animal from art object to living artwork so the borderline between the animal and the aesthetic became much more evidently permeable'; this trend, he suggests, should be understood 'within the shifting visual economy of both animal life and death'. Such a shift has facilitated the exploitation of 'real life' animals for/in art: for instance, in some later 20th-century art involving chickens, the sense of transgression or estrangement has been produced through the use of actual birds (not painted or sculpted substitutes) for the art, by incorporating the skin, feathers, feet, meat or full carcasses of chickens into individual works. Such a ploy is not necessarily motivated by pro-animal sentiment or animal activism, as the art of Pinar Yolacan demonstrates: in her 2004 series entitled *Perishable art*, Yolacan involved chicken intestines, skins, feet, and heads in the formation of Victorian-style fashion garments modelled by women in their 70s.

The dresses, embellished with ruffles, frills, and fancy collars, typical of earlier fashion styles, and made from the flesh of recently killed chickens and other animals, were important to Yolacan's focus on disrupting Western photographic portraiture tradition, not to any critique of the subjugation of animals in human cultures. Likewise, Elpida Hadzi-Vasileva used 3000 chicken skins (obtained from a halal butcher over many weeks) in her 2008 wall hanging 'We are shadows', commissioned for an exhibition by the London Metropolitan University. Hadzi-Vasileva declared that the purpose of this piece was to emphasise the loss, struggle and conflict of immigrant communities (cited in *Bristol Evening Press* 2009).

Hence, chicken bodies can be used in transgressive art that comments more on human concerns and issues; in other words, anthropocentric art which ultimately furthers the exploitation of chickenkind (Potts 2012).[6] However, the same shifting 'visual economy of animal life and death' that results in the use of actual animals in anthropocentric art has also led to the appearance of animal bodies in protest art that deliberately aims to counter animal exploitation. In this context, the practice of incorporating the skin, flesh and offal, heads and limbs of slaughtered animals in art works to draw attention to the living conditions and deaths of chickens themselves, and not to any

---

6   The use of chicken carcasses in 'art' is not exclusive to the 21st century. In 1964 Carolee Schneeman's film *Meat joy* showed a group of people in various stages of undress writhing around together among flayed and featherless dead chickens. The purpose of this art was apparently to celebrate life while acknowledging the certainty of its underside, death, as well as to draw attention to the transience of life (the meat signifying the very visceral decay of the body).

metaphorical or metaphysical human-centred concern. One such activist artist is New Zealand-based Angela Singer who employs discarded
parts of animals in her art in order to disrupt the conventional view that
nonhuman beings are 'naturally' ours to use, kill and eat. For one exhibition in Auckland emphasising the parts of animals (stripped of their
animal identity) that people use and ignore in their homes, Singer created a 'chicken kitchen curtain'. She salvaged discarded chicken claws
from a local butchery and attached these to a sheet comprised of latex
and powder and painted the colour of the orange, fake chicken season-
ing sprinkled on French fries. Here she explains what occurred:

> The chicken kitchen curtain hung in a small space, slightly out from
> the wall, the chicken claws stuck out and caught on people's clothing
> when they walked too close. At the opening of the show I saw people
> react quite angrily, and some were revolted when they realized what
> the curtain was made of. There was another show opening in the
> gallery the same night. The finger food was chicken sushi so people
> were coming out of that show, and walking into my show eating
> chicken and getting upset about chicken claws! (Angela Singer, per-
> sonal communication, 29 September 2008).

The critique of capitalism and animal exploitation is also central to the
art of New York-based animal activist and self-described 'visual journalist' Sue Coe. Coe's easily recognisable works are intended to shock;
they portray explicit cruelty towards animals occurring within scientific laboratories, slaughterhouses, hatcheries, agribusiness and the
entertainment industry. Not shying away from graphic scenes of
chicken processing plants, or the agony of intensive farming practices
such as debeaking and the killing of newly hatched male chicks, Coe's
work is inspired by a deep commitment to socio-political change, as
well as the personal witnessing of such routine procedures in factory
farming situations. In an interview with the *LA Times*, Coe stated: 'I
want [people] to investigate further . . . I'm not proselytizing. I'm saying, "Please see for yourself. Go to a slaughterhouse. See what occurs.
And if you can't, ask yourself why" ' (cited in Vaughn 2009). Many of
Coe's works focus on pain and death. These motifs are common in animal art and representation, according to Burt. They draw attention to
and reinforce an important symbolic – and even more significant prac-

tical – difference between humans and animals: humans assume the right to sacrifice or kill animals: '[sacrifice] is taken as defining the us and the them, it provides the criteria for the "noncriminal putting to death", and the identity of those beings that it is acceptable to subject to total control' (Burt 2008, 8).

Visual culture experts also argue that animal art has the potential to disrupt assumptions about coherent species identity – not just that of the human, but of the animal as well (Burt 2009). In her activist art foregrounding the commodification and exploitation of chickens (as well as other farmed animals), Australian Yvette Watt aims to be confrontational and thought-provoking without unduly alienating the viewer. Watt's series of paintings called *Offerings*, based on real life rescued farm animals, features a portrait of *Sally*, a former battery hen now living on a farm sanctuary. Confusing the place of chicken and human, Sally's face and upper body is painted onto a large white linen tea-towel in Watt's own blood. Because this medium quickly changes to a sepia colour as it dries, Watt is able to ensure the viewer's initial engagement is with the image of Sally, rather than the more sensational connotations of the painting's medium:

> The intention is that, on discovering the nature of the painting medium used, the viewer will be caused to consider the matter of these animals as flesh and blood – and hence as meat. As such it was essential that the blood used was *my* blood, as I see these works as gestures of solidarity with those animals that are killed in their billions for meat; as a kind of offering, a symbolic giving up of my blood, a recognition of the spilling of the blood of these animals for meat production and of the fact that their blood stains the kitchens of most homes (Watt, personal communication, 25 September 2009)

More recently Watt has turned to documentary photography of large scale factory farms across Australia as a means of enabling viewers to engage with chickens (and pigs) as sentient beings rather than objectified commodities. The images of intensive farms are taken by the artist from publicly accessible points such as roadsides; no trespassing is required – for while the 'farm animals' themselves are concealed from the public, the enormous buildings incarcerating them are not. As Watt explains: 'the absence of [chickens] in the imagery serves to highlight the hidden and secretive nature of the unnatural and restricted environments endured by the [birds] housed inside the windowless sheds'. It also places the viewer in the position of having to imagine what 'might be seen inside the sheds' were they able to enter (personal communication, 12 November 2012).[7]

Chicken advocacy in popular music

When image and sound combine, the effect can be powerful. Musicians who are also chicken advocates have used their unique ability to reach out to listeners as well as viewers in their efforts to protest against the contemporary disregard and abuse of chickens. For instance, vegan musician Moby produced a video to accompany his song, 'Disco lies' (a piece whose lyrics focus on betrayal) involving a newly hatched chick who quickly realises, upon witnessing fellow chickens caged, slaughtered, decapitated and dismembered, that his kind has been deceived and abused by humans, and one human in particular. Luckily avoiding a similar fate, and growing up to become a human-sized (and fashionable) rooster, he sets off to seek retribution. The traitor turns out to be a debauched and greedy man closely resembling Colonel Sanders, whom the chicken hero pursues until he catches him by a chicken meat stall. There the Colonel is decapitated by the rooster, the final scene showing the rebellious rooster before a platter of human legs drizzled with gravy on a fine looking salad.[8]

While Moby's music video utilises comedy to get across a much less sanguine message to viewers, English musician Morrissey – formerly of The Smiths – applies a frankly confrontational technique – more like Coe's – to educate his fans about the realities of chicken farming and slaughter. The lyrics in The Smith's 1986 single, 'Meat is murder', from the album of the same name, expose the suffering inherent in meat production while the video accompanying this song features graphic imagery from a variety of farms and slaughterhouses, including broiler

---

7   Watt's project is entitled 'Animal factories: a visual investigation into the hidden lives of animals in industrial agriculture' (2011–2012).
8   Retrieved 13 March 2013 from www.moby.com/discograpy/singles/disco-lies.html.

sheds, battery farms and chicken meat processing plants.[9] During Morrissey's live concerts, performances of 'Meat is murder' are accompanied by shocking footage displayed on a large screen behind the band; this is not the limit of the audience's exposure to the artist's protest, however, as accompanying the live music, poignant lyrics of the song, and the explicit imagery of farms and slaughter, are the actual noises of the animals appearing on film.[10]

Conclusion

Twenty years ago renowned biologist Lesley Rogers, author of *Brain and development in the chicken* (1995, 231), asserted that 'there is a demand to understand the cognitive abilities of the domestic chicken above all avian species, because this bird is the one we have singled out for intensive farming. *Gallus gallus domesticus* is indeed the avian species most exploited and least respected'. Recently, prominent African-American author Alice Walker (2006, 170) questioned humans' continued reticence to acknowledge and truly engage with chickens as sentient beings: ' "Why do you keep putting off writing about me?" It is the voice of a chicken that asks this'. The key to a more compassionate and respectful future for our species' relationship with *Gallus gallus domesticus* lies in re-establishing the kind of esteem in which these birds were once held. The dominance of intensive farming has rendered invisible not just the suffering of the birds it subjects, but also the knowledge and appreciation that many human societies once had of the ways in which chickens lived naturally. As a result, it has become easy to dismiss chickens as unworthy of consideration. Associated with dim-wittedness and cowardice – the very opposite of the traits that humans perceived in hens and cockerels prior to industri-

---

9   See www.youtube.com/verify_age?next_url=/watch%3Fv%3D06c5Srk3fxM.
10 The authors, who attended a Morrissey concert in New York in October 2012, were bemused by the reaction of the audience, many of whom used various tactics to avoid the images and noises derived from the footage on screen. Some people left, others kept their heads down and did not watch the video. 'Meat is murder' was performed for longer than any other song on that night, and afterwards we observed that applause was muted.

alisation – factory-farmed chickens are made easily killable, and their suffering is made inconsequential. For chicken advocates, then, there is still much to be done in returning to visibility not just the suffering and death of farmed chickens, but also their lives, their beings and their natures. For contemporary urban dwellers, whose own lives so often remain distant from those of living chickens, the proliferating and ever-changing world of visual culture offers the most promising domain in which this kind of reconnection can take place.

Works cited

Adams C (2003). *The pornography of meat*. New York: Continuum.

Anderson M (2005). Dissecting 'subservient chicken'. *Adweek*, 7 March [Online]. Available: www.adweek.com/news/advertising/ dissecting-subservient-chicken-78190 [Accessed 12 March 2013].

Armstrong P (2007). Farming images. In L Simmons & P Armstrong (Eds). *Knowing animals* (pp105–30). Leiden: Brill.

Baker S (1993). *Picturing the beast: animals, identity, and representation*. Chicago: University of Chicago Press.

Berger J (1980). Why look at animals. In *About looking* (pp1–26). London: Writers and Readers.

Bramwell S (2006). Fowl play. *The Press* ('At home'), November, p. 23.

Bristol Evening Post (2008). Bristol butcher's chicken skins turned into art. [Online]. Available: www.thisisbristol.co.uk/news/article-232248-details/ article.html [Accessed 10 November 2012].

Burt J (2002). *Animals in film*. London: Reaktion.

Burt J (2008). The aesthetics of livingness. *Antennae*, 5: 4–11.

Davis K (2003). United Poultry Concerns urges President Bush to stop using chickens in Iraq. [Online]. Available: www.upc-online.org/nr/31103iraq.htm. [Accessed 12 November 2012].

Davis K (2010). Chicken–human relationships: from procrustean genocide to empathic anthropomorphism. *Spring*, 83(Summer): 253–78.

Dixon J (2002). *The changing chicken: chooks, cooks and culinary culture*. Sydney: University of New South Wales Press.

Fox MW (1997). *Eating with conscience: the bioethics of food*. Oregon: New Sage Press.

Franklin A (1999). *Animals in modern cultures*. London: Sage.

Genosko G (2005). Natures and cultures of cuteness. *Invisible Culture* 9 [Online]. Available: www.rochester.edu/in_visible_culture/Issue_9/genosko.html [Accessed 15 November 2012].

Hughes R (1990). Codeine analgesic and morphine hyperalgesic effects on thermal nociception in domestic fowl. *Pharmacology, Biochemistry, and Behavior*, 35: 567–70.

Hughes R & Sufka KJ (1990). The ontogeny of thermal nociception in domestic fowl: thermal stimulus intensity and isolation effects. *Developmental Psychobiology*, 23(2): 129–40.

Jasper J (1997). *The art of moral protest: culture, biography and creativity in social movements*. Chicago: University of Chicago Press.

Jones P (2006). I know why the caged bird Sings. *Satya*, February [Online]. Available: www.satyamag.com/feb06/jones.html [Accessed 15 November 2012].

Kubberod E (2005). Not just a matter of taste: disgust in the food domain. Unpublished dissertation, BI Norwegian School of Management.

Malamud R (2010). Animals on film: the ethics of the human gaze. *Spring*, 83 (Summer): 135–60.

Mark P (2006). The importance of being honest: the *Satya* interview with Patty Mark. *Satya*, September [Online]. Available: www.satyamag.com/sept09/mark.html [Accessed 10 November 2012].

Potts A (2012). *Chicken*. London: Reaktion.

Purdy M (2004). First analysis of chicken genome offers many new insights. Press release 8 December. *EurekAlert!* [Online]. Available: www.eurekalert.org/pub_releases/2004-12/wuso-fao120604.php [Accessed 3 May 2013].

Mestel R (2004). The chicken's genetic code is cracked. *LA Times*, 9 December [Online]. Available: articles.latimes.com/2004/dec/09/science/sci-chicken9 [Accessed 23 October 2011].

Rogers L (1995). *The development of brain and behaviour in the chicken*. Oxfordshire: CABI.

Vaughn S (2001). Staying true to a unique vision of art: interview with Sue Coe. *LA Times*, 1 April [Online]. Available: graphicwitness.org/coe/latimes.htm [Accessed 13 March 2013].

Walker A (2004). An open letter to David Novak, CEO Yum! Brands (parent company of KFC), Mothers' Day, 9 May 2004. [Online]. Available: www.scribd.com/doc/98893916/Alice-Walker-on-KFC-cruelty. [Accessed 16 November 2012].

Walker A (2006). Why did the Balinese chicken cross the road. In *Living by the word*. London: Orion.

Walker A (2011). *The chicken chronicles: a memoir*. London: Orion.

10
Learning from dead animals: horse sacrifice in ancient Salamis and the Hellenisation of Cyprus

Agata Mrva-Montoya

> Arguably the most significant [human–animal] interaction, and certainly the most visible archaeologically, is killing them.
>
> *Russell 2012, 144*

Horses were rarely eaten or sacrificed in the ancient Mediterranean. From time to time, however, horse sacrifice was enacted as part of funerary celebrations. Although rare, this custom was widespread culturally and geographically, and typically associated with aristocracy and status display (Carstens 2005). In Cyprus, a series of tombs with remains of horses and donkeys was found in the necropolis of Salamis and dated to the eighth and the seventh centuries BC. Almost all the deposits follow the same pattern with one or more pairs of equids, still yoked to an elaborate funerary chariot or hearse, found lying on the floor of the tomb entrance (Karageorghis 1965, 1967, 1969; Rupp 1988).

Since the tombs were excavated in the 1950s and 1960s, the presence of horse sacrifice in Salamis has been linked with 'Homeric' rituals and woven into the narrative of the Hellenisation of Cyprus. This narrative equates the arrival of people from the Aegean during the 12th and 11th centuries BC with the colonisation of Cyprus. While there

A Mrva-Montoya (2013). Learning from dead animals: horse sacrifice in ancient Salamis and the Hellenisation of Cyprus. In J Johnston & F Probyn-Rapsey (Eds). *Animal death*. Sydney: Sydney University Press.

is no doubt that Cyprus was Hellenised in antiquity, the dating and detailed reconstruction of the process remains contentious and highly politicised.[1]

This chapter aims to investigate what can be learned about the human–animal relationship in ancient Cyprus and the cultural identity of people who carried out and witnessed the public enactments of animal death. Similarly to Russell (2012, 5), I am looking at animals from the anthropocentric perspective, using their remains to understand the people of ancient Cyprus. Through the investigation of the cultural associations and the symbolism of horse sacrifice in Cyprus, I aim to demonstrate that the culture of the Salamis elite in the eighth and seventh century BC was far from being Hellenised.

Looking at dead animals

Bones of dead animals are a frequent occurrence at archaeological sites, in settlement, ritual and funerary contexts. Finds of disarticulated (out-of-natural arrangement) and fragmented bones typically represent what animals were eaten, how they were butchered and how the remains were disposed of. These bones represent the results of human agency and reflect cultural practices of past societies. Once deposited or buried in the ground, the animal bones were affected by post-deposition environmental and human actions as well as natural processes, before the modern excavation and recovery procedures made them available for archaeological interpretation.

Apart from fragmented bones, complete or partially articulated animal skeletons are occasionally found in archaeological excavations. These animals, or their parts, were deposited with some portion of connective tissue in place, causing the bones to remain in anatomically correct arrangement throughout the post-deposition processes. In the past, these 'special animal deposits' were interpreted in connection with

---

1 As Leriou pointed out, the development of Cypriot archaeology in the late 19th and early 20th century against the background of the Ottoman (1151–1878) and British occupations (1878–1960) has been heavily influenced by the idealisation of ancient Greece, the 'enosis' movement and the growth Cypriot nationalism, and in more recent times by the Turkish invasion (1974–present) (Leriou 2007, 566–67).

ritual activities, until Hill (1995, 16) suggested the term 'articulated or associated animal bone group (ABG)'. Considered apart from associations of 'ritual' or 'other special' treatment, the term ABG allows for a functional or mixed interpretation transcending the sacred and profane dichotomy typical of modern thinking.

Although some ABGs discovered in association with human activity may be a result of natural or accidental death, these animals were more likely killed for a specific purpose. Animals and their death have been an intrinsic part of ritual and social transactions in many societies, including contemporary Western culture (for example, the Christmas or Thanksgiving turkey). In the archaeological context, together with other remains of material culture, dead animals allow the reconstruction of the life of past peoples, their economy and subsistence strategies. They can also provide an insight into the social structure of past societies and how it changed over time. Finally, they can contribute to the understanding of past human–animal relations.

In contrast to settlement deposits, both ABGs and disarticulated remains found in tombs (in Cyprus and elsewhere) were typically formed as a result of a single event. The majority of tombs in Salamis, however, were used for a secondary burial, with the remains of an earlier interment subject to disturbance, physical damage or removal and the potential loss of links with the individual burials, related grave goods and animal remains. Apart from the effects of re-use of tombs, some evidence was lost due to looting, or poor excavation techniques of early archaeologists (Rupp 1988, 119).

Depending on their articulation and the state of preservation, animal bones found in a funerary context can elucidate the role that the animals played in the funerary ritual, which otherwise may be invisible in archaeological records (funerary procession, for example). Fragmentary bones are often remains of funerary feasts and sacrifices, food offerings for afterlife, or gifts to appease the gods. Worked bone could have been components of dress or paraphernalia (Russell 2012, 64). Whole ABGs may represent companion animals or status symbols killed to mark the funerary celebrations. Some animals played an active role in funerary ritual providing transport to the final resting place but also, once sacrificed, in the afterlife (Russell 2012, 68).

Horse sacrifice in Salamis

A series of ABGs found in tombs discovered west of Salamis has been
dated to the second half of the eighth and seventh centuries BC on
the basis of pottery types found among the grave goods. Most of the
tombs, with an expansive dromos (entrance)[2] leading to a raised propylaeum (entrance) with an ashlar facade concealing a relatively small
burial chamber, were re-used for a second burial after a period of up to
several decades (except tomb 3 and possibly 50a which contained single
burials).

The absence of systematic bone analyses from Salamis means that
the understanding of tomb demographics, age and gender of deceased
is limited. While the social and biological relationships of the individuals buried in the same tombs is unknown, it seems likely that they were
linked by kinship or other social ties, reinforcing the common ancestry
and group allegiance. The members of these kinship groups or families organised and enacted the funerary ceremonies, which culminated
in a horse sacrifice. The elaborate funerary ritual, accompanied by the
display of 'the Near Eastern and Greek symbols of status, prestige, and
power' (Rupp 1988, 129), could have been seen by a large number of
mourners and spectators.

The horses most likely took part in the funerary procession drawing a cart/hearse or a chariot with the body of the deceased. Two,
three or even four horses wearing elaborate bronze and leather trappings would draw a single vehicle. In three burials (two in tomb 79 and
a single burial in tomb 3) both a cart and a chariot were found and
they most likely played different roles: the cart probably transported the
corpse, while the chariot with horses was part of a funerary equipment
(Karageorghis 1965, 284), meant for use by the deceased in the afterlife. Once the burial rites were performed, the body of the deceased or
his/her cremated remains were placed in the tomb chamber; the grave
goods were arranged in the chamber, the propylaeum or the lower part
of the dromos; the horses were killed while still yoked to the vehicles.
Finally the dromos was filled and a tumulus (mound) may have been

---

2   The dimension of the smallest dromos of tomb 19 are – width min: 3.2 m and
max: 3.7 m and length ca 3.7 m. The dimensions of the largest dromos of tomb 50
are: width min: 6.9 m and max: 12.5 m, and length ca 27.6 m (Rupp 1988, 118).

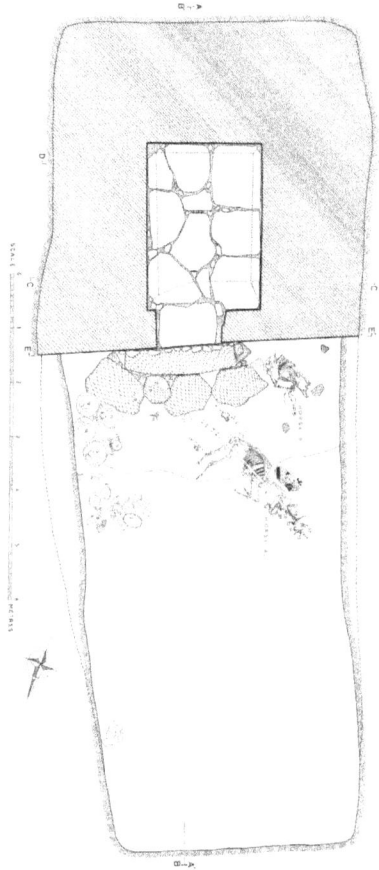

Figure 10.1 Salamis, Tomb 2: plan with finds in the dromos in situ. After Karageorghis 1967, fig. VI. Reproduced with permission of the Department of Antiquities, Cyprus.

built above the tomb. When the tomb was re-used for a second burial, the lower part of the dromos, the propylaeum and the chamber were cleared and the entire ritual was performed again (Rupp 1988, 121–22).

The logistics of how the actual killing of horses was executed have been inferred from the way the ABGs were preserved. While one of the animals associated with a single burial was typically found lying on its side in front of the propylaeum, the other horse or horses had their necks twisted round the yoke and their bodies stretched opposite and not parallel to the first horse. Some horses managed to break loose and they seem to have been stoned to death in other parts of the propylaeum and the dromos. Overall, the position of the skeletons indicates that the animals must have panicked following the death of the first horse (dispatched with a single stroke) and were killed while struggling, some may have even been buried alive in the process of filling the dromos (Karageorghis 1969, 31, 53–54).

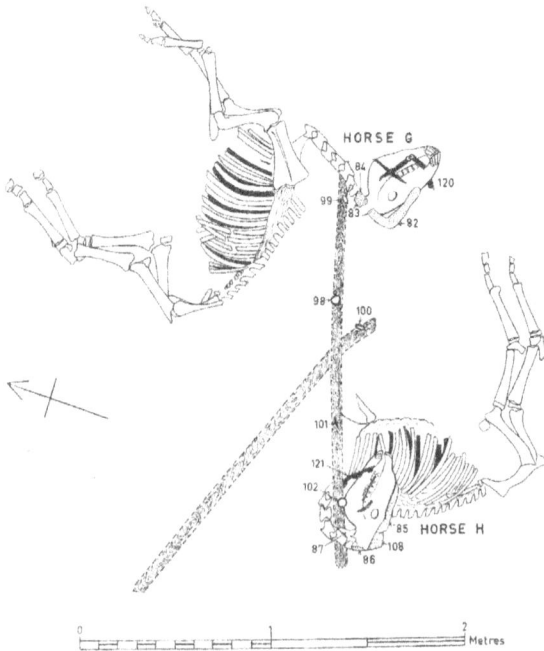

Figure 10.2 Salamis, Tomb 47: skeletons of horses G and H (first burial) in situ. After Karageorghis 1967, fig. XXIX. Reproduced with permission of the Department of Antiquities, Cyprus.

Several of the ABGs were found without traces of harness or vehicles – two horses were found lying on their side in tomb 31 and one in tomb 19. Karageorghis (1965, 284) interpreted them as a sacrifice parallel to the custom described by Homer in the *Iliad*. The horses in Salamis, however, were not burned. Apart from horses, in tomb 2 evidence of human and cattle sacrifice was found. Moreover, in the less wealthy burials of the seventh century BC, asses were killed instead of horses, and then the custom was discontinued.

The violent death of horses and donkeys in Salamis, although gruesome in the context of the invisibility of animal death in the modern West, may not have been anything out of the ordinary. The remains of animals such as cattle, goats and sheep in a ritual context indicate that animal sacrifice was a frequent occurrence in Cyprus from at least the Late Cypriot (LC) period[3] to the end of antiquity (Marczewska 2005, 455). In funerary context, caprids (but also cattle) were usually deposited as joints of meat, but sporadically a whole calf was present in tombs of EC–MC periods. In the LC tombs, ABGs of immature caprids or joints of meat of older individuals were found and the findings of animal remains in tombs of Cypro-Geometric (CG) and later periods confirm that the species continued to play a role in the mortuary ritual (Marczewska 2005, 455). The interpretation of animal remains in a funerary context, especially when only disarticulated and/or fragmented remains are found, requires a thorough investigation of the treatment of the bones, including the traces of burning, cut marks, cut choices etc., to conclude whether the flesh was provided for the journey into the afterlife, or constitute the remnants of a sacrifice for the dead, or leftovers of a ritual consumption as part of mortuary festivities.[4]

In contrast, the ABGs of non-food domesticates like dogs or horses may be the remains of a sacrifice of a companion animal. In the case of Salamis, however, the way the animals were killed and buried does not imply that a special bond existed between them and the deceased, even

---

3 Late Cypriot period is dated to 1600–1050 BC. Please see the end of chapter for the list of abbreviations and chronology.
4 For example, Croft interpreted the lack of cut marks and the occurrence of less edible lower legs in LC tombs at Kalavassos *Ayios Dhimitrios* as an indication that the meat was deposited intact, perhaps even uncooked, rather than representing scraps from the funeral feast (Croft 1989).

though these horses must have been treated as individuals, which was a predominant approach to domestic animals in the preindustrial ancient world (Clutton-Brock 1994, 33–34). The presence of horses in tombs of Salamis can be interpreted in the context of the economic exploitation of animals (Benton 1993, 62). Horses were used in funerary processions as draught animals, as well as symbols of wealth and status. These domestic animals were accorded a high value and a special position in the society. They were hardly ever eaten or sacrificed in a non-burial context. Horses may have also been used as a symbol of social identity. Since the discovery of the 'Royal Tombs' in Salamis, the custom of horse sacrifice has been linked with Mycenaean migrants and the Homeric burial ritual described in the *Iliad* (Karageorghis 1969, 27). But this association is somewhat problematic.

The 'Homeric' origins of horse sacrifice

In the *Illiad* (dated to around eighth century BC but set in the time of Bronze Age collapse in the early 12th century BC) four horses were sacrificed alongside nine dogs and 12 men (sons of the Trojan elite), and burned in the pyre together with Patroclus' body. The discovery of Late Bronze Age horse sacrifices in the Aegean has prompted suggestions that the epic might have been inspired by actual rituals, memory of which was passed down through oral tradition (Carstens 2005, 66). It has also been proposed that the description may have inspired later funerary celebrations of affluent warriors (Carstens 2005, 63). The archaeological records show, however, that in none of the currently known burials in Greece were the horses burned in the pyre (Kosmetau 1993, 32). This is to be expected, as even in the *Iliad* the pyre of dead Patroclus would not burn without the gods' intervention.

Putting poetic invention aside, it is theoretically possible that the 'Royal Tombs' were inspired by actual rituals performed in honour of the noblemen in prehistoric Greece. As Reese pointed out, however, equid remains were known from numerous Cypriot burials of EC (2300–1900 BC) and MC (1900–1600 BC) date, and they pre-date those found in Greece (Reese 1995, 35). In Greece, apart from Dendra, where a pair of horses was found in Tumulus B and C (both burials dated to the Middle Helladic period, 2100–1550 BC), most of the examples come from the Argolid and are dated to the Late Helladic period (1550–1060 BC). Usually a single animal or a pair of horses was yoked to a chariot that escorted a male deceased. The horses were killed after the body of the deceased was interred and deposited in the grave together with the chariot (Kosmetau 1993, 32).[5]

Not only does the presence of horse sacrifice in Cypriot burials predate the known Greek examples, but also the interval between the arrival of Mycenaeans in Cyprus during the 12th and 11th centuries BC (Knapp 2009, 223–24) and the reappearance of the custom in eighth-century Salamis is difficult to explain if the ritual was brought over from the Aegean.

Keeping in mind the insularity of Cyprus and a tendency of isolated societies to develop a strong sense of social identity (Knapp 2008, 29), it is plausible that horse sacrifice in Salamis was a resurfacing of the local custom. Once again, however, there is a long hiatus between LC and CA examples of horse sacrifice, which can only partly be explained by the cyclical pattern of mortuary display discussed below or cultural continuity. The question must be asked: why did the custom of horse sacrifice (re-)emerge at this particular time?

Looking outside Cyprus, an interesting analogy can be found in eastern Anatolia,[6] where an Urartian chamber tomb was discovered in Altintepe near Lake Van. Dated to the early seventh century BC, the tomb's equipment includes a bronze cauldron, remains of a war chariot, horse trappings, furniture and pottery among other items, a similar array of items as found in tomb 79 in Salamis (Carstens 2005, 68). Apart from two so-called Urartian cauldrons, examples of richly decorated furniture decorated in the Assyrian/Phoenician style was associated with the first burial in tomb 79 and the whole assemblage was interpreted as belonging to the north Syrian/Urartian sphere (Karageorghis 1969, 89).

---

5 An example of horse sacrifice found on Crete (dated to Late Minoan IIIA period, ca 1400–1300 BC), associated with the burial of a prominent female and unique in being cut to pieces, seems to belong to a different tradition to mainland Greek or Cypriot models (Kosmetau 1993, 34).
6 Carstens also pointed out to the Phrygian tumuls chamber tombs from Central Anatolia. One of the tombs (KY), dated to seventh century BC and interpreted as Cimmerian, included a pair of horses (Carstens 2005, 69).

The Urartians were known for their horse breeding and training skills as described in a letter on Sargon II's eighth campaign against Urartu in 714 BC (Dalley 1985, 42–43; Carstens 2005, 69). A small group of administrative cuneiform tablets from Nimrud, known as Horse Lists, also dated to the reign of Sargon II (721–705 BC), contains names of many of the top equestrian officers in Sargon's army. Their names indicate that by the late eighth century BC the Assyrian royal army included Urartian experts on cavalry and Samarian experts on chariotry who worked with horses imported from Nubia (Dalley 1985, 47–48).

As Dalley (1985, 47) concluded,

the late 8th century was a time when the Assyrians were increasingly aware of the importance of equestrian technology. Suddenly during this period cavalry in particular developed into a newly powerful weapon of war. Innovation in the form of breeds of horses, methods of harnessing and of importing foreign experts, in particular from Nubia and Samaria for chariotry, from Urartu for cavalry, contributed to that development.

The equestrian elite was responsible not only for disseminating their expertise with horses, but also their culture including ivory styles and techniques, and luxury furnishings (Dalley 1985, 48).

While the horse played an important role in the Assyrian royal iconography, the evidence for horse sacrifice in a funerary context is limited. The sacrifice of at least ten horses, together with 30 oxen and 300 sheep, was part of funerary ritual described in a Neo-Assyrian text dated to the reign of Esarhaddon (681–669 BC) or Ashurbanipal (668–627 BC). The animals served one of three functions: they were used for draught in the funerary procession, killed for a banquet, or as offerings to various deities (McGinnis 1987, 10), in a similar way to the funerary rituals of Ur-Namma, the first king of the Third Dynasty of Ur (2112–2095 BC). The text describing his death also shows that the function of the chariot may have been greater than simply the transporting of the body to the tomb: Ur-Namma used the chariot to arrive in the underworld (McGinnis 1987, 10).

As can be seen from the examples above, the cultural associations of horse sacrifice are complex and cannot be unequivocally used to support a Greek identity of the people buried in the tombs of Salamis.

The ethnicity of the first kings of Salamis

Apart from the 'Homeric' origins of horse sacrifice, other arguments were used to support the hypothesis that the first rulers of Salamis were of Mycenaean extraction and their culture was Greek: the tomb architecture, the provenance of grave offerings, and the foundation legends. The latter were preserved in the works of classical Greek writers according to which Salamis was established by Mycenaean hero Teucer, son of Telamon, king of the Greek island of Salamis (Karageorghis 1969, 20).

The architecture of the tombs – with a chamber built of stone, a facade made of dressed ashlar masonry, and a trapezoidal, gently sloping dromos providing access to a formal display area in front of the main chamber – is unusual in the context of Cypro-Geometric and Cypro-Archaic Cyprus, where tombs are typically small with irregular rock-cut chambers. Rupp suggested that Salamis tombs may have been inspired by the public and religious architecture of Phoenicia (Rupp 1988, 125).

The direct association between the presence of Greek pottery among the grave goods and ethnic identity of the deceased has been attributed to the culture historical approach (also known as an 'equation between pots and people') and methodologically discredited (Leriou 2007, 564). The presence of Greek imports can be better explained in terms of trade or gift exchange of high prestige goods (Rupp 1998, 128–29).

The value of foundation legends for the reconstruction of the ethnic identity of the first rulers of Salamis is undermined by their 'much later date, limited number, Greek origin and association with ancient Greek political propaganda' (Leriou 2007, 574). Interestingly, Iacovou has recently pointed out two minor details of the Teukros/Teucer legend which the proponents of the early Hellenisation narrative omitted and which would indicate that 'the foundation of Salamis was a joint venture of Greek, Phoenician and indigenous people'.[7] It is only in the second half of the sixth century BC that the Greek identity of the king of Salamis becomes irrefutable: Evelthon had a Greek name, issued coins with syllabic Greek legends, and sent a votive deposit to a Greek sanctuary (Iacovou 2006, 45).

A close critique of all the evidence used to support the theory that the first rulers in Salamis were Hellenised is beyond the scope of this chapter. Nevertheless, given the mixture of Aegean, Cypriot and Levantine elements in the available material, this evidence can be interpreted in terms of hybridisation practices (Knapp 2009, 223) and the cultural identity of the rulers of eighth-century Salamis remains ambiguous.

This view is consistent with AT Reyes' suggestion that in the Cypro-Archaic period it is best to speak of 'distinctively Cypriot, as opposed to Greek, culture, without drawing any inferences about the separate survival and existence of Greek or Eteocypriot groups within the island' (Reyes 1994, 12). As Reyes argued,

> the precise extent of the island's Hellenism by the beginning of the Cypro-Archaic period is difficult to gauge. The use of the Greek language, at least in parts of Cyprus, is certain. But although Cypriots claimed kinship with Greeks in their foundation myths, it still seems clear from written sources that the Greeks tended to regard the island as a distinctively foreign place, on the periphery of the Eastern world, if not part of it, with its own peculiar customs and features. (Reyes 1994, 12)

One of those customs was the sacrifice of horses, which seems to have been absent in Greece in the eighth and seventh century BC.

As Carstens (2005, 70–71) already noted, the kings of Salamis were part of the Near Eastern aristocratic culture and palace life. The hunting and war chariots drawn by horses are commonly represented as part of the royal iconography of the Assyrian king in reference to his role as a defender and protector of his lands. In view of Assyrian supremacy on

---

7   According to the version of the legend in Virgil's *Aeneid* (I, 619–626), Belos (king of Phoenician Sidon) assisted Teukros/Teucer in the foundation of Salamis. Later, as stated by Pausanias (1, 3.2), Teukros/Teucer married the daughter of Kinyras, the indigenous king and priest of the Great Cypriot goddess. (After Iacovou 2006, 44–45.)

Cyprus, it is not surprising that the local elite, whatever their ethnic extraction was, adopted a similar set of prestige symbolism.

Orientalisation as an active strategy of employing the Eastern symbolism of power by elites (Knapp 2006, 50) was not a new phenomenon in Archaic Cyprus. The horse sacrifices of the MC period have been linked to the local elite's desire to emulate foreign ideology, transmitted through personal interactions and the Near Eastern iconography present on glyptics and other items. At the time, horses were important status symbols for Syrian and Babylonian elites (Keswani 2005, 392–93). Similarly, the LC elites used Egyptian and Near Eastern objects decorated with complex iconography and ideology of kingship and royal power to 'establish, stabilise and legitimise social power' (Knapp 2006, 48–49).

Killing horses as a status statement

David Rupp (1988, 134–35) argued that the 'Royal Tombs' of Salamis were a 'chronologically and spatially discrete phenomenon' employed by the first rulers of Salamis as conscious symbolic statements of political and economic power. Once their position was consolidated, perhaps during the Persian domination of Cyprus in the mid-sixth century BC, such ostentatious displays ceased to be required and the killing of equids ceased.

The staging of elaborate funerary practices to enhance social standing of kin groups was not a novel phenomenon in eighth-century Cyprus. Keswani interpreted the increasing elaboration of mortuary practices in the Early Cypriot–Middle Cypriot (EC–MC, 2300–1600 BC) period as evidence of the funerary ritual being the focus of conspicuous consumption and competitive display. Later, in tombs of the LC elite (for example, at Enkomi), imported goods were used as symbols of prestige (Keswani 2005, 393–94), which was also the case in Salamis.

Naturally, elaborate funerary practices were not limited to Cyprus. Going beyond the practicalities of burying the dead and dealing with the emotional and social consequences of death, funerary ritual has often played a central role in community life, economy and distribution of inheritance in many societies, becoming a political event at which the status of the deceased, of the funeral organisers and of the mourners 'is actively negotiated and re-evaluated' (Parker Pearson 1999, 32, 84). Already in 1945, Gordon Childe remarked that 'big funerals often went with politically unstable and formative situations, that élite funerary ostentation contributed to political legitimation' (quoted in Parker Pearson 1999, 87), which seems to fit well with the political climate of eighth-century Salamis.

While extravagant mortuary customs were relatively common in Cyprus and elsewhere, horse sacrifice was not. Nevertheless, burials containing horse skeletons, chariots or elements of harness appear in different periods and regions of the ancient Mediterranean and the Near East, and have been consistently linked with wealth and nobility. For example, Vedic horse sacrifice described in the *Rig Veda*, was performed in connection with royalty or noble warriors from the second millennium BC to the 12th century AD (Zaroff 2005, 75, 84).

In Cyprus, equid remains appeared in several EC–MC tombs in Kathydhata, Lapithos *Vrysi tou Barba*, Episkopi *Phaneromeni*; MC tombs in Politico *Chomazoudhia*, Ayia Paraskevi, Kalopsidhia, Tamassos; and LC tombs in Hala Sultan Tekke and Kalavassos where they would have been placed as a status symbol or indication of a particular connection with the deceased rather than as a food offering (Reese 1995, 38–38). In the Cypro-Archaic (CA) period, apart from Salamis where the practice was widespread, horse remains and bronze trappings were found in the chamber of tomb 306 from Amathous (?CG/CA) (Reese 1995, 40). Tomb 2 in Patriki dated to CA II had a horse's skull placed on the roof (Ducos 1972). Moreover, horse and sheep remains were found in a dromos of a CA I tomb at Kouklia (Palaepaphos). All pieces of harness were in pairs so possibly there were originally two equids (Reese 1995, 38). Finally, tomb 4 at Tamassos (dated to the late seventh century BC) produced ABGs of two horses and a fine bronze helmet, but also bones of other animals (cattle, goat and sheep) (Buchholz 1973, 330–36; Nobis 1976–77, 280, 285).

The presence of ABGs of horses in a funerary context in Cyprus is an interesting phenomenon. Equids were probably introduced to the island in the early part of the Bronze Age (EC, 2300–1900 BC). As only small quantities of bone material are ever present in a settlement context and usually do not show evidence of butchery, it seems that the role of equids as either a beast of burden or a steed was far more important than as a dietary contribution.[8] Moreover, equid remains rarely appear in a sanctuary context, indicating that they were not considered suitable for a cult-related sacrifice. They may have been indirectly associated with the religious ritual on account of being used for the transport of cultic statues, priests and officials during religious ceremonies (Marczewska 2005, 455–56).

In contrast to other animals, such as cattle, goats and sheep, which were commonly eaten and sacrificed in Cyprus, the horse seems to have been accorded a special role. This is not an unusual attitude. As Lawrence pointed out, the horse has been strongly associated with aristocracy from the earliest times. The upper classes often not only have had an exclusive right to horse-riding, or the economic means to do so, but this connection extended into the domain of symbolism. The sheer distance from the ground and elevation above the pedestrian sets the rider above the unprivileged (Lawrence 1988, 99).

The growing importance of horsemanship in the emerging aristocracy in Cyprus is also evident in the iconography of Cypro-Geometric III (CG III, 850–750 BC) and CA periods. The practice of horse sacrifice in Salamis coincided with the growing popularity of horse representations among limestone and especially terracotta figurines, so that by the end of CG III the horse became the most commonly depicted animal species in the repertoire of terracotta production and the main type of vota deposited in temples of male deities. It seems that these figurines of horse-riders and charioteers reflected the social prestige conferred by the identification with cavalry, and the association with horse-rearing and horsemanship in general (Marczewska 2005, 456). In this context, the use of horses, chariots and other equipment to frame and identify the person in the aristocratic context in life, at the funeral and in the other world (Carstens 2005, 68), is hardly surprising.

As mentioned earlier, the later tombs of Salamis contained donkey sacrifice and then the custom was discontinued. Mortuary expenditure overall, as measured by the energy investment in the construction of tombs, the value of accumulated goods and sacrificed animals, de-

---

8 Occasionally, however, they may have been eaten, as indicated by the fragmented remains of equids at Marki Alonia (EC–MC I) (Croft 1996, 220, 222) and Maa Paleokastro (LC) (Croft 1988, 449–51). Equids found in LC wells were most likely cases of a carcass disposal (Reese 1995, 35–36).

Figure 10.3 Terracotta horse-and-rider figurine dated to Cypro-Archaic II (600–475 BC), provenance unknown. Nicholson Museum, Inv No: NM 47.378, on long-term loan from the Museum of Classical Archaeology, University of Cambridge. Reproduced with permission of the Nicholson Museum.

creases over time. This change in the level of ostentation display is consistent with the cyclical pattern in mortuary behaviour observed by Aubrey Cannon, among others. He demonstrated that cycles of increasing ostentation and subsequent restraint 'might emerge in any cultural context in which mortuary behaviour is a medium for competitive display' (Cannon 1989, 438). After a period of 'an initial elaboration of mortuary practices as the result of increased affluence, socioeconomic flux, and status uncertainty', mortuary ritual reaches a peak of elaborate display, which is followed by 'subsequent decline and ultimate prohibition of previously sanctioned forms of mortuary expression' (Cannon 1989, 438).

Conclusion

Learning from dead animals allows for insights into how various animal species were used in daily life, religious and community rituals and how the structure and the culture of Cypriot society changed over time, filling the gap created by the scarcity of written sources for the most part of the island's ancient past.

The rarity of horse sacrifice as part of funerary celebrations in the Mediterranean and the Near East in antiquity, especially in burials of females, and its common association with the aristocracy, indicates a custom connected with displaying the social position of the deceased. The examples of ABGs from Salamis correspond to this prestige theory particularly well, as confirmed by both the size of the tomb complexes and the quality of the offerings. The level of ostentation in the funerary ritual decreased over time, and donkeys replaced horses as sacrificial animals. This change and subsequent cessation of the ritual can be interpreted in connection with the cyclical patterns of increasing ostentation and subsequent restraint in funerary ritual. It can also be seen as a sign of increased stabilisation of the elite, associated social order and political organisation on the island.

The horses and donkeys, and indeed all the worldly goods found in the 'Royal Tombs', may have served several functions at the same time: they were used in the funerary ritual, demonstrated the status of the deceased and, once buried, provided food, transport and possessions for life in the underworld. They transcended the sacred and the profane. The Salamis horses and their sacrifice played an important part of the funerary ritual, contributing to the drama and emotional gravitas of the human transition to the other world. Instead of being obscured, minimised and morally distant, animal death was a central and visible part of life, and afterlife, in ancient Cyprus. At the same time, there was nothing ceremonial in the way these horses were killed and buried. They were certainly prized possessions, but even if a personal bond existed in life, the utilitarian functions seem to have prevailed.

The provenance of the custom of horse sacrifice cannot be unequivocally linked to the Mycenaean roots. Rather than evoking the Homeric ritual, the horse sacrifice reflects the growing importance of horsemanship amongst the emerging elites in Cyprus, coinciding with similar developments in the Near East. In fact, the identification of the ethnicity of Salamis rulers as Greek in the eighth and seventh century seems also conjectural, extending into the past later cultural developments and associated legendary claims. It is also symptomatic of projecting modern national identities and political complexities onto a past society. Mortuary rituals in Salamis were drawing on the Near Eastern symbolism of power, in a similar way to the orientalising strategy employed by the Cypriot elite in the earlier periods. In view of the currently available evidence and understanding of ethnicity as a fluid, dynamic and socially constructed category, it seems that the first rulers of Salamis were far more interested in highlighting their social, economic and political power than signalling a distinctive ethnic identity. In the context of the Hellenisation debate, it is clear that the culture of the eighth and seventh century Salamis, and by extension the rest of Cyprus, was far from being Hellenised.

Abbreviations and chronology

EC	Early Cypriot (2300–1900 BC)
MC	Middle Cypriot (1900–1600 BC)
LC	Late Cypriot (1600–1050 BC)
CG	Cypro-Geometric (1050–750 BC)
CA I	Cypro-Archaic I (750–600 BC)
CA II	Cypro-Archaic II (600–745 BC)

After Peltenburg 1989

Works cited

Benton T (1993). *Natural relations, ecology, social justice and animal rights.* London: Verso.

Buchholz H-G (1973). Tamassos, Zypern, 1970–1972, *Archäologischer Anzeiger* 88(3): 295–388.

Cannon A (1989). The historical dimension in mortuary expressions of status and sentiment. *Current Anthropology* 30(4): 437–58.

Carstens AM (2005). To bury a ruler: the meaning of the horse in aristocratic burials (pp57–76). In V Karageorghis, H Matthäus & S Rogge (Eds). *Cyprus: religion and society from the Late Bronze Age to the end of the Archaic period.* Proceedings of an International Symposium on Cypriote Archaeology,

Erlangen, 23–24 July 2004. Möhesse: Leventis Foundation; Institute for Classical Archaeology, University of Erlangen-Nuremberg; Institute for Interdisciplinary Cypriot Studies, University of Mu?nster.

Cassimatis H (1973). *Les rites funeraire à Chypre*. Report of the Department of Antiquities, Cyprus, 116–66.

Clutton-Brock J (1994). The unnatural world: behavioural aspects of humans and animals in the process of domestication. In A Manning & J Serpell, *Animals and human society: changing perspectives* (pp23–35). London & New York: Routledge.

Croft P (1996). Animal remains. In D Frankel & JM Webb (Eds). *Marki Alonia: an Early and Middle Bronze Age town in Cyprus. Excavations 1990–1994* (pp217–23, 315–20, tables 9.1–9.11). Studies in Mediterranean Archaeology CXXIII:1. Jonsered: Paul Åströms Förlag.

Croft P (1989). Animal bones. In A South, P Russell & PS Keswani (Eds). *Vasilikos Valley Project 3: Kalavassos–Ayios Dhimitrios II. Ceramics, objects, tombs, specialist studies* (pp70–72). Göteborg: Paul Åströms Förlag.

Croft P (1988). Animal remains from Maa-Paleokastro. In V Karageorghis & M Demas (Eds). *Excavations at Maa-Paleokastro 1979–1986* (pp449–57). Nicosia: Department of Antiquities.

Dalley S (1985). Foreign chariotry and cavalry in the armies of Tiglath-Pileser III and Sargon II. *Iraq* 47: 31–48.

Ducos P (1972). Le crane de cheval de Patriki. *Report of the Department of Antiquities, Cyprus*, 181–82, pl. XXXI, 3–4.

Hill JD (1995). *Ritual and rubbish in the Iron Age of Wessex*. Oxford: British Archaeological Reports (British series 242).

Iacovou M (2006). 'Greeks', 'Phoenicians' and 'Eteocypriots': ethnic identities in the Cypriote kingdoms. In J Chrysostomides & Ch Dendrinos (Eds). *Sweet land . . .: Cyprus through the ages* (pp27–59). Porphyrogenitus: Camberley.

Karageorghis V (1965). Horse burials on the island of Cyprus. *Archaeology* 18(4): 282–90.

Karageorghis V (1967). *Excavations in the necropolis of Salamis I*. Salamis vol. 3. Nicosia: Antiquities Department.

Karageorghis V (1969). *Salamis in Cyprus: Homeric, Hellenistic and Roman*. Norwich: Thames and Hudson.

Keswani P (2005). Death, prestige, and copper in Bronze Age Cyprus. *American Journal of Archaeology* 109(3): 341–401.

Knapp BA (2009). Migration, hybridisation and collapse: Bronze Age Cyprus and the Eastern Mediterranean. In A Cardarelli, A Cazzella, M Frangipane & R Peroni (Eds). *Scienze dell'antichitá*, Storia Archeologia Antropologia 15 (pp219–39). Roma: Department of Historical, Archaeological and Anthropological Sciences of Antiquity, Rome University 'La Sapienza'.

Knapp BA (2008). *Prehistoric and protohistoric Cyprus: identity, insularity and connectivity*. Oxford: Oxford University Press.

Knapp BA (2006). Orientalization and prehistoric Cyprus: the social life of oriental goods. In C Riva & NC Vella (Eds). *Debating orientalization: multidisciplinary approaches to change in the ancient Mediterranean*. Monographs in Mediterranean Archaeology 10 (pp48–65). London: Equinox Publishing.

Kosmetatou E (1993). Horse sacrifices in Greece and Cyprus. *Journal of Prehistoric Religion*, VII: 31–41.

Lawrence EA (1988). Horses in society. In AN Rowan (Ed.). *Animals and people sharing the world* (pp95–115). Hanover, NH: University Press of New England.

Leriou A (2007). Locating identities in the Eastern Mediterranean during the Late Bronze Age–Early Iron Age: the case of 'Hellenised' Cyprus. In S Antoniadou & A Pace (Eds), *Mediterranean crossroads* (pp563–91). Athens: Pierides Foundation.

Marczewska A (2005). Animals in ancient Cyprus. Unpublished PhD thesis, University of Sydney.

McGinnis J (1987). A Neo-Assyrian text describing a royal funeral. *State Archives of Assyria Bulletin* I(1): 1–13.

Nobis G (1976–77). Tierreste aus Tamassos auf Zypern. *Acta Praehistorica et Archaeologica* 7–8: 271–300.

Parker Pearson M (1999). *The archaeology of death and burial*. College Station: Texas A&M University Press.

Reese DS (1995). Equid sacrifices/burials in Greece and Cyprus: an addendum. *Journal of Prehistoric Religion* IX: 35–42.

Reyes AT (1994). *Archaic Cyprus: a study of the textual and archaeological evidence*. Oxford: Clarendon Press; New York: Oxford University Press.

Rupp DW (1988). The 'Royal Tombs' at Salamis (Cyprus): ideological messages of power and authority. *Journal of Mediterranean Archaeology* 1(1): 111–39.

Russell N (2012). *Social zooarchaeology: humans and animals in prehistory*. Cambridge: Cambridge University Press.

Zaroff R (2005). Aśvamedha: a Vedic horse sacrifice. *Studia Mythologica Slavica* VIII: 75–86.

11
The last image: Julia Leigh's *The hunter* as film

Carol Freeman

The pivotal scene in the film adaptation (Nettheim 2011) of Julia Leigh's book *The hunter* occurs near the end of the narrative, as it does in the book. The story revolves around a hunt undertaken in a vast and wild landscape for what is implied is the last, or close to the last, member of an Australian native species long presumed extinct. We see this elusive animal for the first time observing the hunter and then padding silently away through the snow. She turns to look at her pursuer. The film cuts to the human who raises his gun, hesitates, and then grimly pulls the trigger. The animal falls and the camera very slowly pans in to capture his crunching steps to the body. There he kneels, sobs, and tenderly carries the corpse away as the scene dissolves into mist.

Alternately in Leigh's novel (1999) 'M', as the male hunter is called, ultimately finds the animal with a kill and 'watches, fascinated' as she feeds. Eventually she jerks her head up from the carcass:

> Then snap, suddenly she is staring straight at him, eyes wide, and he watches as her cavernous jaw cleaves open and he listens to an unholy strangled hissing roar.

C Freeman (2013). The last image: Julia Leigh's *The hunter* as film. In J Johnston & F Probyn-Rapsey (Eds). *Animal death*. Sydney: Sydney University Press.

He shoots as soon as she starts to leap and the first bullet catches
her mid-air. The second and third bullets, fired in quick succession,
bring her to the ground.
And that is it. (Leigh 1999, 163)

Soon M has completed the job he was sent to do: he takes out his surgical kit, removes samples of the animal's blood and hair and then her
ovaries and uterus.

The messages conveyed in the book through descriptions of the animal's behaviour and the hunter's actions have been utterly changed,
transforming the significance of this scene and its implications for the
film in its entirety. The differences between the death of the animal in
the book and in the film expose the capabilities and the limitations of
each media and focus attention on their audiences. These differences
may also suggest that a new sensitivity toward species extinction has
arisen between 1999 when the book was published and 2011 when the
film was released.

This chapter will compare the novel and film *The hunter*, concentrating on the scene where the animal is killed and noting how the
process of adaptation can 'redistribute energies and intensities' (Stam
2005, 46).[1] I show how the film illustrates the challenges and also some
of the possibilities that arise when representing an individual animal's
demise, as well as extinction. Finally I evaluate the implications of the
textual differences between novel and film for human–animal relations
and species conservation efforts. As such, this study of an adaptation
will produce 'something new that neither belongs to film nor literature'
(Cartmell & Whelehan 2010, 14) but aims to contribute to the field of
animal studies in the humanities.[2]

---

1   The chapter owes its existence to an unpublished paper co-authored with Sally
Borrell for the Animal Death conference in Sydney, July 2012. It pursues and
extends ideas that arose in the process of writing that paper.
2   Exactly what the term 'animal studies' defines is still being debated within this
new field, but I favour Kim Stallwood's suggestion that it denotes 'various strands
of academic thinking that fall under it, including Human–Animal Studies, Critical
Animal Studies and Animalia Studies' (Stallwood 2012, 8) and, I would add,
anthrozoology.

The hunter

Leigh's book *The hunter* keys into the story of the thylacine or Tasmanian 'tiger', an extinct marsupial carnivore that existed in relatively
small numbers in Australia until about 3000 years ago. The species remained only on the island state of Tasmania, which was isolated by
rising sea levels after the waning of the most recent Ice Age. The last
captive member of the species died there in 1936. It is a compelling
and familiar story about the extinction of a colonial animal following
European settlement.[3] When the very first evidence of the thylacine
was found by white explorers, there arose fantastic ideas about how
the species might look and behave (Freeman 2010). To the present
day the intrigue remains among online enthusiasts and zoologists.[4]
Like the Japanese wolf that also disappeared in the early 20th century,
myths concerning the survival of the thylacine have arisen (Knight
1997), driven by the existence of relatively large tracts of dense and
undeveloped terrain in Tasmania. Numerous reports of sightings have
occurred since the 1950s, with a huge reward for evidence offered by
an Australian national magazine.[5] However, no photographs, verified
scats, or other firm evidence has emerged and, as a relatively large population with genetic diversity is needed to ensure species survival, it is
certain the thylacine no longer exists.

Leigh's novel picks up on these tantalising tales of sightings to
weave a story of what might happen if a thylacine survived into a postmodern world of international rivalry, terrorism and biowarfare. Her

3   For detailed zoological and historical information about the thylacine and
other recent extinctions in Australia, see Guiler (1985), Paddle (2000), and
Johnson (2006).
4   Popular websites and webpages with sometimes sensational material abound.
See, for instance, The Thylacine Museum www.naturalworlds.org/thylacine/;
Wikipedia's thylacine entry en.wikipedia.org/wiki/Thylacine; The Australian
Museum thylacine page australianmuseum.net.au/The-Thylacine; the Emberg's
page on sightings www.tasmanian-tiger.com/thylafiles.html and the Centre for
Fortean Zoology website www.cfzaustralia.com/2012/02/
nsw-thylacine-sightings-update.html.
5   On *The Bulletin*'s 125th birthday, the magazine offered $1.25 million reward for
conclusive proof that a living thylacine existed (Hoy 2005, 16–22). Several photos
were submitted, but none proved authentic.

protagonist is employed by a biotechnology company called Red Leaf to obtain genetic material from a thylacine. There is a hint that this material is to be used for the production of biological weapons, although the nature and process of their manufacture is never mentioned. It is a bleak, spare story of alienation and the determination of the company's agent, resulting in what Drusilla Modjeska calls a 'sense of desolation so utter, so complete, that it seems barely believable' (Modjeska 1999, 9). Leigh's writing is understated, exemplified by the naming of M, and the novel explores an attitude toward animals that sees them as beings to be used for whatever purpose humans desire. The narrative is structured around the hunt and the text focuses almost exclusively on actions and objects relating to the search and pursuit of the thylacine. It often revolves around issues mentioned in Matt Cartmill's seminal study of hunting *A view to death in the morning* that notes: '[the hunter] is a liminal and ambiguous figure, who can be seen either as a fighter against wildness or as a half-animal participant in it' (Cartmill 1993, 31). It also throws up many of the elements Garry Marvin isolates in his chapter 'Wild killing' in *Killing animals*; for instance, the distinction between the intentional hunting of the human and the spontaneous actions of a nonhuman animal, and the cultural aspect of human hunting as opposed to the natural function of animal hunting. Marvin quotes Roger King's comment that the hunter is never just an anonymous cipher, but a member of a particular culture, living in a particular moment in that culture's history. The hunter brings certain technologies to bear on the hunt, together with distinct beliefs and attitudes (Marvin 2006, 15).

Although M shows glimpses of empathy with the thylacine, what he displays is predominantly a hunter's need to understand animal behaviour and habits in order to effectively find and kill his quarry. His identification with the animal is always subsumed by the need to complete his task. For instance, he notes that 'the tiger does not chase her prey. Instead, she persists. She outlasts'. A paragraph later the text notes: 'I am patient, thinks M. I, too, can wait' (Leigh 1999, 38). He mulls over this last thylacine's condition: 'after years of inbreeding does she bear any behavioural resemblance to her forebears? . . . does she even have the energy to kill or has she . . . descended to picking at carrion?' Then, 'discouraged' by this 'ignoble' image, he sets about 'rectifying' the impression:

yes, there is virtue in being a survivor. The last tiger must be wary, she must be strong, she must be crafty and ruthless and wise. And if the mutation has endowed her with any new qualities, they must be qualities which enhance, not detract from, the inescapable drive to survive . . . This is what propels her day after day across the plateau: immortality. (Leigh 1999, 66)

So, in contrast to the film, he imagines an animal worthy of killing – a resilient beast, a hunter's mighty opponent – to avoid the idea that he is pursuing and destroying an old, ill or weak animal that does not deserve to die. Here M is fitting the profile of the sports hunter who engages in a contest to outsmart a cunning or strong animal. For example, 'the hunter competes with himself or herself in terms of attempting to exercise personal hunting skills, with the environment in which hunting takes place, and, finally, with the animal which [sic] is the focus of attention' and the hunted animal is given a chance to escape (Marvin 2006, 19). As he closes in on the thylacine in the latter part of the book, M is described as 'a natural man' who can 'see and hear and smell what other men cannot' (Leigh 1999, 161). As noted by Marvin, this is one of the central tenets of hunting, where the distinction between the human and animal becomes blurred.[6] Soon, M notices his quarry disappearing into the foliage nearby and on the next page he has shot her.

In the film directed by Daniel Nettheim and starring Willem Dafoe, M is called 'Martin David', a pseudonym he is said to assume in the book. This conventional title gives him a less harsh persona compared to the character in the novel. From the beginning of the film it is difficult not to engage with him: he is a sensitive man who listens to the music of Dvořák and Handel and we hear this music – a potent resource for making meaning that does not exist in the book. In one scene he activates the sound of Vivaldi's *Gloria*, with its associations with worship, praise and enlightenment, through speakers hung in the trees surrounding the house where he is staying. This suggests an

---

6   Tony Hughes D'Aeth has a protracted discussion of the *postnatural* man in his article 'Australian writing, deep ecology and Julia Leigh's *The hunter*'. He notes that M is not a natural man nor can he become one because 'he is not a "character", within the humanistic precepts of this idea, but an agent' (Hughes d'Aeth 2002, 25).

appreciation of the natural environment as well as the idea of 'home'. Tony Hughes-D'Aeth contends that although in the book M 'takes on the contours of the natural man' (Hughes-D'Aeth 2002, 25), they are refigured in terms of indeterminacy and conflict. For example, M notes that 'Early explorers ravaged by hunger tried to eat their clothing; another party survived by bleeding one another and drinking blood from a shoe. He admires other men's endurance' (Leigh 1999, 157–58). However, while the film develops to some extent the idea of human survival in a wild environment, it focuses more heavily on a burgeoning concern for the family he is staying with, who come to stand for regeneration and hope, rather than discord. These scenes tend to give Martin an ethical dimension that no-one in the novel embodies.

It is clear that many of the changes from book to film were made in the interests of effective transition to another medium, or selling the film. To quote some metatexts: screenwriter Alison Addison notes that to make the narrative interesting she needed to make more of the relationship between Martin and Lucy – the primarily internal monologue that dominated the book would not have successfully translated to screen. She says: 'the central character in the film goes through a transformation, in a way that he never really does in the book' (Wilson 2011). In terms of the film as a whole, Sue O'Neill, a sales agent with an Australian film distribution company, says that to sell a low budget feature to audiences 'it must have a positive message, a bit of redemption at the end, with a punchy soundtrack ... downbeat films about dysfunctional characters, where it's more depressing at the end than at the beginning, are the biggest turn off' (O'Neill 1996, 214). The protagonist's actions in the film, then, are partly dictated by the practical demands of turning a book into a successful film. As film critic Jonathan Dawson notes, once filming starts and again when the publicity mills are grinding 'the last image respected is a static icon of the writer'. Even the scriptwriter is out of the equation: 'The irresistible momentum of *process* now supervenes' (Dawson 1984, 76–77) and these processes, as Linda Hutcheon and others note, are not only material but social and economic (Cartmell & Whelehan 2010, 10).

The killing

The scenes in the novel that precede the killing of the thylacine describe the days M spends in the animal's 'lair' in a way that underscores his attempt to identify with the animal. Leigh has researched what is known about the thylacine's habitat and behaviour and weaves this into an account of the species' home, noting the signs of her presence and that it is a good spot for dwelling. She mentions the 'cache of bones' under a rock ledge nearby; fresh water close at hand; a 'dry twisted scat' and describes the scene as M enters the lair on all fours. M considers the inter-relation of himself and the thylacine: he finds the bones of a pup 'pale and clean, undisturbed since the creature lay down to die' and lies on the ground in a 'mirror position', imagining 'that he, too, will rot in the cave. In years to come, decades later, an intrepid explorer will find the skeletons and ponder the relationship between the two' (Leigh 1999, 159–60). And he decides to wait, comfortable under wallaby skins, for the thylacine to return.

Eventually he hears a faint rustling and catches sight of a 'dun-brown black-striped animal the size of a large dog, all thin and tattered looking' and he is instantly alert. Then Leigh uses the rhetoric of war. M knows what to do because he is 'an army general with the hard skill of a foot soldier' (Leigh 1999, 162). With his rifle slung over his shoulder, he wants the animal to run to him. Here he is represented as the quintessential hunter: 'the wild animal must be given the opportunity to remain an active and re-active agent' (Marvin 2006, 25). Then with his finger on the trigger he watches the thylacine eat: 'Part of him wants to keep watching, perhaps even walk away, but another part fixes him there, poised and ready, and it is the part of him he recognizes as strong and true'. When the thylacine perceives M's presence she 'stares straight at him', utters a 'strangled hissing roar', and then 'leaps'. Leigh has succumbed to the stereotype of the thylacine provided by many websites and popular mythology. She conjures a dangerous creature. The hunter must expend a second and third bullet to 'bring her to the ground' (Leigh 1999, 163).

Alternately, in the film, the first glimpse of the thylacine by Martin David is of the animal silently watching him as she stands at the opening to the den and he lies inside.[7] She quickly turns and walks away with the hunter in equally quiet pursuit. Her slow and soundless behaviour accurately reflects that noted by those who witnessed the species in the wild – they often saw just a glimpse of an animal who disappeared as suddenly as he/she appeared. Outside in the stony and snowy landscape Martin aims his rifle, then the camera dwells in close-up as she turns again to look at him. He lowers the gun in the face of her gaze and they stare at each other. She twitches her ears and then lowers her head gracefully, an action that could be read as submission, imply an instinct for her fate, or express dignified disinterest. Then the thylacine seems to prepare to move on. The camera has a close-up shot of the hunter narrowing his eyes slightly, then a view of the back of his head as he raises his gun and delivers a single blast.

As Kari Weil notes, the return of the human gaze with the animal about to die is important in JM Coetzee's *Disgrace* 'in which the look of the animal we kill provokes, however disturbingly, a transforming moment in the life of the main protagonist' (Weil 2006, 90). Here Martin exchanges a look that, as Sally Borrell suggests, may link with Lucy's comments earlier in the film: 'It's probably better off extinct. If it's alive people will always want to find it, hunt it down'. Borrell comments that 'although Lucy does not actually suggest it, this introduces the notion of killing the thylacine as an act of mercy' and the performance of shooting the animal becomes a 'mercy killing' (Borrell 2011, 53; see also Borrell & Freeman 2012). But this idea does not entirely explain Martin's grief following the shot, nor all his subsequent actions. Nor does it address the transformative potential of the animal gaze in the context of this film. Martin's demeanour after the act of killing does not suggests he is proud of delivering the thylacine from further suffering, but that he has reached a point when direct connection with the animal through a common sense (sight) has endowed him with an awareness

---

7 Jonathan Burt notes that the film image of an animal usually depends on some form of montage. The thylacine in *The hunter* is a digitally produced moving image that appears to originate from photographs of the species taken in zoos (for examples of photos, see Freeman 2010). The stilted movements of the figure are, at first, cringe-making, but with repeated viewing I acquired a greater acceptance of the figure. Representing an extinct animal is always going to be highly problematic. In terms of this film it is apposite to take into account Burt's comments that this is not the animal made virtual – the corrupt image contained in film signals, in effect, 'the end of nature', although it can also be 'presented as a means of redemption' (Burt 2002, 87, 166–67).

that undermines his hunter's sensibilities and reduces him to a state of humility and pain. It is as if all the cultural conventions surrounding his pursuit and its purpose have been sliced through by this one nonverbal exchange.

When the far-off figure crumples, Martin walks toward the thylacine's body with stumbling gait and kneels, crying, as his hand reaches to touch her bloodied fur. The camera recedes, repositioned to show the animal in the foreground as the hunter bows his head, touching her body again as he sobs. The concern or regret expressed by his actions suggest that a bond between the man and animal, as Jonathan Burt sees in *Amores perros* (2000) 'may enable other kinds of transformations in the future'. But Burt also warns of the complex interplay between 'the emotive simplicity of the animal image, the manner in which it appeals to sentiment and feeling, and its potential for over determination at the level of meaning' (Burt 2002, 178). There are other elements in the film and outside it that I discuss below which interfere with the idea of Martin's complete redemption in the film.

In the book M approaches a body that is still wheezing and shuddering. He watches and 'finds himself unable to do the right thing now and finish her off'. The words he whispers are 'you won't die alone', but any sensitivity is cancelled out as he looks into her eyes and sees there blankness, vacancy – they 'say nothing' to him. And then 'without thinking' he shoots her (again) in the head. When he examines the corpse, 'It galls him that he can press a finger against her wet nose, that he can close her eyes: it feels so wrong. She looks nothing like the creature he knew before. There is an impassable, unimaginable gulf between life and death'. M's reflection is focused on surface appearances, similarity to himself as 'natural' man, and his role as hunter: there is nothing to hunt unless it moves, then he is all action. But now 'her stillness is obscene' and he immediately gets to work to protect the body from scavengers and complete his task (Leigh 1999, 16–64). The contrast between his blunt observations and the racking sobs of Martin David could not be more extreme. Just as M seems to show a hint of remorse, or concern, or identification, it is pulled back into context: he is the hunter and his interest focused only on matters that serve himself and his task. On the other hand, the film version of this crucial event connotes a wider significance. This animal is the last of a species and the event has enormous weight – Martin seems to cry for the last members of all extinct species.

The next scene in the film shows a fire burning and Martin watching the skull of the thylacine through the flames. The shot cuts to a vast and mountainous landscape and pans to Martin looking over the escarpment while holding a water bottle owned by his host family's absent father, Jarrah. Solemn music and the sun highlighting his profile signify that his act of emptying the ashes the bottle contains is of key importance to the film's meaning. The following scene shows Martin phoning his employers at the biotech company to say 'What you want is gone forever'. This line again conveys the idea that, despite or because of his killing of the animal, Martin has experienced some kind of transformation in his attitudes. The novel has a similar burning of the bones, but specifically to destroy evidence and M buries the ashes with the comment that 'now *he* [M] is the only one' (Leigh 1999, 167, my italics). This is total negation of the animal's existence, the importance of her death, and the idea of responsibility. Indeed, the thylacine becomes less a being than a resource as he draws her blood ten times with a sterile syringe and cuts into her groin to surgically extract her ovaries. He 'locks each away in a custom-built vial of liquid nitrogen' (Leigh 1999, 166) and notes that an egg can be fertilised by sperm from a semi-compatible organism.[8] He then removes her uterus and notes that his job is done.

Before and after

The novel's refusal to redeem M is perceived as a difficulty by many critics, but as Hughes-D'Aeth points out 'The unredeemed M is not a failing in the novel, it is the point of the novel'. He contends that the narrative shock of M's actions in killing the thylacine and removing her organs works to question whether a surviving thylacine would be treated any differently now (Hughes-D'Aeth 2002, 22–23). If redemption is a com-

---

8 This reference to cloning is fleeting and insubstantial. An unsuccessful, but widely publicised, attempt at cloning a thylacine was made by Professor Mike Archer and his team at the Australian Museum in Sydney during the years 1999–2003. See Freeman 2009 for more details about this project.

mon theme in environmental literature, as he also notes, it seems to be the perceived expectation of film audiences – a wider group than may be understood to have read Leigh's literary work. Indeed, Martin David's steady change of mind in the film, culminating in his decision not to extract the animal's organs, perpetuates ideas which Hughes-D'Aeth feels are absent from the book, including the notion that as humans become 'more natural' they become 'more humane' (Hughes-d'Aeth 2002, 22). If we follow Hughes-D'Aeth's reasoning, the change from the book could imply that a thylacine would indeed be treated differently in the 21st century but, although awareness of environmental issues such as climate change is now widespread, whether this has translated into a concern for the extinction of species that constitutes social change is arguable. So there is now little shock, but an ending in which a general audience can safely identify with the main character: he becomes a hero, saving the thylacine from exploitation. Also, by extension, he is potentially saving the world from the effects of the particular kind of biowarfare Red Leaf plans to develop.

Hughes-D'Aeth comments in relation to the book that the ideas that 'children . . . can soften the hardest hearts' and that the woman in the family 'will surely find a way to redeem M' hang tantalisingly over the narrative (Hughes-D'Aeth 2002, 23). It could follow also that when Lucy and her daughter Sass die in the film, Martin will revert to the hunter who continues to carry out his assignment. But instead, the way the camera dwells on his exchanges with the family implies his decision not to remove the animal's organs are influenced by desire for continuing involvement with them. We can also consider that his change of heart may have been inspired by knowledge of the father Jarrah's rebellion against Red Leaf, as well as Lucy's suggestion that killing the thylacine will avoid the animal suffering further. These factors create an ethical ambiguity that undercuts the idea of Martin's redemption. Yet the final scene of the film where Martin embraces the family's orphaned son Bike (who has helped him in the search for the thylacine) does endow the hunter with a particularly redemptive characteristic.

Despite the implication that Martin has reflected on his role as exterminator and made an ethical choice to keep the thylacine's body intact, and despite the parallel he draws between human and animal by giving the animal the burial rites/rights usually reserved for humans, he still kills the thylacine. In the film and the book, the protesters who are at Lucy's house to celebrate an anti-logging victory suggest a different action: 'point [the thylacine's] nose dead west and tell him to run like the wind' (Leigh 1999, 155). This is consistent with an approach that leaves nature alone, and introduces the view, so often left out of narratives, that animals should be regarded as subjects with agency. And with Martin's abandonment of Red Leaf, the film also implies that the group made up of conservationists or 'greenies' and academic researchers – to which he seems sympathetic – is capable of influencing events, although it implies they need organisation and consolidation to meet their goals.

In addition, many elements in the film suggest that *The hunter* fits firmly into the profile of animal movies that Jonathan Burt outlines in his historical text *Animals in film*. Again and again Burt finds there is a motif of the incomplete family, orphaned children, threats to the environment and a moral imperative that governs animal imagery, and that these films are instructional on how to behave. He mentions children's films and television series *Flipper's new adventures*, *Lassie*, *Fury* and *Champion* – that feature widowers, young boys, foster fathers, or various ruptures to family cohesion – and that children who are unhappy at the beginning are transformed in the end by their contact with animals (Burt 2002, 177–87). There is a sense, then, that with its interlocking themes of loss and the possibility of change, the film *The hunter* transforms Leigh's bleak book into a standard animal film.

Reflection

If the thylacine in this narrative represents *everyanimal* –

> they are ... killed, gassed, electrocuted, exterminated, hunted, butchered, vivisected, shot, trapped, snared, run over, lethally injected, culled, sacrificed, slaughtered, executed, euthanized, destroyed, put down, put to sleep, and even, perhaps murdered (Fudge 2006, 3)

– the change from having her sexual organs removed for the production of biomedical warfare in the book, to having a ritualistic cremation in the film, carries meanings in relation to the conservation of species and the treatment of animals that are of vital importance to human–animal relations. As far as the book is concerned, M articulates an acute awareness of extinction, which he ponders as he hunts the thylacine:

> What must the plateau have been like before? Ragged and jagged, teeming with animals, giant fauna now extinct . . . it was not, he knows, the last Ice Age that had killed them . . . What made the last one different was a two-legged fearsome little pygmy, the human hunter: a testimony to cunning, to mind over matter.
> But he identifies with that human – what he is doing is what his ancestors have always done, and done well . . . he knows it will come easily, this skill learnt in the schoolyard . . . When you look, you can see it everywhere (Leigh 1999, 30–31)

On the other hand, the film *The hunter* celebrates the wildness and vastness of Tasmanian forest and buttongrass plains, and in its ending implies redemption is possible for a humanity that has destroyed so many natural environments and the animal species that live in them. But it also presents a bleak scenario for the future of species currently facing extinction, managing to convey the idea of absence in a visual trope of an often empty landscape. Less obviously, in both book and film the loss of the human family, with which we can relate so closely because we are human, conveys to the audience the enormity of the loss of the thylacine. They may not be aware, however, that in zoological terms Thylacinidae is an entire taxonomic family of which *Thylacinus cynocephalus* (the thylacine) is the last species to remain. So it is not just the species, nor the genus that is lost: it is the same as losing the whole Canid family – wolves, dogs, jackals and foxes. And because killing the thylacine could also be interpreted as an heroic attempt to save the *human* race from suffering the effects of biowarfare, and the film does not specifically assert humanity's capacity to prevent further extinctions, there remains a void at its conclusion.

Conclusion

The differences between the novel and the film have a number of implications for animal studies. The point central to the novel is that there is little concern for animals or effective protection for any surviving thylacine and that the drives of humanity in the direction of technology, war, and the interests of science produce species catastrophe. The film reinforces this idea, as Lucy sees death as the only way for the individual thylacine to escape persecution. However, the film's sympathetic depiction of Martin and the environmentalist characters conveys far more optimism about human nature than the novel, although it does not raise the same questions about how we perceive extinction, such as M's reflection in response to the idea of life as a cycle: 'If everything is transformed then what is extinction?' (Leigh 1999, 107). While these changes to the text are a function of the need to please audiences who want to see an uplifting film, considering the gap of ten years they may also reflect a shift in interest and attitudes toward animals and the environment – perhaps spurred by wider awareness of global warming and mass extinction – and demonstrate a 'repurposing for a new audience in a different time or cultural context' (Cartmell, 2010, 21).

The film's change in attitude epitomises a move that is beginning, gradually, to infuse popular media. But does the film have the power to change views? Comments on the ABC's *At the movies* webpage imply that this audience came to the movie with set views. For example, 'I disagree with the green movement entirely, but that did not overshadow my enjoyment of this film' (*The hunter*, Gina 19/2/12); 'It is pretty evident how appalling it is to have lost an entire species to human stupidity, and then we have to watch it all unfold for a second time in front of our eyes in the most despairing manner imaginable' (*The hunter*, Matt 16/2/12); 'As a greenie living the dream in Tasmania I thought the film portrayed the logging conflict reasonably. Only cringe for me was the firearm discharge' (*The hunter*, Max 20/11/11). The latter is one of the few comments that even mentioned the killing of the thylacine or the issue of extinction. Most concentrated on the actor Daniel Dafoe, the character development, the scenery (stunning) and cinematography in their reviews. Burt notes that 'when audiences do respond to the plight of animals as a result of a film this response can be highly selective and unpredictable' and cites examples for *Free Willy* and *101 dalmatians* (Burt 2002, 188–89).

However, some reviews for *The hunter* align with the screenwriter's aim for the film to remain 'morally ambiguous' – something the producers were keen to uphold, despite doubts expressed by funding bodies

(Wilson 2011). According to *The Observer's* reviewer Jason Solomons, the film has 'a sparse, allegorical quality that allows for mystery and interpretation' (Solomons 2002). This ambiguity does not mean that a message is necessarily lost to its viewers who may be stimulated to think about issues they have not confronted before and, in addition, it provides many interesting lines of enquiry for animal studies scholars. In terms of films about extinction, while it does show the brutal killing of an individual animal *The hunter* also projects Martin David's concern for the last representative of a species. Perhaps, then, it achieves that delicate balance between conveying the finality and emptiness of death and encouraging its audience to save species currently under threat.

Works cited

Borrell S (2011). Review: mercy killing. *Australian Animal Studies News Bulletin* 14: 53.

Borrell S & Freeman C (2012). Mercy killing: Julia Leigh's *The hunter* as film. Animal Death Symposium, University of Sydney, 12–13 June.

Burt J (2002). *Animals in film*. London: Reaktion Books.

Cartmell D & Whelehan I (2010). *Screen adaptation: impure cinema*. Basingstoke: Palgrave Macmillan.

Cartmill M (1993). *A view to death in the morning: hunting and nature through history*. Cambridge, Mass.: Harvard University Press.

Coetzee J M (1999). *Disgrace*. New York: Penguin.

Dawson J (1984). The writer and the film. In O Zuber-Skerritt (Ed.). *Page to stage: theatre as translation* (pp75–82). Amsterdam: Editions Rodopi.

Freeman C (2009). Ending extinction: the quagga, the thylacine and the 'smart human'. In C Gigliotti (Ed.). *Leonardo's choice: genetic technology and animals* (pp235–56). Dortrecht: Springer.

Freeman C (2010). *Paper tiger: a visual history of the thylacine*. Leiden: Brill.

Fudge E (2006). Introduction. In Animal Studies Group (Eds). *Killing animals* (pp1–9). Urbana and Chicago: University of Illinois Press.

Guiler E (1985). *Thylacine: the tragedy of the Tasmanian tiger*. Melbourne: Oxford University Press.

Hoy A (2005). Eye on the tiger. *The Bulletin with Newsweek*. 2005 Mar 2: pp16–22.

Hughes-D'Aeth T (2002). Australian writing, deep ecology and Julia Leigh's *The hunter*. *JASAL*, 1: 19–31.

The hunter. ABC TV: At the movies with Margaret and David [Online]. Available: www.abc.net.au/atthemovies/txt/s3312287.htm [Accessed 10 February 2013]

Johnson C (2006). *Australia's mammal extinctions: a 50,000 year history*. Cambridge: Cambridge University Press.

Knight J (1997). On the extinction of the Japanese wolf. *Asian Folklore Studies* 56 (1997): 129–59.

Leigh J (1999). *The hunter*. Ringwood: Penguin.

Marvin G (2006). Wild killing: contesting the animal in hunting. In Animal Studies Group (Eds). *Killing animals* (pp10–29). Urbana and Chicago: University of Illinois Press.

Modjeska D (1999) Endangered craft. *Australian's Review of Books*, 4(5): 9–11.

Nettheim D (Dir) (2011). *The hunter*. Richmond: Madman.

O'Neill S (1996). Marketing the low budget feature. In C Knapman (Ed.). *Low means low: the collected papers from the low budget feature seminar* (pp199–221). Sydney: Australian Film Commission.

Paddle R (2000). *The last Tasmanian tiger: the history and extinction of the thylacine*. Cambridge: Cambridge University Press.

Solomons J (2012). *The hunter* – review. *The Observer*, 8 July 2012 [Online]. Available: www.guardian.co.uk/film/2012/jul/08/ hunter-tasmania-daniel-nettheim-dafoe [Accessed 25 October 2012].

Stallwood K (2012). Report by Kim Stallwood on Minding Animals 2. *Minding Animals International Bulletin*, 12: 8–9.

Stam R & Raengo A (Eds) (2005). *Literature and film: a guide to the theory and practice of film adaptation*. Malden MA: Blackwell.

Weil, K (2006). Killing them softly: animal death, linguistic disability and the struggle for ethics. *Thinking with animals*, special issue of *Configurations* 14 (1/2): 87–96.

Wilson J (2011). *The hunter*: solitary soul of the south. *Sydney Morning Herald*, 8 October [Online]. Available: www.smh.com.au/entertainment/movies/ solitary-soul-of-the-south-20111007–1ld94.html [Accessed 25 October 2012].

12
Euthanasia and morally justifiable killing in a veterinary clinical context

Anne Fawcett

Brisbane vet Michael O'Donoghue has seen many people have to give up, or put down, their pets because they could not find a rental property that welcomed animals. 'It's very heartbreaking, people euthanasing their beloved pet because they can't find accommodation', he said. (Nancarrow 2012)

In Australia, urban companion animal-ownership per capita is declining in tandem with falls in living space. Despite this reduced demand, the pet industry uses positive imagery and targeted research to promote pet acquisition, helping to maintain a situation in which supply generally exceeds demand. This results in the annual euthanasia of thousands of excess animals from shelters and pounds. (McGreevy & Bennett 2010)

The quotations above highlight challenges for pet-owners in urban Australia, namely reduced living space and increased difficulty in finding appropriate rental or permanent accommodation that allow pets. But what I would like to highlight in the above is the use of the term 'euthanasia' in both pieces to describe the killing of animals due to lack of space and/or excess supply. In this essay I will analyse what I see

A Fawcett (2013). Euthanasia and morally justifiable killing in a veterinary clinical context. In J Johnston & F Probyn-Rapsey (Eds). *Animal death*. Sydney: Sydney University Press.

as an unjustifiable double standard operating in current thinking surrounding killing animals and killing humans, and the word 'euthanasia' as applied to animals and humans as it enshrines that double standard. The term is traditionally applied to killing aimed at preventing suffering in animals for which reasonable interventions are either exhausted or not available and where quality of life is poor. This might be construed as killing an animal in its interests. But the term is often applied to animal killing in which the above criteria do not apply, or in which killing is not truly in the animal's interests. Veterinarians are trained to kill animals humanely (with minimal suffering) and are often called to do so in practice. Misappropriation of the term 'euthanasia' may be a source of moral stress for veterinarians, as it may not only obscure the motivation for killing, but the interests of the one who is killed. Animals clearly have interests independent of their owners, and these are in a different logical category from imagined projections about how they may or may not fare if their owner surrenders them.

In reality, the killing of an animal is often not a case of 'euthanasia', no matter how painless, dignified and legally sanctioned that happens to be, because the interests of the animal are not served. Like us, animals may be willing to persevere with less than perfect fulfilment of their interests in some conditions. It is only in cases that are analogous to cases of human euthanasia where the animal's interests are served by killing; for example, cases of debilitating or incurable illness. Yet it seems that the term 'euthanasia', where animals are concerned, is synonymous with any death effected by a veterinarian. If the life of your companion animal is ended by a veterinarian, it is likely that service will be invoiced under the category 'euthanasia' regardless of the reason. That is unproblematic if we accept the American Veterinary Medical Association's (AVMA) definition of euthanasia, as defined in its *Guidelines on euthanasia*, as a death 'that occurs with minimal pain and distress. In the context of these guidelines, euthanasia is the act of inducing humane death in an animal' (AVMA 2007). But what this definition fails to explain is that not all humane deaths are equal. It may be possible to induce a painless, rapid death in a healthy person by administering a toxin without that person's knowledge – but we call that murder, not euthanasia. The above use of the term fails to capture the morally significant difference between the killing of an animal to prevent present suffering, killing of an animal to prevent inevitable or at least likely future suffering, and the killing of a perfectly healthy animal because it is unwanted (by a particular owner or society at large). The AVMA guidelines make no claim to pronouncing on ethical dilemmas such as the euthanasia of healthy, unwanted animals – although it states that such concerns are 'complex and warrant thorough consideration by the profession and all those concerned with the welfare of animals' (AVMA 2007). Rather, the authors take the view that 'if an animal's life is to be taken, it is done with the highest degree of respect, and with an emphasis on making the death as painless and disease free as possible' (AVMA 2007).

I support the existence of such guidelines as they ensure that prevention of suffering in bringing about death is a central and critical animal welfare consideration. What is at issue here is whether all forms of humane killing constitute 'euthanasia', and whether it is important to make the distinction. The danger is that the term 'euthanasia' becomes a euphemism, a means of easing moral discomfort we might otherwise have about killing animals in certain contexts. As one colleague who did not wish to be identified commented:

> Using the term in this way does make 'euthanasia' almost pleasant when in practice in many situations it is extremely uncomfortable, weakly justifiable and just feels wrong. It's not very honest but it cushions the blow and helps me cope in the long run. (personal communication 2012)

Lumping all veterinary-effected animal deaths in the same moral basket poses a danger to animals as well as veterinarians, hospital staff and pet owners.

Euthanasia and morally justifiable killing

The term euthanasia is derived from the Greek 'eu', for good, and 'thanatos', or death. Given how much energy living creatures devote to avoiding death, the pairing of the words is intuitively oxymoronic. The term 'good' is philosophically loaded and may be interpreted differently in different contexts. A 'good' death may be used to describe a death ranging from pleasant to the dying individual, to a death that is neutral or free of suffering, to a death that is ethically sound. For some this means accepting one's demise and going peacefully. According to one popular Christian funeral homily, 'the Christian who has suffered long, and who has died in peace and with dignity, has lived the Gospel' (Mulvihill 1990).

For those whose loved one dies in the agonising throes of terminal agitation, such demise is neither good in any physical sense nor good within this belief system. The question of whether one's behaviour in one's terminal moments determines the quality of one's afterlife has been the subject of much religious and philosophical speculation. Not surprisingly, there is no simple answer to what constitutes a 'good' death for humans.

It may, however, come as a surprise to learn that on day one of graduation, veterinarians are expected to be competent in matters pertaining to euthanasia. According to the United Kingdom's Royal College of Veterinary Surgeons, a new graduate must be able to:

1. Recognise when euthanasia is necessary
2. Perform it humanely
3. Be familiar with methods of euthanasia and select the appropriate method
4. Display sensitivity to the feelings of owners and others
5. Perform euthanasia with due regard for the safety of those present
6. Advise on carcase disposal. (RCVS 2006, adapted from section C1.15)

This assumes that euthanasia is performed by veterinarians only when it is 'necessary', but provides no criteria by which a veterinarian may judge euthanasia to be necessary or not. That depends on one's working definition of the term euthanasia.

Pavlovic and colleagues argue that the word 'euthanasia' has been flagrantly misused and abused, most notably by the German Nazi party, and by those killing animals in scientific experiments (Pavlovic et al. 2011). For some, they argue, the word has been irreversibly tainted through its association with crimes against humanity.

The authors point out that it is not satisfactory to define euthanasia as 'the act or practice of killing or permitting the death of hopelessly sick or injured individuals (as persons or domestic animals) in a relatively painless way for reasons of mercy' (Merriam-Webster Online

Dictionary 2011) as this does not take into account the interests of the individual, who, despite being 'hopelessly sick', may wish to live, or at least wish not to die. Furthermore, such a definition may excuse someone – be it a war criminal, or a scientist experimenting on animals, from causing a state of hopeless, irreversible, terminal illness, such that ending the life of that being – when viewed in isolation – appears to be consistent with euthanasia.

To avoid such misappropriation of the term, Pavlovic et al. argue that the entire procedure – including causing that individual to be in that state – must be taken into account (which is why they reject the use of the term 'Nazi euthanasia program'). Instead, they propose a two-pronged definition, suggesting that 'euthanasia' be defined as:

a) an act which fulfils the interests of the one who will die

b) an act motivated by a moral imperative – for example, 'to save from suffering somebody who explicitly expressed such a desire'. (Pavlovic et al. 2011)

Thus the termination of laboratory animals for the purposes of experimentation does not meet the conditions for 'euthanasia'. The authors do not overtly call for the end of terminal laboratory animal experiments, nor do they equate Nazi war crimes with experiments on laboratory animals. Their objective is to preserve the notion of 'a good death' to permit patients to express their desires and ensure others respect their dignity – while protecting the concept from misuse.

Pavlovic argues that it is challenging to apply his work on reorienting the concept of euthanasia to a veterinary clinical context. He feels that the circumstances in which animals are killed – whether in their interests or not – are so different from those of humans that the term 'euthanasia' should be applied exclusively where the patient is human (Pavlovic, personal communication 2012).[1] Unlike a human patient, who may make their wishes known prior to death, either directly or via a will, directions to a family member or legal representative, the nonhuman patient is unable to convey their interests nor consent to or dictate the timing of euthanasia – or even the place. Where a patient cannot convey his or her interests, there is huge scope for error.[2] End-of-life

---

1 He suggests the term 'mercy killing' to apply to situations where the suffering of an animal is deemed to outweigh the benefit of survival. (Pavlovic, personal communication 2012)

care typically requires pet owners and veterinarians to make decisions of monumental consequences (life and death), while feeling that they lack critical information (Shanan 2011). In particular, decision-making around whether to pursue treatment (Is it realistic? Is it fair? Is it likely to result in further or at least prolong suffering?) versus concerns about ending the life of an animal prematurely can be very difficult to address.

Much has been written about, and many schemata formulated for, assessing quality of life, a discussion of which is beyond the scope of this essay. Suffice to say, there remains no consensus on measurement of quality of life, and no clear cut-offs on the quality of life continuum. Most significantly, 'there is no objective point below which quality of life is unacceptable' (Shanan 2011). Furthermore, veterinarians may be called upon to end the life of an animal for a range of reasons including but not limited to:

• terminal illness or injury
• overpopulation (particularly in the context of animal shelters but also in the case of animal hoarding (Joffe et al. in preparation)
• legal issues (a council declaration or court order of a nuisance or dangerous animal)
• change of circumstances (for example, lack of house-training or a requirement for an onerous medication regime; the family member who was caring for that particular animal has passed away or been admitted to hospital/hospice care; the owner is moving to a dwelling that does not accommodate pets etc.)
• financial inability on the part of the owners to fund treatment (often referred to as 'economic euthanasia')
• treatment not available (for example, dialysis for treatment of acute kidney failure is not widely available in Australian veterinary hospitals)

---

2 Of course human patients cannot always communicate their wishes – their physical and/or mental state may prevent them from doing so. In such cases, proxies (close family members, carers and representatives) may be asked to determine that person's interests or wishes. But studies which compare decision-making by proxies to decisions made by patients who can communicate have shown that even close relatives and experienced health professionals have a limited ability to correctly predict what the patient perceives as best for themselves or in their own interests. (Shanan 2011)

- concerns that treatment may reduce quality of life
- failure of an animal to meet the expectations of the owner
- public health concerns (for example, in the event of an outbreak of a zoonotic disease such as Hendra virus, affected animals may be sacrificed to contain spread of the disease)
- biosecurity (for example, where outbreak of a non-endemic disease of economic importance such as Newcastle disease or foot and mouth disease, affected animals may be sacrificed to contain spread of the disease).

Many of the above reasons do not satisfy the aforementioned criteria to be labelled 'euthanasia' – many satisfy (b) but do not necessarily satisfy (a).

In 1984, philosopher Tom Regan posed more stringent conditions for the use of the term euthanasia in application to animals, specifically that:

1. killing must be by the most painless means possible
2. that it must be believed to be in the animal's best interests and this must be a true belief
3. one who kills must be motivated by concern for the interest, good or welfare of the animal involved. (Regan 1984)

Few of the above situations would satisfy these criteria. For example, if a shelter veterinarian euthanases a healthy dog because they believe it is in the dog's best interests, this in Regan's view is not a true belief and therefore does not satisfy (b). It may be well intentioned killing – but it is not euthanasia.

There are situations where killing may be deemed morally justifiable even if it does not meet the criteria for euthanasia. Consider the example of an aggressive dog, declared by the local council to be dangerous after biting a passer-by without provocation. Despite attempts to confine this particular dog, it escapes and attacks a child. In such a case, it is likely that the owners will be fined and the dog will be ordered to be destroyed.

Legal issues aside, when all stakeholders are taken into account (the owner, the dog, the community, legal institutions and so forth), it may be possible to make an argument that terminating the life of that dog is morally justifiable on the grounds that the outcome would lead to the greatest good for the greatest number of stakeholders. The death is not in the animal's interests, but it is motivated by the imperative of preventing the suffering of multiple stakeholders and therefore morally justifiable.[3]

Yeates provides less stringent criteria, suggesting that the term 'euthanasia' may be used when killing is 'contextually justified'. This argument is based on the observation that quality of life is heavily dependent not just on the animal's physical and mental state but the context in which the animal lives. Assessment of quality of life is based on predicting what might happen if the animal continues to live.

[The term] contextually justified euthanasia [applies] where an animal could have a life worth living in an ideal world, but the circumstances mean that the opportunity is not worthwhile. This may be due to an owner's unreasonableness or the fault of society, but the veterinarian should not feel guilty for 'making the best of a bad job'. (Yeates 2010a)

In this model, the killing of an aggressive dog could be justified by arguing that such a dog could not be kept in a comfortable environment which is likely to meet the animal's needs. For example. the dog may need to be locked up and may not be able to exercise, and may suffer

---

3 For many, this is uncontroversial. But if we reason strictly as utilitarians, the above scenario could apply to a human subject if we replace the dog with an unruly teenager. But of course few of us are strictly utilitarian. According to philosopher Bernard Rollin, the predominant social ethic represents a combination of utilitarian and deontological theories. 'On the one hand, social decisions are made and conflicts are resolved by appealing to the greatest good for the greatest number. But in cases wherein maximising the general welfare could oppress the basic interests constituting the humanness of individuals, general welfare is checked by a deontological theoretical component – namely, respect for the individual human's nature and the interests flowing therefrom, which, in turn, are guaranteed by rights' (Rollin 2011b). Rollin gives the example of a terrorist who plants a time bomb in a school. The only way to defuse the bomb without setting it off is to obtain information from the offender. But according to our social ethic, torturing the terrorist to extract that information is wrong – despite the enormous costs on a purely utilitarian analysis of the situation. The problem is that while the unruly teenager is afforded rights, the predominant social ethic does not afford animals rights.

secondary effects such as anxiety, boredom and distress, compromising the dog's quality of life to such an extent that euthanasia would be a better option.

Yeates distinguishes (a) contextually justified euthanasia from (b) 'absolutely justified euthanasia' (where the only alternative to induced death is suffering and where further treatment would be considered unethical) and (c) 'killing that is not truly in an animal's interests' (such as making space available for another animal or killing which may be of great benefit to science).

This model acknowledges the reality of killing an animal for reasons other than prevention of that animal's suffering, but it can be difficult to distinguish (a) from (c). For example, one could argue that killing a shelter animal to make room for another is contextually justified because the animal being killed is one which is unlikely to be re-homed, and therefore doomed to a life of confinement, whereas the animal for which room is being made is more likely to be rehomed, and attempting to accommodate both animals would lead to overcrowding and suffering for all.

But could this be simply a guilt-displacement strategy packaged as an ethical argument? After all, one may counter that killing one animal to make room for another fails to address the greater issue of overpopulation, and man-made dependence of domestic animals on humans, and simply perpetuates the problem (Palmer 2006).

Another deficiency of Yeates' contextually justified euthanasia model is that ending a life is not framed as a morally significant behaviour. The danger here is that this obviates the veterinarian of moral responsibility and therefore potentially ethical reasoning. What is there, then, to stop a veterinarian ending the life of any animal on relatively trivial grounds?

Moral stress and the veterinarian

Veterinarians are around four times more likely to commit suicide than members of the general population.[4] Attitudes of veterinarians towards death and euthanasia are considered by numerous authors to be among key factors behind this increased risk of suicide.

Bartram and Baldwin cite evidence which suggests an association between familiarity with death and dying and attitudes to expendability of life (Bartram & Baldwin 2010). Similarly, an array of studies cited by these authors have demonstrated an association between permissive attitudes towards euthanasia, physician-assisted suicide and unassisted suicide, and suicidal thoughts.

Rollin identifies 'moral stress' as stress arising from the fact that persons such as veterinarians whose life work is aimed at promoting the wellbeing of animals are called upon to kill animals, or 'being complicit in creating pain, distress, disease, and other noxious states' required in research (Rollin 2011a).

> This kind of stress grows out of the radical conflict between one's reasons for entering the field of animal work, and what one in fact ends up doing . . . Imagine the psychological impact of constant demands to kill healthy animals for appalling reasons: 'the dog is too old to run with me anymore; we have redecorated, and the dog no longer matches the colour scheme; it is cheaper to get another dog when I return from vacation than to pay the fees for a boarding kennel,' and, most perniciously, 'I do not wish to spend the money on the procedure you recommend to treat the animal,' or 'it is cheaper to get another dog'. (Rollin 2011a)

Rollin rightly points out that the ability of veterinarians to kill animals is not only a burden but a blessing:

> Whereas human physicians are not empowered to help horribly suffering patients end their pain by providing access to euthanasia, veterinarians are fortunately blessed to be able to end suffering by providing a peaceful, painless death. (Rollin, 2011a)

---

4   A recent study found that veterinarians have a proportional mortality ratio for suicide approximately four times that of the general population and approximately twice that of persons in other healthcare professions (Bartram & Baldwin 2010). That is consistent with Australian data, with the reported suicide rate for veterinarians of 45.2 deaths per 100,000 population in data from Western Australia and Victoria combined – this is 3.9 times the rate in the general populations of these states (Jones-Fairnie et al. 2008).

As a veterinarian who performs euthanasia, I am often thanked by clients who comment that they wish a close family member with a terminal illness or similar condition had died as peacefully as their animal had. Euthanasia, declares Rollin, is a 'double-edged sword'.

One of the major dangers of moral stress generated by euthanasia is that it may alter the attitudes of veterinarians to suicide. According to the theory of cognitive dissonance, conflicting thoughts or beliefs may lead to psychological discomfort, prompting the modification of existing thoughts or the development of new thoughts and beliefs designed to reduce inconsistency (and reduce or eliminate tension) (Harmon-Jones & Harmon-Jones 2007).

Consider, for example, the so-called meat paradox: meat is central to the diet of the majority of Australians, yet most of us like animals and are disturbed by the prospect of harm being done to them (Bastian et al. 2012). Meat eating is a morally significant behaviour, but conceiving it as such creates dissonance for meat-eaters. The authors showed through a series of experiments, that dissonance is resolved by many meat-eaters by denying animals minds – as most people are reluctant to harm things with minds, but less reluctant to harm things without minds.[5]

As the authors state, 'by denying minds to animals, people bring their cognitions in line with behaviour commitments, facilitating effective and unconflicted action' (Bastian et al. 2012). The experiments suggest that a range of cognitive and emotional processes obscure moral responsibility for action by reducing the extent to which an action (in this case meat eating) is viewed as morally relevant.

When it comes to ending the life of an animal, Bartram and Baldwin suggest that veterinarians may experience 'uncomfortable tension' between the desire to preserve life and the inability to treat an animal effectively. Depending on the situation, the tension may be between the

---

5   The authors base their argument on a series of experiments which show that: (a) animals considered for consumption are ascribed diminished mental capacities by prospective consumers; (b) meat eaters are motivated to deny minds to animals when they are asked to consider the link between meat products and animal suffering; and (c) mind-denial is more likely to occur immediately prior to consumption of meat, rather than immediately prior to consumption of a non-animal food product (Bastian et al. 2012).

desire to treat the animal and the desire to fulfil the owner's wishes. For some veterinarians, they argue, this dissonance is overcome by considering euthanasia and/or client satisfaction a positive outcome.

If we accept this argument, the cost to the veterinarian is high. The impact of moral stress is absorbed by the veterinarian, who experiences the cognitive dissonance and resolves this by modifying his or her thinking about an animal's death: 'I didn't have another choice'; 'if I'd treated it, it might not have recovered anyway'; 'if I'd not put that litter of kittens down she would have dumped them in the creek' and so on.

In the longer term the veterinarian is desensitised toward death – specifically, medically or mechanically induced death. Bartram and Baldwin argue that from here it is a smaller leap to considering suicide as a solution to one's own problems.

This argument is challenged by a recent survey of UK veterinarians which found that attitudes to animal euthanasia did not correlate with acceptance of human euthanasia or suicide (Ogden et al. 2012). The findings cast doubt on whether changes in attitudes to animal life affect veterinarian's attitudes to human life. However, the authors suggest that the dissonance between personal values or ideals and the reality of 'convenience euthanasia' may be a stressor which could lead to suicide. Thus, where requests for euthanasia of healthy animals are made, veterinarians who disagree with the procedure may experience psychological distress (Stark & Dougall 2012).

Another major concern is that in lumping all veterinary-effected deaths in the same category, there is less motivation to analyse one's actions, their consequences and potential alternatives. That may negatively impact animals treated in the future. At worst, cognitive dissonance around such matters may lead a veterinarian to consider death as a zero or neutral state. As Yeates argues, this position simplifies end-of-life decision-making and may in some circumstances (for example, where an owner presents a healthy animal for 'euthanasia' with poor contextual justification) avoid conflict with the owner: almost any animal can be killed on welfare grounds if an argument could be made that a small amount of suffering would occur otherwise. According to this argument, death – entailing zero suffering – is better than a life entailing any level of suffering. This position is consistent with current legislation in the UK, the US and Australia – that is, if consent is given and a humane method of killing employed, ending the life of any animal (healthy or sick, young or old) is not illegal.

It is an attractive post-hoc position for a veterinarian who feels compelled to kill an animal for reasons they don't believe are satisfactory. But followed to its logical extreme, this line of thought leads to the disturbing conclusion that any killing can be justified as 'euthanasia', as all life involves some degree of suffering, be it minor discomfort or inconvenience, extreme pain or anything on a continuum in between.[6] The use of 'death-as-a-zero-state' to resolve cognitive dissonance by veterinarians is highly dangerous as it may infiltrate subsequent decision-making processes and lead to situations where ending a life is considered the simplest and most humane option – and is therefore not questioned.

An alternative position holds that death is a welfare state. That is, if living leads to overall bad welfare, death is a positive state as it alleviates suffering. Thus, inducing a humane death in such circumstances meets the criteria for euthanasia. If living leads to overall positive welfare, death is a negative state and inducing the death does not meet criteria to be classed as euthanasia (Yeates 2010a, 2010b).

Where to from here?

Veterinarians are trained to bring about the deaths of animals humanely. They may be called upon to perform this service for a variety of reasons, which may or may not be morally justifiable. Veterinarians sit, often uncomfortably, between professional obligations as espoused in guidelines and broader moral questions. Failure to reflect on this position poses risks to animals, veterinarians and their clients (pet owners).

The term euthanasia, defined as an act which fulfils the interest of the one who will die and motivated by a moral imperative, applies to one form of morally justifiable killing of animals, but we need termin-

---

6   Of course an important presupposition of this position is a sharp human/animal distinction, such that while it may be considered logical for any suffering animal to be killed, it is not understood to follow in the case of humans who are viewed as morally exceptional.

ology that recognises the distinction between these and poorly justified or ethically unjustifiable killing of animals.

The terminological elision, a symptom of discourses on euthanasia which are tied to the broader topic of human–animal power relations, has a real impact on animal lives. Part of the problem is no doubt the absence of a palatable alternative term to apply to deaths which do not meet criteria for 'euthanasia'. The terms 'termination', 'destruction' and 'killing' fail to encompass the obligation of veterinarians to bring about the death of animals in a humane manner. Terminology which facilitates clear ethical reasoning about end-of-life decision-making is important not only to ensure that such decisions are made carefully and transparently, but to ensure that the privilege of euthanasia is not abused.

Acknowledgements

The author would like to thank Professor Bernard Rollin, Dr John Baguley, Dr May Chin-Oh and two anonymous reviewers for their constructive feedback and valuable suggestions.

Works cited

Merriam-Webster online dictionary [Online]. Available: www.merriam-webster.com [Accessed 1 July 2011].

AVMA (2007). American Veterinary Medical Assocation Guidelines on euthanasia [Online]. Available: www.avma.org/issues/animal_welfare/ euthanasia.pdf [Accessed 6 June 2012].

Bartram DJ & Baldwin DS (2010). Veterinary surgeons and suicide: a structured review of possible influences on increased risk. *Veterinary Record*, 166: 388–97.

Bastian B, Loughnan S, Haslam N, & Radke HRM (2012). Don't mind meat? The denial of mind to animals used for human consumption. *Personality and Social Psychology Bulletin*, 38: 247–56.

Harmon-Jones E & Harmon-Jones C (2007). Cognitive dissonance theory after 50 years of development. *Zeitschrift Fur Sozialpsychologie*, 38: 7–16.

Jones-Fairnie H, Ferroni P, Silburn S & Lawrence D (2008). Suicide in Australian veterinarians. *Australian Veterinary Journal*, 86: 114–16.

McGreevy PD & Bennett PC (2010). Challenges and paradoxes in the companion-animal niche. *Animal Welfare,* 19: 11–16.

Mulvihill M (1990). A great relief. In L Swords (Ed.). *Funeral homilies.* Dublin: The Columba Press.

Nancarrow D (2012). Vet pleads for landlords to allow pets. *Sydney Morning Herald,* 11 January.

Ogden U, Kinnison T & May SA (2012). Attitudes to animal euthanasia do not correlate with acceptance of human euthanasia or suicide. *Veterinary Record,* 171: 174.

Palmer C (2006). Killing in animal shelters. In Animal Studies Group (Eds) *Killing animals.* Urbana and Chicago: University of Illinois Press.

Pavlovic D, Spassov A & Lehman C (2011). Euthanasia: in defence of a good, ancient word. *Clinical Research & Bioethics,* 2: 5.

Royal College of Veterinary Surgeons (2006). *Essential competencies required of the veterinary surgeon.* London: RCVS.

Regan T (1984). *The case for animal rights.* London, Routledge.

Rollin BE (2011a). Euthanasia, moral stress, and chronic illness in veterinary medicine. *Veterinary Clinics of North America: Small Animal Practice,* 41: 651–59.

Rollin BE (2011b). *Putting the horse before Descartes:my life's work on behalf of animals,* Philadelphia: Temple University Press.

Shanan A (2011). A veterinarian's role in helping pet owners with decision making. *Veterinary Clinics of North America: Small Animal Practice,* 41: 635–46.

Stark C & Dougall N (2012). Effect of attitudes to euthanasia on vets' suicide risk. *Veterinary Record,* 171: 172–73.

Yeates JW (2010a). Ethical aspects of euthanasia of owned animals. *In Practice,* 32: 70–73.

Yeates JW (2010b). Death is a welfare issue. *Journal of Agricultural & Environmental Ethics,* 23: 229–41.

13

Preventing and giving death at the zoo: Heini Hediger's 'death due to behaviour'

Matthew Chrulew

Recent analyses of contemporary biopower have emphasised the exposure of populations to political technologies aimed at fostering their health and wellbeing. They emphasise that natural biological processes have thereby become the object of power, invested and cared for but at the same time infiltrated by a rationalised administration. Yet, as many have recognised, while the nurture of life itself might have become power's objective, death can never be entirely banished from this biopolis.[1] It is either disavowed and returns in distorted ways, or is in fact an immediate product of scientifico-medical intervention, where one group survives (or indeed lives well) at the expense of another. Nor is it only human populations that are targeted; nonhuman animal life

M Chrulew (2013). Preventing and giving death at the zoo: Heini Hediger's 'death due to behaviour'. In J Johnston & F Probyn-Rapsey (Eds). *Animal death*. Sydney: Sydney University Press.

---

1   Michel Foucault (2003) argued that the continued pairing of sovereign violence with biopower occurs through a logic of biological racism. Giorgio Agamben (1998) maintains the originary correspondence of sovereignty and biopower in the exception of bare life, while Roberto Esposito (2008) develops a rubric of immunisation that conjoins the logics of protection and exclusion. For Achille Mbembe, a global necropolitics still prevails that demands elucidation: 'the notion of biopower is insufficient to account for contemporary forms of subjugation of life to the power of death.' (2003, 39–40)

is also subjected to modes of knowledge and intervention that seek to conserve and cultivate it in a range of forms, from economy to spectacle, while exposing or abandoning other groups to death (Wadiwel 2002; Shukin 2009).

One significant heterotopia of human–animal relations, which has historically been the site of both vital and lethal experimentation in multispecies relations, is the zoological garden. Zoos today are model biopolitical institutions devoted to the reproduction and nurture of life (Chrulew 2010). Interventions in zoo biology throughout the 20th century waged a veritable war against mortality, deploying technologies of surveillance and care to secure captive animals against natural threats such as starvation, disease and predation, while also seeking to minimise the harmful effects of their own interventions. Yet this recreation of Eden and its ordered harmony, which hid and hounded mortality from its domain, could not ultimately except itself from the realm of fallen creatures and angelic swords. Death is a constitutive part of life, as well as a constitutive right of the sovereign power reserved to the human. Zoos produce death not only accidentally – in botched transfers, for example – but also deliberately, in feeding their carnivores, making space for healthy specimens, and today even in facilitating the reintroduction of endangered species. Zoos both prevent death and deliver it in the service of the species life under their care.

Attending to the attitude to mortality of Heini Hediger's zoo biology will help illuminate the foundations of zoos' biopolitical operation, and trace how this life-fostering revolution in turn altered their relationship to death. Hediger (1908–1992) was a mid-20th-century Swiss zoo director whose practical and theoretical writings, as well as his institutional reviews and professional advice, were enormously influential in the worldwide practice of zoo biology (1964, 1968, 1969). His entire life's work was dedicated to understanding and nurturing the lives of animals in captivity (1985). This demanded a meticulous concern with eradicating death, particularly that caused by human intervention or negligence. A close reading of his work will show that his scrutiny of what he dubbed 'death due to behaviour' opened up captive animals' lives to a new domain of knowledge, power and biopolitical intervention.

Heini Hediger's philosophy and practice of animal care was preeminently and entirely biopolitical. Every observation and intervention was directed towards the flourishing of animals' lives in captivity, addressing both their variously capable bodies and their variedly alien minds. As he explained in an autobiographical essay, describing his early childhood collections and biological education, his lifelong interest differed from the typical concerns of scientific dissection or museological display: 'something was missing; I was working exclusively with dead animals when I was oriented toward living animals' (1985, 152).[2] Thus he was drawn to zoological gardens where, directing in turn Bern, Basel and Zürich, he became a renowned expert in the psychology and behaviour of captive animals, and in the techniques of their keeping and display. Joining encyclopaedic knowledge of experimental and naturalistic biology with extensive anecdotal observation of zoo animals' responses to their fabricated environments, his books became bibles for zookeepers worldwide in their endeavours to care for their wards: to lengthen their lives, to improve their physical and psychological health, and to encourage them to behave naturally and especially to reproduce.

Yet while implicit today, such care for life had not always been central to zoos' operations. The capture of exotic specimens had long had deadly consequences among wild populations – for example, in the 19th-century colonial hunting expeditions that would decimate groups in order to capture infants (Rothfels 2002, 44–80). Those captured were left to wounded lives and routine deaths, made to survive yet unable to thrive (Chrulew 2010, 2011). But throughout the 20th century, as changing legal and cultural contexts made wild animals increasingly unavailable, the quality and longevity of the lives of those in captivity assumed an ever greater economic and ideological importance (Donahue & Trump 2006). Hediger played a preeminent role in biologically

---

2   Hediger related that at one point in a collecting expedition, when it was time to preserve in alcohol a tame monitor lizard he had become fond of, 'I was unable to perform my duty' (1985, 149). He elsewhere attributed significance to a biophilic upbringing, such as when, as part of his polemic against the growth of generic automated feeding (emerging from the work of laboratory scientists), he speculated on the effects of a lack of relational contact: 'From the start Ratcliffe worked predominantly or exclusively on dead animals. At the same time, other zoo people (including myself) had been dealing with live animals, often since our childhood days' (1969, 142).

modernising zoological gardens from imperial spectacles with blunt sovereign instruments to the detailed, individualised care of biopower. What was the relationship to death of this life-fostering regime that Hediger helped institute and intensify? Modern zoos, and the intertwined discourses, practices and strategies for governing animals of which they form part, indeed developed a specific attitude to death that it is worthwhile delineating. While certain abject groups remained more useful as corpses than organisms, overall the productive investment in life thoroughly transformed the relationship of power to death, which became no longer its means of operation but an elusive spectre to be prevented and excluded as far as is possible.

'Causes of death in the zoo', a major chapter in Hediger's imposing book *Man and animal in the zoo*, particularly elucidates his mature zoo biology as the theory and practice of fostering life and reducing death among captive animals. Here Hediger addressed many of the common reasons for zoo animal mortality, the historical changes in their makeup, and the best means of addressing and minimising these factors. Indeed the nature of death had already been transformed as a result of Hediger's and his colleagues' interventions:

> Over the years improvements in quarantining, more hygienic accommodation, stricter methods of examination, more effective drugs and more appropriate feeding methods have resulted in a decline in the importance of infectious diseases [such as tuberculosis], parasitic ailments and dietary disorders; in the meantime other categories have come more to the fore. (1969, 169)

He expanded in detail upon many of these newly prominent causes of death, yet what is most immediately apparent is his overriding focus on the *knowledge* and *prevention* of death and mortality.

Death is of course not something that can be entirely eliminated from the zoological garden. Rather it is a common occurrence and a threat to the cohort's overall health and numbers and thus something that the scientific biopolitician must investigate thoroughly. Hediger was extremely concerned to maximise knowledge of mortality. He decried the ignorant past (and its holdovers) when zoos would bury dead animals without autopsy. Such failures to investigate causes of death were incomprehensible to his biopolitical rationality. He insisted rather that death be scrutinised by a class of experts and made known through careful records, and he encouraged the still incomplete progress from the 'occasional ... post-mortems' of the 19th century to 'the establishment of comparative pathological examinations of all the corpses occurring in the zoo on a regular basis' (1969, 166). He made extensive use of the published mortality statistics of certain zoos, and bemoaned the lack of similar data from other institutions:

> corresponding material would undoubtedly be available from virtually every zoo if only such informative reports were to be published; this is unfortunately not possible for the majority of zoos because many of them do not have sufficient scientific specialists available for such work. (177)

Hediger thus lamented the economics preventing maximal knowledge of all aspects of animal health, life, behaviour, disease and death. He criticised not only the quantity but also the quality of zoological knowledge, condemning ignorant or wrongheaded explanations for animal mortality, such as the turn-of-the-century tendency to attribute it to homesickness (53) and later fashionable explanations to do with improper feeding or the new catchword 'stress' (240), as well as other outdated, unscientific and ignorant views.

This will to improve knowledge of animal death was illustrated in a report he compiled reviewing the operations of Sydney's Taronga Park. Hediger was incredulous that its current, somewhat aloof amateur keeper maintained a strange Edenic belief in the perpetual replaceability and irrepressible health of exotic animals: 'the theory of Sir Edward's that his animals do not die and that he has no sick animals is ridiculous and I was surprised that he insisted for a long time on the correctness of this statement' (1966, 8). Animal life was no longer something that could be captured from the outside and 'let live' with sovereign detachment, but a proximate concern that must be understood in its biological reality and *made* to live. Hediger's first recommendation for the reform of the zoo was to insist on pathological investigation, to open up, not a few, but all of their corpses, to compile accurate mortality statistics, and in general to make death and disease visible and knowable in order that it could better be mitigated.

Hediger's concerns correspond to Foucault's description of how the emergence of modern biopower produced a new political relationship to disease and death:

At the end of the eighteenth century, it was not epidemics that were the issue, but something else – what might broadly be called endemics, or in other words, the form, nature, extension, duration, and intensity of the illnesses prevalent in a population. (2003, 243)

The face of death mutated and withdrew, becoming disseminated throughout the processes of life: 'Death was no longer something that suddenly swooped down on life – as in an epidemic. Death was now something permanent, something that slips into life, perpetually gnaws at it, diminishes it and weakens it' (244). The gaze of power turned to mortality, which it problematised as a statistical object affecting the population as a whole. The result was that: 'Death is beyond the reach of power, and power has a grip on it only in general, overall, or statistical terms. Power has no control over death, but it can control mortality' (248). Such biopolitical intervention in mortality is precisely what we see in Hediger's zoo biology.

Despite the inadequacy of pathological records, at Sydney and from zoos in general, Hediger nonetheless made the best he could of the available information, using it to paint a picture where certain causes of death had declined due to improved keeping, while others regrettably remained due to inadequate care. Meanwhile he highlighted new types of mortality not found in the wild but occurring as a result of the conditions and interventions in the zoological garden. In particular, Hediger was concerned to articulate a new category of causes of death neglected elsewhere in the literature, a category 'which is rapidly assuming significance' (1969, 169). For Hediger, what must be attended to is 'death due to behaviour'. By this he referred to death caused not simply by disease, as was visible to a reductive physiological approach and addressed with increasing effectiveness by medicines and other veterinary measures, but death that resulted from the animals' behaviour and actions, from their psychological perceptions of their simulated environments, and thus, importantly, anthropogenic or iatrogenic deaths that are attributable to and preventable by the actions of their keepers. As will become apparent, this category of *death due to behaviour* exemplifies the protective apparatus of human/animal biopower elaborated in these institutions.

'Today', Hediger declared, 'there is a pressing need in zoo biology to analyse "death due to behaviour" in more detail and on the basis of this analysis to achieve an effective prophylaxis' (1969, 178). This category, he argued, had been under-recognised in other zoo mortality reports but could nonetheless be interpreted from among their given categories. He went on to provide a remarkable table cataloguing the 'background' to the different types of causes of death he considered to fall under the category of 'death due to behaviour':

A. Interspecific incompatability
  a) Predator-prey situation (e.g. fox—pheasant)
  b) "Sworn enemy" situation (e.g. dog—cat)
  c) Mobbing, i.e. song-bird—bird of prey
  d) Biological hierarchy (e.g. lion—leopard)
  e) Different reactions to contact and distance
  f) Different behaviour relative to stance (e.g. deer—kangaroo)
  g) Differences in activity rhythms (at the extreme, nocturnal and diurnal animals)
B. Intraspecific incompatibility
  a) Social hierarchy
  b) Territorial disputes
  c) Individual antipathy
  d) Sexual hyperactivity (rut)
  e) Misinterpretation of expressive behaviour
C. Disturbance reactions
  a) Refusal to feed (inanition)
  b) Automutilation
  c) Killing of the young (abandoning, eating)
D. Reactions to man
  a) direct: extreme flight, e.g. when being caught up
  b) indirect: spatial effects (unfamiliarity, fright reactions), injury in transit or transfers
E. Nutritional defects
  a) Quantitative (over-feeding)
  b) Qualitative (toxic effects)
  c) Picking up of foreign bodies

Figure 13.1 Hediger's catalogue of 'death due to behaviour' (1969, 179).

This is not an exhaustive list of causes of death in the zoo but only those Hediger classes as 'due to behaviour', that is, as brought about by what is to him not a biological given but a contingent, relational, knowable and controllable element of all living existence. Most of these causes are for Hediger in principle eliminable: 'The introduction of this term serves the purpose of drawing attention to the need for considering all the possible aspects of behaviour which could have contributed to the causes of death, because some behaviour patterns can be influenced or prevented' (1969, 174). For example, injuries and accidents such as fractured bones and even broken necks were common results of agitation; as opposed to medical diagnoses of infections or senility, often such problems 'can be traced back to fighting and flight, in other words they can be attributed clearly to behaviour patterns' (175). It is the job of the zoo director and his keepers to comprehensively observe the incidence of such dangerous behaviour patterns, and the effectiveness of their own practical interventions.

Foreign bodies are one common yet 'avoidable' (1969, 159) cause of fatalities. The zoo must be cleared of all 'dangerous or pathogenic' (160) objects that might harm the animals by being eaten or otherwise penetrating the skin, whether poisonous plants such as yew, or hazardous metals such as staples, nails and wires left behind by craftsmen, keepers, or the public. Having listed common examples, Hediger provided practical suggestions on how to avoid these dangers, as well as a general exhortation to forethought and scrutiny: 'Cases of this kind can be avoided in principle, providing the greatest care is taken to remove the source of danger. Strict control and inspection of the zoo premises can ensure prevention' (169). It is moreover knowledge of animals' behavioural inclinations that best guides decisions on permissible materials.

It is not only out of place objects within the grounds but all of its structures and buildings that are potentially dangerous if, equally, controllable elements of zoo organisation. In a chapter on 'Building for animals', Hediger expounded on 'the close relation between causes of death and constructional methods in zoos' (1969, 189). Failure to attend to species-specific requirements in building exhibits had often been and remained a regular cause of harm, whether from grooming behaviours such as rubbing horns against unbiological metals, too little or too much bathing, or failure to prevent foxes and other predators from entering the grounds. What is needed for a particular animal's enclosure 'does not lie within the choice of an individual or even of the architect, for it is compulsorily prescribed by the nature of the species' (198). With their expert knowledge of common mistakes and the ways in which architecture can cause or prevent death, reduce or promote health, zoo directors must insist on such biological prescriptions against the habits of architects and builders, however intuitive in aesthetic or practical terms. Enclosures require obtuse angles to assist their occupants to escape from potential pursuers. Animals must always have an auxiliary space to which they can be moved if intervention is required. Both wet and dry ditches have particular disadvantages, increasing the risk of drownings or other accidents. To avoid injurious escapes, barriers have specific height requirements for different species, which must not be underestimated, not only in terms of anatomical leap distances but also from a psychological perspective, given that 'the subjective height of a barrier may be significantly reduced by the so-called mood factor, that is, in conditions of excitement' (Hediger 1969, 191; see also 1964, 53). All aspects of zoo architecture can and should be modulated so as foster life and avoid danger and death.

Some of the clearest and most common causes of 'death due to behaviour' are those direct and indirect 'reactions to man' such as fight or flight in the process of transfers or treatments. Insufficiently tame animals might attempt to escape from perceived human enemies: 'It is possible for an animal to dash itself with all its strength against the cage, thus injuring itself seriously. In this way fractures of the skull or broken necks often result . . . No zoological gardens have been spared losses of this nature' (1964, 44). For Hediger, the act of transferring animals between enclosures within or between zoos should be considered an 'art' that requires skill and knowledge to be performed safely and effectively: 'transfers of this nature provide one of the main sources of "death due to behaviour", and it is imperative that progress should be made in zoo biology so that these fatalities no longer take place' (1969, 228). He related the horrific example of 110 dead monkeys arriving in a box from South America; such mass deaths in transit were, of course, the outcome of unscrupulous dealers and not the practice of the professional zoological garden (222).[3] However, zoos too were known to

---

3   On the development and protection of zoos' credentials as the only professional handlers of exotic animals, see Donahue and Trump (2006).

bungle relocations, such as when a pair of wallabies '[b]oth died of shock as a result of the fright experienced during the move into another enclosure' (227). Hediger spent a chapter advising on the best techniques for performing this art of catching up and transporting without provoking dangerous panic behaviours in the animals. But even when comfortably installed, all forms of contact by keepers must be expertly judged so as not to produce unnecessary disturbance or bring about avoidable harm.

It is, however, not only the most obviously human-caused elements of the zoo – whether artificial building materials or keeper interventions – that serve to produce 'death due to behaviour'. Insofar as the zoo is an entirely anthropogenic environment, this category indeed also covers all interactions between the animals (whether of the same or different species) as well as their responses to their milieux. Insufficient seclusion from disturbing noises or viewing visitors could cause agitation. Refusal to feed, self-mutilation, and the killing or abandonment of offspring were all signs of psychological 'disturbance reactions' to conditions and were thus likewise treatable in numerous ways, from assisted feeding to rehabilitation. Aggression and in-fighting were common, whether due to illness, restricted space, jealousy over food or the onset of breeding season. Roaming cats or other interlopers could cause panic among the immured. Introductions of new animals often produced not loving welcomes but dangerous fights: 'the incorporation of a new member into an existing society is an extraordinarily difficult task . . . Many animals die in the process if the necessary precautions are not observed' (1969, 173). Every level of social structure and all types of interactions, whether territorial, hierarchical, mating or otherwise, were rightly seen as impacted by human zookeeping decisions. Such antipathies and conflicts could thus be avoided by appropriately separating species and properly constituting the mix of cohabitants based not on inherited circumstance but the rational and natural principles of zoo biology.

As these examples indicate, the category of 'death due to behaviour' covers an extremely diverse range of circumstances. Though widespread, it is often not properly recognised or differentiated from among the regular hazards of disease or old age. Yet it is imperative to identify and to intervene to prevent its occurrence. As Hediger indicated,

> The underlying purpose here is not to establish a 'new' category of causes of death for its own sake, but to create a greater awareness of the behavioural components in many causes of death and thus devote greater efforts to establishing effective preventive measures. (1969, 175)

All too aware that mistakes (whether due to insufficient knowledge or inadequate technique) often led to animal losses, Hediger pushed for the professionalisation of animal care and management in zoos. Not only animals' relationships with their keepers but also every aspect of the anthropogenic circumstances in which they live, and of their species-specific behavioural response to this milieu, must be assessed as contributing to the animals' health or 'dis-ease', and must be modified in order to better foster their lives.

To focus on the behavioural and psychological dimension is Hediger's distinctive contribution to zoo biology: while others were more concerned with the enclosures as aesthetic or pedagogical displays for human visitors, or with the animals as physiological beings in objective terms, Hediger ensured the animals' unique subjective *Umwelten* were considered in constructing their new environments and improving their adjustment to them. Yet the result of this attention to animals' points of view and forms of expression – a refusal of mechanomorphic and behaviouristic determinisms – can not simply be understood as resulting in a progressive improvement in their care and welfare. The increased knowledge of varied nonhuman inner worlds opened up at the same time a sphere of practice, discourse and experience that, I propose, can be understood as that of *ethopolitics*. Extending biopolitical power/knowledge over the life of anatomical and species bodies, this emerging ethopolitical problematisation of behaviour produced what Foucault would call new 'domains of intervention, knowledge, and power' (2003, 245) that understood and acted upon animals as agents with unique perceptions and dispositions. Hediger's expertise in ethopower was thus able to even more effectively 'invest [animal] life through and through' (Foucault 1998, 139), penetrating both body and mind, comprehending and managing animals not only as biological organisms but as subjects of phenomenal worlds.

This ethopolitical domain was made intelligible and effectible in order to foster life and, with Hediger's 'death due to behaviour', to minimise mortality. Of course, the relationship of captive animals to a 'natural' death had already been interrupted by their protection from predators and disease and the regular provision of food (Sax 1997). Hediger embraced and celebrated these 'improvements', often favourably comparing the longevity of his wards to their wild counterparts (1964; 1969, 168). Nonetheless he insisted that zoo animals remained 'wild' and, though tame, undomesticated, and that other than in these two important respects (no longer needing to avoid enemies or find food), their behaviour ought to be 'as true to nature as possible' (1969, 63). In the regime of truth that he instituted and perpetuated, zoo exhibits should demonstrate the nature of a species in relation to its environment, not artificially, but by transposing natural conditions so that the animals within mirrored the norm of natural behaviour for their species in the wild (Hediger 1964, 72; 1968, 12; 1969, 20). Such demonstration nonetheless occurred under improved conditions in which dangers were removed and deaths prevented – not only regular accidents and injuries (which wild animals 'are by no means spared' [1969, 175]) but particularly those attributable to anthropogenic causes.

For this biopolitical regime, mortality was something to be eradicated as far as possible in its persistent and aleatory forms, an elusive adversary that could only be temporarily and inadequately held at bay. As Foucault put it:

> Now that power is decreasingly the power of the right to take life, and increasingly the right to intervene to make live, . . . to improve life by eliminating accidents, the random element, and deficiencies, death becomes, insofar as it is the end of life, the term, the limit, or the end of power too. (2003, 248)

Other than safeguarding wildlife through security and provision, the role of the zookeeper was in fact one of self-erasure, to eliminate all injurious anthropogenic impacts on the animals' behaviour, all detrimental changes wrought by captivity, and in particular the morbid factors that might produce illness or death: 'The zoo can only regulate, subdue and avoid excesses caused by confinement' (Hediger 1969, 194). All human influence in zoo animals' lives must be not harmful but salutary. In the case of death due to behaviour, 'we are concerned here not with details or statistics, but with the principle of extending preventative measures in new directions' (178). Through assessing and modifying all elements of the animals' artificially natural environments and their reactions to their significance, the zoo could be optimised towards the ideal of healthy, flourishing, reproducing specimens.

Yet as numerous thinkers of the biopolitical have maintained, the sovereign power to give death was never far removed from the imperative to actively take care (Agamben 1998; Mbembe 2003; Esposito 2008). In order to protect his flock, the shepherd must kill the wolf. Whether through war against external or internal enemies, or the creation of abject categories of certain forsaken subjects – particularly animals – the taking of life was rarely truly abandoned as a sovereign prerogative, even among the emerging medical and ecological managerial vocations. Biopower has preserved an enduring and intimate connection to death, presenting a dual face as a thanatopower that continues to 'make die' certain targets in order to safeguard its subject population. Foucault asked: 'How can a power such as this kill, if it is true that its basic function is to improve life, to prolong its duration, to improve its chances, to avoid accidents, and to compensate for failings?' (2003, 254). He argued that this life-affirming apparatus takes a deathly turn through the logic of racism, which:

is primarily a way of introducing a break into the domain of life that is under power's control: the break between what must live and what must die. The appearance within the biological continuum of the human race of races, the distinction among races, the hierarchy of races, the fact that certain races are described as good and that others, in contrast, are described as inferior: all this is a way of fragmenting the field of the biological that power controls. . . . That is the first function of racism: to fragment, to create caesuras within the biological continuum addressed by biopower. (2003, 254–55)

We witness here the return of sovereign violence in a modified biological form. Racial divisions enable the population that is to be defended, fostered and cared for to be separated from that which (in the name the life of the former) is to be excluded, disallowed or actively killed. Yet such racist divisions often find their originary model in the human/animal divide (Wolfe 2003; Agamben 2004), a divide already present and unremarked in Foucault's reference to the 'human race'. It is not racism but speciesism that here creates caesuras within the *non-human* biological continuum addressed by biopower, introducing 'the break between what must live and what must die', indeed creating multiple breaks and caesuras and allowing multiple contradictory practices to be directed towards each specific category of life, some loved and some unloved, some barely surviving, some living well at the expense of certain others.

Killing was likewise never far away from Hediger's zoological biopower. In his account of a lunch he shared with his good friend Hediger, the American biosemiotician Thomas Sebeok recounted how they were bothered by a pesky fly:

> I idly raised the question how the complex interplay of light, form, color, and motion perception, and so forth, that have steered the fly to our table as a potiential energy source could be deflected? Hediger, who of course well understood the intricacies of the neural network in the eyes of flies, answered with an impish smile, 'Let me show you.' He picked up his table knife and, when they fly next landed, lowered it in the manner of a guillotine precisely between its eyes, bisecting it along its anterior-posterior axis. We could now proceed with our meal. (Sebeok 2001, 16–17)

This rather fascinatingly repellent story illustrates the deadly possibilities opened up by Hediger's 'all but omniscient awareness of behavioral minutiae' (Sebeok 2001, 16). Ethological expertise enabled not only the effective prevention of 'death due to behaviour' among the protected, but also its direct production among unloved others.

In order to provide for the lives of the valued animals under their care, zoos regularly subject certain other groups of animals to death, whether as food, vermin or excess. In taking on the role of securing animals' lives by providing safety and sustenance away from the struggle for survival, zoos also arrogate the natural role of the predatory animals themselves to kill for food, wielding nature's red teeth and claws on its behalf. While it might not be aesthetically or culturally acceptable to feed flesh-eaters live prey – a pacific expectation that zoos themselves have propagated – they must still be provided with fresh meat to maintain their natural behaviour. Thus zoos cater to a wide variety of carnivore diets by producing food from other forms of life. Hediger, however, paid little attention to the deaths of food animals, focusing rather on the potential of diet to cause digestive diseases among his charges (1964, 121), on ensuring food was appropriate to species' needs, and on feeding patterns' possible psychical effects on natural behaviour. After all, as he liked to put it: 'The animal does not live on bread alone' (1969, 129; 1964, 120).

Yet zoo animals must not only be fed but also protected from disease-carrying pests such as mice, who present a particular problem in zoos. Hediger devoted special verve to a discussion of 'Catching mice without bait'. Despite his scientific sympathy for 'these attractive little rodents', they 'are unfortunately one of the creatures – like rats – that must be rigorously controlled in the zoo. Man must declare war on mice, not only in zoos, but everywhere; we have no choice' (1969, 245). These enemies of man were also the enemies of his wards, and it was on their behalf that Hediger went to war in the zoo.[4] What is remarkable is the expert means of his attack. The same skills that elsewhere enabled him to care for his animals so effectively were here put to deadly use. His sophisticated knowledge of their different sensory worlds, his characteristic ability to empathise with their perspectives and predict their needs, with which he helped them adjust to their enclosures and improved their wellbeing in numerous ways, were here deployed to ruthlessly remove their antagonists from his dominion. One can eradicate established populations of mice, he advised with his years of experience, by attending carefully to their behaviour patterns. Indeed they are so predictable that 'it could be regarded as a game, if it were not for the fact that it involves the killing of animals, even though they are of a dangerous and injurious kind' (1969, 251). This interspecies power game – in Foucault's terms, strategically modifying the actions of others – was focused on breaking up the mice's distinctive spatial behaviour. If one knows their 'runs', which function like a network of roads, one can place traps so precisely that bait is unnecessary. By using sympathetic projection to put oneself in the mind of a mouse and understand that it gets around by negotiating the familiar lines of its territory with a precise kinaesthetic sense, one can most effectively

---

4   On war against animals, see Wadiwel (2009).

intervene so as to eradicate it. Ethopolitics, too, becomes thanatopolit-ics.

Perhaps the most notorious of zoological contradictions has been the euthanasia of otherwise healthy animals. The irony of these un-wanted individuals, whom space or other considerations exclude from the zoo, is that they are a result of the exceptional effectiveness of efforts in breeding captive animals, and in extending their lives: 'In these con-ditions they can as it were exhaust their latent capacity for living' (1964, 36). Biopower's success in supporting life here warps into its distortion and occasions the giving of death. In 1963, Hediger had considered the problems and paradoxes of surplus zoo animals, describing how, given that captive longevity exceeds expectations in the wild, to a point were quality of life suffers, 'the question then arises of whether man, who has been responsible for lengthening the life of these animals, should not also bear the responsibility, under certain circumstances, of ending the animal's life by putting it painlessly to death' (Hediger 1969, 181). (It is of course not 'man', but a certain professional class – zoologists, veterin-arians, and other animal experts – to whom this responsibility falls.) Yet not only elderly animals but also the healthy surplus offspring resulting from over-production are at risk of being put down, as a last resort, due to what he calls the 'objective criteria' of 'total lack of accommodation' (182).[5]

Speciesism thus fragments the biological continuum of life, intro-ducing numerous divisions between those who must live and those who must die: not only that massive exception of humans from animality, but also between different species and groups of animals (separating,

---

5   As well as the naïve public outcry against the difficult decision to euthanise them, Hediger rejects the equally naïve suggestion that such animals should be reintroduced to the wild, as anthropogenic behavioural changes, such as the inability to escape predators or find their own food, would equally mean death: 'to believe that surplus zoo lions should be taken to Africa and released there … in practice this remarkable experiment would scarcely bear repeating; … it usually means a painful death for the animals involved' (1969, 181). The biopolitical disavowal of death's intertwining with life has thus utterly altered the animals' form of life. Yet today, in the name of conservation, reintroduction experiments wilfully send animals to likely death in an attempt to boost or re-establish native populations, and in fact go to great lengths to train captive-born animals to survive in the wild (Chrulew 2011).

for example, the exhibited predators and their provided food or contagious enemies), as well as breaks within species, between superior and inferior specimens, or between selected and surplus offspring. The former case divides between loved and unloved species, while the latter privileges the health of the species itself above the lives of its individual members.

Heini Hediger was instrumental in ushering the zoo across its 'threshold of biological modernity' (Foucault 1998, 143) such that the optimal psychological and bodily health of living populations became its chief strategic focus. He sought to create an environment from which all eliminable death was removed: that caused by interactions between animals and humans, between or within animal species, or between animals and their milieux. To prevent such anthropogenic 'death by behaviour', all the controllable elements of the zoo must be regulated and improved to the point where they foster life and disallow death. Death here became power's limit, a creeping adversary that took from it the captive living creatures it wished to nurture and exhibit. Mortality was confronted as a statistically knowable and technically preventable factor to be hounded out of the zoo's enclosures. Just as Hediger could inhibit death, he could also wield it; the sovereign right to kill remained in the form of a speciesist exclusion of certain groups or individuals judged disposable, instrumental, dangerous or inferior. Yet even such violent procedures were conceived and effected in the service of animal life, of those privileged specimens who were valued as spectacles but also, overridingly, as subjects of protection and care.

Works cited

Agamben G (1998). *Homo sacer: sovereign power and bare life*. D Heller-Roazen (Trans.). Stanford: Stanford University Press.

Agamben G (2004). *The open: man and animal*. K Attell (Trans.). Stanford: Stanford University Press.

Chrulew M (2010). From zoo to zoöpolis: effectively enacting Eden. In RR Acampora (Ed.). *Metamorphoses of the zoo: animal encounter after Noah* (pp193–219). Lanham, MD: Lexington Books.

Chrulew M (2011). Managing love and death at the zoo: the biopolitics of endangered species preservation. *Australian Humanities Review* 50: 137–57.

Donahue J & Trump E (2006). *The politics of zoos: exotic animals and their protectors*. DeKalb: Northern Illinois University Press.

Esposito R (2008). *Bíos: biopolitics and philosophy*. T Campbell (Trans.). Minneapolis & London: University of Minnesota Press.

Foucault M (1998). *The will to knowledge*. R Hurley (Trans.). 3 vols. Vol. 1, *The history of sexuality*. London: Penguin Books.

Foucault M (2003). *'Society must be defended': lectures at the Collège De France, 1975-1976*. M Bertani et al. (Eds). D Macey (Trans.). London: Allen Lane.

Hediger H (1964 [1950]). *Wild animals in captivity: an outline of the biology of zoological gardens*. G Sircom (Trans.). New York: Dover Publications.

Hediger H (1968 [1955]). *The psychology and behaviour of animals in zoos and circuses*. G Sircom (Trans.). New York: Dover Publications.

Hediger H (1966). *Report on Taronga Park Zoo from the viewpoint of biology of zoological gardens*. Sydney: Government Printer.

Hediger H (1969). *Man and animal in the zoo: zoo biology*. G Vevers & W Reade (Trans.). New York: Delacorte Press.

Hediger H (1985). A lifelong attempt to understand animals. In DA Dewsbury (Ed.). *Leaders in the study of animal behavior: autobiographical perspectives* (pp144-81). Lewisburg: Bucknell University Press.

Mbembe A (2003). Necropolitics. L Meintjes (Trans.). *Public Culture* 15(1): 11-40.

Rothfels N (2002). *Savages and beasts: the birth of the modern zoo*. Baltimore: Johns Hopkins University Press.

Sax B (1997). Are there predators in paradise? *Terra Nova* 2(1): 59-68.

Sebeok TA (2001). *The Swiss pioneer in nonverbal communication studies, Heini Hediger (1908-1992)*. New York; Ottawa: Legas.

Shukin N (2009). *Animal capital: rendering life in biopolitical times*. Minneapolis: University of Minnesota Press.

Wadiwel DJ (2002). Cows and sovereignty: biopower and animal life. *Borderlands e-journal* 1(2).

Wadiwel, DJ (2009). The war against animals: domination, law and sovereignty. *Griffith Law Review* 18(2): 283-97.

Wolfe C (2003). *Animal rites: American culture, the discourse of species, and posthumanist theory*. Chicago: The University of Chicago Press.

14
Nothing to see – something to see: white animals and exceptional life/death

Fiona Probyn-Rapsey

A white feather becomes attached to my windscreen wipers as I drive along a main road on the outskirts of south-western Sydney. The feather is stuck, thrashing about in the wind in frantic flight. White feathers are symbols of peace, of cowardice and writing's flights of fancy. Another feather appears, this one white as well. It too is a fluffy feather, a young bird's feather. My focus shifts from the feathers accumulating on my windscreen to the truck up ahead that is stopped in traffic. Coming up alongside it, I see it is stacked high with orange-red crates, each stuffed with live, white crouching chickens. This truck sits in the traffic, perfectly visible to all around it, with its white feathery bodies with no room to move, no protection from the elements, stacked like tyres, bricks or any other industrial product. I wonder how many other people in their cars around me want to get on their horns and protest the ordinary violence on display.[1] The lights change and the white mass of feathers stacked high in orange crates lurches off into the hills behind south-western Sydney; the white feathers on my windscreen wave. There is something about the uniformity of those birds squashed into crates, specifically their whiteness, that looms large in my mind; a mass

F Probyn-Rapsey (2013). Nothing to see – something to see: white animals and exceptional life/death. In J Johnston & F Probyn-Rapsey (Eds). *Animal death*. Sydney: Sydney University Press.

of undifferentiated white bodies, stacked and standardised, *visible but also invisibilised at the same time.*

The *standardisation* of the white broiler chick's appearance is, as Karen A Rader explains in relation to the 'iconic', standardised, inbred laboratory mouse, a story of the 'social and scientific meaning of biology' (2004, 7) in the 20th century where a new paradigm of template 'model organisms' are produced alongside and *as* new forms of knowledge. Rader gestures at the ethics of the cultivation of homozygous model organisms by reference to Zadie Smith's novel *White teeth.* The conclusion of *White teeth* raises the question of how to liberate an animal (in this case futuremouse) whose body is composed for death, where 'the damage is done' (Smith Qtd in Rader 2004, 266) by the time the organism is born. Smith goes on to write that the mouse 'carries around its own torture in its genes. Like a timebomb. If you release it, it'll just die in terrible pain somewhere else' (2000, 401). The broiler chicken is similarly placed. Temple Grandin has described the broiler chicken as 'pushed to the point where [their] physiology is totally pathological' (Grandin & Johnston 2009, 219). They are bred to make flesh fast, with depleted bones, collapsing legs and in pain. The whole question of their liberation necessarily involves a critique of standardisation, and here standardisation's meanings include not only the reproduction of model organisms,[2] template beings, but also what Grandin describes as a culture of 'bad becoming normal' (223). The industrial production of animals for human use requires standardisation in both these senses: genetically modified animals that produce meat *efficiently,* as well as the normalising of a certain view that animal life is secondary to that principal aim. This standard results in the chickens

---

1 Siobhan O'Sullivan's *Animals equality and democracy* (2011) calls for the development of a 'visibility framework' (69) for animal protection. Her work highlights how an animal's visibility correlates with its legal protection: the more visible, the greater the legal protection. Agricultural animals and laboratory animals have the least protection and least visibility. Here I wonder how whiteness (as standardisation) increases the invisibility of the agricultural and laboratory animal, while also making other white animals visible spectacles.

2 Rob Kirk describes *Standardised laboratory animals,* a publication from the Laboratory Animals Centre (UK) from 1971, as something that 'allowed users to choose a standard animal suitable for their purposes as easily as they might choose any other piece of technology or equipment from a trade catalogue' (2010, 93).

stacked in crates, stuck in traffic, to be taken to slaughter. When I see the meat chicks, I see them as, in some senses, *already dead.*

On top of their collapsing bodies, their standardised *whiteness* is another element in my perception of them as already dead. Whiteness in human-centred critical whiteness studies is exposed as a form of invisible privilege[3] and also, importantly, as a category of being that is haunted by absence and death. These associations can be brought to bear on the lives of white animals who also appear as extraordinary, or disappear in a standardised mass, depending on the context in which they are placed by humans: industrial farm, laboratory, zoo, wildlife sanctuary, breeding stock and/or companion. Whiteness is thus relevant to the ways in which animals are traded, treated, kept or killed. It is, as I hope to show, an important factor that makes them 'exceptional' both in Agamben's sense of living in a state of exception, but also extraordinary in the case of white animals displayed for their rarity, their freakishness, their *it would ordinarily be dead in the wild* 'value' to humans. Whiteness is both a tool for making invisible (the uniformity of the mass of broiler chickens) and for making spectacles (the display of albino animals in countless zoos around the world). The white animal is *nothing to see* and *something to see* depending on the context, including the conditions under which their whiteness is produced.

One way in which the white broiler chicken, like the iconic white lab mouse and rat, is exceptional, is in its designation within industry as *owing* its life to humans ('they would not exist without us'), and as therefore expendable (by us) within a discourse of sacrifice and 'noncriminal putting to death' (Derrida 1995, 278). As Derrida implies and Nicole Shukin makes plain, Agamben's 'state of exception' (which renders specific human lives in the concentration camp an example of 'bare life'), finds its 'zoopolitical supplement' in the 'modern industrial slaughterhouse' (Shukin 2009, 10). And prior to this, it is the paradigm of standardisation that leads to the idea that the animal *belongs* in captivity (laboratory or factory farm) and not in an alternative space where it can be liberated. Shukin observes that Agamben's 'bare life' and Foucault's account of biopolitics (that can reduce humans to a mere species body) 'presupposes the prior power to suspend other species in a state

---

3   Invisible in the sense of being hegemonic. That is, anyone who is not white can see white privilege, but white privilege is not necessarily seen by those who have it.

of exception within which they can be noncriminally put to death' (2009, 10). The whiteness of these animal bodies is one aspect of their standardisation that leads to this state of exception.

Their whiteness *in the billions* makes the broiler chicken an example of what Derrida refers to as 'regimentalization at a demographic level unknown in the past'[4] that includes

> [the] organization and exploitation of an artificial, infernal, virtually interminable survival, in conditions that previous generations would have judged monstrous, outside of every supposed norm of a life proper to animals that are thus exterminated by means of their continued existence or even their overpopulation. (2002, 394)

Part of the 'self evidence' in this 'industrial, mechanical, chemical, hormonal, and genetic violence' is in the uniformity and de-individuating of the animal bodies produced for consumption. Their conformity to a breeding standard, colour being only one element, assists in their assimilation into a machine-like state of de-animation, something which the industrialisation of animal bodies for meat production accelerates. Regimentalisation is another way of thinking about standardisation, in that it works to conceal by overproduction, to hide by multiplication and uniformity, a *something* that is then made into *nothing to see* uniformity. Derrida notes that this is a process that began 200 years ago and Noelie Vialles' anthropological study of the abattoir provides the evidence. Vialles' analysis traces modernity's exiling of the abattoir beyond the city limits and she finds that in its very architecture, the abattoir brings together the elements of conformity, whiteness, death, asepsis, acceleration and exception:

> If everything is up to standard, there is *nothing to be seen* anymore; indeed, the effect of standards and of conformity to standards is to render invisible what used to be a bloody spectacle. At the same

---

4   Andrew Knight points out that genetically altered animals now make up the majority of animals used in animal experimentation: 'The proportion of genetically altered animals used has been steadily rising since at least 1995, and in 2009 exceeded the number of normal animals used for the first time: in 2009, 52.4 percent of procedures involved animals that were genetically altered' (2011, 13).

time the colour of blood has been everywhere ousted by white: white walls, white accessories, white clothing from head to foot. This logic of an external, explicit, normative asepsis making everything commonplace forms the basis of a code in hygiene ... if anyone ever doubted the fact, it is clear from this that the effect of appearances is never without significance. (1994, 66; my emphasis)

When *white* meat is rendered from the blood red animal body, it is also being rendered as in *re-presented*, as Shukin points out. Its life form is rendered chromatically as a colour of aseptic industry (blankness, hygiene) in which there is a promise of 'nothing to see': no blood, feathers, death. As Vialles writes, 'the colour of blood has been everywhere ousted by white' (1994, 66). But add to this the fact of the *white* bird itself. An affective whiteout is part of the reason for the use of white birds for meat, as Annie Potts points out: white 'pinfeathers missed during plucking are less likely to be noticed by consumers' (Potts 2012, 150). Potts points out that backyard chicken fanciers did not favour white chickens for their risk to predators, but that 'once hens were contained indoors the colour of their plumage no longer mattered' (145). The chicken's uniform whiteness is also used as a reason for their intense captivity: broiler chickens are reared in barns for six weeks of rapid growth, seeing the outside world only when they are sent for slaughter. Producers can claim that the barns that hold these chickens keep them safe from predators, who otherwise would make targets of these starkly visible chickens in the open. This preference for white birds tells us something important about whiteness itself – that there is something about its disappearance (white pin feathers less likely to be noticed by customers) and its visibility (to predators) that together exceptionalise it for making white meat. The bird's whiteness is a form of disappearance/absence (the feather we can't see), and a form of hypervisibility (the feathers we predators see above all else). When these two come together as defining characteristics of the white meat bird, it is the human-predator who also disappears. The sensitive consumer who prefers not to see feathers on their flesh, and the sensitive farmer who 'protects' his flock from predators outside the barn,[5] both situate the bird's whiteness as a standard way of denying the relationship to the bird being eaten. Allowing a situation of 'bad becoming normal' (Grandin & Johnson 2009, 223), such conditions are also emblematic of a logic of protection: the protection of consumers from seeing lively feathers, the protection of birds from other predators. The logic of protection is, as Iris Marion Young and Wendy Brown observe, deeply contradictory. This is summarised best by Wendy Brown's observation (in a non-animal context) that 'to be "protected" by the very same power whose violation one fears perpetuates the very modality of dependence and powerlessness' (1995, 170).

If, as Vialles points out, modernity sends abattoirs into exile, then postmodernity makes their cargo visible again, only in the form of standardised, multiplied masses which in 'life' appear already dead. The making invisible of animal death also comes with the (over-)production of white birds, to be hidden in barns, but also *in* whiteness and because of their whiteness. They are the most hidden and the most numerous, as Potts describes: 'though they exist in the billions, layer hens and broiler (or meat) chicks are the breeds of Gallus least on show; that is, until they appear on supermarket shelves or in cans of pet food' (2012, 29). They are, in the sheer scale of their exile, like the 'subject without properties' (Dyer 1997, 80) that Richard Dyer describes in *White*. Dyer points out that in Western culture (his particular focus is film) white skins conjure up the 'living dead' (211) and forms of disembodiment (4) (hegemonic whiteness is invisible to those who benefit from it). Whiteness appears as a proximity to death not as in transcendence, but in immanence and 'mere' animality. Such 'necrological whiteness', as Joseph Pugliese writes, informs even our 'seemingly neutral scientific illustrations of forensic pathology' where the 'template body' of the dead subject is a white one (2006, 350).

Critical race scholars point out the long association between whiteness and death in Western and non-Western cultures. Alistair Bonnett's analysis of non-European whiteness highlights this association:

The association of whiteness with positive qualities was far from being universal in pre-modern societies. Moreover, in many societies whiteness was embroiled in more than one set of connotative traditions. In China, for example, as in many other societies (both

---

pre-modern and modern), whiteness was (and is) seen as the colour of death and mourning. Similar traditions exist in South America and Africa (Chevalier and Gheerbrant 1996). Describing 20th-century Kongo cosmology MacGaffey (1994, p. 255) explains that the 'dead ... contrast sharply with the living in some respects, one of which is that they are white in color ... This same whiteness, contrasting with the organic and domestic blackness of charcoal, appears in masks all over Central Africa'. A similar example is offered by Robert Harms (1981) in his study of identity constructions among the peoples of the central Zaire basin in the 19th century. Harms (1981, 210) notes that, 'White people were ... associated with spirits of dead ancestors ... Indeed, Mpoto, the name generally taken to mean "the country where white people came from", actually means 'the land of the dead' (Bonnett 1998, 1036).

Toni Morrison's discussion of chromatism, whiteness and racialisation in American literature finds that: 'Whiteness, alone, is mute, meaningless, unfathomable, pointless, frozen, veiled, curtained, dreaded, senseless, implacable' (1992, 59). Morrison's reading of whiteness locates it in its ideological as well as corporeal form, finding a profound fear and anxiety at its strange absence. Her work focuses on white people, but also includes white animals, for instance the white whale in Melville's *Moby-Dick* (1851). The whale's exceptional whiteness renders him more freakish, more spectacular, frightening and also more readily accessible to be 'filled up' by with the accumulative strategies of fetishisation. The white animal (sometimes on the spectrum of albinism) is prone to such fetishisation, which continues the association between whiteness and death by the fact that their lives become of special interest to humans as specimens, as forms of 'animal capital', to use Shukin's term. Animal capital can fetishise death, as well as expand our claims to act as 'protector' of the vulnerable. Albino animals, or the birth of white animals where colour is the norm, confirm the worst and best of human interest in animal life, and the fact that very often the two come together.

Albino animals very often make national headlines. 'Casper' the albino echidna, 'a rare and extraordinary addition to the unique wildlife of Tidbinbilla', was 'rescued off the side of a busy Canberra road' and then photographed, written about and celebrated in national news.[6] Casper's ghostly uniqueness, his exceptional treatment (rescue and pro-

tection) trades on his spectacular whiteness. Through Casper, Australian viewers get to experience the simultaneity of the 'semiotic currency of animal signs and the carnal traffic in animal substances'
(Shukin 2009, 7). Casper was released into the wildlife park, whereas
many albino animals become attractions in captivity. The emphasis on
rescuing wild albino animals from a life of hypervisible vulnerability to
predators persists in zoos and wildlife sanctuaries. The animals that are
in need of rescue (because hypervisible) are put on display, made hypervisible as spectacles, extending the point made by John Berger that
the gaze *between* man and zoo animal atrophies in spectacle-making
conditions (1980). And while the discourse of rescue makes much of
the vulnerability of the white animal in the wild (such that one might
think them grateful for their protective custody), this does not prevent
breeding programs designed to capitalise on and accelerate the production of these exceptional, 'extraordinary', vulnerable creatures.

Bordertown in South Australia has a population of kangaroos
which are all white (in fur) but are not albino. The Bordertown Wildlife
Park started up in 1968 with a 'selection of Australian Wildlife; grey
kangaroo's, emu's, ducks and other native animals [sic]' and now also
about 50 or so white kangaroos. In the 1980s, the wildlife park's owners
heard about the presence of two white kangaroos in a neighbouring
property, one of which had been recently shot and killed by goat shooters. The Park owner and local man Bill Hole decided to organise to
catch the last remaining white kangaroo:

His son Barry duly captured the kangaroo off his motorbike, a trick
he had perfected catching other kangaroos over the years, to show
the animals to visitors, without the kangaroo's [sic] being hurt. The
animal was sedated and brought to Bordertown by his sister Sandra,
in the back of her panel van. On arrival in Bordertown, the other
buck kangaroo's were shut away and the white male released into the
enclosure with the females. Suffering some stress, but otherwise unharmed, he took about six weeks to fully recover his strength and
move around normally. The first white joey was born in 1984, followed by a second two years later. There have been about fifty white

---

6   Rare albino Echidna released at Tidbinbilla [Online]. Retrieved on 19 Octover
2012 from www.tidbinbilla.com.au/.

individuals born at the park over the years. A number have been sent to parks and reserves around the country and there are currently fifteen in the Bordertown Park, proving indeed to be of great interest to tourists and visitors to the area. (Editor, 2010).

The kangaroo is an iconic Australian animal and this mob of exceptional white kangaroos, in which there is 'great interest', cannot help but draw attention to the simultaneous oddness and naturalness of a 'white Australian'. What is on show here is an exceptional icon of persistent vulnerability, but how much this 'great interest' comes close to white settler nationalism, where whiteness has always been an issue of vulnerability and violence, is not clear. In the period following the Second World War, 'Digger' the white kangaroo was a present to the London Zoo from the Stockowner's Association of South Australia and, in 'shaking hands' with Winston Churchill, made headlines back home. Digger's 'grey skin' companions would not 'have any part of Churchill. They loped away each time he approached' (*The Advertiser* [Adelaide], 12 September 1947, 1). Digger's whiteness made him extraordinary, and somehow a better match for the ex-British PM than his two 'grey skin' companions. Two other 'iconic' Australian breeds – the Australian sheepdog and the Australian cattle dog – are marked out and haunted by a problematic, unhealthy whiteness, as the 'White Aussies' website proclaims: 'we feel it would be best if these dogs were no longer produced . . . White is not a color that any responsible Australian Shepherd breeder would strive for or advertise about' (White Aussies Project 2003–2005) because it is associated with deafness: ear hairs need pigment in order to function. The 'White Aussies Project' is, like many sites and clubs devoted to breeding, heavily inflected by the rhetoric of (human) race and, in this context, whiteness is both a 'project' for standardisation and a source of fear and anxiety. In the sphere of domestic, companion animals, albino animals are to be avoided: 'No decent breeder would EVER breed an albino dog. You are a moron' (Answerer 6, 2012). Such disputes and controversies also persist in the reptile breeders' online discussions: 'Albinos which were once the Ferrari of the reptile world are now ending up in shelters because new "prettier" snakes are out there' (Razoraze 2007). Such discussions highlight the nothing to see – something to see dynamic at play in and around the white-bodied animal, on show as spectacle of freakish vulnerability, to be carefully managed, bred out, bred in, controlled, hidden, culled and worried over. The white animal portrays ambivalence between life and death, not least in the form of the laboratory mouse, the white lab rat, an animal that belongs to science almost completely. They are often depicted as little heroes of science because they are 'human symbionts' (Rader 2004, 124), because they make life abundantly (they are spectacularly successful breeders) and have been made to make it so exactly, with generations of brother to sister inbreeding producing homozygous 'individuals' that epitomise standardisation. The lab rat and mouse, sometimes albino, often not, sometimes 'pink-eyed whites', sometimes not, are also sometimes described as 'creepy'. One website devoted to pet rats suggests that: 'They are the hardest to find homes for in rescue's [sic] because they are "plain" or because they fit the Hollywood stereotype of evil lab creatures' (Random Rats 2007). Such 'evil' connotations persist around humans with albinism as the National Organization for Albinism and Hypopigmentation points out. Hollywood depicts people with albinism as villains; the nasty sidekick in *Cold mountain* and the twins in *Matrix reloaded* and more recently Silas in *The Da Vinci code*. There is also the very white Lucius and Draco Malfoy ('mud-blood haters') in the Harry Potter films. Activist Luna Eterna (2006) catalogues the negative accounts of people with albinism in literature, film and other popular culture texts. The Skinema website also criticises the stereotyping of albinism in films which situate people with albinism as vampiric, with red eyes, and as associated with death, sadomasochistic cruelty, fascist eugenicism and evil: 'There have been 67 movies since 1960 where the protagonist is an evil albino' (Waugh quoted in Reese 1997–2008). Such stigmatising of people with albinism is, according to Natalie Wan, 'embedded in our society' (2012, 278). She notes that these Hollywood depictions indicate that 'prejudice towards persons with albinism is socially acceptable' (278). Albinism is, because of its chromatism, linked to racialisation, something that the film *Powder* (1995) plays upon.[7] On finding a supernaturally gifted[8] albino boy called Powder in the basement of his grandparent's home, the Sheriff tells his aggressive deputy, Harley Duncan: 'never thought we'd

---

7   Thanks to Matt Chrulew for bringing this film to my attention.

find someone *too white for you'* (Salva 1995). Albinism makes whiteness highly visible in societies where ideological whiteness is often invisible to those who identify with it. As Richard Dyer points out, the whole point of the privilege of whiteness is that it goes unnoticed, that there is *nothing to see*. Albinism, however, invokes the opposite response: *look!*

Spectacularisation and hypervisibility of albino animals is something well known to zoos and wildlife parks. Examples abound, from my local wildlife park with its all-white kookaburra, to the internationally renowned Snowflake,[9] an albino western lowlands gorilla at the Barcelona Zoo after his capture in Equatorial Guinea in the 1960s. Snowflake was a hugely popular attraction and the zoo attempted, unsuccessfully, to breed more 'white gorillas' just like him. Cincinnati Zoo has selectively (in)bred white tigers since 1974, from original white tigers on loan from India. Through selective inbreeding across generations (brother to sister) the Cincinnati zoo has become a principal trader in white tigers, exporting them over the world and in exchange for other species. The Executive Director of Cincinnati's zoo, Edward Maruska, explains: 'Everywhere they go they increase attendance. Without people coming through the gate we are nothing . . . they are footing the bill. The people would run me out of town if we got rid of the white tigers' (Qtd in Cohn 1992, 654). The inbreeding programs and the breeding of animals with these recessive genes that would possibly, in the wild, compromise their survival is intensely controversial:

> The only conceivable legitimate reason for exhibiting a white tiger would be for educational purposes to clearly and unequivocally illustrate to the public the process of natural selection and how, when a deleterious recessive genetic mutation randomly occurs that is disadvantageous for the survival of the animal, such as white color in

---

8 *Al Jazeera* reported on the trade in the body parts of albino men, women and children in Burundi, on 23 July 2009, and in Tanzania in 2007. They report that the body parts of people with albinism are believed to have medicinal, magical properties. Available at: www.youtube.com/ watch?feature=endscreen&NR=1&v=9F6UpuJIFaY.
9 See also the children's movie *Snowflake: the white gorilla* (Schaer 2011). The film depicts Snowflake as desperate to fit in with his fellow gorilla captives, but reassured of the value of his difference by the human children who love him for 'what he is'.

a tropical jungle environment, the animal does not survive to pass on that genetic mutation or disadvantageous characteristic to its offspring. (Laughlin 2012)

In other words, the legitimate display of the white tiger would be in the context of it appearing as an example of the living dead – that which *naturally* would be dead but has life in confinement. The proximity of these lives/deaths is reflected in the following defence of breeding white tigers:

> One thing is for sure, we humans see our world in full colour and white attracts our attention, our admiration, and our desire – the desire to possess, especially anything rare. Some seek to take possession of the living being, others want the trophy body. Either way, over time the white tiger was selectively removed from nature whenever man observed it. (Culver 1955–2013)

To be 'removed from nature' brings together the themes of nothing to see / something to see in the form of: captivity, desire, death, beauty, attraction, observation and possession. Shukin's analysis of 'animal capital' – the 'animal meme and animal matter' that circulates today – expresses this sad love for a lost object, already gone but substituted by some unsettling semblance of what once was, or what shouldn't *be*. In their proximity to whiteness, these animals are 'meme and matter' in different ways to other captives. This is because they are marked by the (non-)colour of whiteness, caught not just *within* but *as* the space between death and life: whiteness as vulnerable hypervisibility and as exceptional life; to be made *more of* in order to be continually unmade.

Works cited

Answerer 6 (2012). How much does Albino poodles (puppies) are sold for now in days? [sic] *Yahoo Answers* [Online]. Available: answers.yahoo.com/question/index?qid=20111115201237AAinYJM [Accessed March 2012].

Berger J (1980) Why look at animals? In *About looking*. New York: Pantheon.

Bonnett A (1998). Who was white? The disappearance of non-European white identities and the formation of European racial whiteness. *Ethnic and Racial Studies* 21(6): 1029–55.

Brown W (1995). *States of injury, power and freedom in late modernity*. Princeton: Princeton University Press.

Cohn JP (1992). Decisions at the zoo. *BioScience* 42(9): 654–59.

Culver L (1955–2013). 9 generations of white tigers. *Feline Conservation Society* [Online]. Available: www.felineconservation.org/fcf/ 9_generations_of_white_tigers.htm [Accessed 11 March 2013].

Derrida J (2002). The animal that therefore I am (more to follow). *Critical Inquiry* 28(2) Winter: 369–418.

Derrida J (1995). Eating well, or the calculation of the subject. In E Weber (Ed.), P Kamuf (Trans.). *Points: interviews 1974–1994* (pp255–87). Stanford: Stanford University Press.

Dyer R (1997). *White*. London: Routledge.

Editor (2010). The origin of Bordertown's white kangaroos. *Borderonline* 16 July 2010. Available: www.borderonline.com.au/?p=218 [Accessed 11 March 2013]

Eterna, L (2006). Albinism in popular culture [Online]. Available: web.archive.org/ web/200101240804/http://www.lunaeterna.net/popcult/ [Accessed 23 November 2012].

Grandin T & Johnson C (2009). *Animals make us human*. Boston: Houghton Mifflin Harcourt.

Laughlin D (2012). Zoo vet on white tiger fraud. Big Cat Rescue blog [Online]. Available: bigcatrescue.org/abuse-issues/issues/white-tigers [Accessed 7 September 2012].

Knight, A (2011). *The costs and benefits of animal experimentation*. London: Palgrave.

NOAH (The National Organization for Albinism and Hypopigmentation) (n.d.). A call for Hollywood to retire the evil albino character [Online]. Available: www.albinism.org/ [Accessed July 2006].

Kirk, R (2010). A brave new animal for a brave new world: The British Laboratory Animals Bureau and the constitution of international standards of laboratory animal production and use, circa 1947–1968. *Isis* 101(1): 62–94.

Morrison T (1992). *Playing in the dark: whiteness and the literary imagination*. Cambridge: Harvard University Press.

O'Sullivan S (2011). *Animals, equality and democracy*. London: Palgrave Macmillan.

Potts A (2012). *Chicken*. London: Reaktion.

Pugliese J (2006). Necrological whiteness: the racial prosthetics of template bodies. *Continuum: A Journal of Media and Cultural Studies* 19(3): 349–64.

Rader KA (2004). *Making mice: standardizing animals for American biomedical research, 1900–1955*. Princeton: Princeton University Press.

Random Rats (2007). 'PEW awareness' website [Online]. Available: www.freewebs.com/jazztherat/pewawareness.htm [Accessed March 2012].

Reese V (1997–2008). Albinism controversy featured on *Inside Edition* [Online]. Available: Skinema.com [Accessed March 2012].

Razoraze (2007). Should we breed albinos? *Redtailboa.net*, 8 February [Online]. Available: Redtailboa.net [Accessed January 2012].

Salva V (1995). *Powder*. Hollywood Pictures.

Schaer AG (Dir.) (2011). *Snowflake: the white gorilla*. Filmax International.

Shukin N (2009). *Animal capital: rendering life in biopolitical times*. Minneapolis: University of Minnesota Press.

Smith Z (2000). *White teeth*. New York: Random House.

Vialles N (1994). *Animal to edible*. Cambridge: Cambridge University Press.

Wan N (2012). Orange in a world of apples: the voices of albinism. *Disability & Society* 18(3): 277–96.

White Aussies Project (2003–2005) [Online]. Available: www.lethalwhites.com [Accessed 22 April 2013].

15
'Death-in-life': Curare, restrictionism and abolitionism in Victorian and Edwardian anti-vivisectionist thought

Greg Murrie

This chapter focuses on the state of death-in-life which Victorian and Edwardian anti-vivisectionists considered vivisection under curare – a neuromuscular blocking drug which prevents nerve impulses from activating voluntary muscles – to effect in laboratory animals. Although death-in-life is a metaphor that can easily be extended to the vivisectional process *in toto*, it was the pain nonhuman animals were considered to experience under curare, and their helplessness to fight back or signify their distress under its influence, that caused it to serve as a powerful symbol and propaganda tool for the totality of suffering Victorian and Edwardian anti-vivisectionists believed was associated with vivisection. I situate curare within the struggles British anti-vivisectionists had amongst themselves as to the wisdom and efficacy of an abolitionist versus a restrictionist stance in their fight against vivisection.

In addition, my chapter explores the influence that evolutionary theory had on the restriction/abolition question by its highlighting of the consanguinity between humans and other animal species, and investigates various ways in which anti-vivisectionism, both then and now, has risked being trivialised by a tendency for its detractors and

G Murrie (2013). 'Death-in-life': Curare, restrictionism and abolitionism in Victorian and Edwardian anti-vivisectionist thought. In J Johnston & F Probyn-Rapsey (Eds). *Animal death*. Sydney: Sydney University Press.

historians alike to psychopathologise its propelling force as a projection of human anxieties. Despite this, it is undeniable that anti-vivisection-ism and the burial reform movement shared many of the same actors; in my penultimate section I explore the late Victorian and Edwardian fear of premature burial and how this links with anti-vivisectionism, particularly in regards to the spectre of the laboratory animal under the influence of curare. In conclusion I argue that due to the overreach-ing emphasis on the *pain* experienced by animals during vivisection, particularly under curare, an abolitionist debate about the ethics of us-ing animals at all for human experimentation based around the *moral status* of nonhuman animals – parallel to the 19th- and early 20th-cen-tury challenge of vegetarianism to all killing of animals for food – was largely neglected.

Restriction versus abolition

The history of Victorian and Edwardian anti-vivisectionism, both in the way contemporary anti-vivisectionists understood their own move-ment while it was extant, and in subsequent historiography, particularly over the last 40 years, has often worked within a binary opposition which pits activists who fought for the restriction of vivisection against those who fought for its abolition. This is an opposition which is plainly demonstrable in late 19th- and early 20th-century anti-vivisectionist literature as it caused prominent activists to leave anti-vivisectionist so-cieties when the policy of the society shifted from a restrictionist to an abolitionist stance, and others to leave societies and begin entirely new ones on the basis of an abolitionist stance when the former society opened the door to fight vivisection on the basis of restriction, albeit with the ultimate end of abolition in view.[1]

Historiographically it is evident, for example, in Richard D French's seminal source on anti-vivisectionism in the Victorian period, *Antivivi-section and medical science in Victorian society*, in which the opposition operates as one of its chief structuring devices.[2] For the crucialness of the abolition versus restriction distinction one need only consider the titles of some abolitionist anti-vivisectionist organisations of the period (the Society for the Abolition of Vivisection and the International As-sociation for the Total Suppression of Vivisection for instance) and of some anti-vivisectionist journals (*The Abolitionist*), and the heated debates which emerged between The National Anti-Vivisection Society, The British Union for the Abolition of Vivisection and the Animal Defence and Anti-Vivisection Society in the last years of the 19th and first decades of the 20th century.[3]

In parallel with this, some animal activists in this period argued against vivisection explicitly on the basis of rights and others employed an animal protectionist model of the need for humans to care for other species according to a model of *noblesse oblige*.[4] If one were to take one's bearings from late 20th- and 21st-century animal activism, a likely assumption would be that Victorian and Edwardian rights activists would have been far more likely to have made a strong case against vivisection based on the claim that humans had no right to use other species for selfish purposes, and also to have made an argument against vivisection based on the concept of the equality of all species. The lit-

---

1   As an example of the former, Dr George Hoggan (1837–91), the co-founder and co-Honorary Secretary (with Frances Power Cobbe) of the Society for the Protection of Animals Liable to Vivisection (commonly referred to as 'The Victoria Street Society') from its inception until 1878, left the Society in 1878 because it adopted the stance of total abolition; as an example of the latter, Cobbe (1822–1904) herself left the Victoria Street Society (by this time The National Anti-Vivisection Society) in 1898 when a policy of 'Lesser Measures' was introduced, and formed a new society, The British Union for the Abolition of Vivisection, in the same year. The policy of 'Lesser Measures' was introduced in order to present a bill to parliament which could control the abuses of vivisection, as a series of bills presented in 1877, 1879, 1880 and 1884 based on abolition had all either been defeated or failed to receive a second reading. See French (1975, 88); Cobbe (1904, 644, 657, 662–63, 668–69, 689–92); and Great Britain (2005–2012).
2   French (1975, 84, 89–90, 107, 114–15, 129–30, 138–9, 160–65, 169–70, 282, 287, 302).
3   For the latter, see, for example, Coleridge (1902).
4   For the concept of animal 'rights' in this period, see Salt (1980 [1892]). In regards to anti-vivisectionism and *noblesse oblige*, from the outset of the agitation British anti-vivisectionism enjoyed the strong support of the aristocracy, both local and foreign. The briefest perusal of the list of the Victoria Street Society's Executive Committee and Vice-Presidents, for example, anytime in the late 19th century, reveals such luminaries as the Archbishop of York, Cardinal Manning, Lord Mount-Temple, the Earl of Shaftesbury, the Bishop of Gloucester and Bristol, the Bishop of Manchester and Lord Chief Justice Coleridge.

erature on vegetarianism, a parallel arena of animal advocacy in this period with advocates who overlapped strongly with anti-vivisectionism, would lead one to expect to find a strong correlation between those fighting for abolition and having a rights agenda, versus those fighting for restriction and operating from a protectionist model.

This neat alignment of abolition and rights versus restriction and protection, in fact, does not exist in the anti-vivisectionist discourse of the period. It is not that Victorian and Edwardian animal rights activists did not argue both that humans do not have the right to use other species for selfish ends *and* that all species should be given equal moral consideration; these arguments were particularly prominent amongst anti-vivisectionists who were also vegetarians. Rather, it is that these arguments made almost no appearance in any mode of *anti-vivisectionist* discourse. It is important when considering Victorian and Edwardian anti-vivisectionist activism not only to guard against projections from late 20th-century and subsequent animal politics, but also against making too easy a slippage between it and the, on the whole, more radical vegetarian political ideology of the period.

Instead, what is found in an examination of almost all 19th- and early 20th-century anti-vivisection literature is an overwhelming emphasis on the spectre of animal pain and suffering, or torture as a very common trope of the time puts it, and not on the fact that the end of the process of vivisection was invariably the death of the animal. This is evident, for example, in the two bills presented to parliament in 1875 for the regulation of vivisection. The bill for 'Regulating the Practice of Vivisection', proposed by Cobbe and presented in the House of Lords by Lord Henniker (1842–1902), stipulated that anaesthetics be used in all experiments. The alternative bill, devised by the scientific lobby which was anxious to forestall more prohibitive legislation, and presented in the House of Commons by Lyon Playfair (1818–98), focused solely on the regulation of *painful* experiments on animals. In neither case was the taking of the life of the animal being experimented upon an explicit cause for concern (French 1975, 69–73). The emphasis in anti-vivisectionist discourse of this period, if not on the effect of vivisection on its practitioners, onlookers or the human race in general, was typically firmly fixed on the experience of the nonhuman animal on the vivisecting table and the desire to reduce the potential pain associated with this, not that the animal was there in the first place.

In particular, especially at the outset of the anti-vivisectionist agit-ation in the 1870s, it was the use of curare, a poison that affected the nerves of motion but not sensation, so that it completely paralysed the animal but yet had no anaesthetic properties, that was the particular bane of anti-vivisectionists.[5] In this state the animal remained alive – artificial respiration was applied – in a state of excruciating pain, but was unable to struggle or voice its distress. As such, the focus of anti-vi-visectionists when they contemplated the scene of vivisection was more strongly on the hope that the animal would die and be relieved from pain, rather than a strong rights position holding that it was unethical for humans to experiment on other species per se. Paradoxically there is often more focus on animal death per se in the writings of experimental physiologists than in that of anti-vivisectionists, and a corresponding deliberate *lack* of attention in physiological discourse on the spectre of the suffering of the animal in the process of vivisection.

Historical overview

In order to make sense of these particularities, I will outline extremely briefly the histories of vivisection and British anti-vivisection up until the controversy over vivisection resulted in the Royal Commission on the Practice of Subjecting Live Animals to Experiments for Scientific Purposes being conducted in 1875 and the Cruelty to Animals Act being instituted in 1876.[6] By observing how the anti-vivisectionist agit-ation was transposed to Britain from English concern over vivisectional atrocities on the Continent in the mid-19th century, it can be under-stood how the later anti-vivisection debate in Britain came to be framed

---

5   For the history of curare as a poison, muscle paralysant and relaxant, and clinical drug, see McIntyre (1947) and Hoffman (2009). I take the 1870s as my starting point in discussing anti-vivisectionism in this paper as, although there had been English opposition to vivisection in Italy and France in the decades before that, it was only in the 1870s that English anti-vivisectionist activists began to focus on the practice in their own country.
6   For the Royal Commission, see Great Britain (1876), *Report of the Royal Commission*. For the Cruelty to Animals Act, see Great Britain, An Act to Amend the Law Relating to Cruelty to Animals, No. 39 & 40, 15 August 1876 in Great Britain (1876), *The law reports*.

around questions of the degree of pain to which animals were subjected, rather than on their status as experimental subjects per se.

As Henry Salt outlines in *Animals' rights*, vivisection is an ancient
practice stretching back thousands of years (Salt 1980 [1892], 93n).
Galen practised it; Celsus refers to human vivisection; and it was practised on both animals and humans in the Middle Ages (Salt 1980
[1892], 93n–94n). With the birth of modern experimental physiology
in the 19th century, which particularly flowered in France and Germany, François Magendie was famous, or notorious, early in the century in France for his experiments on the nervous system of animals in
which he demonstrated the different functions of the sensory and motor nerves in the spinal cord.[7] It was Magendie's former assistant Claude
Bernard, however, who in his 1865 *Introduction to the study of experimental medicine* became the *bête noire* for many in the anti-vivisection
movement (Bernard 1927).

Bernard, writing at the high point of scientific positivism in France,
and at the crucial point at which experimental physiology was establishing itself as a scientific endeavour with a professional identity
separate from the practice of medicine, announces in his section on vivisection:

> A physiologist is not a man of fashion, he is a man of science, ab-
> sorbed by the scientific idea which he pursues: he no longer hears the
> cry of animals, he no longer sees the blood that flows, he sees only
> his idea and perceives only organisms concealing problems which he
> intends to solve. (Bernard 1927, 103)

Bernard draws the conclusion that it is useless to argue against those
opposed to such experimentation as their frame of reference is so di-
vorced from that of the man of science that no agreement could ever
be broached, even if they are physicians. As such, the 'man of science'
should only take heed of the opinions of others like him and follow his
own individual conscience (Bernard 1927, 103).

---

7   For the development of experimental physiology on the Continent during the
course of the 19th century, see Coleman and Holmes (1988), Cunningham and
Williams (1992) and (for France) Lesch (1984). For Magendie, see Olmsted
(1944).

Vivisection was practised in Britain at this time and had been for centuries, but no scientific institutions existed that sanctioned the practice, so it was easier for British people with anti-vivisectionist sympathies to focus on particularly flagrant acts of what they perceived as cruelty on the Continent. As such, Frances Power Cobbe – feminist, theologian, journalist and woman of letters – who was to become the most high profile anti-vivisectionist of the 19th century, became involved in the agitation in 1863 when reports of vivisections on horses at veterinary schools in Alfort in France, performed by veterinary students to acquire surgical skill, began to appear in English newspapers.[8] She wrote an article attempting to deal with the ethical questions involved in human rights trumping nonhuman in this way. In addition, living near Florence as a foreign correspondent upon the month of the article's publication, Cobbe was the recipient of eyewitness reports of mangled live dogs and pigeons emanating from the laboratory of Moritz Schiff there.[9]

It was not until the early 1870s that British anti-vivisectionists focused on what was occurring in vivisectional laboratories within Britain itself. British physiologists by this time were well aware that they lagged far behind their Continental *confrères* in establishing the presence of experimental medicine in their own country (French 1975, 36–41). In 1870, at a British Association for the Advancement of Science meeting in Liverpool, a committee was formed to deal with the subject of physiological experimentation, and the following year guidelines for physiologists were published in an attempt at self-regulation of the practice (French 1975, 44–46; Cobbe 1904, 624–25).

Around this time those who were to become the leading British experimental physiologists of the 19th century were establishing themselves as such: John Burdon-Sanderson at University College and The Brown Institution for Animals at the University of London; Michael Foster at University College and Cambridge University; and Edward Schäfer (who changed his name in 1918 to Sharpey-Schafer in honour

---

8 For Alfort, see French (1975, 25, 30–31, 44–6). For Cobbe's specific association with the issue, see Cobbe (1904, 620–21). For a background to Cobbe in general, see Cobbe (1904) and Mitchell (2004).
9 Cobbe (1865); Cobbe (1904, 622–24). For Schiff (1823–96), see Guarnieri (1987).

of his physiologist mentor William Sharpey) at University College.[10] Cobbe considered that the attempts of the profession to self-regulate were not being enforced in any way; she was particularly opposed to the fact that advertisements for medical schools in the mid-1870s sought to attract potential students by promising them the ability to perform their own vivisections (Cobbe 1904, 625).

In 1873 and 1874 two events transformed this unease into a full-scale controversy. First, in 1873 *Handbook for the physiological laboratory* was published. Edited by Burdon-Sanderson with sections by himself, Foster, Emanuel Klein and Lauder Brunton – Klein was assistant professor at the Brown Institution and Brunton was a lecturer at St Bartholomew's Hospital, London, so all four practised in Britain – it clearly announced itself in the preface as being for 'beginners in physiological work' and almost completely failed to mention anaesthetics in the course of its many hundreds of pages.[11]

Anti-vivisectionists, after the publication of the *Handbook*, perceiving rank amateurs to be vivisecting without anaesthetics all over the country, were then mobilised in 1874 when Valentin Magnan, a French psychiatrist who did research on the effects of absinthe, was invited to lecture at the annual British Medical Association meeting in Norwich, and then induce epilepsy in two dogs by injecting them intravenously with the spirit.[12] The meeting turned into a debacle when, the first dog having been injected, a protest ensued amongst the medical men and one layman present, and one of the dogs was set free; two months later the RSPCA charged Magnan and the three Norwich doctors who had arranged the demonstration with wanton cruelty to a dog. The prosec-

10   French (1975, 42). For further information on Burdon-Sanderson, see Romano (2002); for Foster, see Geison (1978); for Schäfer, see Marshall (2009).
11   Klein, Burdon-Sanderson, Foster and Brunton (1873, i, vii). Burdon-Sanderson at the Royal Commission claimed that 'It is generally understood that we use anæsthetics whenever we possibly can, and consequently that is a thing taken for granted' (Great Britain 1876. *Report of the Royal Commission*, Question 2265), but this attitude to anaesthetics was not shared by all the contributors to the volume; see my later discussion of Klein's evidence at the Commission. For the controversy over the *Handbook,* see French (1975, 47–50). For Emanuel Klein (1844–1925), see Atalić & Fatović-Ferenčić (2009). For Brunton (1844–1916), see Gunn (2004).
12   For Valentin Magnan (1835–1916), see Luauté (2007).

ution failed as Magnan was back in France and did not appear, but the publicity the case generated ensured that vivisection remained on the press' agenda, two bills were put before parliament to regulate vivisection – one inspired by Cobbe and the other by the scientific fraternity – and a Royal Commission on the subject was called in May 1875.[13]

The Royal Commission and curare

At this point I leave my potted history of vivisection in Britain and focus upon one of the key elements of vivisection upon which both the Royal Commission and anti-vivisectionists concentrated: the experience of the nonhuman animal in the act of being vivisected, and particularly the experience of the animal under the influence of curare.

Curare is a poison inducing paralysis that was traditionally used by South American indigenes in tandem with arrows or darts as a weapon. The arrow or dart was dipped in curare and shot at the victim who died of asphyxiation as his or her respiratory muscles became paralysed and failed to contract. By 1781 Felix Fontana, the Italian physicist and naturalist, had discovered that it only acted on the voluntary muscles, not the nerves or heart, and in a series of experiments in 1811–12 Sir Benjamin Brodie, an English physiologist, demonstrated that curare did not kill an animal, but it recovered completely if its respiration was maintained artificially.[14]

Claude Bernard frequently used curare; in his essay 'Physiological studies on certain American poisons', published in 1864, he described his first use of curare on a frog, in which he discovered the motor nerves became paralysed, whereas other parts of the body retained their physiological functions. He later went on to apply curare to birds and mammals with the same results.[15]

---

13   For the Norwich incident, see French (1975, 55–60) and Cobbe (1904, 627–28). French incorrectly refers to 'Eugene' Magnan. For an account of the Royal Commission, see French (1975, 91–111) and Cobbe (1904, 640, 642–44, 646–47).
14   McIntyre (1947, 1, 6–7, 87–88). See also Fontana (1781) and Brodie (1811).
15   Bernard (1864); Black (1999). For Bernard, see also Olmsted and Olmsted (1952).

Bernard's experiments were significant within the British anti-vivi-sectionist context. George Hoggan, a doctor who after having received his Bachelor of Medicine from Edinburgh University spent four months as an assistant in Bernard's laboratory in Paris, published in the London *Morning Post* in February 1875 an extraordinarily powerful letter, just over a week after the RSPCA had had presented to it a memorial signed by 600 of the most influential men and women in Britain urging it to fight to restrict vivisection.[16]

Hoggan's letter described the secrecy with which physiological ex-periments were conducted. He drew on his personal experience in Bernard's laboratory without naming him: in this laboratory one to three dogs were vivisected each day, in addition to rabbits and other animals; Hoggan's belief was that not one of those experiments was jus-tified. He claimed that 'the good of humanity' as the motivation for vivisection was an idea laughed at:

the great aim being to keep up with, or get ahead of, one's contem-poraries in science, even at the price of an incalculable amount of torture needlessly inflicted on the poor animals. (Hoggan 1883, 1)

Dogs were described as being brought up from the cellar where they were kept before vivisection, and being seized with terror upon enter-ing the laboratory. They would approach the three or four staff in the laboratory 'appeal[ing] for mercy' (Hoggan 1883, 2). Even after being thrown on what Hoggan terms a 'torture trough' they continued to lick the hand that bound them until gagged (Hoggan 1883, 2). Still they wagged their tails in what Hoggan interprets as 'the last means of excit-ing compassion', and this continued even through what was assumed to be the excruciating pain of vivisection (Hoggan 1883, 2). Hoggan states only patting the dogs calmed them, and projects onto them the thought that only this reassured them their suffering would come to an end: an end, he states, only possible through death.

Hoggan witnessed animals being slapped and rebuked when writh-ing through a painful vivisection and, if a particular animal had faced its ordeal without struggle, it being 'rewarded' by death (Hoggan 1883,

---

16 George Hoggan, 'Vivisection', *Morning Post*, 2 February 1875, reprinted as Hoggan (1883); French (1975, 64–68); Cobbe (1904, 628–39).

2). Otherwise it might be let loose to crawl about the laboratory await-
ing another day's vivisection or, if its tissues on one side were too
obscured by clotted blood to allow further experimentation, its other
side might be operated on, or another animal operated on so as not to
be 'so economical' (Hoggan 1883, 2). An animal upon which Bernard
had completed his experiment could be given to the assistants for practice in finding body parts, or for performing further basic experiments
from laboratory handbooks.

Hoggan clearly stated that anaesthetics were generally not relied on
as they altered animal bodies too much to give accurate results and, indeed, he casts doubt upon the degree of their efficacy. It is then that
Hoggan revealed Bernard's use of curare, a poison little known at this
time in Britain; Hoggan believed that curare actually *increased* sensation in the animal rather than just paralysing its motor nerves. He
described the 'double torture' that animals underwent under curare; vivisections employing curare were performed before Continental audiences who were lulled into believing the animal was experiencing no
pain (Hoggan 1883, 2).[17]

The effect of Hoggan's letter was, predictably, immense, not just
because it was a recent eyewitness account of vivisection whereas few
other anti-vivisectionists could claim to have actually observed the
practice, but because the witness had a medical degree. Cobbe, for example, opined:

> I have never ceased to feel that in thus nobly coming forward to offer
> [such valuable testimony] spontaneously, he struck the greatest blow
> on our side in the whole battle. (Cobbe 1904, 639)

The *British Medical Journal*, for its part, displayed its nervousness about
the influence of Hoggan's medical qualifications:

> where is it that Dr Hoggan writes these letters? [two letters which
> Hoggan wrote to the *Spectator* in June 1875]. Not in a medical public-

---

17 What exactly an animal experienced under the influence of curare was the
subject of great disagreement; see French (1975, 68) and my later discussion of the
Royal Commission. *The British Medical Journal* responded to Hoggan's assertions
in *The British Medical Journal* (1875a and b).

ation, where the readers, possessed of professional knowledge, could at once detect the incorrectness of his statements, but in the pages of a journal intended for the general public, the readers of which, learning from Dr. Hoggan himself that he possesses a medical degree, and has worked some time in a physiological laboratory, are willing to accept his doctrine as authoritative, and can hardly distinguish between him and the illustrious Bernard whom he reviles. (*The British Medical Journal* 1875b, 829)

The letter was to be used again and again in anti-vivisectionist propaganda well into the 20th century. Hoggan was called as a witness when the Royal Commission on the Practice of Subjecting Live Animals to Experiments for Scientific Purposes got underway in July of that year, and the use of curare itself became one of the special subjects of concern for the commissioners.

The evidence given at the Royal Commission on the use and effects of curare is a patchwork of conflicting testimony which demonstrates how little was known about the poison at that time in Britain – even by those who regularly employed it in vivisection – and how much perception of the effects of the drug was dependent on the perceiver's attitude towards vivisection.

Emanuel Klein, one of the contributors to *Handbook for the physiological laboratory*, was questioned by Richard Holt Hutton, one of the commissioners, the editor of the *Spectator* newspaper, who was an ardent anti-vivisectionist.[18] In asking Klein whether he had ever performed the operation in the *Handbook* on the mesentery of the frog (the membrane that attaches the intestines to the anterior wall of the abdomen) and suggesting that it would be painful, Klein replied that it would always be performed under curare (Great Britain 1876. *Report of the Royal Commission*, Questions 3717–18). Hutton questioned whether curare could be considered to have anaesthetic qualities when applied to a frog. Klein thought it *could* according to recent experiments by Moritz Schiff, the German physiologist whom Cobbe had encountered in 1863 in Florence (Question 3719). When asked why Bernard then thought it *could not*, Klein made the curious reply that

---

18   For Hutton, see Orel (2006) and Dixon (2008, 137, 139, 141, 143, 173, 179–80, 235, 368).

'Those that believe in experiments will . . . agree that it is [an anaes-thetic]' (Question 3720). Klein believed that, as the frog was by this time not breathing through its lungs, it would be feeling less pain due to the comparative lack of oxygen it would be receiving which would lower its sensitivity (Questions 3721–22).

Klein had not impressed the commissioners earlier in his evidence by his complete disregard for the suffering of animals. He had stated that he had no regard for the suffering of animals at all:

I think that with regard to an experimenter, a man who conducts special research, and performs an experiment, he has no time . . . for thinking what will the animal feel or suffer. His only purpose is to perform the experiment, to learn as much from it as possible, and to do it as quickly as possible. (Question 3540)

As such, he later said, he only used anaesthetics for his own conveni-ence if, for example, there was a danger he might be scratched by a cat upon which he were experimenting (Question 3642).

Contrary to Klein, Lauder Brunton stated that curare was '[t]o a certain extent' an anaesthetic and a 'partial anaesthetic', but admitted that there was no certainty about this (Questions 5694–97). William Rutherford, professor of physiology at Edinburgh University, stated that the evidence as to whether curare diminished pain or not was in dispute, but he tended to believe it caused a 'state of insensibility'.[19] Burdon-Sanderson claimed that ordinary doses of curare had no effect on the sensory nerves (Question 2381). Sir George Burrows, President of the Royal College of Physicians from 1871–75, did not consider cur-are to be an anaesthetic at all; nor did Hoggan, who quoted Alfred Vulpian, the French physiologist, in a publication from that very year, claiming curare had no effect on nerves of sensation.[20]

Hoggan, helpfully for the anti-vivisectionist cause, produced Bern-ard's account from *Revue des deux mondes* in which Hoggan, para-

19   Question 2909. For William Rutherford (1839–99), see Richards (1986).
20   Questions 136–37, 4115–16, 4126–29. For Burrows, see Webb (2004) and for Vulpian (1826–87), Cousin (2002). The Vulpian publication Hoggan quoted from, which is referred to in the report as *Lecons* [sic] *sur l'appareil locomoteur,* is Vulpian (1874–75).

phrasing Bernard, stated that for any animal to be vivisected under curare would be 'horrible beyond all conception' (Question 4117; Bernard
1864). William Sharpey, former professor of physiology at University
College concurred with Bernard that 'the patient suffers just as much
as ever' under the influence of curare; Foster, in contrast to this, dis-
agreed with Bernard and other Continental physiologists and claimed
that curare *did* destroy consciousness in frogs and their central nervous
system, thus causing pain to be an irrelevant issue.[21]

Cobbe and evolutionary discourse

If experimental physiologists equivocated about the efficacy of curare
as an anaesthetic, anti-vivisectionists too were somewhat indecisive in
their views on the legitimacy of vivisection based on their changing understandings of the relationship between humanity and other species.
Cobbe, writing her first article on vivisection four years after the publication of Charles Darwin's (1859) *Origin of species*, having determined
that vivisection was permissible under some circumstances as humanity is 'of a rank so much higher, that our interests must always have
precedence', nevertheless tentatively opened herself to an evolutionary
perspective:

> It may be that we shall come to see that sentient life and conscious-
> ness and self-consciousness are mysterious powers working upward
> through all the orders of organic existence; that there are rudiments
> in the sagacious elephant and the affectionate dog of moral qualities
> which we need not consign hopelessly to annihilation. It may be
> that we shall find that man himself, in all the glory of his reason,
> has sprung, in the far-off ages of the primeval world . . . from some
> yet-discovered creature which once roamed the forests of the elder
> world, and through whom he stands allied in blood to all the beasts
> of the field. (Cobbe 1865, 252–54)

---

21 Questions 440, 2324–26. William Sharpey (1802–1880) was professor of
anatomy and physiology at University College, London from 1836 to 1874 and
Secretary of the Royal Society from 1854 to 1872. See Sykes 2001.

By 1875, after the publication of Darwin's (1871) *The descent of man*, when she wrote her essay *The moral aspects of vivisection*, Cobbe was employing evolutionary theory as a weapon in her fight against experimental physiologists, castigating them as hypocritical in their assignation of nonhuman animals to a lower moral status:

> that the disciples of Darwin should themselves be the teachers and leaders in a new development of most exquisite cruelty to the brutes whom they believe to share our blood, our intelligence, and our affections, is indeed a portent of strange and threatening augury. (Cobbe 1889b, 6)

By 1884, in *The future of the lower animals*, she was speculating on animal immortality as a consequence of the working out of divine justice due to the 'calamity' of the suffering of sensitive creatures subject to vivisection. She imagined anti-vivisectionists lying awake at night contemplating the fate of a particular animal they had read about: 'they almost see it lying on the vivisecting table in the laboratory' (Cobbe 1889a, 258–59). As such, she concluded that:

> It is absolutely necessary to postulate a future life for the tortured dog or horse or monkey, if we would escape the unbearable conclusion that a sentient creature . . . incapable of offence, has been given by the Creator AN EXISTENCE WHICH ON THE WHOLE HAS BEEN A CURSE. (Cobbe 1889a, 259; original emphasis)

The psychopathologisation of anti-vivisectionism

As psychological explanations were proffered in the 19th century for what was considered to be the overwhelming affective investment by anti-vivisectionists in the spectre of vivisection, so too some later anti-vivisectionist historiography – even if sympathetic to animal activism – has tended overly to focus on what it perceives as the overdetermined nature of anti-vivisectionist concern for animal pain. Among the former, Magnan, the French psychiatrist who injected absinthe into the dog at Norwich, even invented an 'anti-vivisectionist syndrome', explicitly gendered female, as an explanatory mechanism by which he psychopathologised what he perceived as female hyper-emotionalism when considering the subject of vivisection.[22] Among historians, Coral Lansbury, proceeding from the oft-cited observation that the rank and file of Victorian and Edwardian anti-vivisectionists were disproportionately women, has advanced speculative explanations of the fervour of anti-vivisectionism in women's fear of and distaste for new gynaecological procedures conducted by male doctors, gynaecology being increasingly professionalised at this time, or in alleged parallels of the role of the vivisector with the male gaze of Victorian pornography (Lansbury 1985, 112–29).

This mode of historiography runs the risk of trivialising anti-vivisectionist activism by implying that humanitarian sentiment for animals is always a symptom of an anthropocentric projection of purely human concerns. What is far less present in the historiography of anti-vivisectionism, and in scholarly writing on vivisection in general, is a psychopathological investigation of the *lack* of affective investment by experimental physiologists in the living subjects of their investigations. There are exceptions to this, however. A few contemporary writers on vivisection have turned the critique of female anti-vivisectionists as overly emotional back onto experimental physiologists as *insufficiently emotionally invested*. Among these, for example, is Lynda Birke, who in *Feminism, animals, science* provided a gendered analysis of late 20th-century vivisection from the perspective of a feminist biologist, and Hilda Kean, who has done the same from a historical viewpoint for the late 19th-/early 20th-century context (Birke 1994; Kean 1995). The title of Kean's article, 'The "smooth cool men of science" ', draws on a quotation from Frances Power Cobbe when she states she had better not say what she feels 'towards the smooth, cool man of science who stands by that [vivisectional] torture-trough' (Cobbe 1889c, 56).

Fear of premature burial

With these cautions in place, one historical parallel worth investigating is between the feelings of horror at vivisection, particularly if experi-

---

22 Magnan (1893). The French feminine ending on 'antivivisectionnistes' clearly genders the 'madness' accordingly.

enced under curare, and Victorian and Edwardian fears of premature human burial which seem to be over-represented among anti-vivisectionists.[23] Anna Kingsford, one of the most prominent anti-vivisectionists of the late 19th century, a Catholic although by no means an orthodox one, nevertheless claimed that, due to the fact that her horror of burial was greater than her attachment to the Church, she wished to be cremated (Pope Leo XIII having forbidden cremation to Catholics in 1886).[24] Her particular fear was that she be buried in a trance state (Maitland 1913, ii, 396).

Frances Power Cobbe had a morbid fear of being buried alive and, every night towards the end of her life in 1904, placed a letter to her doctor, Walter Hadwen, a fellow anti-vivisectionist, at her bedside (Mitchell 2004, 366, 412). Her instructions therein, reproduced in her will, could not have been more explicit:

> to perform on my body the operation of completely and thoroughly severing the arteries of the neck & windpipe (nearly severing the head altogether) so as to render my revival in the grave absolutely impossible (Cobbe, cited in Behlmer 2003, 222).

Hadwen himself, who was to succeed Cobbe as President of the British Union for the Abolition of Vivisection, published a second edition of William Tebb and Edward Vollum's *Premature burial and how it may be prevented* the year after this.[25] Yet a third head of an anti-vivisectionist society, Louise Lind-af-Hageby, who founded the Animal Defence and Anti-Vivisection Society in 1909, was one of the most active members of the London Society for the Prevention of Premature Burial, founded by Arthur Lovell in 1896 with the involvement of Tebb and Vollum, which was extant until 1936 when its dwindling membership merged with that of a like-minded society, the Council for the Disposition of the Dead.[26]

---

23 For the fear of premature burial in the 19th century (and more generally), see Bondeson (2001).

24 Maitland (1913, ii, 326); Bryant (2003, i, 772). Kingsford, in fact, ultimately *was* buried, supposedly to avoid inconvenience to her husband who was an Anglican clergyman (Maitland 1913, ii, 396).

25 Bondeson (2001, 195). For Hadwen, see Kidd and Richards (1933).

If anti-vivisectionist discourse focused on the limitations anti-vi-visectionists believed experimental physiologists should impose upon themselves in the scientific investigative use of other species, and concluded that these should be greatly increased or experimentation curtailed altogether, activists associated with burial reform focused on the medical and scientific limitations in their determination of the moment of human death, particularly foregrounding the concern in many cases as to whether death had in fact occurred at all. Both discourses were preoccupied with questions of liminality: for anti-vivisectionists, at what point did humans transgress upon the rights of other species and, perhaps, deface their own humanity by so doing?; for campaigners against premature burial, to what extent and at what point could Victorian and Edwardian medical expertise accurately pronounce a body truly to have passed from a state of life to death? In regards to the latter, both the *British Medical Journal* in 1885 and Sir Henry Thompson, First President of the Cremation Society of Great Britain, in 1901, stressed that decomposition of the body, or more specifically putrefaction, was the only foolproof single sign (*The British Medical Journal* 1885 and Thompson 1901, both cited in Tebb & Vollum 1905, 4).

The association between the experience of vivisection for an animal and premature burial for a human was at least latent in the comments of campaigners against premature burial such as the American physician and author of *Our Darwinian cousins* (1873) Alexander Wilder (both anti-vivisectionism and burial reform being the subjects of transatlantic dialogue). In 1899 when he claimed that 'The thought of suffocation in a coffin is more terrible than that of torture on the rack, or burning at the stake', torture being a common trope adopted by anti-vivisectionists, and experiments to gauge animal endurance of hy-

---

26   For Lind-af-Hageby, see Gålmark (1997) and Bondeson (2001, 195–97, 202). Sources differ as to the year of foundation of the Animal Defence and Anti-Vivisection Society between 1903, 1906 and 1909 but Westacott partially provides an explanation of the discrepancy when he explains that the Society was a reconstitution of Lind-af-Hageby's Anti-Vivisection Council founded in 1906 (Westacott 1949, 193, 196). For the London Society for the Prevention of Premature Burial, see Bondeson (2001, 184, 191–92, 194–203, 258) and Behlmer (2003, 207, 228, 232–34).

perthermia being a speciality particularly of French physiology (Wilder 1899, 181).

Conclusion

Speculations about to what extent Victorian and Edwardian anti-vivisectionism derived motive force from human projections aside, the vivisection debate, occurring as it did immediately after Darwin's *The descent of man* (1871) and *The expression of the emotions in man and animals* (1872), provided a context within which to reassess the similarities and differences between humans and all other animal species. The outcome, I submit, was on the whole a *widening* conceptual gap paradoxically being drawn between the two as a means of reaffirming supposed human exceptionalism. Specifically as regards vivisection, the number of experiments on living animals performed in England, Scotland and Ireland in 1878, the first year for which such statistics are available, was 505; by 1910, at the close of the era considered here, this had ballooned to 95,985 (Great Britain 1878–79; Great Britain 1911). Ideology needed to be harnessed to justify the burgeoning amount of animal experimentation, and the Cruelty to Animals Act furnished the bureaucratic regulation that, while ostensibly in place to forestall scientific abuses, in fact operated as a means of lulling the public conscience and keeping the status quo in place. The progressively production-line nature of the vivisectional laboratory into the 20th century further served to objectify and commodify nonhuman laboratory animals which, along with their factory farm counterparts in the realm of food, became increasingly conceptually distanced from the human.

Although pain is still a potent factor in 21st-century discussion of vivisection, the philosophical range and sophistication of animal ethical discourse since the birth of the animal liberation and revival of the animal rights movements in the 1970s has allowed the focus to shift to questions of the moral status of the nonhuman animal that bring into question the human/animal divide. Peter Singer's popularisation of Richard Ryder's term 'speciesism' in *Animal liberation* allowed the conceptual gap between humans and other animal species to be bridged by drawing an effective parallel between contemporary gender, race and other discrimination and that which favoured the human species, and

Tom Regan in *The case for animal rights*, by his concept that nonhuman animals were 'subjects-of-a-life', granted them a status far beyond the instrumental (Singer 1977, 18, 42; Regan 2004, Chapters 8 and 9).

Subsequent theorists have refined these positions; the animal activist Gary Francione, for example, interestingly uses sentience (and thus animals' ability to experience pain) as the sole basis for his rights and abolitionist position, thus avoiding the Victorian emphasis on reduction or cessation of pain in the process of vivisection by questioning why an animal is being experimented on in the first place (Francione 1993, 253).

Despite the increased philosophical sophistication of modern discussions of the ethics of vivisection, there is much that can still be drawn from the Victorian and Edwardian context and its focus on the rawness of pain of the animal undergoing vivisection. 'The truth' of which Cobbe spoke,

> that Science, by the aid of exquisitely delicate machinery and far-fetched drugs, and skill, and patience, and ingenuity worthy of a God-like instead of a Devil-like task, has achieved the creation of AGONY such as simple Nature never knew (Cobbe 1889a, 258; original emphasis)

may not contain the same shock value as it did in the Victorian period, but the insight it affords clearly speaks to issues crucial to questions in contemporary human–animal studies concerning the status of the 'human' as opposed to the 'animal' and, regardless of the level of pain, whether one species has the right to consign others to a sub-class of experimental raw material.

Works cited

Atalić B & Fatović-Ferencić S (2009). Emanuel Edward Klein: the father of British microbiology and the case of the animal vivisection controversy of 1875. *Toxicologic Pathology* 37(6): 708–13.

Behlmer G (2003). Grave doubts: Victorian medicine, moral panic, and the signs of death. *Journal of British Studies* 42(2): 206–35.

Bernard C (1864). Études physiologiques sur quelques poisons américaines. I. le curare. *Revue des deux mondes* 53(2): 164–90.

Bernard C (1927). *An introduction to the study of experimental medicine.* Henry Copley Greene (Trans.). New York: The Macmillan Company.

Birke L (1994). *Feminism, animals, science: the naming of the shrew.* Bristol, PA: Open University Press.

Black J (1999). Claude Bernard on the action of curare. *British Medical Journal* 319(7210): 622.

Bondeson J (2001). *Buried alive: the terrifying history of our most primal fear.* New York: WW Norton & Company.

The British Medical Journal (1875a). Vivisection and anæsthetics. *The British Medical Journal* 1(753): 749.

The British Medical Journal (1875b). Notices to correspondents. *The British Medical Journal* 1(755): 829–30.

The British Medical Journal (1885). Death or coma. *The British Medical Journal* 2(1296): 841–42.

Brodie BC (1811). Experiments and observations on the different modes in which death is produced by certain vegetable poisons. *Philosophical Transactions of the Royal Society of London,* 101:178–208.

Bryant CD (Ed.) (2003). *Handbook of death and dying.* 2 vols. Thousand Oaks, CA: Sage Publications.

Cobbe FP (1865). The rights of man and the claims of brutes. In *Studies new and old of ethical and social subjects* (pp209–57). London: Trübner & Co.

Cobbe FP (1889a). The future life of animals. In *The modern rack: papers on vivisection* (pp257–66). London: Swan Sonnenschein & Co.

Cobbe FP (1889b). The moral aspects of vivisection. In *The modern rack: papers on vivisection* (pp1–17). London: Swan Sonnenschein & Co.

Cobbe FP (1889c). The right of tormenting: an address delivered at a meeting of the Scottish Anti-Vivisection Society. In *The modern rack: papers on vivisection* (pp49–60). London: Swan Sonnenschein & Co.

Cobbe FP (1904). *Life of Frances Power Cobbe as told by herself.* 2nd edn. London: Swan Sonnenschein & Co., Lim.

Coleman W & Holmes FL (Eds) (1988). *The investigative enterprise: experimental physiology in nineteenth-century medicine.* Berkeley: University of California Press.

Coleridge S (1902). *The folly of our subdivisions: an appeal for unity to all anti-vivisectionists.* London: Privately printed.

Cousin MT (2002). Vulpian and not Claude Bernard first proposed the hypothesis of the motor end-plate as the site of action of curare. *Anesthesiology* 97(2): 527–28.

Cunningham A & Williams P (Eds) (1992). *The laboratory revolution in medicine.* Cambridge: Cambridge University Press.

Darwin C (1859). *On the origin of species by means of natural selection, or the preservation of favoured races in the struggle for life.* London: John Murray.

Darwin C (1871). *The descent of man, and selection in relation to sex.* London: John Murray.

Darwin C (1872). *The expression of the emotions in man and animals.* London: John Murray.

Dixon T (2008). *The invention of altruism: making moral meanings in Victorian Britain.* Oxford: Oxford University Press.

Fontana F (1781). *Traité sur le vénin de la vipere sur les poisons américains sur le laurier-cerise et sur quelques actress poisons végétaux.* 2 vols. Florence.

Francione G (1993). Personhood, property and legal competence. In P Cavalieri & P Singer (Eds). *The great ape project: equality beyond humanity* (pp248–57). London: Fourth Estate.

French RD (1975). *Antivivisection and medical science in Victorian society.* Princeton: Princeton University Press.

Gålmark L (1997). *Shambles of science: Lizzy Lind af Hageby & Leisa Schartau, anti-vivisektionister 1900–1913/14.* Älvsjö: Nordiska samfundet mot plågsamma djurförsök.

Geison GL (1978). *Michael Foster and the Cambridge school of physiology: the scientific enterprise in late Victorian society.* Princeton, NJ: Princeton University Press.

Great Britain (1876). *The law reports. The public general statutes, passed in the thirty-ninth and fortieth years of the reign of Her Majesty Queen Victoria, 1876: with a list of the local and private acts, tables showing the effect of the year's legislation, and a copious index. Vol. XI.* London: William Clowes and Sons.

Great Britain (1876). *Report of the Royal Commission on the practice of subjecting live animals to experiments for scientific purposes; with minutes of evidence and appendix.* London: Her Majesty's Stationery Office.

Great Britain (2005–2012). House of Commons Parliamentary Papers [Online]. Available: parlipapers.chadwyck.co.uk/home.do [Accessed 16 June 2014].

Guarnieri P (1987). Moritz Schiff (1823–96): experimental physiology and noble sentiment in Florence. In N Rupke (Ed.). *Vivisection in historical perspective* (pp105–24). London: Croom Helm.

Gunn JA (2004). Rev. MP Earles. Brunton, Sir Thomas Lauder, first baronet (1844–1916). *Oxford dictionary of national biography.* Oxford: Oxford University Press [Online]. Available: www.oxforddnb.com/view/article/32139 [Accessed 16 June 2014].

Hoffman P (2009). Fatal attractions: curare-based arrow poisons, from medical innovation to lethal injection. Unpublished PhD thesis, University of California, Berkeley.

Hoggan G (1883). Vivisection. In Victoria Street Society for the Protection of Animals from Vivisection, united with the International Association for the Total Suppression of Vivisection. *The vivisection controversy: a selection of speeches and articles by the Earl of Shaftesbury . . . [et al.] from the publications of the Victoria Street and International Society* (pp1-2). London: Victoria Street Society for the Protection of Animals from Vivisection, united with the International Association for the Total Suppression of Vivisection.

Kean H (1995). The 'smooth cool men of science': the feminist and socialist response to vivisection. *History Workshop Journal* 40(1): 16-38.

Kidd BE & Richards ME (1933). *Hadwen of Gloucester: man, medico, martyr.* London: Murray.

Klein E, Burdon-Sanderson J, Foster M & Brunton TL. Burdon-Sanderson J (Ed.) (1873). *Handbook for the physiological laboratory.* 2 vols. London: J & A Churchill.

Lansbury C (1985). *The old brown dog: women, workers and vivisection in Edwardian England.* Madison, Wis.: University of Wisconsin Press.

Lesch J (1984). *Science and medicine in France: the emergence of experimental physiology, 1790-1855.* Cambridge, Mass.: Harvard University Press.

Luauté J (2007). L'absinthisme: la faute du docteur Magnan. *L'Évolution Psychiatrique* 72(3): 515-30.

McIntyre AR (1947). *Curare: its history, nature and clinical use.* Chicago: The University of Chicago Press.

Magnan V (1893). De la folie des antivivisectionnistes. In *Recherches sur les centres nerveux: alcoolisme, folies des héréditaires dégénérés, paralysie générale, médecine légale.* 2nd series (pp269-77). Paris: G. Masson, Éditeur.

Maitland E & Hart SHH (Ed.) (1913). *Anna Kingsford: her life, letters, diary and work.* 2 vols. 3rd edn. London: John M. Watkins.

Marshall FHA (2009). Rev. Anita McConnell. Schafer, Sir Edward Albert Sharpey (1850-1935). *Oxford dictionary of national biography.* Oxford: Oxford University Press [Online]. Available: www.oxforddnb.com/view/article/35967 [Accessed 16 June 2014].

Mitchell S (2004). *Frances Power Cobbe: Victorian feminist, journalist, reformer.* Charlottesville: University of Virginia Press.

Olmsted JMD (1944). *François Magendie: pioneer in experimental physiology and scientific medicine in XIX century France.* New York: Schuman's.

Olmsted JMD & Olmsted EH (1952). *Claude Bernard & the experimental method in medicine.* London: Abelard-Schuman.

Orel H (2006). Hutton, Richard Holt (1826–1897). *Oxford dictionary of national biography*. Oxford: Oxford University Press [Online]. Available: www.oxforddnb.com/view/article/14312 [Accessed 16 June 2014].

Regan T (2004). *The case for animal rights*. 2nd edn. Berkeley: University of California Press.

Richards S (1986). Conan Doyle's 'Challenger' unchampioned: William Rutherford, F.R.S. (1839–99), and the origins of practical physiology in Britain. *Notes and Records of the Royal Society of London*, 40(2): 193–217.

Romano TM (2002). *Making medicine scientific: John Burdon Sanderson and the culture of Victorian science*. Baltimore: Johns Hopkins University Press.

Salt HS (1980 [1892]). *Animals' rights considered in relation to social progress*. Clarks Summit, PA: Society for Animal Rights, Inc.

Singer P (1977). *Animal liberation: towards an end to man's inhumanity to animals*. London: Paladin/Granada Publishing.

Sykes AH (2001). *Sharpey's fibres: the life of William Sharpey, the father of modern physiology in England*. York: William Sessions.

Tebb W & Vollum E (1905). *Premature burial and how it may be prevented with special reference to trance, catalepsy, and other forms of suspended animation*. 2nd edn by W Hadwen. London: Swan Sonnenschein & Co., Limited.

Thompson H (1901). *Modern cremation, its history and practice*. 4th edn. London.

Vulpian A (1874–75). HC Carville (Re-ed). *Leçons sur l'appareil vaso-moteur (physiologie et pathologie) faites à la Faculté de Médecine de Paris*. 2 vols. Paris: Gerner-Baillière.

Webb WW (2004). Rev. Michael Bevan. Burrows, Sir George, first baronet (1801–1887). *Oxford dictionary of national biography*. Oxford: Oxford University Press [Online]. Available: www.oxforddnb.com/view/article/4113 [Accessed 16 June 2014].

Westacott E (1949). *A century of vivisection and anti-vivisection: a study of their effect upon science, medicine and human life during the past hundred years*. Ashingdon: The CW Daniel Company Ltd.

Wilder A (1899). Premature burial. *The Metaphysical Magazine* 10(3): 178–81.

16

Huskies and hunters: living and dying in Arctic Greenland

Rick De Vos

This chapter looks at the lives of, and the practices surrounding, Green-land huskies in Ilulissat and Qaanaaq, two towns in Arctic Greenland that I visited between May and July in 2011. It argues that attitudes to-wards dogs and their welfare, regulation and legislation, and towards hunting in Greenland, contribute, along with environmental changes, to a situation in which Greenland huskies are confined spatially, tem-porally and physically, and their perspectives, welfare and ultimately their deaths are concealed and forgotten. The chapter is instigated by a particular instance of death I encountered in Qaanaaq and found hard to understand and discuss. In part this chapter is a way of critically re-flecting on my own response to what I saw, as well as attempting to understand the significance of the death of animals, specifically that of huskies, in Greenland.

Greenland huskies, or Greenland dogs, are large huskies character-ised by their strength, speed and endurance. They are believed to be one of the oldest breeds of dogs, and to have accompanied the Saqqaq people from Siberia to Greenland between four and five thousand years ago (Meldgaard 2004, 88–90). Approximately two-thirds of Greenland lies above the Arctic Circle. Legislation prohibits Greenland Huskies

R De Vos (2013). Huskies and hunters: living and dying in Arctic Greenland. In J Johnston & F Probyn-Rapsey (Eds). *Animal death*. Sydney: Sydney University Press.

from being moved south of the Arctic Circle and other dog breeds from being brought into the Arctic Circle, ensuring that Greenland huskies are the only dogs in the region. The dogs are kept as working dogs rather than pets, with most dog-owning households keeping a pack of between eight and sixteen dogs. Greenland huskies have been used by explorers on Arctic and Antarctic expeditions, being renowned for their hardiness, their ability to withstand extreme cold conditions and survive on virtually any source of food, and their willingness to work to exhaustion.

Ilulissat is situated at the mouth of a 40 km ice fjord in Disko Bay on the west coast of Greenland. It is the third largest town in Greenland, with a population of around 4000 people. The town is also home to about 6000 huskies, almost all of whom live in designated areas on the outskirts of the town. In the summer months of July and August it is a popular tourist destination, with most visitors flying in from Denmark and Germany as part of tour groups, or sailing in on cruise ships. For the rest of the year Ilulissat is comparatively quiet. The town is dotted with a number of children's playgrounds, scattered around the residential areas. The equipment in them is brightly coloured, and each playground is surrounded by a white or coloured picket fence. The fences, while providing a pleasant border to the colourful structures, also serve a more serious purpose, calling attention to a sadder past. Greenland huskies, particularly when in packs, occasionally attacked small children playing in the streets or in playgrounds. A number of deaths and serious injuries have been recorded, especially before 2000. While laws now enforce that all huskies over the age of five months be chained up in permitted areas, there is always the danger that one or more may escape.

Between May and late August, Arctic Greenland experiences 24 hours of daylight each day, meaning that it is possible to move around easily and see the surroundings all night as well as all day. The dogs in Ilulissat are not immediately evident, their shapes emerging from the rocks as they stretch and stand up, sniffing the air. On my second night in Ilulissat I watched a dog escape its tether and wander off, exploring the rocks nearby, looking for food and other diversions. The sight filled me with interest but also with fear for the dog. Huskies that wander off into the town area of Ilulissat are likely to be shot by rangers if they are seen. Over the next few days, on two occasions, I saw stray dogs exploring the central area of Ilulissat. I gave them a wide berth without feeling too much concern for my safety, and they reciprocated. The one or two other people in the general vicinity did not pay them any particular heed either. However, I still had the sense that I was watching a dog that was soon going to die.

Ilulissat is the birthplace of Knud Rasmussen, the best known of Greenland's modern explorers. Rasmussen was of Greenlandic and Danish descent, born in 1879, the son of the local Lutheran pastor. His childhood was spent in and around Ilulissat, playing with the local Greenlandic children. His first language was Greenlandic, the language of his Inuit mother. He only became fluent in Danish after commencing studies at the University of Copenhagen. He accompanied the other children and their families on hunting trips, learning to drive dog sleds. In 1910, after returning to Greenland from Copenhagen, he established the Thule trading post at Dundas (Uummannaq), which became the base for seven major anthropological expeditions led by Rasmussen between 1912 and 1933. The expeditions made major contributions to the mapping of northern Greenland, and collected a vast amount of ethnographic, archaeological and biological data. During the Fifth Thule Expedition, Rasmussen and two Inuit hunters travelled for 16 months across North America to Alaska by dogsled, crossing the Northwest Passage (Rasmussen 1999, 216–17). His exploits are celebrated by both Greenlanders and Danes. He was a prolific writer, and his journals display a deep interest in Inuit stories and culture, a love of the Arctic landscape, and an almost dismissive attitude to the hardships and privations of Arctic exploration. Both tourist and historical accounts of his life and adventures quote his most famous utterance: 'Give me winter, give me dogs, you can have the rest' (Ehrlich 2001, 8).

I met a young Danish tour guide who had lived in Ilulissat for a number of years, attracted to the town because of the promise of a dogsledding lifestyle. He recalled learning about Knud Rasmussen in school, and acknowledged him as a source of inspiration in coming to Greenland. He now owned a team of dogs, and took every opportunity to go sledding. He said that while fishing by boat was the main source of both income and recreation for most Ilulissat residents, the majority of families still kept dogs, and took the opportunity to go hunting in the winter months. Indeed dogsleds are a common sight in the streets of Ilulissat in winter, with road signs showing that dogsleds have right of way over cars and pedestrians. Paintings in the local art gallery depicted Ilulissat in earlier times with people and dogs living in close proximity. Dogs lived outside their owners' homes or camps in scenes contrasting sharply with the reality that now presented itself outside the gallery.

The Ilulissat Museum, housed in the family home of Knud Rasmussen, juxtaposes representations of the area's hunting past, underlying its cultural significance, with representations of Ilulissat's future, characterised by receding icefields, longer summers, shorter winters and rising temperatures. Audiorecordings of residents' attitudes to these changes are made available via installations with on/off buttons. While detailing older people's memories of past winters and their changing experiences over ensuing decades, the installations also include the attitudes of other residents who see advantages in the climatic and environmental changes, including less time confined indoors in winter, and the opportunity to grow plants, and have small gardens. However, these changes are also seen as restricting the activities and wellbeing of the huskies around Ilulissat. Where dogs worked in sleds for eight to nine months of the year, the lack of suitable ice for sledding meant that they were now tethered for eight to nine months each year. Combined with their largely being restricted to designated dog areas on the outskirts of the town, these changes constituted a dramatically more adverse experience for the Greenland huskies. Where once they lived in packs or teams in close proximity to the men they hunted with, and perhaps their families, they were now tethered just out of reach of their fellow pack members with little knowledge of where and when they might be visited by their owners or fed. While there was general agreement that winter was the time during which the huskies were happiest, it was acknowledged that that time was becoming shorter each year, testing the patience of both the helpless dogs, and their owners who had to visit them each day to feed them.

The day before I left Ilulissat I saw four primary school students, three boys and a girl, walking back to school after lunch. The children were walking past a house outside of which a mother husky was tethered, with four puppies playing around her. As they walked by, the little girl stopped and approached the puppies, petting them and picking one up. The boys called out to her to leave the puppies alone and come with them, but she lingered as long as she could, quite clearly taken by the puppies she cuddled, before eventually joining her class-

*Figure 16.1 Dogs tethered in the designated dog yard, Illulissat, June 2011.
Photo: Monika Szunejko.*

mates. I found this very affecting. Upon reflection I realised that it was the first time I had seen anybody in Greenland show physical affection towards dogs. My own natural response before coming to Greenland was to pat any dog that approaches or appears friendly. I understood what I had read and had been told: Greenland huskies are working dogs and should not be handled by anybody but their owners. While walking past huskies in Greenland without fear or apprehension, respecting their space and careful not to stand and stare at them, I was also resisting the desire to make closer contact with them.

Qaanaaq is the main town in the northern part of the Qaasuitsup municipality in northwestern Greenland, 1066 km north of Ilulissat. Situated on the northern bank of the Inglefield Fjord, it is one of the northernmost towns in the world. It has a population of around 650, and was established in late 1953 when the United States expanded their airbase at Thule, which it was given permission to build in 1951, and forcibly relocated the people living in the settlements of Pituffik and Dundas to the north during the height of the Cold War. As no roads existed in the area, and no airstrip had been constructed yet in the new town site, the majority of residents made the 130 km trip north, along with their possessions, by dogsled. At Qaanaaq, people were forced to live in tents from May 1953 until November 1953, well into the polar winter, while new houses were constructed for them. The cost of the relocation was shared by the United States and Danish governments. The first houses built were very rudimentary, single-room dwellings without raised floors. The dogs lived immediately outside the dwellings (Ehrlich 2001, 142–43).

On 21 January 1968, a United States Air Force B-52 bomber carrying four hydrogen bombs on a Cold War alert mission over Baffin Bay crashed onto sea ice in North Star Bay, Greenland, causing the nuclear payload to rupture and disperse, which resulted in widespread radioactive contamination. The United States and Denmark governments launched an intensive clean-up and recovery operation, but the secondary of one of the nuclear weapons could not be accounted for after the operation was completed. Strategic Air Command operations were discontinued immediately after the incidents. Radioactive plutonium from the 1968 bomber crash contaminated the nearby ancient hunting grounds, affecting the livelihoods of the region's inhabitants. There is evidence both of genetic deformities in land and marine mammals in the area, as well as a spike in cancer among Greenlanders employed in service duties at the air base (Ehrlich 2001, 176).

On my first morning in Qaanaaq I was filled with a sense of dread and impending death. As I walked along the stony shoreline in front of the Inglefield Fjord, I could see men in their familiar blue overalls working on the hulls of fishing boats. Unlike the streets of the main town area of Ilulissat, Qaanaaq does not give any impression of being open to visitors or tourists. People studiously ignored us. I felt that I had no place being there. Unlike Ilulissat, where at least a few tourists were always present, Qaanaaq did not appear to rely on foreign visitors or be used to engaging with them. Along the shore I saw remnants of fish and the signs of previous catches, skin and fur. I was reminded of an online posting I had recently read which had mentioned that the icy ground was too hard to bury animals in Qaanaaq. Further up the beach I saw a structure upon which what appeared to be two small bodies were hanging. As I approached I saw that they were harpoon bladders made from sealskins. The flippers of the seals were still attached. Unlike floats I had seen in museums, where the skin was old and weathered, these floats appeared to be recently made, resembling two small, inflated seals.

Looking out over the frozen fjord I was able to make out two or three small teams of huskies on the ice. Most were lying down, making them difficult to see. That evening I was told by the hotel owner that most of Qaanaaq's dogs were now starting to be taken from the ice, where they had remained during the winter and most of the spring. June was proving to be a month of waiting – the ice was too thin and unpredictable to be negotiated by dogsled or for anyone other than the most experienced hunters to walk on, but still thick enough to prevent boats from getting through to the open water where fish and marine mammals could be found. I watched and listened to the dogs, largely silent earlier in the day except for singular growls or whimpers, howling together as they lay on the thin ice.

People I spoke to in Qaanaaq expressed resentment that their families had been moved from Pituffik and Dundas, as well as a strong desire to move back.[1] Historically the people of these settlements were subsistence hunters, and while a considerable proportion of the population now depend on welfare payments, hunting and fishing still constitute the major source of employment for residents. While hunting and fishing had proved to be good around Qaanaaq for a few decades after the move, numbers of both land and sea mammals had dwindled since the 1990s (Hansen 2002, 75; Ehrlich 2006, 4). This in turn has increased the resentment towards both the US and Danish governments, and the urge to return to Thule, even though some acknowledge that their historical home has been contaminated by radioactive waste, making hunting difficult and hazardous.

The cemetery at Qaanaaq, lying to the east of the town site within sight of the town's Danish Lutheran church, draws to mind both those

---

1 My partner and I were the only non-residents of Qaanaaq on our flight north to the town. About half an hour before our scheduled arrival, I became aware that all the other passengers on board had gotten up and were looking through their windows or moving into the aisle to get a better view west. One passenger pointed out a tiny speck, suggesting two or three small buildings, near the coast in the distance. 'Thule!' he said. The passengers started to smile and exclaim, expressing both joy in sighting their historical home, and a longing to return there.

Figure 16.2 Dogs tethered on the ice, Inglefield Fjord, Qaanaaq, June 2011.
Photo: Monika Szunejko.

that have passed away in the past 60 years and those that lie buried in the old settlements. A front end loader is employed in the burial of humans and of waste in the icy soil of Qaanaaq.

Hunting plays an important part in both the social organisation and the imagination of Greenlanders. While only about 3000 Greenlanders are registered as professional hunters, most residents have engaged in recreational hunting from a young age. Teaching children hunting skills, including the handling of dogs and sleds, is seen as a parental duty. Children can be seen walking around towns in Arctic Greenland with dog whips, practising their technique. While in Ilulissat residents mix hunting and fishing with paying day jobs, such as fish factory work and tourist services, Qaanaaq and its surrounding settlements still place great importance on subsistence hunting and fishing. Dogsleds are used throughout the winter to hunt seals, narwhal, beluga and walrus. In the spring they hunt polar bear. Municipality restrictions in north-western Greenland prohibit the use of motorboats and snowmobiles by hunters, meaning that hunters must rely on dogsleds and kayaks. In

Figure 16.3 Cemetery, Qaanaaq, June 2011. Photo: Rick De Vos.

addition, marine mammals other than seals can only be hunted and struck with spears and handheld harpoons, with rifles only to be used for finishing off a wounded animal. In the spring and summer, birds, including dovekies and ptarmigans, are hunted and their eggs collected. Seals continue to be hunted from boats and kayaks in the open water. Small halibut, capelin and other fish are caught for at least half the year in the fjords near the settlements. Musk oxen are hunted in late summer and in the spring a large proportion of the Greenland population takes time off to hunt reindeer.

Huskies facilitate hunting in the winter by pulling sleds but also by keeping predators, primarily polar bears, at bay, working as a pack to surround or distract bears in order to alert hunters and allow them to shoot the bear. While hunting, dogs and hunters share food, with dogs being fed the same meat as the hunters, albeit more scraps and bones.

While not everyone is a hunter, most men in Arctic Greenland aspire to be hunters, or consider themselves part-time hunters. Hunters enjoy a high social status, and demographic figures suggest that they are the healthiest and richest people in Arctic Greenland, possessing the most respect among their fellow Greenlanders. Access to what is known as Greenlandic or country food, that is, meat derived directly from hunting (bowhead whale, narwhal or beluga meat and skin, seal and walrus meat, polar bear, musk ox and reindeer meat, and local birds and their eggs) is seen as the source of this physical, social and emotional wellbeing. The lack of access to these foods has been identified in studies as a major cause of illness and other problems in older people, women and other social groups removed from contact with hunters and hunting activities (Ford 2011, 4; Golhar, Ford & Berrang-Ford 2009). My comments to locals regarding my desire to see narwhal, beluga and walrus, generally led to exclamations and responses praising the deliciousness of these animals as food, with little understanding of my wanting to spend time with these animals without hunting and eating them.

While hunting remains socially and culturally significant to Greenlandic people, it makes a negligible contribution to Greenland's annual revenue. Fishing and fish processing, principally Greenland halibut and prawns, constitute the main industries in Greenland, as well as providing the second largest source of employment after public administration. The Greenland economy, however, is still dependent on considerable subsidies and financial support from Denmark. The annual block grant from the Danish state was set at 35 billion Danish kroner (approximately 5.9 billion Australian dollars) in 2010. This represents approximately 40 percent of the total revenue. According to the Act on Self-Government which came into force in 2009, this amount is now fixed until Greenland establishes regular income from oil or minerals (Statistics Greenland 2012).

Both hunters and Greenland's wildlife have been adversely affected by environmental changes that have been most strongly felt since the 1990s. The sea ice has receded along with the polar ice cap as temperatures have increased throughout Greenland. Summers have increased in duration while winters have contracted. Marine mammal numbers have decreased in the fjords and coastal waters, with the higher temperatures and thinning of the sea ice leading to a lack of ice ledges, on which walrus and seals feed, rest and give birth. Polar bears are affected both by habitat loss, as they move with the sea ice, hunting ringed seals from the edges of ice floes, as well as from a shortage of prey, with less seals present in hunting areas. Beluga whale and narwhal numbers, decimated by commercial practices which continued until 1987, decrease each year, with populations becoming increasingly vulnerable to indigenous hunting. Like the hunters, huskies in Greenland are witnesses to this changing environment and the disappearance of animals. Traditional hunting in northern Greenland faces both a loss of hunting grounds as well as a loss of animals and species. Hunters are forced to fish more and to supplement their diet with food bought from shops, which is often expensive and subject to limitations in supply. This in turn leads to a loss of face, and perceived status. Specialised dog food also needs to be bought when food from hunting is scarce. While keeping dogs represents the promise of hunting, the reality of feeding and maintaining working animals is leading many to reconsider the worth of doing so.

There is a noticeable loosening of the spatial arrangements made for dogs in Qaanaaq when compared to those in Ilulissat. Adult dogs still remain tethered, but most packs remain within sight of their owners' homes, and puppies wander the streets more frequently. While the Danish Home Rule government, in the face of increasing complaints about the neglect and abuse of Greenland huskies, has introduced legislation in regard to dog welfare, and instituted an action plan aimed at educating hunters and dog owners about disease, living conditions and access to veterinary advice and medicine, only two veterinary officers have been employed to patrol the whole of the area of Greenland above the Arctic Circle and carry out inspections and information sessions. The difficult relationship between local municipalities and the Home Rule government, combined with hunters' resentment at legislation drawn up in the south, far removed from the realities of life in northern Greenland, means that enforcing minimum standards of care is currently impossible (Ray 2006, 1). A hunter in Qaanaaq told me that a neighbour of his complained to him that each generation of his dogs was getting smaller in size and were less healthy. The neighbour poured scorn on this hunter's advice that he needed to find dogs outside the pack to breed with, in order to increase his pack's genetic diversity and lessen the effects of in-breeding. I noticed that the dogs in each pack bore a strong and distinct resemblance to each other in terms of their markings and colour. The hunter told me that while many hunters in the Qaanaaq/Thule area held a preference for dogs with darker markings, dog owners in Ilulissat often sought to obtain dogs that were almost pure white in colour, believing that such dogs more closely met the expectations of tourists looking for a dogsledding experience.

Walking along the edge of the frozen fjord, less than an hour from Qaanaaq, I noticed a shape along the shoreline that did not appear to be a rock. As I looked closer, I saw the decomposing body of a husky, its ribcage still intact, the blue straps of its harness still in place. In that moment the inexplicable sense of dread I had felt when first walking along the beach had been confirmed and starkly clarified. Dogs lie where they die. They become sick on hunting trips, or weak from fatigue and hunger. At this point they are often killed by the rest of the pack or shot by the hunter. The alternative to dying on a hunting trip is to be put down at the age of four or five, when huskies are believed to become too aggressive and independent to work in a sled team, or when keeping and feeding them through increasingly long summers proves too expensive. While the killing of hunted wildlife is celebrated, marking a time of sharing, and the death of Qaanaaq's residents is marked by funeral services and burials, the deaths of dogs are ignored and forgotten, lacking in significance. Seeing the husky's body stopped and silenced me. I could not point it out to my partner some distance away, nor could I discuss it at the time. In Greenland I felt a social pressure not to photograph local people. To do so was to contravene an unspoken tolerance, the camera being viewed as the weapon of the tourist, one that often breaches the bounds of respect and equality. At this moment, for the same reason, I could not photograph the dead husky, but retreated, the sight of the body committed to my memory.

I concede that my response to the death and to the lives of huskies is shaped by my own metropolitan perspective, devoid of the social and cultural experiences connected to traditional subsistence hunting. I do not believe that the treatment of huskies is viewed as unethical by the majority of hunters in Arctic Greenland. However, I maintain that where such a lifestyle is so markedly subsidised and represented as romantic, fragile and exotic in the face of growing evidence that it is unsustainable, then those that choose to support it must take responsibility for its victims. In Ilulissat, where traditional subsistence hunting has disappeared and dogsledding is more aligned with tourism, huskies have begun to take on a more symbolic role in their relationship with humans and their environment. For tourists, a hunting experience or long-distance dogsledding trek may include the death of the hunted

Figure 16.4 Hunters and huskies, Inglefield Fjord, Qaanaaq, June 2011.
Photo: Monika Szunejko.

animal, but not the death of the hunting dog, whose death occurs in an occluded space. A more profound relationship between hunter and husky is ceding to one that is more fleeting: the production of a memorable, commercial experience rather than an everyday one. The space that was once shared is now increasingly segregated.

Greenland huskies possess a liminal status, afforded neither the status of hunters nor the attention and respect given to hunted wildlife. They are neither celebrated nor mourned. They facilitate dogsledding and hunting, and as working animals are viewed as property and transportation, despite having helped to shape the social environment in which they live and die and despite being active participants in human life. Their space is restricted by the sea ice and changing climate, the geographical limits of settlements, designated dog areas, and by physical tethers and harnesses. Their time is restricted by the seasons and the opportunities for hunting, and by their perceived ability to work effectively, and their future generations are restricted by selective and ill-informed breeding control.

Figure 16.5 Dogs look out over Inglefield Fjord, Qaanaaq, June 2011. Photo: Rick De Vos.

Since returning to Australia I have reflected regularly on the image of the lone husky's death on the outskirts of Qaanaaq. The blue traces of the dog's harness signify restriction and control of the dog's movements, even in death, and yet at the same time show that the dog was working at the time of its death, part of a pack and a hunting party, and not one of thousands of dogs languishing in the designated dog areas of Ilulissat. Despite the harshness of working life for huskies in Arctic Greenland, a way of life threatened by social and environmental changes, to die while hunting would appear far preferable to dying isolated and separated from one's pack and fellow hunters.

Works cited

Ehrlich G (2001). *This cold heaven: seven seasons in Greenland*. New York: Pantheon Books.
Ehrlich G (2006). Living on thin ice. *National Geographic* [Online]. Available: ngm.nationalgeographic.com/2006/01/arctic-hunters/ehrlich-text [Accessed 16 June 2014].

Ford J (2011). *Qeqertarsuaq: 'Access to food' study 2008–11.* Montreal: McGill University.

Goldhar C, Ford J & Berrang-Ford L (2009). Food security in western Greenland: a case study from Qeqertarsuaq. In J Oakes, R Riewe, R Bruggencate & A Cogswell (Eds). *Sacred landscapes: linking people, environment and world views* (pp17–34). Winnipeg: Aboriginal Issues Press, University of Manitoba.

Hansen K (2002). *A farewell to Greenland's wildlife.* Copenhagen: Gads Forlag.

Haraway DJ (2008). *When species meet.* Minneapolis: University of Minnesota Press.

Hastrup K (2007). Ultima Thule: anthropology and the call of the unknown. *Journal of the Royal Anthropological Institute* 13(4): 789–804.

Leane E & Tiffin H (2011). Dogs, meat and Douglas Mawson. *Australian Humanities Review* 51: 185–99.

Meldgaard M (2004). *Ancient harp seal hunters of Disko Bay: Subsistence and settlement at the Saqqaq Culture Site Qeqertasussuk (2400–1400BC), West Greenland.* Copenhagen: Danish Polar Centre.

Morey DF (2006). Burying key evidence: the social bond between dogs and people. *Journal of Archaeological Science* 33: 158–75.

Pearson SJ & Weismantel M (2010). Does the animal exist? Toward a theory of social life with animals. In D Brantz (Ed.). *Beastly natures: animals, humans, and the study of history* (pp17–37). Charlottesville: University of Virginia Press.

Rasmussen K (1999). *Across Arctic America: narrative of the Fifth Thule Expedition.* Fairbanks: University of Alaska Press.

Ray J (2006). Improving a dog's life in Greenland [Online]. Available: www.iol.co.za/scitech/technology/ improving-a-dog-s-life-in-greenland-1.274400#.UE8BxbKwzSg [Accessed 16 June 2014].

Statistics Greenland (2012) [Online]. Available: www.stat.gl/default.asp?lang=en [Accessed 16 June 2014].

17

On having a furry soul: transpecies identity and ontological indeterminacy in Otherkin subcultures[1]

Jay Johnston

> That which is Other is a constant part of the person; s/he is the Other
> at all times.
>
> *Lupa 2007, 27*

Conceptualising otherness as radical difference (alterity) has been the
joyous *bête noir* of innumerable humanities debates. The dark beast
evoked here is not accidental, as the other – understood as either internal or external (or both) to the ontological subject – has famously
and relentlessly been viewed in various threatening guises. Indeed, at
a civic level the modern 'West' has three main modes of engaging
with that deemed other: aggression (annihilate it), accommodation (on
terms set by the dominant culture) or render it peripheral and unim-
portant (ignoring and ridicule are common techniques here). Hence

J Johnston (2013). On having a furry soul: transpecies identity and ontological
indeterminacy in otherkin subcultures. In J Johnston & F Probyn-Rapsey (Eds).
Animal death. Sydney: Sydney University Press.

---

1   This chapter is dedicated to Suzie Johnston who departed this life the day the
call for papers for the Animal Death conference was first sent out. A truly gentle
furry soul.

the significant calls to cultivate a different range of response mechanisms to the other (Oliver 2001; Johnston 2008).

However, as many theorists note, otherness is wondrously unruly and productive and continues to destabilise the ontological ground of subjectivity. This chapter enters into this discussion by considering the 'other' of a transpecies spiritual subculture Otherkin. In particular, it examines the use the concept of the 'animal' is put to in the construction of Otherkin (Therian) identity and the ramifications of this figuration for conceptualising animal and human ontology. Does an Otherkin presence paradoxically require the erasure of the 'animal'?

To commence this inquiry, the concept of subjectivity found in Otherkin discourse will first be elaborated, with particular focus on the conceputalisation of both 'other' and 'animal.' This will then be considered in relation to Derrida's work on ontological absence and presence, and questions found in his work and that of Kelly Oliver concerning meeting animal difference.

Otherkin: fluid definitions

According to Lupa, a self-identified Therianthrope and author of *A field guide to Otherkin,* an Otherkin is:

> a person who believes that, through either a nonphysical or (much more rarely) physical means, s/he is not entirely human. This means that anyone who relates internally to a nonhuman species either through soul, mind, body, or energetic resonance, or who believes s/he hosts such a being in hir [a non-gender specific pronoun] body/ mind. (Lupa 2007, 26)

Otherkin are a heterogeneous subculture in which individuals consider themselves to be only partially – or something other than – human. The nonhuman element includes a variety of real and fictional species. Indeed one of the delights of Otherkin subjectivity is the destabilisation of the real–fiction binary their concept of self proposes. Sharp distinction cannot be drawn between the 'real' and the 'imaginary.' When considering Otherkin engagement with the 'animal', this is not purely a case of an imaginary relation. The type of subjectivity evoked elicits the death of a pure proposition of human or animal. Otherkin's 'other' includes – but is by no means limited to animals – the type of Otherkin focused on herein and known as Therian – faery, machines, media characters, anime characters, vampires and mythological beasts. Otherkin identity can not only be comprised of two-part combinations, but can also be 'multiple', wherein subjectivity is understood to be comprised of numerous parts of different species; for example, rat, human, elf simultaneously. This is certainly no wholly human self.

In this discussion, Otherkin will be considered as proposing (and living) a form of transpecies identity.[2] This term is employed to represent a fluid subject position that questions normative categories including concepts of species and dimorphic concepts of gender. Further, transpecies identity undermines the categorical distinction of 'human' and 'animal.' The ways in which the terms are effected in this particular subculture is the focus of later discussion.

Otherkin identity is largely articulated in online forums and, as indicated by Lupa's aforementioned definition, members of the community challenge normative concepts of the human including dimorphic gender distinctions (Otherkin subcultures are not to be confused or equated with Furrie Fandom). Even the categories employed by Lupa herself to identify kin types are not universally used or applied and many individuals understand themselves to belong to several groupings simultaneously. Nonetheless, the recognition of the 'other within', according to the data amassed by Lupa, is core to individual self-understanding and provides a narrative or a reason for 'feeling different' and is considered an *ontological* aspect of the self. These are selves that embrace a ubiquitous haunting; that one's lived, felt subjectivity is not 'normal.' 'Otherkin', writes Lupa, 'is a safe haven for us to express the aspects of ourselves that do not fit into the everyday world but that need to have a place nonetheless . . .' (2007, 30). In Otherkin discourse, the

---

2   Although this chapter focuses on animal–human subcultures – Therianthropes rather than other types of Otherkin – this is not because animalkin are assumed more important. There are some very serious questions to be asked of the more supernatural Otherkin, not in the least regarding the way in which medical diagnostic measures are utilised in the identification processes (for example, Fey exhibit an allergy to iron) and the way in which they subvert definitions of not only the human and gender dimorphism, but also the 'real'.

'other' aspect is often equated with concepts of soul or spirit. As Lupa writes further about hir self: 'I look, sound, and smell human, and I cannot change that. But the spirit of Wolf still resides within me' (2007, 27).

The capitalisation of 'W' and the concept of 'wolf spirit' alerts one to the obvious influence of universal forms of contemporary shamanism, especially the type popularised by Michael Harner (shamanism as constituted by techniques and practices that can be taught to anyone regardless of their cultural background) (Harner, 1980). This concept of the animal spirit or totem is also found in publications like Ted Andrew's *Animal speak* (2002), where a range of animals are presented, behaviours described and symbolic associations detailed. Such 'dictionaries' run along the lines of either offering ways to decode the meaning of a particular animal 'showing up' in one's life (either physically or as an image) and/or as describing the characteristics of a human individual for whom the animal is a 'totem'. Individuals identify with a specific animal species, for example, as 'bear people', or (less commonly) 'moth people', and these guides list the mostly psychological attributes allocated to that species in human form. There are also guides for calling on particular animal spirits to assist with specific tasks or life crises (for example, beavers if one is lacking in attention to detail). In general, such texts are contemporary articulations of reading the 'book of nature': a hermeneutic approach historically associated with Western esoteric discourses and Renaissance hermeticism in particular (Faivre 2006). Here, with Lupa's self-description, a legacy of these traditions is found. We have a generic wolf, a wolf born of universal shamanism, and so it is that one meets the first ethical hurdle found in Therian identity – the other as generic rather than the specific animal (a discussion of which is taken up in more detail the last section of the paper).

For Otherkin in general, both the other and the human are part of their lived subjectivities. Unsurprisingly the communities have offered a varying array of beliefs about their origins, many of which use popular science, religious belief and mythological discourses as the foundation narratives. For example:

> Our biological father, when he was young, would tell people that he wanted to be a fox when he grew up. He also had eyes that, under average circumstances are green, but 've [sic] been known to randomly

turn very yellow, and he has rather pronounced canines (qtd in Lupa
2007, 69)

Overall, shared physical characteristics do not seem to feature as much
in the 'origins' discourse as do energetic or soul connections. The 'other'
is most usually understood to be 'present' in soul or spiritual matter. For
example, energetic appendages – tails and talons for example – figure in
the lived embodiment of some Therians (Lupa 2007, 127). This reflects
the influence of popular contemporary adaptations of energy bodies
(subtle bodies found in yoga, tantra and Theosophical traditions) that
extend the self – in invisible energetic ways – beyond the limits of the
physical skin. Subtle anatomy is presented as an ontological substance –
that is *real* not imaginary – which comprises both the material and im-
material aspects of the individual. For Therians it also comprises their
animal subjectivity.

Accompanying these discussions about identity are claims for specific epistemological practices and knowledges. The role of the imagination (not in the sense of derisory fantasy but as a significant epistemological tool for recognising and relating to one's own species alterity) and
creativity are privileged as modes for communicating with the other aspects of self and for working with the Otherkin subjectivity in everyday
life.

However, the prime concern herein is not to present a categorisation or even outline community debates and dynamics, but to consider
the forms of subjectivity being proposed – a 'subjectivity' built on the
demise of the 'human' and 'animal' as ontologically distinct categories – and the ethics which emerge. These ethics are considered both
in terms of recognition of that which falls outside of the normative,
but also, and especially, with regard to how this 'other', this nonhuman
element, is conceptualised. To achieve this, two types of discourse are
drawn together: on the one hand statements of individuals who consciously self-identify as Therianthropes, and on the other hand discussions of the 'animal' by Jacques Derrida and Kelly Oliver. Specifically,
the questioning now turns to consider what concept of the 'animal,' is
being employed by Otherkin communities and how this plays out with
conceptualisations of the 'other' from within the domains of Continental animal philosophy (so often built upon concepts of the feminine

other). To commence, the ontological 'foundation' (however nebulous and slippery) will be discussed.

Tracing the demise of both presence and absence: Derrida's *différance*

Already we have had to delineate *that différance is not*, does not exist, is not a present-being (on) in any form . . . and consequently that it has neither existence or essence. It derives from no category of being, whether present or absent . . . *Différance* is not only irreducible to any ontological or theological – ontotheological – reappropriation, but as the very opening of the space in which ontotheology – philosophy – produces its system and its history, it includes ontotheology, inscribing it and exceeding it without return. (Derrida 1982, 6)

As the above quotation illustrates, in his proposition of the concept of *trace* Derrida critiques Heidegger's own critique of metaphysics, proposing *différance* as the only 'solid' step outside the discourse of metaphysics. As is well-known, Derrida's proposition of *différance* presents difference as outside of, alien to, the discourse of absence and presence.

It is thus that the difference between Being and beings, the very thing that would have been 'forgotten' in the determination of Being as presence, and of presence as present – this difference is so buried that there is no longer any trace of it. The trace of difference is erased. If one recalls that difference (is) itself other than absence and presence, (is) (itself) trace, it is indeed the trace of the trace that has disappeared in the forgetting of the difference between Being and beings. (1982, 65–66)

This *différance* is a constantly erased trace, ineradicable but forever beyond the grasp of known presence (or absence). Paradoxically, this *trace* presences – without presencing – the other: radical alterity. It is a mobile, impartial interface that undermines the logic that proposes the dichotomy absence–presence. It is: 'A writing exceeding everything that the history of metaphysics has comprehended in the form of the Aristotelian *grammē*, in its point, in its line, in its circle, in its time, and in its space' (1982, 67).

At its mercurial 'foundation' the *trace* which signals *différance* within discourse marks it as always beyond encapsulation in the metaphysics of absence–presence and as an always 'present' but inherently unknowable alterity – an alterity that is neither present nor absent. However, as has been argued elsewhere (Johnston 2008, 48):

> In a desire to move out from within dialectical bounds, Derrida still – with the untraceable trace – remains within the dialectic of knowable–unknowable: originary–secondary. Postulating that *différance* is of a different 'order' to Being/beings raises the question of how is (it) ever to be discernible? In his quest to escape the presence–absence polarity, Derrida's *différance* and its trace are still conceptualised as a movement of erasure: a continual oscillation between present/absent – a movement between.

It is here, suspended betwixt presence–absence that alterity as perpetual erasure is evidenced (albeit still locking it in the discourse of metaphysics). As a 'map' for understanding the dynamics of ontological difference, the relation to the other, one wonders whether Otherkin's dual and multiple aspects of self can similarly be figured to operate in such a (unstable) relation. Can the 'other' – Therian alterity – also be considered to take part in a similar dance of absence and presence? Or is its ontology, while fluid, still a rather conservative ontology of the One?

Meeting the animal-other

In moving into this next section in which Otherkin subjectivities are reframed within the rubric of contemporary philosophical discourse, it is imperative to make clear that in no way are these more critical comments deployed to denigrate the individual experiences or beliefs of any Otherkin, Therian or indeed any individual who participates in contemporary shamanism. These are real, valuable and meaningful subject positions and experiences for numerous people. But, they are also experiences that are filtered through dominant concepts of 'soul' and of

'spirit' and especially of 'animal'. In asking the question 'What is this animal Other of Otherkin?', it is at least superficially clear that this animal
is conceptualised from within the discourse of contemporary shamanism, including the magical and healing aspects associated with animal
species. However, tracing this conceptual linage with more precision
is the task of another publication. Herein, arguments are restricted to
pondering: How can we conceptualise the Otherkin's ontological relationship to their Other? Does such a conceptualisation enact a death of
both the 'animal' and the 'human'?

To enter into these issues, Jacques Derrida's The animal that therefore I am (2008) is discussed, with specific focus on the ethics of engagement that he articulates. This will be considered with feminist
philosopher Kelly Oliver's text *Animal lessons: how they teach us to be
human* (2009), which is by and large an exploration of the way in which
within philosophies of alterity, as Oliver puts it: 'the *abstract* concept of
the animal continues to work along with animal metaphors, examples,
illustrations, and animal studies to support alternative notions of a split
or de-centred subject' (2009, 4). Oliver argues that the general concept
of the animal is a foundation for the proposition of the decentred subject – including the subject of sexual difference. Similarly, as noted in
the previous section, Otherkin, the decentred subject (the subject that
is not even wholly human), is still predicated upon an abstract and universal concept of the animal: it is this general 'animal' that provides the
individual with their particularity (even at the edge of the human). And
to put it as succinctly as possible, like Derrida, what is advocated for
herein is an acknowledgment, a presencing of the particular animal, as
he articulates in his meditations of the (female) cat's gaze upon his nakedness:

> I must immediately make it clear, the cat I am talking about is a real
> cat, truly, believe me, *a little cat*. It isn't the *figure* of a cat. It doesn't
> silently enter the bedroom as an allegory for all the cats on earth,
> the felines that traverse our myths and religions, literature and fables.
> (2008, 7)

Likewise, Oliver argues that philosophies of difference exclude animal
difference: 'Animal difference is too different, too other, too foreign,
even for thinkers of alterity' (2009, 5). This may be so (historically)

but it is exactly this difference (in all its multiplicity) that needs to be grappled with – however impartially – to meet the *particular* animal.

It is most certainly well recognised that much animal rights discourse has been modelled on women's rights discourse and the conceptual coupling of women–nature still lurks within it (Calarco 2008, 6–13). However, this does not necessarily result in the re-inscription of a predictable dualism (male-culture/female-nature) onto species relations. Indeed, the question of the 'animal' offers serious challenges to such normative logics.

Elsewhere, work has been done to problematise Derrida's concept of the Sexual Otherwise that emerges from his consideration of whether 'one thinks difference *before* sexual difference or taking off from it' (1997, 31). A significant aspect of the critique of this concept is identifying its reliance on linear logic and proposing that 'difference' not be presented as either separate from temporal flux or attributed fixed ontological status (indeed a Deleuzian multiplicity is a potential framework for rethinking such a difference). Therefore as akin to the *trace* this is a concept of alterity that emphasises the creative capacity of difference, its inherently unknowable status, which posits difference not as singular and as not existing in a negative relation (or indeed a relation of erasure or absence) with regard to the 'present' normative subject (Johnston 2008, 36–54). The relation to animal difference proposed herein is one in which – like Levinasian 'radical proximity' – the one and the other are mutually imbricated at an ontological level in relations that confound the presence–absence dualism.

While questioning Derrida's rendering of relations with difference, Kelly Oliver notes that thinking animal difference enables a critique of dualism:

Rather than separate women from animal and align her with the otherside of the divide, whether it is man or human, I explore sexual difference from the side of the animal. (2009, 131)

In short, for Oliver, thinking about animal sexual difference (and animal difference) unravels binary thinking: 'the binary opposition man/animal and man/woman are so intimately linked that exploding the first has consequences for the second' (2009, 133). Oliver goes on to advocate the 'unimagined possibility of pansexuality'. While there is much to support in Oliver's critique, especially the understanding that troubling the man/woman and man/animal dualism necessarily leads to a radical rethinking of subjective (and ontological) difference, one is wary of the employment of a term like 'pan' (in 'pansexuality') and its potential to evoke the universal, or at an ontological level a concept of sameness. And does not the claim to 'take the side of the animal' contain the assumption that one can speak for the subject of difference? Is this not yet another form of appropriation? That said, Oliver makes evident the usefulness and inherent politics of thinking animal difference, precisely for the way in which such thinking troubles concepts of the human and normative subject positions.

Donna Haraway has made clear in her work on cyborgs and simians that the boundaries between such terms as 'human,' 'animal' (and 'machine') are so nebulous that the maintenance of the terminology no longer makes any sense. There is no pure 'animal', no pure 'human' (1991, 149–81). One can glean her work at play in Derrida's concept of the animot, the animal–machine:

> Neither animal nor non-animal, neither organic nor inorganic, neither living nor dead . . . This quasi-animal would no longer have to relate itself to being *as such* (something Heidegger thinks the animal is incapable of), since it would take into account the need to strike out 'being'. But as a result, in striking out 'being' and taking itself beyond or on this side of the question (and hence of the response) is it something completely other than a species of animal? Yet another question to follow up. (2008, 39)

That is, the animot is the 'animal' outside of ontologies of presence, ontologies upon which human subjectivities are premised. Would 'animal' cease to exist in such a conceptual frame? In illustrating the *animot*, Derrida gives the example of the echidna and the *chimaera:* 'the proper name of a flame-spitting monster. Its monstrousness derived precisely from the multiplicity of animals, of the *animot* in it (head and chest of a lion, entrails of a goat, tail of a dragon)' (2008, 41).

Is this also the ontology of Otherkin? A subjectivity, which in its multiplicity, pushes on the boundaries of prescribed human ontologies (neither process nor substance; but something betwixt and between).

Questions no doubt designed to confound dominant logic. Such questions also rupture the life–death relation.

Here again, Otherkin self-description meets philosophical mediation as in both discourses are found deferrals to the poetic, to the mystic, to that which escapes language, in order to partially presence and articulate the animal-other.

> I first felt my tail in my childhood (my second memory from this life was me trying to insist I had a tail), and when I was in Junior High School I remember sitting in a chair relaxing and entering an [sic] meditative state where I felt my ears, tail and muzzle. (Kitsula, qtd in Lupa 2007, 43)

Derrida claims that: 'For thinking concerning the animal, if there is such a thing, derives from poetry' (2008, 7). Further, he contends that there is a link between the specific animal and the seer: that the animal's gaze (in this instance the cat) if met in its particularity, opens one to an alterity that exceeds the individual subject.

Oliver, building upon previous work regarding response-ability (2001) (cultivating an ability to respond to difference), argues that ethical relations with the animal can only be entered into if the individual pays particular attention to their own capacity to respond to this 'gaze' of the particular animal. She writes: 'Echoing Derrida's sentiment, if we want to assimilate what animals can teach us, perhaps we should attend to how we learn from, and how we should thank, our teachers' (2009, 11). Can such relationships be, or are they already taken up, in Transpecies forms of subjectivity, such as Otherkin? Are the animal 'other(s)' of Otherkin teaching the subject to be human or animal?

Transpecies selves and the life–death of the particular

In conclusion, a series of disparate relations remain. Paradoxically, while challenging the boundaries of the human, Otherkin identities simultaneously desire to maintain the definitions and borders given to animal and human in dominant discourse: otherwise the construction of their own difference (from the 'norm') disperses. Can such a proposition of human–animal identity be proposed in a way in which radical difference is not elided? Would this require the death of both the 'human' and the 'animal'? Such a death would seem a constructive creation. That is, a proposal of Transpecies identity where 'Other' ceases to be the operative word: for it is always 'other to what?' Such politics are notoriously difficult, and perhaps it is enough that animal–human subcultures push at the boundaries of the human, of normative subjectivity. Central to this 'pushing' for Otherkin are concepts of spirit and soul. This accords a reanimation of spirituality in the public sphere that knits together religion, art and media creations and personal experience that questions both the role of the animal in religion and the individual relation to an eclectic world. Such developments require rethinking both the personal and political role of contemporary religious belief. Accompanying this are questions as to what type of metaphysical and/or ontological 'grounds' these subjectivities are built upon. Discourses of presence–absence would seem to sit uneasily underneath such heterodox selves.

And then there is the issue of the singular: surely the ethical endeavour requires seeing/meeting the individual, not the 'animal' universal, generic or plural. This link of looking and alterity is made apparent in Haraway's discussion of the etymology and definition of the term species:

> Rooted in *specere*, 'to look' and 'to behold', species takes us to the image impressed on a wax tablet. To the idea impressed on a receptive mind, and to the sovereign stamped on metal coins. Referring both to the relentlessly *specific* or particular and to a class of individuals with the same characteristics, species contains its own opposite in the most promising – or special – way. Species means radical difference as well as logical, classificatory kind. (2008, xxiii)

Both meeting species and/or understanding one's identity as Transpecies or as Otherkin do therefore require a certain vision, a responseability and a continual questioning: How does one enter into ethical relations with the animal-other: that one is and yet is not? For what does this gaze call?

In answer, Derrida proposed:

As with every bottomless gaze, as with the eyes of the other, the gaze called 'animal' offers to my sight the abyssal limit of the human: the inhuman or the ahuman. (2008, 12)

Here is a productive recognition of limit – this limit is also potentiality. This is simultaneously the death of the animal and the death of the human as well as their re-birth as an elusive limit. Although it has been noted herein that Therianthrope subjectivity can be read as employing a universal concept of the animal that does not ethically take into account radical difference (an alterity not premised upon the human or dimorphic concepts of gender), it is equally evident that the questioning of the human and of normative identity categories that the subculture embraces is valuable. It is a more complex, creative and respectful approach to subject identity than that which is currently found in normative anthropocentric discourses of the human. To consider oneself inherently and ontologically betwixt and between species is perhaps not so much pathological as political. At first glance Otherkin may seem a faddish, perhaps even quaint or fashionable subculture. However, rather than simply dismiss or ridicule the subcultures, what is argued herein is that these individual's relationships and their critique of the human can offer potentially useful renegotiations of the concept of subjectivity and how relations with radical difference (alterity) are lived. These negotiations are underlined by the productive death of both the animal and the human.

Works cited

Andrews T (2002). *Animal-speak*. Woodbury: Llewellyn.
Calarco M (2008). *Zoographies: the question of the animal from Heidegger to Derrida*. New York: Columbia University Press.
Derrida J (2008). *The animal that therefore I am*. D Wills (Trans.). New York: Fordham University Press.
Derrida J (1982 [1972]). *Margins of philosophy*. A Bass (Trans.). Chicago: University of Chicago Press.
Derrida J (1997). Choreographies: interview. In NJ Holland (Ed.). *Feminist interpretations of Jacques Derrida* (pp23–41). University Park: Pennsylvania State University Press.

Faivre A (2006). Naturphilosophie. In WJ Hanegraaff (Ed.). *Dictionary of gnosis and Western esotericism* (pp823–24). Leiden and Boston: Brill.

Haraway DJ (2008). Foreword: companion species, mis-recognition, and queer worlding. In N Giffney & MJ Hird (Eds). *Queering the non/human* (ppxxiii–vi). Aldershot: Ashgate.

Haraway DJ (1991). *Simians, cyborgs and women: the reinvention of nature.* London: Free Association Books.

Harner M (1980). *The way of the shaman.* New York: Harper and Row.

Johnston J (2008). *Angels of desire: esoteric bodies, aesthetics and ethics.* London and Oakville: Equinox.

Lupa (2007). *A field guide to Otherkin.* Stafford: Megalithica Books.

Oliver K (2009). *Animal lessons: how they teach us to be human.* New York: Columbia University Press.

Oliver K (2001). *Witnessing: beyond recognition.* Minneapolis and London: University of Minnesota Press.

About the contributors

Philip Armstrong is an associate professor in the School of Humanities and Co-Director of the New Zealand Centre for Human–Animal Studies at the University of Canterbury in Christchurch, New Zealand. His most recent books are *What animals mean in the fiction of modernity* (Routledge, 2008) and *Knowing animals* (co-edited with Laurence Simmons, Brill, 2007). His next book, jointly authored with Annie Potts and Deidre Brown, is entitled 'A New Zealand book of beasts: animals in our culture, history and everyday life'; it will be published by Auckland University Press in December 2013.

Tarsh Bates completed a Master of Science (Biological Arts) in 2012. She has worked variously as a pizza delivery driver, a fruit and vegetable stacker, a toilet paper packer, a researcher in compost science and waste management, a honeybee ejaculator, an art gallery invigilator, a bookkeeper, a car detailer, a lecturer, and a life drawing model. Tarsh is currently a candidate for a PhD (Biological Arts) at SymbioticA UWA where her research is concerned with gentleness, evolutionary aesthetics, and the aesthetics of interspecies encounters. She is particularly enamoured with *Candida albicans* and the human body as a multispecies ecology.

Jill Bough is currently a research fellow at the University of Newcastle in the Faculty of Humanities and Social Sciences. She combined her

lifelong passion for animals with her academic career when she completed her PhD in 2008, 'Value to vermin: the donkey in Australia'. *Donkey* (2011), published by Reaktion Books, follows the donkey across
many human societies. She continues her research into the significance
of the donkey to human societies and the way that those societies represent and, ultimately, treat them. Jill was co-convener of the inaugural
Minding Animals conference in Newcastle in 2009.

Melissa Boyde is a research fellow in the Faculty of Law, Humanities
and the Arts at the University of Wollongong. Melissa works in the
fields of modernist art and literature, and human–animal studies. She
manages the *Replace animals in Australian testing* website, is the editor
of the *Animal Studies Journal* and chairperson of the Australian Animal
Studies Group (AASG).

Matthew Chrulew is an associate of the School of Humanities at the
University of New South Wales. His essays have appeared in *New Formations, Foucault Studies, Australian Humanities Review, Humanimalia*
and elsewhere. He is editing (with Dinesh Wadiwel) the volume 'Foucault and animals', and (with Brett Buchanan and Jeffrey Bussolini)
three forthcoming special issues of *Angelaki* on 'Philosophical etho-
logy'.

Rick De Vos is an adjunct research fellow in the School of Media,
Culture and Creative Arts at Curtin University. His research interests
include the cultural significance and practices of extinction. He is currently working on a monograph on this topic. He has previously lec-
tured and conducted research in cultural studies, performance, television, literature and Indigenous studies in Australia and Wales.

Anne Fawcett is a companion animal veterinarian and lecturer at the
University of Sydney. After completing a Bachelor of Arts degree ma-
joring in philosophy, with an honours thesis on Spinoza, she completed
a Bachelor of Veterinary Science and Bachelor of Science (Veterinary)
at the University of Sydney. Since then she has worked in both veterinary practice and academia, completing her Masters in veterinary studies (small animal medicine and surgery) through Murdoch University
in 2012. Anne is passionate about all aspects of veterinary medicine and

surgery, and as an academic has interests in the study of human–animal interaction and veterinary ethics. She is the author of numerous peer-reviewed journal articles and book chapters, and manages the *Small Animal Talk* website.

Carol Freeman is an associate in English at the School of Humanities at the University of Tasmania. Her work on representations of animals, bioethics, and the role of popular culture in wildlife conservation has appeared in zoological, museum and animal studies journals, as well as essay collections such as *Leonardo's choice: genetic technologies and animals* and *Rethinking Chaucerian beasts*. Her book *Paper tiger: a visual history of the thylacine* was published by Brill in 2010. She is co-editor of an international collection of essays, *Considering animals: contemporary studies in human–animal relations* (2011), and editor of the quarterly *Australian Animal Studies Group News Bulletin*.

George Ioannides is a PhD candidate, tutor, and research assistant in the Department of Studies in Religion at the University of Sydney. His thesis aims to examine the study of religion and material culture at the critical junctures of new materialism and various posthuman conceptualisations of the human and nonhuman body. His broader research interests include the study of religion and material and visual culture, posthumanism and human–animal studies, theories of culture and Continental philosophy, and the intersections surrounding religion, gender and sexuality, with forthcoming publications on all these topics. He is currently co-editing an issue of the *Journal for the Academic Study of Religion*, and was guest co-editor of an issue of *Literature and Aesthetics*, where he also published an article on the aesthetics of sex and sacrality in film.

Jay Johnston is senior lecturer (religious studies) at the University of Sydney and senior lecturer (art history and art education) at CoFA, the University of New South Wales. She has researched in the areas of Continental philosophy of religion (especially theories of embodiment and desire), Western esoteric traditions, contemporary art and curatorial studies for many years. Publications include *Angels of desire: esoteric bodies, aesthetics and ethics* (Equinox, 2008) and the co-edited volume with Geoffrey Samuel, *Religion and the subtle body in Asia and* *the West: between mind and body* (Routledge, 2013). She is the Chief Investigator for the project: 'The function of images in magical papyri and artefacts of ritual power from late antiquity' funded by the Australian Research Council (2012–2014) and is currently completing a monograph – 'Stag and stone: archaeology, religion and esoteric aesthetics'. Her other scholarly obsessions include animal–human subcultures (especially Otherkin) and the body in alternative medicine.

Hilda Kean FRHistS is adjunct professor at the Australian Centre for Public History, UTS, and former dean at Ruskin College, Oxford. Hilda has published widely on cultural/public history and on non-human animals. Her many books include *Animal rights: political and social change in Britain since 1800*. Her numerous articles on animals (and their representation) include those published in *Anthrozoös, Australian Cultural History Journal, History Workshop Journal, International Journal of Heritage Studies, London Journal*, and *Society and Animals*, where she is history editor. She is on the advisory board for Minding Animals International and the Oxford Centre of Animal Ethics. She is currently writing a book on the animal–human relationship during the 1939–45 war.

Agata Mrva-Montoya is a member of Human Animal Research Network (HARN). She completed a PhD in archaeology exploring the role, meaning and symbolism of animals in ancient Cyprus. Research interests include: the human and animal relationship in the ancient Mediterranean; the social and symbolic value of 'cultural fauna'; the role of animals in religious and community rituals; the relationship between symbolism, attitude and treatment of animals, and the ethnic makeup of people in ancient and modern Cyprus.

Greg Murrie is completing a PhD thesis in the Department of History at the University of Sydney on the interrelationship between British animal rights (particularly in the areas of vegetarianism and anti-vivisectionism), esotericism and evolutionary theory in the long 19th century (1789–1919). One of its arguments is that the modern animal rights and liberation movement that emerged in the 1970s had a vested interest in forgetting its esoteric roots and the creative evolutionary speculations of this earlier period in its desire to present itself as a 'rational', secular philosophical discourse allied with other contemporary liberation struggles of the New Left.

Annie Potts is an associate professor in cultural studies and co-director of the New Zealand Centre for Human–Animal Studies at the University of Canterbury, Christchurch, New Zealand. She is the author of *Chicken* (Reaktion, 2012) and co-author, with Philip Armstrong and Deidre Brown, of *A New Zealand book of beasts: animals in our culture, history and everyday life* (Auckland University Press, 2013). She is currently completing an illustrated book called 'Animal earthquake stories', which focuses on the fate of Christchurch city's wild and domesticated animals following the devastating earthquakes of 2011 (to be published in 2014 by Canterbury University Press).

Fiona Probyn-Rapsey is a senior lecturer in the Department of Gender and Cultural Studies at the University of Sydney. Since 2011 she has been the coordinator of Human Animal Research Network (at Sydney University), and is on the Executive Committee of the Australian Animal Studies Group (AASG). Working primarily at the intersection of human–animal studies and critical race studies, her work has been published in *Humanimalia, Society and Animals, Feminist Review, Australian Feminist Studies, Cultural Studies Review, Australian Literary Studies, ARIEL, Antipodes, Journal of Australian Studies* and *Postcolonial Studies*. She is also the author of *Made to matter: white fathers, Stolen Generations* (Sydney University Press, 2013). She is on the editorial boards of *Australian Humanities Review, Environmental Humanities* and *Animal Studies Journal*.

Deborah Bird Rose, FASSA, is an adjunct professor in environmental humanities at the University of New South Wales where her research focuses on multispecies ethnographies in this time of extinctions. A prize-winning author, she is a founding member of the extinction studies working group (www.extinctionstudies.org), and of Kangaloon – creative ecologies (www.kangaloon.org), as well as co-editor of the newly formed journal *Environmental Humanities*. Her influential books include *Wild dog dreaming: love and extinction, Dingo makes us human, Reports from a wild country, Country of the heart, Nourishing terrains* and *Hidden histories*.

Megan Schlipalius is interested in interdisciplinary exhibitions that generate interactions between arts, science, history and anthropology. Her research focuses on audience research, museology and ephemeral aspects of arts and culture. Megan has a background in anthropology, human biology and social ethics and holds a Master of Arts (Cultural Heritage). She currently works for the Janet Holmes à Court Collection.

Peta Tait is professor and chair in theatre and drama at La Trobe University, and publishes on the practice and theory of theatre, drama, and body-based performance including by animals and on social languages of emotion. She is a playwright and her most recent books are *Circus bodies: cultural identity in aerial performance* (Routledge, 2005) and *Wild and dangerous performances: animals, emotions, circus* (Palgrave Macmillan, 2012).

Chloë Taylor is assistant professor in the departments of Philosophy and Women's and Gender Studies at the University of Alberta. She has a PhD from the University of Toronto and was a postdoctoral fellow in the Philosophy Department at McGill University. She is the author of *The culture of confession from Augustine to Foucault* (Routledge, 2008, 2010) as well as a number of articles in journals such as *Hypatia, Philosophy Today, Ancient Philosophy*, and *Postmodern Culture*. She is currently working on two book manuscripts, entitled 'Bucolic pleasures? Foucault, feminism, and sex crime' and 'Abnormal appetites: Foucault and the politics of food'.

Index

abandonment 11–12
abattoirs 152, 242, 244
Aboriginal worldviews 89
absinthe 260
Adams, Carol 93
Addison, Alison 194
advertising campaigns 154
afterlife, human understandings of the 139, 139, 172, 178
Agamben, Giorgio 221, 241–241
ageing 151
agribusiness 151, 163
agriculture 157
albinism 245
albino animals 241, 245, 247, 249
albino humans 248
National Organization for Albinism and Hypopigmentation 248
Allen, Mary 120
alterity *see* Nwoga, Donatus
American Veterinary Medical Association (AVMA) 206–207
anaesthetics 260, 260, 263, 264
anatomy 45
Anderson, Pamela 161

Anderson, Wallace 30
animal conservation 236
animal memes 250
animal shelters 85
Animal Studies Group 107
Animal Studies 131, 190, 201
animal welfare work and activism 85, 87, 97, 132, 154, 158, 207, 255; *see also* Vint, Sherryl
animal liberation movement 98
Animal Liberation Victoria 159
animal welfare organisations 124–125
Chickens' Lib 155, 155–157, 158
in the 1970s 271
open rescue 155, 158–160
Open Rescue 159
People for the Ethical Treatment of Animals (PETA) 158, 161
Save Animals From Exploitation 160
'imagery' activism 155–161
animal, concept of the 300
animals eating humans 91, 94–95
animals killed on the road 129, 131–132
Anthropocene period 10, 11, 14, 17

anthropocentrism 33
anthropomorphism 8, 33, 104, 104, 157
Anzac legend 137, 147
appearance of animals xxi; *see also*
    Watt, Yvette
Aquinas 90
archaeology xix
    excavation techniques 171
    interpreting the bones of dead anim-
    als 170–171, 175
Ardlethan (NSW) 128
Aristotle 90–91
    Natural Law theory 91
Armstrong, Philip xix
articulated or associated animal bone
    group (ABG) 171–172, 174, 175,
    175
Association de Défense du Cimetière
    de Chiens et Autres Animaux 26
At the movies (ABC) 202
attachment to non-domesticated or-
    ganisms 44–47
Australian cattle dog 247
Australian identity 121
Australian Kelpie Muster, The 128
Australian kelpies 119, 127, 128
Australian sheepdog 247
Australian War Memorial (Canberra)
    30, 144–144

Baker, Steve 107
barbecuing 154
Barcelona Zoo 249
Bataille, Georges 107
Bates, Tarsh xvii
bearing witness 4
bears 90
Belvoir St Theatre (Sydney) 77
Bentham, Jeremy 34–35
Berger, John xviii, 103, 104, 110, 157,
    246

Berkshire Park pet cemetery (near
    Sydney) 36
Bernard, Claude 258–258, 261–262
Bietak, Manfred 139
bioart 61
biological racism 221; *see also* Simons,
    John
biopolitics 222, 226, 241
biopower 221, 226, 233, 236
biosecurity 147, 211
biotechnology 192
biowarfare 199, 200, 201
birds 87
Birke, Lynda 268
black bears 91
Bonnett, Alistair 244
Bordertown (SA) 246
Borrell, Sally 196
botanical illustrations 48
Bough, Jill xix
Bovell, Andrew 78
Boyde, Melissa xix
Boyle, Peter 17
Brakhage, Stan xviii, 104
    Sirius remembered xviii, 104, 110–115
breeding animals 57
    breeding albino animals 247
    inbreeding 248, 249
    reptile breeding 247
    selective breeding 160
British Association for the Advance-
    ment of Science 259
British Columbia (Canada) 91
British Medical Association 260
British Medical Journal 263, 270
Brodie, Sir Benjamin 261
Broken Hill (NSW) 119, 124, 125
Bronze Age 140, 176, 182
brown bears 80
Brown Institution 260
Brown, Wendy 244

Brunton, Lauder 260, 265
The Bulletin 191
Bulliet, Richard 140
Burdon-Sanderson, John 259, 260, 265
Burger King 154
Burrows, Sir George 265
Burt, Jonathan 103, 107, 108, 110, 147,
    161, 197, 200
Bush, George W 98
Butler, Judith 11, 86, 97–98
    grievable lives 86

Cambridge University 259
candida 50–55, 55
Cannes Film Festival 120
cannibalism 89, 90, 93
Cannon, Aubrey 184
capitalism 104, 157
care of nonhuman organisms 43, 50–55
Carlyle, Jane 22
carnivorous animals 235
Cartmill, Matt 192
Casterton (Victoria) 128
Caterson, Robert 28
Catholic Church 269
cats, feral *see* western lowlands gorillas
Catts, Oron 50
cemetery, function of in Wester culture
    33
Chekhov, Anton 75
chickens
    battery hens 152, 155–156, 159,
        239–240
    broiler chickens 152, 159, 240, 240,
        241, 242, 243, 244
    caged chicken farms 76, 155, 157, 161
    Chickens' Lib *see* anaesthetics
    commercial exploitation of 152
    depicted in art 161–165
    depicted in popular music 165–166
    Kentucky Fried Cruelty 158

Open Rescue *see* Anderson, Wallace
chromatism 245, 248
Chrulew, Matthew xx
Churchill, Winston 247
Cincinnati Zoo 249
civilization 127
Clark, David 12
Clark, Dick 153
climate change 199, 280, 286, 290
    changing animal habitats 10, 78–78,
        80
    rising sea levels 10
co-existence 17, 17
Cobbe, Frances Power 256, 256, 259,
    260, 261, 263, 266–267, 268,
    269–269, 272
    The future of the lower animals 267
    The moral aspects of vivisection 267
cockroaches 55, 78, 79
Coe, Sue 163
Coetzee, JM 85, 86, 94, 96
cognitive dissonance 215, 216
Cohen, Stanley xv
Cold War 281–282
colonisation 15
commemoration of animals after death
    see genetic coding
companion animals 86, 97
    domestication of animals 72, 80, 280
    naming of 33
    overpopulation of 210, 213
    ownership 205, 207
    pet industry xx
    status of 21
concentration camps 241
containment of nonhuman organisms
    48
contamination 52–53
Cook, Kenneth xix, 124, 125
    Wake in fright (novel) xix, 119, 120,
        127

Corlett, Peter 30, 144
Cornelius, Patricia 74, 76
cows 123
Craske, Matthew 21
crazy love xvii, 5, 10, 12, 17
cremation 269
critter, definition of 44
crocodiles 94
Cronin, Keri 35
Cruelty to Animals Act (1876) 257, 271
cruelty towards animals 16, 35, 37,
    123–125, 143, 159, 163, 260; see also
    veterinary surgeons: moral stress ex-
    perienced by
cultural acceptance 125
cultural responsibility 132
curatorial studies 56
cyborgs 302
Cyprus xix, 169–186, 170

Dafoe, Daniel 202
Dalai Lama 161
Dalí, Salvador 87–87, 94
Dampier (WA) 119, 128, 128
Darwin, Charles
    evolutionary theory 48, 249
    Origin of species 266
    The descent of man 267, 271
    The expression of the emotions in man
        and animals 271
Dawson, Jonathan 194
de Bernières, Louis xix, 130
    Red Dog (novel) 127, 129, 130
De Vos, Rick xxi
de-animalisation 153–155, 157
death
    relationship between death and life 2,
        303
    stories about the origin of 1–5
death zone xvi–xvi, 5, 11, 12, 13, 17
deers 88

defamiliarisation 112
Deleuze, Gilles 46
deontology 86, 94
Derrida, Jacques 47–48, 241, 242, 242,
    297
    animot 302–302
    différance 298–299
    Sexual Otherwise 301
    'The animal that therefore I am' 120,
        130, 300
Desmond, Jane 32, 67, 71
différance see de Bernières, Louis: Red
    Dog (novel)
disease 222
dislocation 15
display of human status, animals as a
    169, 176, 181, 181, 181–184
DNA 151
dogs, working see whiteness: symbol-
    ism associated with
Donald, Diana 22, 38
donkeys 137–148
    domestication of 139, 140, 145
    Donkey Sanctuary (Sidmouth,
        Devon) 138, 142, 143
    featuring in the Bible 141–142, 144
    hunting 145–148
    sacrifice of see RSPCA
    symbolic function of 137, 140, 147
    use in war 143–144
    working donkeys see wild / feral an-
        imals
drinking / getting drunk 123
Druce, Clare 155–156
ducks 75
Durand, Marguerite 25
Dvořák, Antonín 193
Dyer, Richard 244

eating animals 86, 89, 127, 157, 158,
    160, 164, 170, 178, 182, 183, 254

as an act of respect 87–89, 92
breeding animals for food 60, 76, 96,
98, 152–155, 240, 241, 244
ethics of live food 60
echidnas 245
ecocide 15
Edinburgh University 265
Edison, Thomas 106
Ehrenreich, Ben 87, 93
electricity 106
elephants 106
Enlightenment 48
entertainment, using animals for 48
animals in zoos 231, 241, 246, 249
animals on stage 74–78
trained animal acts 69, 75, 77
environmental changes *see* chickens:
Chickens' Lib
environmental conservation 45, 200,
202
epidemics 226
epilepsy 260
Esposito, Roberto 221
Eterna, Luna 248
ethics xviii, 4, 10, 11, 60, 65, 67, 71, 76,
80, 85–86, 87, 92, 96, 99–99, 194
environmental ethics 88
moral stress suffered by veterinary
surgeons 213–217
of 'euthanising' animals 207, 211, 212;
see also epilepsy
of 'mercy' killings 196, 199, 202, 209
of defining 'human' as distinct from
'animal' 297, 305
of keeping working animals 288
of vivisection 272; *see also* Vint,
Sherryl
ethnic cleansing 15
ethopolitics 231–231, 236
euthanasia xx
definition of 205–218

euthanising animals xx, 236
euthanising dangerous animals 210,
211, 212
Everett, Mick 147
excavation of tombs 169
experimental medicine 259
exploration 279
extinction of animals xv, xx, 6, 13, 78,
104, 105, 189, 190, 201, 201,
202–203, 202; *see also* Strand, Chick,
identity politics

farming industry 37
cattle farming 128
educating the public about 159
factory farms, animals in xx, 76, 159,
166, 241
standardisation of animals in the 241
Fawcett, Anne xx
feminism 259
feral animals *see* western lowlands gorillas
Fertile Crescent 140
film
as a medium 13
representing animals in 103, 105,
106–108, 110–113
First Nations Canadians 88
First World War 143
fish 78
fishing 282, 283, 284
Flanagan, Richard 12, 13
flies 122
fruit flies 56–57
flying foxes, extermination of 15–17
Fontana, Felix 261
food chain 89, 90
Foster, Michael 259, 260
Foucault, Michel xxi, 221, 226, 231,
232, 233, 233, 235, 241
Abnormal 96

foxes 123
Francione, Gary 272
Franklin, Adrian 36
French, Richard D 254
funerary rituals, human 169, 172,
  181–183, 185, 199
  role of animals in 139–141, 140–141,
  171, 175, 178

Gardiner, Michael 64
gaze
  human 196, 268
  of the non-human Other 47–48, 196,
  303, 304–305
gelatine 109
genetic coding 151
genetically modified animals 240, 242
genocide 15
goats, sacrifice of see Rose, Deborah
  Bird
Goodall, Jane 77
gophers 88
Gosling, Ryan 161
Grandin, Temple 240
Greenland huskies xxi, 277–290
greyhounds 123
grief 1, 5
  animals grieving for animals 8–9, 37,
  109
  grievable lives 86
  humans grieving for animals 21, 31,
  31, 34, 35, 37, 97, 109, 138–139,
  143–144, 196, 200
  humans grieving for humans 96, 98
  obligations to the dead 96
grooming, animal 6
Guattari, Felix 47
gynaecology 268

Hadwen, Walter 269–269
Hadzi-Vasilev, Elpida 162

Hancock, Lang 127
Handel, George Frideric 193
Haraway, Donna 44, 47–48, 64, 302
Hardy, Thomas 36
Harmois, Georges 25
Harner, Michael 296
Harris, Elizabeth 137
Harris, Emmylou 161
Hatley, James 2
Hauser, Jens 61
Hawaii 6
Heaney, Seamus 1
Hediger, Heini xx, 222–237
  death due to behaviour see working
  animals: donkeys
  Man and animal in the zoo 224
Heidegger, Martin 47, 107, 113, 298
heroes, animals as 28–30
heterosexuality 133
heterotopia 222
Hillside Animal Sanctuary (England)
  37
Hinchliffe, Steve 30
Hirst, Damien 71
Hoggan, George 262–264, 265–265
Holland, Steve Mark 30
Holmes à Court Gallery 55
Homer 175
homosexuality 125, 126–127
horses 123
  horse sacrifice see Royal Botanic Gar-
  dens (Sydney)
  horse-riding 183–183
  vivisection on horses 259
Hospice of Great St Bernard (the Alps)
  28
House Rabbit Society 37
Hughes-D'Aeth, Tony 194, 198–199
Human Animal Research Network
  (HARN) xvi

Index

human habituation to nonhuman
deaths 54
human sacrifice *see* Royal College of
Physicians
humans as animals 49
humans, dominance of 13, 90; *see also*
McCartney, Sir Paul
human–animal relations xv, 222
human–animal boundary 36
human–animal intimacy xvii, 32, 138;
see also climate change: rising sea
levels
human–animal studies xvi
hunting
endangered species 189
for pest control 145
for sport 88, 119, 123–124, 223, 284,
286
humans as hunters 197, 201
in Australia 119, 145
in Canada 91
in Greenland xxi, 283, 284
in Québec 88
subsistence hunting 86, 88, 92, 93,
127, 283, 284, 284, 286, 288
Hutcheon, Linda 194
Hutton, Richard Holt 264
Hyde Park, London 143
hydra 57–62

Ibsen, Henrik 75
Ice Age 191, 201
identity politics 71
ignorance, deliberate 12
Ilulissat (Greenland) 277, 278–280, 287
immunisation 221
in vitero (artistic research project)
43–65
indifference, cultivation of xvi
infectious organisms 51
insectivorous plants 90

insects 87
intelligence of animals 22
interdependency of species 79
Ionesco, Eugene 75
Irigaray, Luce 64

Japanese wolf 191
Jasper, James 156
Jennings, Kate 121
Johnston, Jay xxi

kangaroos 119, 121, 126, 129, 131,
246–247
Kaua'i (Hawaii) 5
Kaua'i Albatross Network 10
Kean, Hilda xvii, 50, 268
Kelpie Dog Festival 128
Kemp, Jenny 80
KFC 158–158, 160
killing humans 93
Kimberley, the 119, 146–146
King, Roger 192
Kingsford, Anna 269
Klein, Emanuel 260, 264–265
Knight, Andrew 242
kookaburras 249
Kotcheff, Ted xix
Wake in fright (film) xix, 119,
120–127
Kundera, Milan 87
Kuzniar, Alice 97

labradors 121
Landseer, Sir Edwin Henry 21
language 33–35, 107
Lansbury, Coral 268
LA Times 163
Laurence, Janet 12–15, 17
Laysan albatross 5–10
Lazaroo, Kit 74, 78
leeches 90

Leigh, Julia xx
The hunter (novel) xx, 189, 191–193,
    195, 197, 198–198
Lévinas, Emmanuel 10–11, 48, 301
life cycles 57, 202
lifespans 46, 47, 50
Lim, David 28
Lind-af-Hageby, Louise 269
Lingara 3
Lippit, Akira xviii, 103, 105, 107
    Electric animal 108
live animal export 128
live burial 174
logging 202
London Metropolitan University 162
London Zoo 247
looking at dead animals 68–70
Lovell, Arthur 269
Luna Park (Coney Island) 106
Lunney, Dan 132
Lupa 294, 296–297

Macdonald, Sharon 71
Magendie, François 258
Magnan, Valentin 260, 267
Magnotta, Luca 93
Mangum, Teresa 35
Mark, Patty 159
Maruska, Edward 249
Marvin, Garry 192
massacre of animals 119, 123–124, 126
massacres of Australia's Indigenous
    peoples 119
mateship 121
Mbembe, Achille 54
McCartney, Sir Paul 161
McDonald's 158
McHugh, Susan 120
McMahan, Jeff 99
memorialising dead animals *see* genetic
    coding

Merleau-Ponty, Maurice 69
mice 240, 241, 248
Midway Island (Hawaii) 10
Miller, Stephen 128
mining industry 127–127, 133–133
Moby 165
modernity 5, 104, 105, 105
Modjeska, Drusilla 192
moral status of nonhuman animals
    254; *see also* Homer
Morrison, Toni 245
Morrissey, Steven Patrick 166
mosquitos 55, 90, 90
Mrva-Montoya, Agata xix
multispecies relationality xvii
Munt, Sally 127
murder, definition of 206
Murrie, Greg xxi
Museum of Natural History (London)
    68
musicals 128

Nagel, Thomas 47
natural history museums 48
naturalism 74
nature's spaces 30
Nettheim, Daniel xx, 193
    The hunter (film) xx, 189, 193–194,
    195–197, 201
Newfoundland dog 35
Ngarinman people xvii, 3
noblesse oblige 255
Novak, David 160
Nozick, Robert 99
Nussbaum, Martha 99
Nwoga, Donatus 1

The Observer 203
Oliver, Kelly 97, 297, 300, 301–302
open rescue *see* Anderson, Pamela
organ donation 86

Index

Osterlund, Hob 10
Otherkin xxii, 302
  communities 297
  definintion of 294–295, 299, 303, 305
  identity as 294–294, 295–295, 304, 304
  physical characteristics of 297
  role of the imagination 297
  Therian 294–295, 296, 299, 299, 305
otherness 47, 48, 293, 297–297, 299
outback, myths of the Australian 120, 128, 132
oxen, sacrifice of *see* Royal College of Veterinary Surgeons (UK)
O'Neill, Sue 194

P!nk 161
pain, animals in 16, 16, 132, 157, 253–254, 256, 258, 270
Palmer, Clare 96–96, 98
pansexuality 302
pedigree animals 31
People for the Ethical Treatment of Animals (PETA) 158
Perdue Farms Incorporated 158
Perth Institute of Contemporary Art 44
pet cemeteries xvii, 21; *see also* genetic coding
  Cimetière des Chiens (Asnières-sur-Seine, Paris) 21, 25, 31
  Federal Park (Annandale, Sydney) 37
  Hartsdale pet cemetery (outside New York) 21, 23, 28, 31, 33
  Hyde Park pet cemetery (London) 21, 22, 31, 32, 33
  PDSA cemetery (Ilford) 23
Petit, Eugene 25
pets *see* climate change: rising sea levels
phenomenology of the body 67
physiology 258
Pick, Anat 105

Pilbara region (Australia) 127, 128, 129, 129, 132
plastination 71–71, 73
Plumwood, Val 89–90, 94
Plutarch 142
polar bears 80
Pomeranz, Margaret 121
Pope Leo XIII 269
pornography 268
post-mortems of dead animals 225, 225
poststructuralism xxi
Potts, Annie xix, 243
predation 222
premature burial, fear of 254, 268–271
  Council for the Disposition of the Dead 269
  London Society for the Prevention of Premature Burial 269
preservation of dead animals 73
Probyn-Rapsey, Fiona xxi
prophylaxis 227
public health 211
Pugliese, Joseph 244
Pulkara, Daly 3

Qaanaaq (Greenland) 277, 281–290
quality of life for animals 72, 210, 212

rabbits 87–87, 123, 127
racism 233–233
  racialisation 245, 248
radioactive contamination 282, 283
rape 126
Rasmussen, Knud 279–280
rationality 5
rats 248
Red Dog 127, 127, 128, 130
Red Jungle Fowl 151
Regan, Tom 211, 272
religious belief, role of 304
religious ceremonies 183

religious sentiments 26
representation of animals 104
reproductive strategy 45
respect for dead animals xviii, 62–65, 85, 100
Reyes, AT 180
rhinoceroses 75
right to kill animals 55
Rindner, Sandra 24
Rinehart, Gina 127
Rio Tinto 127, 128, 133
ritual killing of animals see Rogers, Lesley
Ritvo, Harriet 72
Rivière, Pierre 97–97
Rogers, Lesley 166
Rollin, Bernard 212, 214–215
roman à clef xix, 120, 125, 126, 130, 131
Rose, Deborah Bird xvi–xvi, 148
Royal Botanic Gardens (Sydney) 15, 16, 17
Royal College of Physicians 265
Royal College of Veterinary Surgeons (UK) 208
Royal Commission on the Practice of Subjecting Live Animals to Experiments for Scientific Purposes (1875) 257, 264
RSPCA 37, 260, 262
Rupp, David 181
Rutherford, William 265
Ryan, Chris 77
Ryder, Richard 271

sacrifice, animal 105, 120, 164, 171
cattle sacrifice 175, 183
donkey sacrifice 169, 175, 183, 185; see also flies
goat sacrifice 183
horse sacrifice 169–186
human sacrifice 175

oxen sacrifice 178
sheep sacrifice 178, 182, 183
Salt, Henry 258
sanctuaries for animals 37
sandflies 90
Schiff, Moritz 259, 264
Schlipalius, Megan xvii, 44
Schäfer, Edward 259
scientific experiments, using animals for 46, 48, 49, 50, 99, 106, 153, 163, 208, 209, 223, 240, 242, 248, 254, 256, 260–266; see also veterinary surgeons: moral stress experienced by
scientific experiments, using humans for 99, 208, 209
scientific positivism 5, 258
seagulls 75
Searby, Rose 31
Sebeok, Thomas 234
Second World War 23, 247
Sedgwick, Eve Kosofsky 133
self-representation 120
sentinent beings, animals as 32, 35, 107, 164, 166, 200, 231, 266, 267, 272
Serpell, James 31
sexism 121–121
sexual difference 300, 301
shamanism 296, 299
shame and shamelessness 120, 125, 125–127, 132–134
sharks 71
Sharpey, William 260, 266
sheep, sacrifice of
Sherman Contemporary Art Foundation 12
Sherman Gallery (Sydney) 12
Shestov, Lev 5
Shrine of Remembrance (Melbourne) 30, 144

Shukin, Nicole 106, 241, 243, 245, 250
Simons, John 121
Singer, Angela 163
Singer, Peter 271
Sitney, P Adams 112
Skinema 248
slaughterhouse *see* overpopulation(particularly in the context of animal shelters but also in the case of animal hoarding (Joffe et al. in preparation)
Smith, Julie Ann 37
Smith, Zadie 240
The Smiths 165
Smuts, Barbara 48
Solomons, Jason 203
Spalding, Violet 155–156
species, definition of 304
speciesism 0–236, 78, 236, 255, 271; *see also* barbecuing
speciocide 15
spectrality 103, 105, 111, 113
spirituality 304
squirrels 87
St Bartholomew's Hospital (London) 260
Stalin 17
starvation 222
Stender, Kriv 133
Stenders, Kriv xix
Red Dog (film) xix, 119, 127–134
sterilisation of animals 99
Stockowner's Association of South Australia 247
Strand Magazine 22
Strand, Chick 114
Stratton, David 121
strychnine poisoning 119, 129, 129, 132, 132
subculturing 53
subjectivity 297

suicide 213–214, 215–216, 215
surveillance 222
Svendsen, Elizabeth 143
Swinney, Geoffrey 38
symbiosis 50

Tait, Peta xviii
Taronga Park (Sydney) 225, 226
Tasmanian tiger 14, 189–203
Tate Modern (London) 71
taxidermy 13, 22, 38, 67, 70, 71, 76
Taylor, Chloë xviii
Tebb, William 269
technoscience 157
theatre
   animal impersonations in 79
   animals in 74–78
   visual realism in 67, 74, 76
Threatened Species Day (Queensland) 16
Thule (Geenland) 281, 283, 283, 287
thylacine *see* Strand, Chick
tigers 249
Tissue Culture and Art Project (tc&a) 50
tombs
   architecture of 179
   re-use of 171, 172, 173
Tomkin, Silvan 125
torture of animals 154; *see also* White Australia
totems 296
transpecies identity *see* Nettheim, Daniel: *The hunter* (film)
trauma 15, 17, 17

University College (London) 260
University of Copenhagen 279
University of London 259
University of Sydney xvi
University of Western Australia 44

urbanisation 104
utilitarianism 86, 86, 93–94, 99–99, 185

van Dooren, Thom 4
veganism 87, 165
vegetarianism 254, 256, 256
veterinary surgeons xx, 23, 129, 133, 236, 259
  as more likely to commit suicide 213–214, 215–216, 215
  'euthanising' animals 205–218
  moral stress experienced by 213–217
Vialles, Noelie 242–244
Victoria River District (NT) 146
Vint, Sherryl 48
violent death of animals 175
violent realism 120
Virgil 180
visual art
  modern visual art 77
  postmodern visual art 77
  Turner Award 80
Vivaldi 193
vivisection
  anti-vivisation societies 254, 269, 269
  anti-vivisection propaganda 35
  anti-vivisection 253–272
  history of 257–261
  on birds 261
  on chickens 153
  on dogs 259, 262–262
  on frogs 261
  on horses 259
  on humans 258
  on pigeons 259
  on rabbits 262
  purpose of 265
  restriction versus abolition of vivisection 254–257
  self-regulation of 259
  use of curare during 257, 261–266

vocalisation, animal 6
Vollum, Edward 269
von Hagens, Gunther 67
  'Animal inside out' 67–74, 82
  'Body worlds' 68, 71
Vulpian, Alfred 265
vultures 78, 79

Walker, Alice 160, 166
wallabies 131
Wallinger, Mark 80
Wan, Natalie 248
war crimes 208, 209
Wardian case 49
warfare 143–144
Wari' 89, 95
Watt, Yvette 164
Way, Kenneth 139
Weil, Kari 196
western lowlands gorillas 249
Westinghouse, George 106
Westrac 128
whales 80
Wheeler, Wendy 43
White Aussies Project 247
White Australia 247
white privilege 241, 241
whiteness 244, 244, 244
  animal xxi, 241–250
  human 241, 244, 245, 248
  symbolism associated with 244, 248
wild / feral animals 26, 36, 129, 132, 147, 223, 229
  longevity of wild animals 232
Williams, Howard 138, 138, 142
Wills, David 130
Wilson, Richard 151
Winfrey, Oprah 161
witnessing death, animals 148, 174
women, bodies of 50
women's rights 301

Woodside 128
working animals
dogs 278, 279–279, 281–282, 283,
284, 287, 288
donkeys 137, 140–141, 143–144, 144
World Trade Center bombing xvii, 28,
98
Wunderkammer 48

Yarralin 3
Yeates, JW 212–213, 216
Yolacan, Pinar 162–162
Young, Iris Marion 244
Yum! Brands 160

zoologists 236
zoos xx, 56; *see also* Hadzi-Vasilev,
Elpida
behaviour of animals in 228

buildings that comprise 228–228
death due to behaviour 226–233, 234,
237
death of animals in xx, 222, 228–231
function of 222
interactions between animals in 230
longevity of animals in 232
professionalisation of animal care in
231
reducing death among captive animals 224–224
social structures in 230
stress of animals in 225
transfer of animals within and
between 222, 229
zoo animals reintroduced to the wild
236
Zurr, Ionat 50